WOMEN IN MANAGEMENT

WOMEN IN MANAGEMENT

Current Research Issues

Edited by

MARILYN J. DAVIDSON
*Manchester School of Management
University of Manchester
Institute of Science and Technology, UK*

RONALD J. BURKE
*Faculty of Administrative Studies
York University, Canada*

P·C·P
Paul Chapman
Publishing Ltd

Paul Chapman Publishing Ltd
144 Liverpool Road
London
N1 1LA

British Library Cataloguing in Publication Data

Women in Management: Current Research
Issues
 I. Davidson, Marilyn J. II. Burke, R.J.
 658.0082

 Hardback ISBN 1-85396-235-x
 Paperback ISBN 1-85396-289-9

Typeset by Dorwyn Ltd, Rowlands Castle, Hants
Printed and bound by Athenaeum Press, Gateshead, Tyne & Wear.

A B C D E F G H 9 8 7 6 5 4

Contents

Contributors

MARILYN J. DAVIDSON, *Editor*, Senior Lecturer in Organisational Psychology, Manchester School of Management, University of Manchester Institute of Science and Technology, PO Box 88, Manchester, M60 1QD, UK.

RONALD J. BURKE, *Editor*, Professor in Organizational Behaviour/ Industrial Relations, Faculty of Administrative Studies, York University, 4700 Keele Street, North York, Ontario, M3J 1P3, Canada.

BEVERLY ALIMO-METCALF, Senior Lecturer in Occupational Psychology, The Nuffield Institute, University of Leeds, Fairbairn House, 71–75 Clarendon Road, Leeds, LS2 9PL, UK.

JEANNE M. BRETT, DeWill W. Buchanan, Jr, Professor of Dispute Resolution and Organizations, J. L. Kellogg Graduate School of Management, Northwestern University, Evanston, Illinois, 60208, USA.

SUSAN SCHICK CASE, Professor, Organizational Behavior, Department of Organizational Behavior, Weatherhead School of Management, Case Western Reserve University, Cleveland, Ohio, 44106, USA.

MONIQUE CHALUDE, Management Consultant and 'Assistant Chargée d'exercices à l'Université Libre de Bruxelles', Chalude Vandecapelle & Associates, 103, rue Franz Merjay, 1060 Brussels, Belgium.

JEANETTE N. CLEVELAND, Professor, Department of Psychology, Colorado State University, Fort Collins, Colorado, 80523, USA.

ROBIN J. ELY, Professor of Organizational Behaviour, John F. Kennedy School of Government, Harvard University, 79 JFK Street, Cambridge, Massachusetts, 02138, USA.

ELLEN A. FAGENSON, Professor, Management Department, George Mason University, Fairfax, Virginia, 22030, USA.

MARGARET FERRARIO, Senior Research Fellow, Manchester School of Management, University of Manchester Institute of Science and Technology, PO Box 88, Manchester, M60 1QD, UK.

ROB GOFFEE, Associate Professor of Organizational Behaviour, London Business School, Sussex Place, Regent's Park, London NW1 4SA, UK.

JEFFREY H. GREENHAUS, Professor, Department of Management, College of Business and Administration, Drexel University, Philadelphia, Pennsylvania, 19104, USA.

VALERIE HAMMOND, Chief Executive, Roffey Park Management Institute, Forest Road, Horsham, West Sussex, RH12 4TD, UK.

JEFF HEARN, Head of Department and Reader in Applied Social Studies, University of Bradford, West Yorkshire, BD7 1DP, UK.

ATTIE DE JONG, Management Consultant, De Jong en Van Doorne-Huiskes, Management Consultants, Singel 226, 3311, Dordrecht, The Netherlands.

ROBIN KRAMAR, Senior Lecturer, Industrial Relations and Human Resource Management, University of New South Wales, Kensington, NSW 2033, Australia.

JACQUELINE LAUFER, Professor, Département Management et Ressources Humaines, Groupe HEC School of Management, Jouy-en-Josas, 78350, France.

MARY DEAN LEE, Professor, Organizational Behaviour, Faculty of Management, 1001 Sherbrooke Street West, Montreal, Quebec, H3A 1G5, Canada.

SUZAN LEWIS, Senior Lecturer in Psychology, Department of Psychology and Speech Pathology, The Manchester Metropolitan University, Elizabeth Gaskell Campus, Heathersage Road, Manchester, M13 OJA, UK.

SU MADDOCK, Quality/Equality Consultant, 52 Brookburn Road, Chorlton, Manchester, M21 2FE, UK.

CAROL A. MCKEEN, Professor, Accounting, School of Business, Dunning Hall, Queen's University, Kingston, Ontario, K7L 3N6, Canada.

MARY C. MATTIS, Vice President, Research and Advisory Services, Catalyst, 250 Park Avenue South, New York, 10003–1459, USA.

NIGEL NICHOLSON, Professor and Chairman, Organizational Behaviour, Director, Centre for Organizational Research, London Business School, Sussex Place, Regent's Park, London, NW1 4SA, UK.

SAROJ PARASURAMAN, Professor, Department of Management, College of Business and Administration, Drexel University, Philadelphia, Pennsylvania, 19104, USA.

BARBARA PARKER, Professor, Organizational Behaviour, Albers School of Business and Economics, Seattle University, Seattle, Washington, 98122–4460, USA.

DI PARKIN, Equal Opportunities Consultant, Corporate Management and Policy Services, 17 Kinder Road, Hayfield, SK12 5WJ, Cheshire, UK.

VIRGINIA E. SCHEIN, Professor and Chair, Department of Management, Gettysburg College, Gettysburg, Pennsylvania, 17325–1486, USA.

LINDA K. STROH, Associate Professor, Organizational Behaviour, Institute of Human Resources and Industrial Relations, Loyola University Chicago, 840 Wabash Avenue, Chicago, Illinois, 60611, USA.

Acknowledgements

I would like to acknowledge the support provided by the Manchester School of Management, University of Manchester Institute of Science and Technology, and the assistance of Michelle Brierley for typing assistance and correspondence. I am also most grateful to all the contributors and, finally, the support and encouragement given by Nick Sanders.

MARILYN J. DAVIDSON

I would like to acknowledge the general support provided by Dean Dezso Horvath and the Faculty of Administrative Studies, York University, and the specific assistance of Bruna Gaspini and Louise Coutu in co-ordinating manuscripts and correspondence. I am obviously indebted to all our international contributors. Finally, I am particularly grateful for the support of my children – Sharon, Rachel and Jeff.

RONALD J. BURKE

CHAPTER 1

Women in Management: Current Research Issues[1]

RONALD J. BURKE AND MARILYN J. DAVIDSON

INTRODUCTION

During the past two decades there has been a dramatic increase in the number of women who are pursuing managerial and professional careers (Davidson and Cooper, 1992, 1993). Many of these women have prepared themselves for careers by undertaking university education where they now comprise almost half of the graduates of professional schools such as accounting, business and law. Research evidence suggests that these graduates enter the workforce at levels comparable to their male colleagues and with similar credentials and expectations, but it seems that women's and men's corporate experience and career paths begin to diverge soon after that point (Morrison et al., 1987).

It is evident that although managerial and professional women are at least as well educated and trained as their male counterparts and are being hired by organizations in approximately equal numbers, they are not entering the ranks of senior management at comparable rates. Women are gaining the necessary experience and paying their dues but still encounter a 'glass ceiling' (Morrison and von Glinow, 1990). The relative failure of these women to move into the ranks of senior management, in both private- and public-sector organizations, in all developed countries has been documented (Adler and Izraeli, 1988).

Why should organizations be interested in developing and utilizing the talents of women? Schwartz (1987, 1988) summarizes reasons why supporting the career aspirations of talented and successful managerial women makes good business sense. These include obtaining the best people for leadership positions, giving the chief executive officer (CEO) experience in working with capable women, providing female role models for younger high-potential women, ensuring that companies' opportunities for women will be noticed by both women graduates in recruiting and women customers, and guaranteeing that all ranks of management will be filled with strong executives. The recruitment, hiring and development of managerial

[1] Preparation of this introduction was supported in part by the Faculty of Administrative Studies, York University, and the Manchester School of Management, UMIST.

women is increasingly seen as a bottom-line issue related to corporate success.

AIMS OF THIS BOOK

The overall aim of this book is to present a comprehensive overview of the current international findings pertaining to women in management. This volume brings together an international group of eminent contributors who highlight the major barriers and problems facing women managers, the individual and organizational consequences and recommendations for organizational and legislative changes.

The book is divided into five sections. Part I reviews major issues related to the negative effects of organizational culture (with its predominantly white, male ethos) on women managers. Part II concentrates on some of the main barriers hampering career development prospects and covers prejudicial attitudes and behaviours relating to stereotyping, selection bias, and issues of gender in management/leadership styles. Part III investigates some of the relationship and communication problems at work for women managers, particularly those inherent in interactions between women and men. Part IV presents issues concerning the role conflict between work, home and family: the ways in which female managers combine these roles and how work can be restructured to accommodate and relieve some of this stress. Finally Part V concentrates on positive approaches, strategies and recommendations for helping women into management, particularly in relation to shattering the glass ceiling, and evaluates affirmative action policies and equal opportunity programmes in the USA, Australia, Belgium, France, The Netherlands and the UK.

Throughout the book, while the contributors concede that on the whole organizations seem to be doing a good job at recruiting and hiring capable women, they appear to have difficulty in developing and retaining managerial women and advancing them into ranks of senior management. The 'glass ceiling' that women encounter refers to a subtle and almost invisible, but strong, barrier that prevents women from moving up to senior management. It is also apparent that women experience bias the moment they enter organizations. Schwartz (1992) argues that it is the impact of these subtle, and not so subtle, experiences that limits women's career opportunities.

Three broad hypotheses are offered in this book to explain why this ceiling has remained impenetrable and kept most women from senior levels of organizations. The first builds on ways in which women are different from men and concludes that these deficiencies in women are responsible for their lack of career progress. This hypothesis suggests that women's characteristics, such as attitudes, behaviours, traits, and socialization, handicap them in particular ways. It also suggests that women may lack the education and job training necessary to qualify for managerial and professional jobs. However, research support for this explanation is limited (Morrison and von Glinow, 1990). Almost all the evidence shows little or no difference in the traits, abilities, education and motivations of managerial and professional women and men (Powell, 1990).

A second hypothesis builds on notions of bias and discrimination by the majority towards the minority. It suggests that managerial and professional women are held back as a result of bias towards, and stereotypes of, women. The dynamics of this situation are well explained by Kanter (1977) in *Men and Women of the Corporation*. Such bias or discrimination is either sanctioned by the labour market or rewarded by organizations despite the level of job performance of women (Larwood *et al.*, 1988a, 1988b). In addition, there is widespread agreement that the good manager is seen as male or masculine (Schein, 1973, 1975; Schein and Mueller, 1992). Thus there is some research support for this hypothesis.

The third hypothesis emphasizes structural and systematic discrimination as revealed in organizational policies and practices which affect the treatment of women and which limit their advancement (Morrison, 1992). These policies and practices include women's lack of opportunity and power in organizations, the existing sex ratio of groups in organizations, tokenism, lack of mentors and sponsors, and denial of access to challenging assignments. This hypothesis has also received empirical support (Burke and McKeen, 1992).

In attempting to identify specific reasons for women's lack of advancement, it is important to remember that managerial and professional women live and work in a larger society that is patriarchal, a society in which men have historically had greater access to power, privilege and wealth than women. The mechanisms by which this has occurred and is perpetuated are the subject of feminist theory and research (Marshall, 1989). A useful analogy for conceptualizing the intricacy of the structure enforcing this status quo is presented by Frye, quoted by Code (1988). She envisions a bird cage in which if one examines each individual wire one cannot understand why the cage is so confining. It is only by stepping back to contemplate the entire structure, the interconnected and mutually enforcing system of barriers, that one can see why the bird is trapped.

The appearance of *Breaking the Glass Ceiling* (Morrison *et al.*, 1987) gave renewed energy to women in management research. This book, with its attendant publicity, captured the attention of women managers and professionals, researchers interested in women in management issues, and organizations interested in furthering the careers of managerial and professional women.

This interest, coupled with increased research attention, highlighted the importance to business leaders and educators of understanding the impact of large numbers of managerial and professional women entering the workplace (Jamieson and O'Mara, 1991). These demographic changes are some of the most significant organizational changes taking place in the individualized world (Naisbitt and Aburdene, 1990). They have the potential for creating new ways of thinking about work, careers and organizational purposes and policies as well as family and leisure. Organizations must grasp the significance of these changes, adjust to them, and focus on the positive opportunities these forces offer. The economic success of business hinges on their efforts.

Understanding the experiences of this large and growing segment of the workforce, in whom education, effort and hopes have been invested, is critical for economic survival. Organizations cannot afford to underutilize or lose this talent. Educators need to understand the barriers encountered by women, both in the organizations employing them and in their own educational institutions, and managerial and professional women need to understand why they are encountering particular work experiences.

THE DEMOGRAPHIC IMPERATIVE

Organizations have no choice in coming to grips with the utilization of the competencies and abilities of their female workforce. Projections of the demographic make-up of new workforce entrants during the next 20 years indicate that white males – the traditional managerial and professional pool – will constitute only 15% of this group. The remainder – non-traditional professionals and managers – will be made up of women and members of various minority, ethnic and racial groups. During this time period, organizations may, in fact, experience a shortage of particular skills, for example engineering or computer technology.

This situation is also affected by increasing pressures for greater productivity, effectiveness and innovation. Organizations will be increasingly on the look-out for their most talented and able performers. Thus broadening of the talent pool to include the future projected 50% of the workforce that has often been ignored will become a bottom-line issue – a business imperative.

COSTS OF BUSINESS AS USUAL

There are a variety of costs to organizations of failing to address the needs of their managerial and professional women which are highlighted throughout the book. These include:

- *Not mobilizing your best people at the top.* There is considerable evidence to suggest that the 'old boy' network, men's greater comfort with other men, and subtle biases and prejudices make it more difficult for equally (or more) talented women to reach these levels.
- *Not maintaining quality at every level.* Men have 'advantages' at every organizational level which make it more difficult for equally talented women to receive development, recognition and rewards.
- *Treating a big proportion of your employees as dead weight.* On average, women represent about 40–45% of an organization's workforce. Failing to respond to the developmental needs of such a large number of employees is a huge cost.
- *Limiting the contribution women can make.* The failure fully to utilize the talents of women artificially limits their responsibilities and roles.
- *Undervaluing promising people who wish to take a role in family caregiving.* Failure to be sensitive to the needs of talented women who have families, and want to spend time with their families, penalizes highly educated, committed and productive women who also want to produce the next generation of women and men.
- *Not an employer of choice.* When a woman employee leaves because of difficulties, sometimes modest, that she attributes to the fact she is a woman, she may share her frustrations with others, both inside and outside the organization. Morale of other women inside the organization may suffer; women are very interested in what happens to other women. In addition, 'word on the street' may discourage women, and some men, from joining such organizations or using the services of such organizations.
- *Could be capitalizing on a tremendous opportunity.* Each of the above suggests that organizations that are serious about developing and fully

utilizing the talents of their managerial and professional women can reap substantial benefits from unleashing a group of people who have not been encouraged to contribute.

BENEFITS OF A NEW APPROACH

Organizations that are successful in developing practices and policies that support the career aspirations of their managerial and professional women – that is, create an environment where women and men are judged on their merit – can expect certain competitive advantages as a result. These include:

- *Attract the best talent.* There is some evidence that the most talented women and men are likely to be attracted to organizations that reward merit. Talented women, in particular, would be likely to seek out such organizations. As academic staff members in schools of management, we often have women students ask us about how particular organizations treat their women employees.
- *Retain the investment (cost savings).* Organizations have done reasonably well at recruiting and hiring women; they have done less well in developing and retaining the women they have hired. Fewer women are likely to 'bail out' as organizations become more women-friendly.
- *Optimize potential and productivity.* Organizations that reduce the barriers and 'extra challenge' faced by managerial and professional women will reap advantages in performance and productivity. The talents of women will be developed to the fullest and fully utilized. Feelings of frustrations and 'being stuck' should be reduced, and complete focusing of energy on the job will be realized.
- *Attract and retain clients (market share).* Organizations that unleash the talents of their managerial and professional women will become more attractive to potential clients. There are several reasons for this. First, the women themselves will be more capable and effective. Second, the organization will have a more favourable image to potential clients. Third, women managers may be better able to relate effectively to women in the client groups. Fourth, some clients may respond more favourably to organizations that have capable women and men in them. Fifth, organizations that are women-friendly may encourage such initiatives in their clients as well and serve as models and agents of organizational (and societal) changes.
- *Better quality of management.* The development of an organizational culture that is more merit based, one in which no individual is advantaged or disadvantaged, should increase the quality of management at all levels. Abilities, skills and performance – not the 'old boy' network or comfort – become the criteria for development and promotion.

RESEARCH AND PRACTICE

We believe that the field of women in management has both research and practical relevance. Because this area has only gained research attention within the past 10 years, many research questions remain unanswered or have been only partially addressed. In addition, supporting the career aspirations of managerial women has practical implications for women, men, families, organizations and social policy.

Let us first consider the research agenda. From the research evidence presented in this book, the following questions and issues seem important to us if further progress in creating a level playing field in organizations is to be made.

(1) What career models fit the experience of managerial and professional women?
(2) What responsibilities do these women have for 'second shift' work?
(3) What are the implications of career breaks and part-time work in career progress?
(4) What role do mentors and sponsors have in career development?
(5) What is the role of interpersonal network, both inside and outside of organizations, in career development?
(6) How do women find success in general, and work and career success in particular?
(7) How do managerial and professional women successfully balance their multiple commitments?
(8) What supports and demands exist in the relationships these women have with their spouses/partners and children?
(9) What supports and demands exist in the relationships these women have with their parents and elderly dependents?
(10) What aspects of masculine organizational culture, both subtle and not so subtle, are problematic for women?
(11) What are some of the responses by men to initiatives by organizations to create a level playing field?
(12) What documentation and evaluation is being carried out on attempts by organizations which are supportive of women's aspirations?
(13) Do managerial women of different racial and ethnic groups face additional challenges?
(14) Do women experience the same developmental opportunities in their jobs as their male colleagues in similar jobs?

Let us now move to the practical agenda. These areas, involving action research projects in field settings, are equally important because the topic of women in management has obvious practical implications. All research in this area does not have to have *immediate* practical value – though this might be desirable – but some of our research needs to have usefulness.

The following issues need further attention.

(1) We need greater understanding of the sources of motivation that leading organizations in levelling the playing field have used to launch their efforts. Why have some organizations attempted to be leaders in this area?
(2) Can such motivations be transferred to other organizations, and in what ways?
(3) What types of educational efforts are useful in helping men to understand their roles and attitudes, and to change them?

(4) What contributes to 'best practice' in this area? What are innovative organizations doing? What works? What doesn't work, and why?
(5) What organizational practices and policies are supportive of women's career aspirations?
(6) In what ways, if any, are men benefited by these initiatives?
(7) How can the results of both the organizations' successes and failures be shared with the wider business community?

CONCLUSION

One of the great social paradoxes of the past two decades involves the massive influx of women into managerial and professional ranks and the continuation of inequality in both employment and family responsibilities. Women now represent over 40% of the workforce in Western countries and will be an even more significant component in the future, but organizations have been slow to capitalize on the potential of their women employees. In particular, competent, promising female professionals and managers represent a human resource that is frequently left underdeveloped. It is important that organizational leaders recognize the valuable resource that women represent in management and administrative positions and use them effectively. Managers at all levels need to develop the attitudes and expertise to make full use of their female managers and professionals. Research can provide a recognition of the major issues involved and the knowledge of how to deal with them that will make managers more effective in their roles.

This collection of chapters examines the varied issues covered by the broad term 'women in management'. It includes 20 contributions by authors from 7 countries. Contributors were selected according to their expertise and interests in issues of women in management, their ability to provide a variety of perspectives, and their capacity to cover specific content areas.

We hope that this book contributes to a greater prescriptive understanding of what true employment equality is and how it can be achieved. Many different issues are addressed, which we hope will add to the knowledge and practical experience of managers, more of whom are becoming increasingly aware of their responsibilities in increasing the women-friendliness of their organizations. As for researchers, research on women in corporate management should lead to increasing the satisfaction and well-being of both women and men in management.

A pressing need in this regard is to document efforts by organizations to develop the talent of women managers and professionals. This will serve to identify what works and does not work, and why. In addition, the successful efforts of some organizations will provide a blueprint for others in their own efforts. Efforts by organizations in this area will be more credible to senior corporate leaders. It is also important to have successful CEOs committed to full partnership for women at senior ranks, so that they can influence others at those levels.

We hope this book will serve to interest more organizational researchers to consider the issues of women in management. We also hope that it will encourage organizations to develop positive and effective equal opportunity programmes that will have value to the individuals whose work and life experiences we are trying to understand better – namely women and men in managerial professional jobs.

REFERENCES

ADLER, N. J. and IZRAELI, D. N. (1988) *Women in Management Worldwide*, M. E. Sharpe, Armonk, NY.

BURKE, R. J. and MCKEEN, C. A.(1992) Women in management, in C. L. Cooper and I. T. Robertson (eds) *International Review of Industrial and Organizational Psychology*, Wiley, New York, pp. 245–84.

DAVIDSON, M. J. and COOPER, C. L. (1992) *Shattering the Glass Ceiling: The Woman Manager*, Paul Chapman, London.

DAVIDSON, M. J. and COOPER, C. L. (eds) (1993) *European Women in Business and Management*, Paul Chapman, London.

FRYE, S., cited in CODE, L. (1988) Feminist Theory, in S. Burt, L. Code and L. Dorney (eds) *Changing Patterns: Women in Canada*, McClelland & Stewart, Toronto, pp. 18–50.

JAMIESON, D. and O'MARA, J. (1991) *Workforce 2000*, Jossey-Bass, San Francisco.

KANTER, R. M. (1977) *Men and Women of the Corporation*, Basic Books, New York.

LARWOOD, L., SWAJKOWSKI, E. and ROSE, S. (1988a) Manager–client relationships: applying the rational bias theory of managerial discrimination, *Sex Roles*, Vol. 18, pp. 9–29.

LARWOOD, L., SWAJKOWSKY, E. and ROSE, S. (1988b) When discrimination makes 'sense': the rational bias theory, in B. A. Gutek, A. H. Stromberg and L. Larwood (eds) *Women and Work: An Annual Review*, Vol. 3, Sage, Beverly Hills, CA, pp. 265–88.

MARSHALL, J. (1989) *Women Managers: Travellers in a Male World*, Wiley, London.

MORRISON, A. M. (1992) *The New Leaders*, Jossey-Bass, San Francisco, CA.

MORRISON, A. M. and VON GLINOW, M. A. (1990) Women and minorities in management, *American Psychologist*, Vol. 45, pp. 200–8.

MORRISON, A. M., WHITE, R. P. and VAN VELSOR, E. (1987) *Breaking the Glass Ceiling*, Addison-Wesley, Reading, MA.

NAISBITT, J. and ABURDENE, P. (1990) *Megatrends*, Warner, New York.

POWELL, G. N. (1990) One more time: do male and female managers differ? *Academy of Management Executive*, Vol. 4, pp. 68–75.

SCHEIN, V. E. (1973) The relationship between sex role stereotypes and requisite management characteristics, *Journal of Applied Psychology*, Vol. 57, pp. 95–100.

SCHEIN, V. E. (1975) The relationships between sex role stereotypes and requisite management characteristics among female managers, *Journal of Applied Psychology*, Vol. 60, pp. 340–4.

SCHEIN, V. E. and MUELLER, R. (1992) Sex role stereotypes and requisite management characteristics: a cross cultural look, *Journal of Organizational Behavior*, Vol. 13, no. 5, pp. 439–77.

SCHWARTZ, F. N. (1987) Don't write women off as leaders, *Fortune*, Vol. 115, pp. 185–8.

SCHWARTZ, F. N. (1988) Corporate women: a critical business resource, *Vital Speeches*, Vol. 54, pp. 173–6.

SCHWARTZ, F. N. (1992) *Breaking with Tradition: Women and Work, The New Facts of Life*, Warner, New York.

PART ONE

Negative Effects
of Organizational Culture

CHAPTER 2

An Introductory Overview of Women in Corporate Management

BARBARA PARKER AND ELLEN A. FAGENSON

INTRODUCTION

A new United Nations study says that there is apparently no country in the world that treats its women as well as its men. Researchers in 33 countries including the USA admit . . . that they haven't found a place where women have education, employment and health opportunities equal to those available to men.

(*ABC News*, 25 May, 1993)

Between 1985 and 1991, the percentage of women managers increased in 39 of the 41 countries that report comparative labour statistics (ILO, 1993). Yet at the same time, as noted in the quotation above, authors of the United Nations Study found that among those countries where gender-based statistics are collected no country treats its women as well as its men (UN, 1993). These reports demonstrate two themes to be explored in the following review of research and practice for women in management: progress has occurred, but much more progress is possible both within and across nations.

Although the review to follow shows that progress towards achieving managerial equity for women and men has been slow, it also demonstrates that reducing and eliminating some of the barriers to equity has resulted in more women in managerial positions. Accordingly, this review also examines the ways in which various barriers to equity have been reduced, particularly in the USA. While some progress made in the USA is due to the environmental context, that is to equal rights activities, to the relative abundance of well-educated women in the USA – particularly white, middle-class women – and the shrinking proportion of traditional male entrants to the workforce, there is increasing evidence that these same conditions are emerging worldwide (Cox, 1993; Fernandez, 1993). Similar environmental change elsewhere may be a harbinger that development in the global century will provide increased opportunities for women worldwide (Adler and Izraeli, 1994).

Organizational leaders increasingly acknowledge that their ability to compete worldwide depends on their ability to hire and retain the best employees they can find. Organizations are aware that many of their best employees are those who represent some aspect of diversity, whether it be gender, race, nationality, sexual orientation, physical abilities, or any of the other and many aspects of diversity (Schwartz, 1992). Even more than a competitive advantage, organizations are finding that a diverse workforce is a demographic imperative (Morrison, 1992; Schwartz, 1992). The labour force is shrinking and the highest percentage of new entrants into it are women (Johnston and Packer, 1988). Moreover, while women were once barred from higher education, as the century draws to a close they are receiving more Bachelors and Masters degrees than men (Fagenson and Jackson, 1993; Schwartz, 1992). The US economy has also changed, shifting from a manufacturing to a service- and information-based economy, which relies on brain power rather than brawn (Schwartz, 1992). The marketplace, also in flux, is populated with diverse customers, customers who prefer to interact and transact with employees who look and think just like them (Morrison, 1992).

While organizations are aware of the advantages that hiring women, or minorities, offers, many have not yet fully embraced this practice or these individuals. Many organizations still do not recruit, promote, value or support women workers on a par equal to men (Fagenson, 1993). Instead, they choose to ignore a valuable resource in a competitive global business environment (Schwartz, 1992).

While some companies 'waste' an important resource others have expanded their selection pool to include women. These companies have a competitive edge because they select the most talented, creative and experienced employees regardless of gender. In fact, research has shown that diversity helps organizations reduce costs, increase productivity, improve management quality and increase and maintain market share. Empirical evidence demonstrating that diversity is a 'bottom-line' business imperative has led some companies to initiate new equity programmes. For example, Ortho Pharmaceuticals reports that their programme for managing diversity realized savings of $500,000, mainly in turnover among minority group members (Bailey, 1989). In a broader study, Covenant Investment Management found that Standard and Poor (S&P) 500 firms that had hired and advanced women and minorities, and complied with EEOC and regulatory requirements, outperformed firms that had poorer equal employment track records. For example, 5-year annualized returns for the 100 firms with the best equal employment track records were 18.3% as compared to 7.9% for the 100 firms with the worst equality track records; overall S&P returns for the period were 15.9% (Covenant Investment Management, 1993).

Researchers have explored a number of the opportunities and barriers to managerial work for women in the USA, and in doing so they have helped build a foundation for assessing additional opportunities and barriers for female and male managers in an equitable world (Fagenson, 1993). The body of literature on women in management is rich in diversity and, as the review to follow indicates, there are few universals. This diversity of opinion is reflected in the two primary themes developed here: progress made, and barriers confronted and reduced.

Progress towards achieving equal access and representation of women in management positions to date has been least in developing countries, where women as a group hold few managerial positions and generally have poor access to educational opportunities to prepare them for management (ILO,

1993). In addition to holding few decision-making positions at work, many women in developing countries also have poor access to basic safety, security, nutrition, or healthcare resources (ILO, 1993). Thus, advancing women to managerial positions is but one of a number of challenges women in developing countries may face.

Among the industrialized countries, the percentage of women managers is highest in north America and northern Europe and lowest in Australia, Japan, New Zealand, and southern and western Europe (ILO, 1993). While women in the industrialized countries are less likely to go without food, healthcare or education than their sisters in the developing world, women who aspire to managerial positions in the industrialized world also face barriers to full participation in management. Included among these barriers are limited access to resources, especially to jobs offering promotional opportunities and wages comparable to those of men in similar positions. In many cases the height and breadth of barriers for women in management varies according to race and ethnicity, employing industry, or level of the managerial position. While legal remedies have been brought to bear on some of these barriers, other, more subtle barriers can remain high for women managers, and included among these are lack of equal opportunities, the need to balance work and personal life, and stereotyping.

PROGRESS

Statistics reported by the International Labor Organization indicate that the percentage of women holding managerial positions is as much as 40% or more in Australia, the USA and Canada, but only 1.4% in Bangladesh (ILO, 1993). While it is discouraging to learn that Bangladeshi organizations employ few female managers, it is at the same time astounding to see such high percentages reported for women managers in the USA, particularly in view of US Department of Labor data indicating that women held only 6.3% of managerial positions in 1978 (US Department of Labor, 1989). A simple comparison between data available for these two time periods might suggest that US women have made phenomenal progress in attaining managerial jobs in the last 15 years. This would be an erroneous assumption. While progress has occurred, part of what appears to be an improvement in this instance is differences in data collection techniques. The example is offered as a caution for those who study women in management. Whether one intends to compare the numbers of men to women in management, to assess women's managerial progress over time or across nations, a frequent challenge is the very broad ways in which the term 'manager' or 'management' might be used. Even within countries, data can vary widely because what one considers a manager, another considers a sales clerk. Thus, measuring progress for women in management requires comparable and reliable data. These data are not always available, or as has frequently occurred in the USA, information may be collected or reported in different ways over time. For example, before 1983 the US Department of Labor category now called 'executives, managers and administrators' appeared under several headings, including 'managers, officials and proprietors, non-farm', 'managers and administrators except farm' and so on.

INCREASING NUMBERS OF WOMEN AT WORK AND IN MANAGEMENT

According to the best comparative US data available, women's rate of participation in management has grown from 4% in 1940 to 11.4% in 1992, but the number of managerial positions for men has also grown, rising from 9.6% of all jobs held by men in 1940 to 13.5% of employed men in 1992 (US Department of Commerce, 1953; US Department of Labor, 1992). Using these data, one can conclude that while the percentage of women holding managerial positions increased between 1950 and 1990, the number of total managerial jobs also increased. In addition, available data show that the percentage of US jobs held by women has also increased, and expanded the female pool from which managers can be drawn. Thus, part of the increase in the numbers of managerial women employed in the USA is due to the phenomenal growth in female employment in the last 40 years. For example, while only 33.9% of US women were employed outside the home in 1950 (Johnston and Packer, 1988), 57.8% were similarly employed by 1992 (US Department of Labor, 1992).

According to the US Department of Labor, during the 1980s the number of women in executive, administrative, and managerial fields nearly doubled in the USA to number about 6.2 million, or about 42% of the number of people employed in such positions. Of the 6.2 million women employed in the executive, administrative, and managerial fields, about 83% are white women, 8% are black women and about 4.5% are women of Hispanic origin (Bulletin to Management, 1993). As these data would indicate, women of colour are not well represented in managerial ranks.

THE GLASS CEILING TO ADVANCEMENT

Overall, women have made their greatest gains in attaining lower-level managerial positions. Women face greater difficulty in attaining middle- to upper-level management positions, holding only 3% of senior management jobs by 1991 (US Department of Labor, 1991). In the 1970s, when there were few women in the managerial pipeline, a ready explanation for their absence at top managerial levels was that women with the appropriate skills could not be found. In view of the fact that organizations have had more than 20 years to groom women for management, this same excuse persuades fewer people today. Instead, many assert that a 'glass ceiling' has been built on a foundation of groupism still practised among the power élite of most organizations (Morrison et al., 1987). Organizational leaders have discovered that promoting women above the glass ceiling takes more than talk, and several have made such progress by following the management adage of 'what gets done is what gets rewarded'. Tenneco witnessed a 25% increase in the number of women and minorities hired after they tied a part of the executive bonus to progress in promoting women and minorities (Garland, 1991), and other companies like Xerox and Motorola also tie compensation to progress on organizational diversity goals. Morrison (1992) asserts that her interviews with top managers indicate there are six major organizational barriers that constitute the glass ceiling. These include a lonely and non-supportive working environment, treating differences as weaknesses, excluding people from group activities because of their differences, and failure to help individuals prepare for management, to balance work/personal life issues, and to develop organizational awareness or savvy.

According to a recent International Labor Organization report, men all over the world hold the highest management positions, with greater inequalities occurring between men and women the closer they get to the top of organizational hierarchies (ILO, 1993). This suggests that the glass ceiling, as well as 'glass walls' for lateral movement into line positions, are both features of the organizational landscape for women in many nations. In the USA, the barriers to top-level jobs are perceived to be numerous although many are subtle, and well imbedded in organizational culture and life (Fagenson, 1993). Overcoming 'hidden' or less obvious organizational barriers to managerial equity may be difficult. According to one estimate, attaining full economic integration for women at every organizational level would take 75–100 years at the current rate of change (Women's Research and Education Institute, 1992).

In addition to encountering barriers to advancing toward senior-level positions, women also face barriers associated with position and industry sector. For example, according to Catalyst's *Women in Corporate Management Survey*, women were more likely to hold senior management positions in human resources and communications, and were far less likely to hold senior positions in production or plant facilities functions (Catalyst, 1990). According to a study conducted by the UCLA Anderson Graduate School and Korn/Ferry International in 1990, only 5% of top executive positions in 1,000 of the largest corporations in the USA were held by women and minorities (US Department of Labor, 1991). Women in managerial positions frequently perceive that they have fewer opportunities to be promoted to senior management positions. For example, a *Business Week* poll of 400 women executives at corporations with $100 million or more in annual sales revealed that 53% do not believe they have the same chance for promotion to senior management positions as equally qualified men, and 59% think American companies are showing no improvements or losing ground in hiring and promoting women executives (Editorial, 1992). However, there is some evidence to show that opportunities for women in management may be greater in industries like computers and telecommunications that are experiencing a rapid pace of change. Fisher (1987) suggests this occurs because emergent industries simply have not been in existence long enough to have established rules about who is or should be a manager, relying more on managerial ability than on gender to make employment decisions.

In general, women are not equally represented in all segments of the labour force. Employed women are most frequently found in those professions that have traditionally been considered appropriate for women, particularly in the helping professions such as nursing, teaching and clerical work (US Department of Labor, 1992). Women also tend to be concentrated in sales, particularly at the retail level. For example, in 1992, women held 79.3% of administrative support jobs, 98.4% of secretarial, typist and stenographer positions, and 65.5% of all sales, retail and personal service jobs; 94.3% of registered nurses were women in 1992 (US Department of Labor, 1992).

EARNINGS

The US Equal Pay Act of 1963 addressed a myriad of pay equity concerns, but chief among them was that, on average, women were earning about 58% of what men earned for the same work. Interestingly, executive, professional, and administrative jobs were not covered by the Equal Pay Act until June of 1972. Thirty years after the original equal pay legislation, women on average now earn more than they once earned relative to male wages, but progress has been slow. By 1993, women on average were earning about 70% of the amount men earned for the same jobs (Rigdon, 1993).

It was shown earlier that gains for women in management have been greatest at lower managerial levels, and earning gains show a similar profile. That is, female cashiers earned about 95 cents to every male dollar in 1992 as compared to female securities brokers who earned only 52 cents for every dollar men earned from the same profession (Rigdon, 1993). The biggest gender gaps occur for sales employees where women earn 57% of male earnings, and in executive and managerial positions where women earn 64% of male earnings (Pennar, 1991). Rigdon (1993) also reports that gender disparities are greatest for women from ethnic minorities, particularly black and Hispanic women who earned 62 and 54 cents respectively as compared to every dollar white men earned in 1991. One explanation for the persistence of earnings disparities for women is that wage scales for lower-level positions are fairly well known and publicized among some groups, particularly members of the dominant culture, while secrecy policies and practices more frequently cloak earnings information for managerial and professional employees in the private sector. Union representation is often higher among lower-paid workers, and this too may explain why pay for men and women is more nearly equal in lower-paid occupations.

The annual median income reported for white women managers in 1992 was $26,944; this number compares unfavourably to the average income of white male managers at $41,526, and to all other male managers at $40,746 (US Department of Labor, 1993). While African–American women earned $27,029 – slightly more than white female managers and slightly less than black male managers ($28,264) – their earnings were only 65.1% of those of white male managers (US Department of Labor, 1993). Female managers of Hispanic origin were paid least among female managers for whom comparative earnings were reported, earning $24,951 per year (US Department of Labor, 1993). Wage disparities for male and female managers vary across professions. Using unpublished data appearing in the 1993 *Current Population Survey*, Fagenson and Jackson (1994) calculate that female property and real estate managers earn 87% of the salary of male managers in that field, whereas female financial managers earn only about 62.4% as much as male financial managers.

Despite overall increases in earnings in some sectors, gains in comparative earnings for women overall are slow, and particularly at senior management levels. In 1990 *Fortune* magazine conducted a compensation study of the 1,000 largest industrial and service businesses in the USA to discover that only 19 women (0.005%) were counted among the highest paid officers and directors (Fierman, 1990). Similarly, a recent Korn/Ferry International Study showed that while individual women had made wage progress, on average there had been no group progress in wage increases among executive women when comparing their earnings with those of executive men (Korn/Ferry and UCLA Anderson, 1993). According to the report, the disparity between wages for male and female executives is estimated to be somewhere around $100,000 based on comparing data from a predominantly male sample in 1989 and a female sample in 1992. In 1989 the average base salary plus bonus for men was $290,000 as compared to an average base salary plus bonus compensation of $187,000 for women executives in 1992.

As compared to the rest of the world, working women in the USA are paid proportionately less than working women in most industrialized nations. According to a report prepared by Francine Blau and Lawrence Kahn (1993), the female-to-male weekly wage ratio ranged from 80 to 90% in Australia, Denmark, France, New Zealand, Norway, and Sweden; while other countries in western Europe also had ratios of roughly 65–75%, US wages proportionately tended to be on the low side for women.

This review of women's progress toward managerial positions and toward more equitable pay for similar or the same work shows how much room for improvement is possible, but at the same time it illustrates that considerable progress has been made to this point. The following section identifies where and how progress has been made, and it begins with the basic theoretical assumptions that have been made about women at work and as managers.

THEORETICAL ASSUMPTIONS ABOUT WOMEN AS WORKERS AND MANAGERS

A Significant Case of No Significant Differences is the subtitle of a 1980 study of male and female managers that revealed few differences between the two at work (Donnell and Hall, 1980). The subtitle of the article and its findings sum up overall findings from comparative studies of managers and gender in the USA. Dobbins and Platz's (1986) review of 17 studies comparing leadership effectiveness similarly found that leadership styles were not different, nor did gender influence perceived effectiveness of leadership in organizations. Nevertheless, male and female managers have been and continue to be perceived as different (Freedman and Phillips, 1988; Heilman *et al.*, 1989; Powell, 1990) and a small number of studies have supported this contention (Helgesen, 1990; Rosener, 1990). As the review of progress above would indicate, organizations also treat men and women differently in terms of managerial and pay opportunities. While explanations for perceived or actual differences between men and women vary widely, three primary perspectives have been proposed to direct action. These theoretical perspectives are useful not only as research frameworks, but also because they describe the perspectives organizational leaders implicitly or explicitly adopt when addressing gender equity issues.

One approach to understanding gender differences is known as the 'person-centered' or 'gender-centered' approach (Horner, 1972; Terborg, 1977; Riger and Galligan, 1980). The basic argument for this approach is that gender, whether due to biological roots or socialization influences, determines many if not most of one's preferences, abilities, and skills, and that these characteristics largely drive behaviours. Accordingly, one might expect men to think and act in certain prescribed ways and women to act in other prescribed ways. Organizational practices prior to the mid-1960s in the USA favoured men almost exclusively as managers, operating on the gender-centered belief that men alone possessed suitable qualities for managerial positions (Schein, 1973, 1975). According to this line of thinking, women managers are believed less likely to possess the skills, abilities and attributes needed for management than are their male counterparts, and the research evidence shows that this perspective remains alive and well in the minds of male managers in today's workplace (Brennan et al., 1989; Heilman et al., 1989).

Another variation on the gender-centered approach to management is that women have different, and even better skills than men for managing the demands of the global workplace. Important managerial skills for the global century are likely to be many, but according to some theorists the particular skills women bring to global workplaces are associated with traditional sex-role expectations that women are more nurturant and caring. For example, Lunneborg (1990) studied 204 women in a variety of male-dominated jobs to conclude that themes for women in these jobs included a nurturant approach to co-workers, and a desire to use power differently to how men use power, that is more collaboratively. Following her interviews and diary studies of women managers, Helgesen (1990) also concluded that managerial women have a unique perspective, but she argued that this perspective makes women better managers than men. In particular, women have greater concern for relationships, disdain complex rules and structures, and emphasize process over product or task.

Yet a third gender-centered approach is represented in what has been called the complementary contributions approach (Adler and Izraeli, 1988). This approach to gender differences is described as pervasive in Europe, but it is also found in many US firms and among individuals who believe that while men and women as managers are different, each has an equally valuable contribution to make to the organization. Thus, while it argues that differences are gender based, this theory does not suggest that women or men are inherently better managers, but perhaps better at certain managerial tasks.

A second perspective on women as managers argues that observed or observable differences in managerial behaviour for men and women are due to situational differences in the workplace. This perspective has been called the situation or organizational structure approach, and it argues that differences in how women manage at work may be due to features of the organization. For example, the way women use power might be due to the fact that there are relatively few women in managerial positions, the positions they occupy are vested with little power and those reaching such positions have limited job opportunity or mobility (Kanter, 1977). According to Kanter, those with limited power and few prospects for attaining more powerful positions are likely to act differently to those who expect to attain additional power.

Structural differences for gender differences generally reject the notion of a feminine style of leadership, or a masculine style of leadership, arguing instead for situational forms of leadership that adapt to the demands of the situation. Freeman's (1990) interviews with 40 women managers provided support for this perspective, showing that many of the women in the sample were inclined to play down their femininity so as to be perceived as a manager first and a women second, and to take on traits traditionally considered more masculine, such as being more task oriented than considerate, or more ambitious, at work. Thus, Freeman argues that personality traits (or at least the behaviours that seem to express personality) can change according to the situation.

Yet a third approach has been used to explain gender diversity in management; this approach has been called the 'gender–organization–system' (GOS) approach because it adopts aspects of the situational and gender-centered approaches described above by arguing that situations affect individual behaviour but that individuals *also* may differ from one another on the basis of gender (Fagenson, 1990, 1993). In the latter case, the emphasis is not so much on gender as an imperative for difference, but simply a belief that some women differ from some men. The gender–organization–system approach also makes two additional assumptions about work:

(a) an individual and his or her organization cannot be understood separate from the society (culture) in which he or she works, and (b) when the individual, the organization, or the system in which they are embedded changes, the other components change as well.

(*Fagenson, 1993, p. 6*)

This theory provides a more systems-oriented view of organizations, because it views the status of men and women in organizations simultaneous with the organizational and societal context from which those status differentials or equalities emerged. Rather than arguing that women are better than men or men are better than women, as is possible with the gender-centered approach, or that organizations particularly need to change, which is a central argument for the situational approach, the GOS approach suggests that people, organizations, roles, and societies all change simultaneously in response to environmental shifts, albeit at different paces. The fact that there are these different paces might explain why progress toward managerial equity for women has differed around the world.

As compared to the gender-centered and situational theories, the systems-oriented aspect of the GOS theory approach does not so much assign blame for past inequities as suggest directions for future equity. An organization following a GOS approach would view managerial equity for women as part of a systemic change requiring some amount of adaptation on the part of organizational members, organizational design, and organizational strategy and vision. Ideally, this vision would define equity as a strategic imperative for would-be world-class competitors. According to Taylor Cox, 'Since the diversity of workforces is growing throughout the world, the costs of *not* managing diversity well will escalate greatly in the coming years' (Cox, 1993, p. 26).

In suggesting that change occurs simultaneously and at different rates at all levels of society, the GOS theory alone has the potential to capture the complex person/organization/societal interaction that has led to the progress described above. Accordingly, progress occurs not as the result of singular action, but rather because of interaction among social forces, including political and legal activity, societal beliefs and values, and organizational and individual action. The following review of important (due to space limitations, not all inclusive) barriers to managerial equity simultaneously acknowledges the contributions societal, organizational, and individual initiatives have made to reduce barriers for women as they earn managerial positions.

EQUAL OPPORTUNITY

One result of considerable political agitation for civil rights in the USA was a number of Executive Orders and Acts which have subsequently been tested and developed as the result of court decisions. As was mentioned earlier, the Equal Pay Act, as amended in 1972 to cover executive, administrative and managerial workers, and the Civil Rights Act of 1964 (Title VII) provide basic guarantees for equal opportunity in jobs and pay. However, as was shown above, neither law has been able perfectly to balance opportunity in the USA. This is in part due to the fact that other aspects of society interact to prevent full implementation.

WORK/PERSONAL LIFE CONFLICT

In the USA, managerial work has traditionally made high demands on the individual, but perhaps no demand is higher than the belief that managerial work comes before family or personal concerns (Bartolome and Evans, 1980). While this assumption was sometimes questioned by the men who traditionally held managerial positions, it has come under greater scrutiny as increasing numbers of women entered the managerial workforce. This scrutiny results from the fact that while men in management were expected to be at work and not with family when work demanded it, managerial work for women did not provide the same choice. Instead, whether explicitly or implicitly stated, organizations which hired women for management slots in the 1970s generally expected women in management not to have families. As the review to follow indicates, this is one choice that many women in management did make, but their experiences have led others subsequently to seek different resolutions to conflict between work and personal life.

One approach to managing work/personal life conflict is to make a choice between one or the other. Those choosing a personal life, perhaps a family, were then lost as organizational employees, while those women choosing work life more often postponed or bypassed some aspect of personal life or family. Hennig and Jardim's (1977) study of managerial women showed that few in their sample were married or had children. Similarly, a 1986 study (Heidrich and Struggles, 1986) of corporate officers in the Fortune 1,000 largest industrial and service companies found that the average woman was married but childless, and spent less than 10 hours per week on homemaking tasks. Areas affected by their careers for these women included decisions about having children (30%), the success of their marriages (17%), and the decision to marry (15%).

In 1992, Korn/Ferry International and the UCLA Anderson Graduate School of Management conducted a survey of 400 senior women executives which they then compared to similar surveys of women in executive positions in 1982 and to current senior male executives (Korn/Ferry and UCLA Anderson, 1993). In the 1982 sample, about 49% of the women executives were married and 61% had no children, but by 1992 nearly 70% of the women were married and, among them, most had children. Most men (90%) in the sample were married, and 91% had children, leading the study's authors to conclude that women 'continue to make concessions that men do not seem to face' (p. 2). The authors further posit that balancing work and family concerns has taken a toll on women executives because the overwhelming majority (77%) want to retire before age 65.

Results from the Korn/Ferry report – *Decade of the Executive Woman* – suggest a second strategy has emerged to lower barriers to managerial work associated with work/personal conflict. These women want both to work and to have families. Women in pursuit of this co-called 'have it all' strategy find it can be a very stressful one to pursue without accommodation from family, organization, or both. According to research on the topic, women pursuing the 'have it all' strategy experience a great deal of stress at home and on the job (Davidson and Cooper, 1986; Greenglass, 1987; Offermann and Armitage, 1993), although these stressors are not immutable and can be relieved.

For example, one stressor is likely to be house- and childcare: as much research shows, women are expected to and do perform the majority of such work (Hochschild, 1989; Parasuraman and Greenhaus, 1993). Personal resolutions of these dilemmas include selecting a partner who will take major responsibility for house- and childcare responsibilities, or in the case of executives paid at the high end of the scale, paying others to perform associated tasks. According to reports on a Census Bureau study released in 1993 (Merzer, 1993), social and economic changes in the USA have included increases in the number of fathers providing in-home daycare. That is, fathers provided primary care for 1 in 7 children under the age of 5 in 1988 as compared to 1 in 5 by 1991.

Organizations have also been successful in reducing some amount of work/personal life conflict by providing on-site programmes for childcare and household tasks, and supporting flexible work schedules and job sharing for women and men alike. Unfortunately, despite evidence to show that on-site childcare results in lower employee absenteeism, lower job turnover, and greater job satisfaction and commitment (Dawson *et al.*, 1984; Milkovich and Gomez, 1976; Youngblood and Chambers-Cook, 1984), only 13% of *Fortune* 1,000 companies have on-site childcare programmes (Mathews, 1993). Thus, this is an area where organizations have lagged behind individuals in finding ways to reduce barriers to women in management. Flexible time benefits and work–family benefits programmes seem to appeal more to organizations, with 77% of *Fortune* 1,000 companies reporting that they sponsor these initiatives (Mathews, 1993).

In 1989 Schwartz suggested that organizations could help women balance their work and family lives by providing separate career tracks for women with children. The career track for women choosing to have children was later dubbed the 'mommy track' (Ehrlich, 1989). The article and the concept of the 'mommy track' generated a great deal of debate, with some feeling it tracked women unfairly and others believing it provided a viable option for women and men alike in organizations (Schwartz, 1992). In addition, the 'mommy track' debate carved out a new perspective on 'having it all', which was to suggest that women and men could have it all, although not necessarily at the same time.

The Family and Medical Leave Act was enacted in the USA in February 1993 in response to concerns from men and women that they could not exercise choice to nurture children, or care for sick or ageing family members, without sacrificing their jobs. Prior to its enactment, the USA had no family leave law. In this regard the USA compared poorly to other countries where opportunities to balance work and family were well institutionalized (Lee, 1993). For example, Finland provides 35 weeks of fully paid family leave; Austria provides 20 fully paid weeks; Canada provides for 15 weeks of family leave time at 60% pay (*Seattle Times*, 1993a). Although the Family and Medical Leave Act represents an improvement over the void preceding it, the Act provides no guarantees of paid leave, and allows for many exemptions on the basis of organizational size and for employees viewed as 'key' to their firms. What this is likely to mean is that women who are in higher managerial positions may not be permitted family leave if their positions are perceived as critical or key to the organization. This example also suggests that society and its social institutions are by no means universal in their support for families or a personal life for workers. The work/personal life conflict remains a significant challenge for individuals, and particularly for women who aspire to managerial positions.

STEREOTYPES AND ASSUMPTIONS ABOUT WOMEN

Images of women in advertisements, newspapers, books, television programmes and other instruments of popular culture depict women as less competent than men when women are visible at all (Faludi, 1991). For example, Kuiper (1988) analysed pictures in a sample of *Fortune* 500 annual reports to find that relative to female–male labour force participation, 'females were underrepresented in those reports by approximately 27%, whereas males were overrepresented by approximately 39%' (p. 89). Eighty-one per cent of 200 female chief executive officers (CEOs) identified stereotyping and preconceptions of women managers as a primary factor impeding progress for women in managerial positions (Heidrich and Struggles, 1986). Negative images of women, or their absence from depiction as organizational members, may explain why perceived gender differences draw much attention in the face of empirical evidence showing that such differences are not typical (Powell, 1993). Increasing the number of women managers and their interaction with male colleagues would help counter this process (Powell, 1993; Northcraft and Gutek, 1993), but since women have progressed slowly toward senior executive positions, other strategies should be encouraged. For example, programmes that examine and discuss sex-role stereotypes would help sensitize men and women to one another (Powell, 1993).

Other organizational actions that may serve to reduce stereotypes and overcome erroneous assumptions are including women in networks and providing mentors to assist women in acquiring knowledge of the organization's culture. Many studies indicate that women have been largely excluded from 'old boy' networks which traditionally are composed of individuals who hold power in the organization (Hennig and Jardim, 1977; Kanter, 1977; Fagenson,

1986). While women have successfully formed their own networks (Welsh, 1981; Northcraft and Gutek, 1993), these networks do not necessarily provide access to the 'old boy' networks where power is held. Accordingly, it is also important for women to penetrate male networks to a greater extent if they wish to become sufficiently visible to win organizational promotions. Finding a mentor has been suggested as one way to develop one's political awareness in an organization, and many women who have secured high-level positions acknowledge that they did so in part with help from their mentors (Hennig and Jardim, 1977). Research shows that people who are protégés of powerful people secure more promotions and power themselves, have greater job mobility, recognition, satisfaction, and easier access to powerful individuals in the organizations than do non-protégés, and that women become protégés at the same rate as men (Fagenson, 1988, 1989; Dreher and Ash, 1990; Ragins and Cotton, 1991). At the same time, women perceive that they face great barriers to obtaining mentors (Ragins and Cotton, 1991).

THE ROLE OF WOMEN IN RESEARCH

Stereotypes and assumptions constraining equal opportunity have been overcome in a number of other ways as well. One of the more important methods has been to challenge traditional assumptions about women's place in research, organizations, and in society. Calvert and Ramsey (1992) argue that progress for women has come at a high cost, and that research reflects the price paid because the focus of attention is still on how work has traditionally been organized and how women can fit into existing structures. These authors argue that research on women in management has been forced to adapt and become incremental, focusing on smaller and smaller issues to fit into the existing mainstream. Accordingly, research practices have reinforced the 'maleness' of current organizations where women are expected to do most of the adapting that occurs. Calvert and Ramsey propose a different set of assumptions for research, organizations and individuals that include defining: competition as 'doing excellently' instead of 'excelling over' (Lugones and Spelman, 1987; Calas and Smircich, 1990); power as a way to enhance all rather than diminish some (Miller, 1976); and social change as an organizational responsibility (Marshall, 1984). Diversity as an organizational value and goal could be added to this list (Cox, 1993). In arguing for a different voice, these authors suggest that the voices worth hearing are not just those of white females. Similarly, the major voices from US organizations have been those of white males in powerful positions, individuals who represent just a few of the hue of perspectives found in any organization.

THE ROLE OF ORGANIZATIONS

Challenging the status quo produces resistance to change and this factor alone impedes progress to managerial equity. In addition, results are difficult to achieve because while it is challenging to imagine organizations that are equitable, it is even more challenging to structure those organizations.

Nevertheless, change may occur by adapting current models and developing new ones.

As was indicated earlier, a variety of tactics have been pursued successfully to lower barriers to women in management. In a study of corporations with $100 million or more in annual sales, among the 400 women executives polled, 64% believe large companies have improved in the last five years in hiring and promoting women managers, but most assert that many barriers remain (Editorial, 1992). According to this group, these barriers will be overcome by various actions, including agreeing that women should take a strong public stand on hiring and promoting women executives (70% in agreement) and they should take legal action when they see evidence of discrimination (76%), but many also agreed that they should build networks with other women to help one another (83%). Thus, some amount of progress will be made by individuals acting alone.

In the early years of civil rights and equity initiatives in the USA, many believed that once women or minorities were part of organizations, they would be promoted to managerial positions, and the problems of inequity would disappear. One result was organizational emphasis on recruiting women, but more recent evidence shows that organizational initiatives for gender equity in management are broader, and now include development and retention. Organizational action that has retained more women in management includes developing workplaces that are more congenial for women. According to a *Business Week* report on 'woman-friendly' companies (*Business Week*, 1990), criteria that make a company friendly include the numbers of women in key executive positions and on the board of directors, efforts to help women advance, and sensitivity to work/family issues.

Implicit to Calvert and Ramsey's (1992) description of traditional organizational assumptions is the belief that organizations operate on a zero-sum basis. This assumption has played a significant role in many equity initiatives to date, particularly those where few opportunities have been available to women or minorities. Organizations have been encouraged to rethink their zero-sum assumptions, and replace them with innovative and creative management tools believed better able to improve productivity among all employees. Empowerment, improved teamwork, and creativity are several common themes found among newer management theories. For example, the emphasis on customer service implicit to total quality management requires employees who are able to evaluate alternative options, while a learning organization requires all its members at every level – not just managers – to break down their defences, and employ new approaches to their jobs. Re-engineering asks all members of the organization to reevaluate what has been done traditionally and to question why that tradition is in place, while diversity management argues that productivity depends on every organizational member feeling a part of the inclusive workplace and their differences valued by the organization. The common theme among these theories is that the success of each adopting organization depends upon employees being fully informed and fully involved in the life of the organization. Clearly the latter cannot occur when organizational members feel that the advancement of one group comes at the expense of another's progress. In view of increasing diversity in the US labour force (Cox, 1993), organizations cannot afford to sacrifice any individual productivity. Therefore, organizations must strive to reduce any and all barriers to productivity.

CONCLUSION

Legal remedies to inequitable opportunity and treatment are one means society has of correcting past wrongs or creating future opportunities, but such remedies often are very slow in the USA when they emerge from court cases that take many years to try. Moreover, progress to date would suggest that legal remedies alone do not make for an equitable world. Action from non-governmental organizations and other entities also has a role to play, and they increasingly view equity for women as an issue of worldwide social importance. For example, in September of 1993, representatives of 20 presidents of the worlds' religions signed a document of core values which precludes discrimination against women worldwide. Signers include the Dalai Lama, and the Reverend Wesley Ariarajah, deputy general secretary of the World Council of Churches, which includes most major Protestant sects (*Seattle Times*, 1993b). Those who signed this agreement, as well as those individuals and organizations participating in achieving managerial equity, all have a role to play in realizing a future where the world's women are treated as well as its men.

REFERENCES

ADELMAN, C. (1991) *Women of Thirtysomething: Paradoxes of Attainment*, US Department of Education, Office of Educational Research and Improvement, Report OR 91–530, New York.

ADLER, N. J. and IZRAELI, D. (1988) Women in management worldwide, in N. J. Adler and D. Izraeli (eds) *Women in Management Worldwide*, M. E. Sharpe, Armonk, NY.

ADLER, N. J. and IZRAELI, D. (1994) *Competitive Frontiers: Women Managers in a Global Economy*, Blackwell, Cambridge, MA.

BAILEY, J. (1989) How to be different but equal, *Savvy Woman*, November, p. 47.

BARTOLOME, F. and EVANS, P. A. L. (1980) Must success cost so much? *Harvard Business Review*, Vol. 58, pp. 137–48.

BLAU, F. and KAHN, L. (1993) Working paper no. 4224, National Bureau of Economic Research, University of Illinois Institute of Industrial Labor Relations, Champaign–Urbana.

BRENNAN, O. C., TOMKIEWICZ, J. and SCHEIN, V. E. (1989) The relationship between sex role stereotypes and requisite management characteristics revisited, *Academy of Management Journal*, Vol. 32, no. 3, pp. 662–9.

BULLETIN TO MANAGEMENT (1993) Datagraph: women in the workforce, 25 February, pp. 60–2.

BUSINESS WEEK (1990) Welcome to the woman-friendly company, *Business Week*, 6 August, pp. 48–55.

CALAS, M. and SMIRCICH, L. (1990) Thrusting toward more of the same with the Porter–McKibbin report, *Academy of Management Review*, Vol. 15, no. 4, pp. 698–705.

CALVERT, L. M. and RAMSEY, V. J. (1992) Bringing women's voice to research on women in management, *Journal of Management Inquiry*, Vol. 1, no. 1, pp. 79–88.

CATALYST (1990) *Women in Corporate Management Survey*, Catalyst, New York.

COVENANT INVESTMENT MANAGEMENT (1993) Equal opportunity, stock performance linked. Press release, 21 April, Chicago.

COX, T. JR (1993) Cultural Diversity in Organizations, Berrett-Koehler, San Francisco.

DAVIDSON, M. J. and COOPER, G. L. (1986) Executive women under pressure, International Review of Applied Psychology, Vol. 35, no. 3, pp. 301–26.

DAWSON, A. G. et al. (1984) An Experimental Study of the Effects of Employer-Sponsored Child Care Services on Selected Employee Behaviors, CRS, Inc., Chicago.

DOBBINS, G. H. and PLATZ, S. J. (1986) Sex differences in leadership: how real are they? Academy of Management Review, Vol. 11, no. 1, pp. 118–27.

DONNELL, S. M. and HALL, J. (1980) Men and women as managers: A significant case of no significant differences, Organizational Dynamics, Vol. 8, no. 1, pp. 60–77.

DREHER, G. and ASH, R. (1990) A comparative study of mentoring among men and women in managerial professional and technical positions, Journal of Applied Psychology, Vol. 75, no. 5, pp. 539–46.

EDITORIAL (1992) The gains are slow, say many women, Business Week, 8 June, p. 77.

EHRLICH, E. (1989) The mommy track, Business Week, 20 March, pp. 126–34.

FAGENSON, E. A. (1986) Women's work orientation: something old, something new, Group and Organization Studies, Vol. 11, no. 1, pp. 75–100.

FAGENSON, E. A. (1988) The power of a mentor: proteges and non-proteges' perceptions of their own power in organizations, Group and Organization Studies, Vol. 13, no. 2, pp. 182–94.

FAGENSON, E. A. (1989) The mentor advantage: perceived job/career experiences of proteges vs. non-proteges, Journal of Organizational Behavior, Vol. 10, no. 4, pp. 309–20.

FAGENSON, E. A. (1990) At the heart of women in management research: theoretical and methodological approaches and their biases, Journal of Business Ethics, Vol. 9, no. 2, pp. 267–74.

FAGENSON, E. A. (1993) Diversity in management: introduction and the importance of women in management, in E. A. Fagenson (ed.) Women in Management: Trends, Issues and Challenges in Managerial Diversity, Sage Publications, Newbury Park, CA, pp. 3–18.

FAGENSON, E. A. and JACKSON, J. (1994) The status of women managers in the United States, in N. J. Adler and D. Izraeli (eds), op. cit.

FALUDI, S. (1991) Backlash: The Undeclared War Against American Women, Crown Publishers, New York.

FERNANDEZ, J. P. (1993) The Diversity Advantage, Lexington Books, New York.

FIERMAN, J. (1990) Why women still don't hit the top, Fortune, 30 July, pp. 40–62.

FISHER, A. B. (1987) Where women are succeeding, Fortune, 3 August, pp. 78–86.

FREEDMAN, S. and PHILLIPS, J. (1988) The changing nature of research on women at work, Journal of Management, Vol. 14, no. 2, pp. 231–63.

FREEMAN, S. J. M. (1990) Managing Lives: Corporate Women and Social Change, University of Massachusetts, Amherst, MA.

GARLAND, S. B. (1991) How to keep women managers on the corporate ladder, Business Week, 2 September, p. 64.

GREENGLASS, E. R. (1987) Anger in Type A women: implications for coronary heart disease, Personality and Individual Differences, Vol. 8, no. 5, pp. 639–50.

HEIDRICH and STRUGGLES (1986) The Corporate Woman Officer, Heidrich and Struggles, Chicago.

HEILMAN, M. E., BLOCK, C., MARTELL, R. and SIMON, M. (1989) Has anything changed? Current characteristics of men, women and managers, Journal of Applied Psychology, Vol. 74, no. 6, pp. 935–42.

HELGESEN, S. (1990) The Female Advantage: Women's Ways of Leadership, Doubleday/Currency, New York.

HENNIG, M. and JARDIM, A. (1977) The Managerial Woman, Anchor/Doubleday, New York.

HOCHSCHILD, A. (1989) The Second Shift: Inside the Two-Job Marriage, Penguin, New York.

HORNER, M. (1972) Toward an understanding of achievement related conflicts in women, Journal of Social Issues, Vol. 28, pp. 157–76.

ILO (INTERNATIONAL LABOUR OFFICE) (1993) Unequal race to the top, World of Work-US, no. 2, pp. 6–7.

JOHNSTON, W. and PACKER, A. (1988) Workforce 2000: Work and Workers for the 21st Century, Hudson Institute, Indianapolis, IN.

KANTER, R. M. (1977) Men and Women of the Corporation, Basic Books, New York.

KORN/FERRY INTERNATIONAL (1993) *Board of Directors Annual Study*, Korn/Ferry, New York.

KORN/FERRY INTERNATIONAL and UCLA ANDERSON (1993) *Decade of the Executive Woman*, Korn Ferry and UCLA Anderson Graduate School of Business Administration, Los Angeles, CA.

KUIPER, S. (1988) Gender in annual reports, *The Journal of Business Communication*, Vol. 25, no. 3, pp. 87–94.

LEE, B. (1993) The legal and political realities for women managers: the barriers, the opportunities, and the horizon ahead, in E. A. Fagenson (ed.) *op. cit.*, pp. 246–73.

LUGONES, M. C. and SPELMAN, E. V. (1987) Competition, compassion, and community: models for feminist ethos, in V. Miner and H. E. Longino (eds) *Competition: A Feminist Taboo?*, Feminist Press, New York.

LUNNEBORG, P. W. (1990) *Women Changing Work*, Greenwood Press, New York.

MARSHALL, J. (1984) *Women Managers: Travellers in a Male World*, Wiley, Chichester.

MATHEWS, J. (1993) Easing an employee's family strain reaps benefits for employers too, *Washington Post*, 2 May, p. H2.

MERZER, M. (1993) More fathers taking care of America's children, study says, *Seattle Times*, 22 September, p. A5.

MILKOVICH, G. T. and GOMEZ, I. R. (1976) Day care and selected employee work behaviors, *Academy of Management Journal*, Vol. 19, no. 1, pp. 111–15.

MILLER, J. B. (1976) *Toward a New Psychology of Women*, Beacon, Boston.

MORRISON, A. M. (1992) *The New Leaders: Guidelines on Leadership Diversity in America*, Jossey-Bass, San Francisco.

MORRISON, A. M., WHITE, R. P. and VAN VELSOR, E. (1987) *Breaking the Glass Ceiling*, Addison-Wesley, Reading, MA.

NORTHCRAFT, G. and GUTEK, B. (1993) Discrimination against women in management: going, going, gone – or going but never gone? in E. A. Fagenson (ed.) *op. cit.*

OFFERMANN, L. and ARMITAGE, M. (1993) The stress and health of the woman manager, in E. A. Fagenson (ed.) *op. cit.*, pp. 131–61.

PARASURAMAN, S. and GREENHAUS, J. (1993) Personal portrait: the lifestyle of the woman manager, in E. A. Fagenson (ed.) *op. cit.*, pp. 186–211.

PENNAR, K. (1991) Women are still paid the wages of discrimination, *Business Week*, 28 October, p. 35.

POWELL, G. N. (1990) One more time: do female and male managers differ? *Academy of Management Executive*, Vol. 4, no. 3, pp. 68–75.

POWELL, G. N. (1993) *Women and Men in Management* (2nd edn), Sage, Newbury Park, CA.

RAGINS, B. and COTTON, J. (1991) Easier said than done: barriers to mentorship among women and men in organizations, *Academy of Management Journal*, Vol. 34, no. 4, pp. 939–51.

RIGDON, J. E. (1993) Three decades after the Equal Pay Act, women's wages remain far from parity, *Wall Street Journal*, 9 June, pp. B1, B10.

RIGER, S. and GALLIGAN, P. (1980) Women in management: an exploration of competing paradigms, *American Psychologist*, Vol. 35, no. 10, pp. 902–10.

ROSENER, J. (1990) Ways women lead, *Harvard Business Review*, November–December, pp. 119–25.

SCHEIN, V. E. (1973) The relationship between sex role stereotypes and requisite management characteristics, *Journal of Applied Psychology*, Vol. 57, no. 2, pp. 95–100.

SCHEIN, V. E. (1975) The relationships between sex role stereotypes and requisite management characteristics among female managers, *Journal of Applied Psychology*, Vol. 60, no. 3, pp. 340–4.

SCHWARTZ, F. (1989) Management women and the new facts of life, *Harvard Business Review*, Vol. 67, no. 1, pp. 65–76.

SCHWARTZ, F. (1992) *Breaking with Tradition: Women and Work, the New Facts of Life*, Warner, New York.

SEATTLE TIMES (1993a) Family leave: US vs. other countries (Women at Work, International Labor Office), *Seattle Times*, 5 February, p. 76.

SEATTLE TIMES (1993b) World's clerics draft global ethic, *Seattle Times*, 1 September, p. A12.

TERBORG, J. (1977) Women in management: a research review, *Journal of Applied Psychology*, Vol. 62, no. 6, pp. 647–64.

UN (UNITED NATIONS) (1993) *The Human Development Report*, Oxford University Press.

US DEPARTMENT OF COMMERCE, BUREAU OF THE CENSUS (1953) Census of the population: 1950, in *The Report of the Seventeenth Decennial Census of the US*, Vol. 2, pp. 1–267, Characteristics of the Population, Part I. US Summary.

US DEPARTMENT OF LABOR (1989) *Women in Management. Facts on Working Women*, No. 89–4, US Government Printing Office, Washington, DC.

US DEPARTMENT OF LABOR (1990) *Employment and Earnings*, US Government Printing Office, Washington, DC.

US DEPARTMENT OF LABOR (1991) *A Report on the Glass Ceiling Initiative*, US Government Printing Office, Washington, DC.

US DEPARTMENT OF LABOR (1992) *Tabulations from the Current Population Survey*, US Government Printing Office, Washington, DC.

US DEPARTMENT OF LABOR (1993) Unpublished tabulations from the current population survey. US Government Printing Office, Washington, DC.

WELSH, M. S. (1981) *Networking: The Great New Way for Women to Get Ahead*, Warner Books, New York.

WOMEN'S RESEARCH AND EDUCATION INSTITUTE (1992) *The American Woman 1990–1991: A Status Report*, WREI, Washington, DC.

YOUNGBLOOD, S. A. and CHAMBERS-COOK, K. (1984) Child care assistance can improve employee attitudes and behaviors, *Personnel Administrator*, Vol. 19, pp. 44–5.

CHAPTER 3

Gender Cultures: How they Affect Men and Women at Work

SU MADDOCK AND DI PARKIN[1]

INTRODUCTION

Labour market studies show that women lack status and are segregated at work, but women are also subjected to a more personal form of treatment because of their gender. Everyone knows the atmosphere at work can be either stressful or reinforcing and that organizational culture can affect all employees in work. What is less discussed is how organizational cultures are also gendered and how they influence both men and women's expectations of themselves and of each other.

Men and women's attitudes towards each other and their interpersonal relations constitute a gender culture peculiar to each work environment. Gender cultures are not as vague or imprecise as they might first appear. They may be difficult to quantify, but they are clearly recognizable and understood by every woman we have interviewed.

This chapter describes the gender cultures we have identified during the course of conducting equality audits, training sessions and discussions with men and women managers in British public authorities in the early 1990s. We have both worked for many years in local government and in developing women's organizations. We have felt continually frustrated by the marginal nature of equality work and the narrow interpretation of equal opportunities, which usually failed to grasp what women wanted from work and how women's opportunities are influenced by other women, as well as men. So, we started to analyse gender relations through equality audits to give voice to what women themselves felt about work organization and service delivery, as well as to what they wanted for themselves in terms of career development. Equality audits illustrate how subtle the web of internal gender cultures is and show how all women operate strategically, to combat resistance to them as women, in order to be effective. At work, women have to manage gender, as well as do their job.

Women tend to be more aware than men of gender culture at work, precisely because they are more aware of how it restricts their behaviour and

[1] Parts of this chapter originally appeared in an article in *Women in Management Review*, 1993, (8)2, MCB University Press and are reproduced with permission.

expression. Men, on the other hand, usually feel more comfortable with the prevailing atmosphere at work and are therefore less aware of cultural norms (Kanter, 1977; Freeman, 1992). Women, in our experience, complain as much about the way they are treated by managers and preconceptions about them, as they do about pay and position. Women either 'go along with' or challenge gender cultures; those that have least power have little choice but to collude with cultural norms and are often resentful of other women who appear to have more opportunities than they do.

Equality audits (CMPS Audits, 1992–3) reveal that it is common for male managers to believe that gender bias only exists in blue collar or male trades, that discrimination and job segregation are remnants of a bygone age, and that equality will come naturally through the mere passage of time. The strength of this popular view was shown in the work of Ulla Ressner (1987) in Sweden. But evidence suggests the contrary is the case and even though there may be a greater awareness of gender, when people do not challenge cultural norms, they persist. The fact that powerful gender cultures remain in the public sector, even after 20 years of equal opportunities programmes, illustrates their power (Cockburn, 1991; Cabinet Office 1991; Goss and Brown, 1991). It is therefore necessary to look at why gender cultures are so persistent, how gender cultures affect both men and women, how sexes both concur with them, and why women find it so difficult to articulate their gendered perspective within organizations.

Each organization has its own specific variety determined by both male and female, managers and employees. Although the tone of a company or organization is usually set by corporate management, individual departments develop their own local cultures reflecting the complexity of the web of power relations between employees. Although gender is only one factor influencing power relations, an individual may assume power through formal status, as well as through other personal identity tags of class, race, etc. A person's gender continues to determine where they work and the type of work they do. As social attitudes change towards women, so the expectations of women change and increase. All the cultures we mention can often be seen to be at work within one organization.

Gender cultures tend to reflect two different attitudes to women and men's similarities or differences. Traditional cultures, as seen in the 'Gentleman's Club', the 'Locker Room' and the 'Barrack Yard', all reflect the view that men and women are fundamentally different and have different roles in society. More recent cultures as witnessed in the 'Gender Blind', the 'Smart Macho' and the 'Pretenders', show how the dynamic of gender relations persists even when participants proclaim men and women equal and no different in their capabilities. This polarization of views was acknowledged by suffragettes and reformers in the 19th century and persists today. A more gender-sensitive perspective would acknowledge that women are different in the actual condition of their lives and in many characteristics, but in others are similar – they would assert that women's voice, views and rights should not in any case be dependent on their similarity or otherwise with men. The sole reason for this enduring dichotomy is because women and others have feared that women were not acceptable in the public arena unless they were like men. American feminism and women's ways in management affirm this belief (Gordon, 1991).

Men and women in more traditional cultures assume that the differences between them are natural and ordained and in Britain they hanker after a 'Janet and John'[2] type land, where the woman does the chores and cares for her children, whilst her partner earns the money. For many men used to such a clear-cut division, encountering women at work can be unsettling, if not disturbing. Alison Halford (1993) noticed this when she first arrived in Liverpool to take up her post of assistant chief police officer (one of the highest ranking female police officers in Britain).

Where men have grown up relating only to other men, they believe many myths about women which are never challenged or refined by more mature contact. Myths about women's emotions, competences and desires are further compounded by the very strong belief that women and men are so different that it is impossible to comprehend or empathize with members of the opposite sex. The most comfortable culture which confines women to this separate sphere of femaleness is known as the 'Gentleman's Club'.

THE GENTLEMAN'S CLUB

The 'Gentleman's Club' reinforces the notion that the woman's role as mother and homemaker and the man's role as breadwinner are natural and preordained. This culture not only affects managers in their selection procedures, but also the women in their choices about hours of work, promotion and the caring of their children. It is as hard for women to resist such a culture as it is for men, particularly if their peers believe in it. The traditional stereotype is projected on to all women. One manager honestly commented that 'We have a tendency to think of all women employees as white, middle class, married with children.'

This perspective creates a myth about women and hides the reality of black women, single parents and those working people in need of full-time employment, irrespective of domestic arrangements. This type of a working environment clearly determines women's expectations, sense of ambition and general confidence. Those who think that women lack ambition should understand the source from which ambition springs and how it can be thwarted. A survey in one authority revealed that male managers thought that women lacked ambition, whilst the majority of women said they lacked encouragement and were waiting for the 'green light' to contemplate promotion as a possibility (CMPS Audits, 1992–3).

Women find this exclusive culture extremely hard to challenge and many indeed are happy within it. The Gentleman's Club is polite and civilized, women are kept firmly in established roles by male managers who are courteous and humane. They patronize in the nicest way; the 'old paternalist' is one of the few men who will ask after an employee's welfare and remembers when a secretary's child is sick.

> It's so difficult asking Mr . . . about promotion or re-grading as he's always so sweet and friendly. I think he may be upset and think I'm unhappy here.
>
> (Secretary, CMPS Audits, 1992–3)

---

2 *Janet and John* books were a 1950s reading scheme which was so gender stereotyped it made many young girls gender aware.

The Chief Education Officer is always very polite and is embarrassed if anyone swears in front of me – he always looks to me for moral support in meetings and I convey my feelings about a policy by looking 'prim', 'cross' or 'upset'.

(principal officer, Maddock, 1993)

Alison Halford (1993) notes in her book how even when on the streets of Toxteth during the riots she was treated to a cup by her male colleagues who thought it unseemly for a woman to drink from a mug:

I treasure a moment of pure comedy. As I was briefed, mugs of hot steaming tea were brought for us. I reached over to grab one but before I could someone shouted, 'For God's sake not a mug. Go and find a cup for Ma'am!' Here we are in an urban war zone, bricks are flying, abuse ringing in my ears from the streets outside and Assistant Chief Constable Alison Halford must have her tea from a cup.

(Halford, 1993, p. 125)

Another woman we interviewed was extremely determined to be a surveyor but her boss thought site visits might be too dangerous for her. She had not wanted to 'nag' her boss, so she wasted two years of her training being restricted to the office. The whole point of her traineeship was to experience site opportunities. Older men frequently say they feel it is their duty to restrict younger women to protect them. This attitude is very common in the construction industries, where white-collar managers are fearful of and exaggerate the sexual prowess of building workers, creating a sense of sexual danger for those women who want to venture out (Maddock and Parkin, 1993).

The gentlemanly culture is not hostile to women who conform. Women are valued in the jobs they do, but they are not expected to break barriers or move outside of traditional women's work. Overprotected women frequently conform to type. The 'gentleman' expects women to be 'caring and moral' at work and if they behave appropriately they are rewarded by warmth and concern. Women recognize that if they become too demanding, too assertive or ask for change and promotion, they will lose the friendly 'gentlemanly' boss and, instead, he will become difficult and they will become outsiders. This culture relies on women understanding what they have to lose if they seek to challenge common practice. In this way, women are warned that if they seek less traditional work or more decision-making power, men and women may become antagonistic to them (CMPS Audits, 1992–3).

Those women 'at home' in the 'Gentleman's Club' can be and often are antagonistic to other women who seek promotion or who are brought into management. Many professionals are serviced by women part-timers who feel valued by their male bosses, they receive birthday presents, days off for shopping, and flowers for extra work. In return, they work late, hard and beyond their job descriptions. Women secretaries, nurses, technicians and administrators often have boundless 'goodwill' for male consultants, lawyers, academics and managers. Yet, these same women are frequently very hard on women managers. Women in all senior positions are aware of having to manage the gendered culture of the 'Gentleman's Club' – this is the culture of the professions and of senior management. Women are assumed to serve and not to direct. If a woman reaches such status, she is advised to 'watch her back', for gossip will soon follow about her personal life and her capabilities. Baroness Perry noted as soon as she became a vice chancellor, the gossip started around the university that she had put gold taps in her bathroom ᴄ. other such nonsense (*Guardian*, 1993). Another senior woman in education had to take her committee chairman to a tribunal – she refused him the use of her office. He had assumed that as a woman she would service him, not run the education service (Maddock, 1993). Certainly, being a senior woman manager in the Gentleman's Club involves skill, for here a woman is out of place and exposed not only to the backlash from threatened men, but also venom from some aggrieved women.

THE BARRACK YARD

The Barrack Yard culture dominates in hierarchical organizations where a chain of command exists from top to bottom. This culture is associated with the military, although in reality the armed services in 1992 had more sophisticated management structures than many other public-sector organizations. The Barrack Yard is a bullying culture, where subordinates are shouted at and rarely listened to – it leads supervisors and managers to bawl at people when they make mistakes and to despise those beneath them. Juniors are frequently women, manual workers or people from ethnic minorities for whom managers have little respect.

> He shouts at everyone, he's known as the Führer.
> *(secretary, local government, CMPS Audits, 1992–3)*

> It's not just the women who are scared of him, so are some of the managers – but he blocks women and says things like no women will work above scale 5 in this department.
> *(finance admin. worker, DSO, CMPS Audits, 1992–3)*

Barrack Yard managers disregard training and development and assume people are either 'top' or 'bottom' candidates. This leaves those in part-time and junior posts vulnerable and unable to progress. The Barrack Yard hides a real hostility towards women, manual workers, black people and anyone possessing little institutional power, but it tends to be led by a few people and most other employees are merely responding to them out of fear. The Barrack Yard can be vicious and is an authoritarian culture where power delivers respect. As women rarely have senior status within organizations, their interests and comments are ignored and they are rendered invisible.

Bullies are not confined to supervisor posts or middle management, although many executives and senior managers have learnt that charm is more persuasive that autocracy, many bosses at senior levels bully colleagues and employees alike. They frequently shout at men and humiliate women. Robert Maxwell was clearly one such example, he bullied journalists, managers and staff alike. Such behaviour in a woman would not be tolerated.

THE LOCKER ROOM

This is an exclusion culture, where men build relationships on the basis of common agreements, common assumptions and frequently talk about sport

...erences to confirm their heterosexuality. Although this
...e male culture, male outsiders can join the group through
...innuendo. It is more difficult for women to join the club: 'I
...out the sport and talk about it, then they would change the
...y didn't want me, a woman, in the group' (chief officer, CMPS
...2–3).

...t just junior women who are subjected to Locker Room culture;
...with power but who are isolated as chief executives or directors tell
...t they have to listen to endless references to sport and sex in both
for...al and informal situations: 'Men still exclude women from 'drinks-in-the-pub' and evening socialising, it's difficult asking a woman because everyone assumes you must fancy her even if all you want to do is talk about work' (male director of housing, CMPS Audits, 1992–3).

A man at home with the Locker Room culture justifies 'pin-up' calendars as harmless and fun, but then he puts them on full view to intimidate younger women. Although 'girly' pictures and calendars are rarer in public-sector organizations than private companies (policy statements have made it clear that they are not endorsed by management), even today, some men in local government have them on filing cabinets and behind doors (CMPS Audits, 1992–3).

Another form of masculine domination exaggerated by the Locker Room culture is body language. Men feeling in control in meetings will lean back-wards on chairs with arms outstretched, rocking backwards and forwards and drawing attention to their bodies – detracting attention from other people. A few women managers have told us that they have developed their own tactics to match this behaviour, for instance: 'I spray myself with per-fumes in meetings and wear low cut dresses and generally flaunt myself' (public relations officer, Maddock, 1993). But most women say that they find this overt physical body flaunting either too threatening to challenge or too trivial to imitate. Some women, perhaps more aware of gender dynamics, feel that mirroring male behaviour is both dangerous and inappropriate (Mad-dock, 1993): 'I think too many women managers are either taming or exag-gerating their sexuality at work – and that encourages men to think of women as sex objects not as managers' (woman officer in Education, Maddock, 1993).

THE GENDER BLIND

In the 1980s one of the arguments used to persuade managers that women were capable and should be promoted at work was that there were no dif-ferences between men and women (Rosener, 1990), that a woman could func-tion in exactly the same way as could any man. But, when we pretend that women live the same lives and have the same experiences as men, a gender blindness develops. Although this perspective has been challenged by many feminist writers (Gilligan, 1982), the perspective is very persistent as it allows people to ignore the significance of gender at work.

Gender-Blind persons make no mention or reference to a colleague's home life or personal experiences. They assume or assert that there is a 'level playing field' at work and men and women can excel if they try. Those managers who are Gender Blind ignore a woman's identity and experience, and they probably also deny racial differences and disabilities. Such blindness usually grows out of an illusion that everyone is white, able-bodied and male. The Gender Blind do not want to discriminate, but instead they deny reality and difference.

For instance, one manager organized 24-hour shifts for all employees in the computer pool, without any reference to the difficulties that most women had with this. Women are more likely to be anxious about working late, being alone in buildings or walking to car parks at night. A gender blindness to the reality of women's lives is to ignore the fact that domestic responsibilities and social realities do affect the choices women can make (Maddock and Parkin, 1993).

The Gender Blind can be sincere in their commitment to remove barriers for women but, by ignoring reality, they encourage women to aspire to a super-woman status – of the perfect mother and model manager – without providing support or flexibility. Only those single-minded and well-supported women manage this juggling act and then usually at great cost to themselves. Women's magazines have also encouraged this romantic notion that women can be everything – that they can overcome all obstacles by sheer willpower. Fortunately this is changing and magazines such as *She* and *Options* now stress the importance of women making priorities, relaxing and having time off. Those that deny the difference that gender makes to a person's life are naive and ostrich-like in their belief that patriarchal relationships will disappear overnight without challenge. Such an attitude illustrates the convenience of the illusion of 'sameness'; if more information was sought on why women were not applying for posts, the obstacles women face would become more obvious.

THE SMART MACHO

The current commercial climate in the National Health Service and elsewhere, which encourages economic efficiency at the expense of all other criteria, is a breeding ground for Smart and Macho managers.

Managers dominated by the Smart Macho culture feel under such pressure to reach performance and budget targets that they have no desire to block or obstruct employees who can work 80 hours a week and deliver on time. These new managers are driven by extreme competitiveness, they discriminate against those who cannot work at the same pace or those who challenge economic criteria. If you cannot keep up you are likely to be sacked, demoted or passed over, whoever you are. Superficially this appears not to be a gendered culture and many women managers are known to be as ruthless as male managers, sometimes more so.

> She was known throughout the region as focused totally on objectives and meeting them within deadlines, there was no point in explaining difficulties to her, she wouldn't listen.
>
> (*NHS manager, CMPS Audits, 1992–3*)

> Some of the new women unit managers have ended up sacking the old gentlemen in cardigans and replacing them with young ruthless yuppies, and most of them are male with no domestic responsibilities or interest in staff development.
>
> (*local government middle manager, CMPS Audits, 1992–3*)

But this type of management culture is actually a more ruthless form of the Gender Blind. If you work hard and fast and can focus on narrow targets, your gender or ethnic origin is irrelevant. Of course, most women over 35 years do have 'caring' responsibilities whether they be for parents or children. A recent audit showed that women still do over 75% of housework (CMPS Audits, 1992–3).

It has not gone unnoticed by other people in the NHS that this new breed of macho managers, men and women, are often childless and highly mobile. Although of course men can continue to function in the same way even when they do have children, women are faced with the same choices in 1993 as they were in 1903: if you want a career you have to forgo other aspects of your life. This type of management style is being challenged by both older men and women, because both are having to adapt to fit into it. One woman said:

> The trouble is we got a new dynamic woman unit manager and she sacked all the men in cardigans. Now we've got young macho managers with Gucci shoes and Armani clothes, who are much worse. They never listen, they rush about competing with each other over performance targets – and seem to care little about the service.
>
> *(NHS woman manager, CMPS Audits, 1992–3)*

In many hospitals in Britain there is a mix of cultures. The new women managers are proving themselves and flexing their muscles and appear hostile to other women who cannot make the grade. The most common phrase uttered by hospital doctors is that 'whingers' will not get promoted. 'Whingeing' is frowned upon by male and female doctors alike, yet it is this reluctance to voice difficulties with medical training that ossifies medical practice. The dedicated and single-minded make the grade, but those who want a family and social life are left by the wayside feeling like failures:

> The trouble with hospital medicine is that you are always proving yourself to be invincible, you don't complain for fear of getting a bad reference. Then eventually, when you reach consultant level, I suppose you've had such an onerous training yourself you think, 'Well I've done it why shouldn't they?' It's a very macho environment at medical school, and it's even worse in the hospital.
>
> *(fourth-year medical student, CMPS Audits, 1992–3)*

PAYING LIP SERVICE

Some public sector organizations which have well-developed equal opportunities policies have also developed a new breed of men – men who are well versed in feminism and think of themselves as non-sexist. There are those who pay lip service to equality programmes and declare themselves to be equal opportunities employers, but do little to promote or develop women or black people. As equality work becomes more respectable, the number of people espousing support for equal opportunity policies grows. Those that pay lip service produce policies and charters and then ignore them or fail to put them into practice.

Then there are also those who are adept at manoeuvring around equal opportunity policies. They have learnt the language and have learnt to use it to their own advantage. Some authorities have developed highly politicized administrations where officers criticize and judge each other on the basis of their political perspectives, behaviour and their own personal identities (that is whether they are white, black, able-bodied, female or male).

The culture of political correctness (more visible in the USA than in the UK) is one where men and women will attempt to outdo each other and correct each other over the smallest details of differences in treatment between people, whilst laying claim to a special moral ground because of their own personal identity. Hierarchies of oppression have developed where a person's status is determined by their position on the ladder of oppression – female, black, gay, working class, etc.

New forms of oppression develop in such a culture, victims are martyred and are absolved of all responsibility. Individuals who do not belong to a valued group are belittled and patronized, old stereotypes give rise to new. There is a tendency to think all women must speak in meetings and must be confident, or that all black people must have a position on black politics: 'I think Mary should be more assertive, I've suggested she should read . . .' (comment on woman in Careers Service, CMPS Audits, 1992–3). Such advice between colleagues, who are mere acquaintances, is often insulting. It also perpetuates the idea that women are victims in need of male assistance. Women are not assisted by being directed to where they might find liberation, particularly not by those keenest to lead them and who have social power over them. Many women find men espousing feminism more irritating than traditional bullies. The 'Feminist Pretenders' create a myth of 'equality' based on a form of gender or ethnic determinism. This results in the idea that all women make good managers, are always right, have a greater emphatic sense, when what is actually more likely is that oppressed people have a tendency to be more sensitive because they have had to be astute, more aware and more on their guard. The Pretenders are rather like missionaries who cannot distinguish between individuals within the oppressed group who are their pupils; everyone represents the group and is treated not as a person but as a representative of a class, gender or ethnic group. This creates a dangerous culture where some individuals are persuaded that because they are victims, they have no responsibility for events and blame other people instead of developing themselves (CMPS Audits, 1992–3).

WOMEN AS GATE-KEEPERS

Too often the blocks or resistance to women managers or professional advancement come from other women. There is a clear unspoken division between women who are career oriented and those more home oriented. The wives of senior managers are often as vitriolic about women managers or younger career women as are their husbands. Several women academics have commented that they think the block to women into senior academic posts is because the wives of board members are against it.

The prevailing culture dominates and determines women's behaviour as well as men's. Women may collude or fail to resist stereotypes and prejudices which undermine their own sex. Their self-esteem and survival may be so closely connected to traditional norms that they see no advantage in changing common practice. In many county councils in the UK, for instance, women still form the backbone of the support services and administrative structures and yet very few have reached senior middle management. We have found from equality audits that the majority of women within the organization do not consider this to be odd or something to question. The lack of opportunities for women results not just from male managers' resistance to women but also from women's own sense of place.

Those cultures which are firmly rooted in people's sense of the naturally ordained, where patriarchal relations are firmly embedded and men continue to be confident of their natural right to manage, are hard for individual women to challenge. They therefore collude and conform, even if they do not want to.

Dr Helena Daly (*Independent on Sunday*, 1993), who was dismissed by a hospital Trust in Cornwall for alleged rudeness, fell victim to a powerful gender culture where many female support staff resented her. Nurses and secretaries were encouraged by managers to write notes on Dr Daly, reporting all incidences and occasions where she demanded more work, refused coffee or was off-hand. Such grievances of support staff are common in hospitals and male hospital consultants are reportedly rude to staff frequently (CMPS Audits, 1992–3), yet none have been dismissed. All the nurses who gave evidence about Dr Daly had previously worked for her elderly male predecessor and were long-standing middle-aged staff. He was paternalistic to them and, in all probability, reinforced them rather than patients. Nurses and secretaries felt aggrieved when Dr Daly wanted them to work harder for the patients and didn't want them to fuss over her with coffee, etc. They were confused and offended by her attitude to them and became vengeful. Managers appeared to flame the situation and were quick to spot this feeling and exploited it, in pursuance of their own interests. This mix-match of gender cultures resulted in Dr Daly losing her job and the hospital losing a good doctor.

Many junior women hospital doctors have mentioned to us that nurses can be more supportive to junior male house officers than to their female counterparts (CMPS Audits, 1992–3). They also add that if a woman doctor is of a brusque or stern disposition, she should expect antagonism from nursing staff. Although many nurses do work well with female doctors, who can be more understanding than their male counterparts, most are very reluctant to accept firm orders and rudeness from a women boss whereas, unfortunately, most accept it as natural from a man.

The pressure on senior women is great. Many younger women have high expectations of other women in senior positions, which when dashed give rise to added resentment and anger. Women are expected to be good listeners, managers and mothers and when they are not they are penalized or attacked for not fulfilling their caring role. 'Junior women expect me to always be available for coffee and for support but I no longer have the time, I don't always agree with them and I'm not a counsellor' (principal of college, Maddock and Parkin, 1993).

CONCLUSION

In gender cultures, behaviour is coded male or female. Individual attitudes towards assertiveness are clearly influenced by the view that it is natural for men to be irritable and irascible, whereas women, no matter how pressured or tired, should conform to the gendered stereotype of being 'sweet' and even-tempered:

> In the no nonsense world of macho detective work, Ernie and his men had seen it all. They had mopped up after murders, gatecrashed domestic violence, attended stabbings and shootings. They had had insults and missiles hurled at them but this was the last straw. No woman A.C. C. had ever called Ernie a pratt to his face and he did not like it. . . . . He sat there, red in the face trembling with rage and near to tears.
>
> (*Halford, 1993, p. 101*)

If a senior woman shows her emotions at work it is likely to make her vulnerable, whichever emotion it is. If a man shows anger or compassion, it merely reinforces his status: 'My bosses and colleagues did not expect me to take a firm line at work, thinking that a woman manager would be more compliant and reticent' (local government director, CMPS Audits, 1992–3).

Corporate managers can play a significant part in creating 'gender cultures' and gender dynamics (CMPS Audits, 1992–3). Although there are common themes, each organization has its own brand of leadership and its own characteristic work culture, and each in turn develops its own peculiar resistance to equality proposals. The lack of attention to the spirit, informal norms and values of an organization has led to many equality programmes being sabotaged by both management and male and female staff. Equality audits reveal that some gender cultures are understood to reflect a natural order, illustrated by the Gentleman's Club, in which women feel valued if they conform to female stereotypes. The Barrack Yard and the Locker Room are more authoritarian versions of the Gentleman's Club, where men and women's collusion is out of fear as well as being based on a cultural agreement.

In organizations where there is an acceptance of women in the workplace and an acceptance that women have a right to promotion, cultures develop where 'lip service' is paid toward equality, or perhaps a more positive environment develops where women are judged on merit and in their own right. The Gender Blind and the Smart Macho cultures acknowledge the justice of equality but ignore from where disadvantage springs. Corporate rather than natural agendas tend to determine these cultures. Managers in organizations driven by profit and the need for greater efficiency are not interested in sustaining patriarchal power if it conflicts with economic interest. Smart Machos in particular are interested in economics rather than patronage. If barriers to women hinder performance targets then inequalities become a management problem as well as a problem for women. However, the force of the economic argument appears to be influencing executives rather than middle-managers, and it is the middle-managers and other women who are the 'gate-keepers' for women seeking change. Whilst executives are looking to promote women in middle management, they still protect their exclusive male culture at board level (Handy, 1991).

The Feminist Pretenders are committed to the theory of equality but, in reality, are reluctant to relinquish their power over women. These men are often using women in their own battles with other men. The Feminist Pretenders push women in the direction they want them to go in – the result being that they are often more oppressive than managers in the Gentleman's Club, who leave women alone to get on with their jobs.

Gender stereotypes are clearly not just perpetuated by men. Women in most organizations have positive or negative attitudes towards other women, especially those in 'unusually senior' positions. Gender cultures tend to divide, as well as restrict women. Those women who have accepted 'their place' are sometimes not well disposed to those who are claiming new ground. And those senior women who do not acknowledge the fact that most women are tied by children and lack of opportunities are not likely to be liked by women in more junior positions. Similarly, women who do not struggle against age-old rhetoric that the women's roles are determined and unchanging, cannot expect much support from those women who are attempting to transform social realities. Too many statements are made in the name of women, when women themselves are often in conflict over how to react to a gendered culture at work. Gender dynamics, frequently unnoticed by men, create psychological walls for women. They are also disastrous for organizations. Not only do they waste women's energy and potential, they also damage and distort communication which in turn affects performance and productivity – but that's another story. Suffice it to say, democratic organizations will only develop when the power of gender cultures is acknowledged and challenged by both men and women.

REFERENCES

CABINET OFFICE FOR THE CIVIL SERVICE (1991) A Review of Equal Opportunities for Women in the Civil Service, HMSO, London.

CMPS AUDITS (1992–3) Commissioned research on barriers to women staff in public sector organizations. Corporate, Management and Policy Service, Stockport.

COCKBURN, C. (1991) In the Ways of Women: Men's Resistance to Sex Equality in Organizations, Macmillan, London.

FREEMAN, S. J. M. (1992) Managing Lives: Corporate Women and Social Change, University of Mass. Press, Amherst, MA.

GILLIGAN, C. (1982) In a Different Voice: Psychological Theory and Women's Development, Harvard University Press, Boston.

GORDON, S. (1991) Prisoners in Man's Dreams: Striking out for a New Feminine Future, Little, Brown & Company, Boston.

GOSS, S. and BROWN, H. (1991) Barriers to Women in the National Health Service, The Foundation of Public Sector Management, London.

HALFORD, A. (1993) No Way Up the Greasy Pole, Constable, London.

HANDY, C. (1991) Informal discussion with Maddock.

Independent on Sunday (1993) Dr Helena Daly (Jenny Cuffe), Independent on Sunday, 24 July, p. 18.

KANTER, R. M. (1977) The Men and Women of the Corporation, Basic Books, New York.

MADDOCK, S. J. (1993) Women's frustration with and influence on local government management in the UK, Women in Management Review, Vol. 8, no. 1, pp. 3–7.

MADDOCK, S. J. and PARKIN, D. (1993) Gender cultures: women's choices and strategies at work, Women in Management Review, Vol. 8, no. 2, pp. 3–9.

RESSNER, U. (1987) The Hidden Hierarchy: Democracy and Equal Opportunities, Gower Publishing, Avebury.

ROSENER, J. (1990) The ways women lead, Harvard Business Review, Nov–Dec, pp. 118–25.

CHAPTER 4

Managerial Sex Typing: A Persistent and Pervasive Barrier to Women's Opportunities[1]

VIRGINIA E. SCHEIN

INTRODUCTION

The existence of stereotyping of the sexes has long been documented by researchers (e.g. Anastasi and Foley, 1949; Maccoby, 1966; Rosenkrantz *et al.*, 1968). Sex-role stereotyping can impede the progress of women in management through the creation of occupational sex typing. According to Merton, 'occupations can be described as "sex-typed" when a large majority of those in them are of one sex and there is an associated normative expectation that this is how it should be' (Epstein, 1970, p. 152). In a sex-typed occupation the characteristics required for success tend to be those seen as more commonly held by the majority sex occupant.

In the early 1970s the managerial position appeared to be a male sex-typed one in the USA. The ratio of men to women managers was extremely high and there was an informal belief that this is 'how it should be'. As such, the managerial position, viewed as a 'masculine' one, would be seen as requiring characteristics more commonly held by men than by women. All else being equal, a male candidate would appear more qualified by virtue of such sex typing of the position than a female candidate.

Despite the probable negative influence of stereotypical attitudes on the selection, placement and promotion of women into managerial positions, Schein (1971) found a paucity of studies dealing with psychological barriers preventing women from achieving in the workforce. Schein (1973, 1975) designed and implemented two studies to demonstrate the existence, or lack thereof, of a relationship between sex-role stereotypes and the perceived requisite personal characteristics for the middle-management position. Specifically, the research hypothesis was that successful middle-managers are perceived to possess those characteristics, attitudes and temperaments more commonly ascribed to men in general than to women in general.

---

[1] Sex role rather than gender role is used throughout the chapter so as to maintain consistency across research studies. In the early 1970s a distinction between sex role and gender had not yet been made.

THE SCHEIN STUDIES

The sample consisted of 300 male middle-line managers (Schein, 1973) and 167 female middle-line managers (Schein, 1975), from a total of 13 US insurance companies.

Three forms of the Schein Descriptive Index (SDI) were developed to define both the sex-role stereotypes and characteristics of successful middle-managers (see Schein, 1973). All three forms contained the same 92 descriptive terms and instructions, except that one form asked for a description of women in general (Women), one for a description of men in general (Men), and one for a description of successful middle-managers (Managers).

The instructions on the three forms of the Index were as follows:

> On the following pages you will find a series of descriptive terms commonly used to describe people in general. Some of the terms are positive in connotation, others are negative and some are neither very positive nor very negative.
>
> We would like you to use this list to tell us what you think (women in general, men in general or successful middle managers) are like. In making your judgments, it might be helpful to imagine you are about to meet a person for the first time and the only thing you know in advance is that the person is (an adult female, an adult male, or a successful middle manager). Please rate each word or phrase in terms of how characteristic it is of (women in general, men in general, or successful middle managers).

Ratings on each of the 92 terms were made according to a 5-point scale, ranging from 1 (not characteristic) to 5 (characteristic of (women in general, men in general or successful middle-managers)). Each manager received only *one* form of the SDI and was unaware of the purpose of the study.

Intraclass correlation coefficients (r) from two randomized groups' analyses of variance were computed to determine the degree of resemblance between the descriptions of Men and Managers and between Women and Managers. The analyses were performed separately for male and female managers.

The results revealed that for male managers there was a large and significant resemblance between the ratings of Men and Managers and a near zero, non-significant resemblance between the ratings of Women and Managers, thereby confirming the hypothesis.

Similarly, among female managers there was a large and significant resemblance between Men and Managers. Although there was also a significant resemblance among Women and Managers, this degree of resemblance was significantly less than the one between Men and Managers. As such the hypothesis was confirmed in the female sample as well as the male sample.

This association between sex-role stereotypes and perceptions of requisite management characteristics would seem to account, in part, for the limited number of women in managerial positions in the early 1970s. All else being equal, the perceived similarity between the characteristics of managers and men increases the likelihood of a male rather than a female being selected for or promoted into a managerial position. A woman, by virtue of her gender alone, was viewed as less qualified than her male counterpart.

Managerial sex typing produced entry and advancement barriers that were stronger and higher for women than for men. Unknown numbers of qualified women were denied access to managerial positions, ignored in the recruitment process, not considered for management development programmes and passed over for promotion, simply on the basis of sex-role stereotypical thinking on the part of decision-makers.

Those women who did make it over the hurdles were more likely to 'buy into' the masculine success model, suggesting possible internal conflicts. Other women opted out of the managerial race, acknowledging the possible conflict between a feminine self-image and a masculine model, denying themselves and corporations an opportunity to exercise their talents and skills.

The work of Schein and others on women in management was used in the 1970s to demonstrate that women's limited participation in the managerial ranks was not 'as it should be'. Psychological barriers existed which made it more difficult for women, in comparison to their male counterparts, to enter into and advance in the managerial ranks. Such research showed that women and men were not being treated equally and that these psychological barriers needed to be acknowledged and dealt with if women were to have equality of opportunity in the workplace.

SEX ROLE STEREOTYPING AND MANAGEMENT TODAY

Twenty years after Schein's initial research, the composition of the US managerial workforce has changed. The percentage of women in management has risen dramatically. Of all managerial positions, close to 40% are now held by women (Bureau of Labor Statistics, 1989). Does this increase indicate that the psychological barriers have been lowered? Is the managerial position no longer a sex-typed one?

Despite the gains, the 'glass ceiling' has been noticeably difficult to crack. The participation of women in positions of power and influence in the USA remains limited. Most women are still concentrated in lower management levels. Women represent only 11% of high-level directors and managers, and no more than 3% at the 'top level' of management of large companies in the private sector (World of Work, 1993). Is stereotypical thinking still a barrier, operative only in the realm less likely to be impacted by government pressures? Have managerial attitudes changed over the last 15 to 20 years?

CORPORATE MANAGERS – THE PAST AND THE PRESENT

Brenner et al. (1989) replicated Schein's earlier work in order to answer these questions. They hypothesized, again, that male and female managers perceive successful middle-managers as possessing characteristics, attitudes and temperaments more commonly ascribed to men in general than to women in general.

The sample consisted of 420 male middle-line managers and 173 female middle-line managers, drawn from 4 manufacturing companies, 4 service-oriented companies and 1 combined service and manufacturing company in the USA. The procedures were exactly the same as in the original studies.

The results show that the attitudes of male managers are remarkably similar to those held by male managers in the early 1970s. For the males, there was a large and significant resemblance between the ratings of Men and Managers whereas there was a near zero, non-significant resemblance between the ratings of Women and Managers. As with Schein's (1973) earlier results, the outcomes confirmed the hypothesis among males. In the same year Heilman *et al.* (1989) replicated the research among 268 male managers. Their results also confirmed the hypothesis that requisite management characteristics are perceived as more likely to be held by men than by women.

The Brenner *et al.* (1989) study also included female managers in its sample and here it was found that female managers' attitudes differ from their earlier counterparts. Among the females there was a large and significant resemblance between the ratings of Men and the ratings of Managers. There was also a similar resemblance between the ratings of Women and Managers. Unlike Schein's (1975) earlier findings, however, these outcomes were not significantly different. Thus, for the females, the research replication did not confirm the hypothesis that managers are seen as possessing characteristics more commonly ascribed to men than women.

Compared to attitudes held in the 1970s, there has been a major change among female managers. They no longer sex type the managerial position. Today's female managers see women as more likely to hold some traits necessary for managerial success and see men as more likely to hold others. No longer influenced by stereotypical thinking, these managers would be expected to treat men and women equally in selection, placement and promotion decisions.

On the other hand, today's male managers hold attitudes similar to those of male managers in the 1970s. Despite all the changes that have occurred, male managers continue to perceive that successful managerial characteristics are more likely to be held by men in general than by women in general.

That male managers' attitudes have not changed, speaks directly to the importance of legal and structural interventions as necessary to improving the status of women in management. In the USA the strong emphasis placed on hiring women into management in the mid-1970s were fuelled by compliance reviews, threats of class action discrimination suits, high financial penalties and the possibility of loss of Federal funds.

The results of the Brenner *et al.* (1989) study suggest that had the legal pressures been less, and these attitudes gone unchecked, women's gains today would be less dramatic. The psychological barriers, at least among male decision-makers, are still present. They lost their force when governmental pressures for equal opportunity and concomitant corporate structural changes to ensure such equality were introduced. Increased recruiting efforts, more objective measurement of managerial abilities, rewards for affirmative action compliance, and constant monitoring of the number of women in the managerial pipeline, among other efforts, decreased the opportunity for stereotypical thinking to enter into decisions on selection and promotion.

As stated by Brenner *et al.* (1989), 'That male managers have not changed their attitudes over the last fifteen years is a message to corporate leaders and legislators as to the importance of maintaining the affirmative action pressures' (p. 688). Ironically, Federal attitudes and actions in the mid- to late 1980s took some of the bite out of the equal opportunity laws and affirmative action requirements in the 1980s. Some corporate leaders act as if 'the heat is off'. Given the persistence of psychological barriers, dismantling of corporate structural changes could slow down or even move backwards women's progress in management.

Finally, as concluded by Brenner *et al.* (1989),

> the effect that stereotypical attitudes have when no major legal or structural pressures exist can be seen in the scarceness of women in senior positions: affirmative action efforts rarely reach upper levels, and opportunities for subtle discrimination are far greater. The attitudes of male managers, the predominant decision makers at upper levels, have not changed, and those attitudes may well be negatively affecting women's opportunities to advance into positions of power and influence.
>
> *(Brenner* et al., *1989, p. 668)*

MANAGEMENT STUDENTS – A LOOK AT THE FUTURE

No researcher has a crystal ball. However, interest in the future led Schein *et al.* (1989) to replicate Schein's work using management students. Do today's management students sex type the management position or do they see men and women as equally likely to possess the characteristics necessary for managerial success? Schein *et al.* (1989) again hypothesized that males and females would perceive successful middle-managers as possessing characteristics, attitudes and temperaments more commonly ascribed to men in general than to women in general.

Their sample consisted of 145 male and 83 female management students enrolled in a small private liberal arts institution in the USA.

For males there was a large and significant resemblance between the ratings of Men and Managers and a non-significant resemblance between the ratings of Women and Managers, thereby confirming the hypothesis. For females, there was a significant resemblance between the ratings of Men and Managers, and between Women and Managers. These intraclass coefficients were not significantly different from each other. As such, the hypothesis was not confirmed among females.

The most notable outcome of this research is the similarity in the pattern of attitudes between management students and managers in today's US corporations. Female management students do not sex type the managerial position, but see women and men as equally likely to possess characteristics necessary for managerial success. More than likely, this gender-free view of requisite characteristics fostered women's entry into the field.

Male management students, on the other hand, view the management position in the same way as do today's male managers and male managers in the 1970s. All three groups believe that men are more likely than women to possess characteristics necessary for managerial success. As managers of the future, then, they would be expected still to view women as less qualified for selection into and advancement in management positions.

The eternal hope that change will be easier in the future generation is only half borne out by the Schein *et al.* (1989) results. Similar to her current corporate counterpart, the woman manager in the future will be far less influenced by stereotypical thinking than the woman manager in the 1970s. She will tend to treat men and women equally in the selection and promotion process. The male manager of the future, however, will hold the same stereotypical views of the managerial job requirements as his counterpart in the mid-1970s. He will continue 'to think manager – think male'.

SEX-ROLE STEREOTYPING AND MANAGEMENT: INTERNATIONAL

To what extent does sex-role stereotypical thinking of the managerial job exist in other countries and how does it compare across countries? Now that the globalization of management is an accepted fact, it seems imperative to explore psychological barriers to the advancement of women worldwide.

Internationally the barriers to women in management appear to be strong. According to a survey by the Management Centre Europe (1982) of 420 companies in 9 western European countries, fewer than half (49%) had ever employed a female manager. Of the remaining 51%, 15% stated they would never promote a woman into management. Antal and Izraeli (1993), in an overview of women in management worldwide, state that 'probably the single most important hurdle for women in management in all industrialized countries is the persistent stereotype that associates management with being male' (p. 63).

Two international multi-country replications have been conducted by Schein and her colleagues examining managerial sex typing. Schein and Mueller (1992) selected Germany and the UK as research sites for replication of the stereotyping research done in the USA. According to Antal and Krebsbach-Gnath (1988), there are very few women in management in (West) Germany. On the other hand, while the female management population in the UK is less than that of the USA, it is at least 20% and increasing (Davidson and Cooper, 1987). Schein et al. (1994) recently extended this international investigation to the People's Republic of China and Japan. China has about 9% women in management (Hildebrandt and Liu, 1988) and only 5% of all managers and professionals in Japan are women (Sato, 1990).

Management students were studied in each country. The samples were: Germany, 167 females and 279 males; UK, 78 females and 73 males; China, 123 females and 150 males; and Japan, 105 females and 211 males.

The hypothesis that managers are seen as possessing characteristics more commonly ascribed to men than to women was confirmed for males in Germany and the UK (Schein and Mueller, 1992) and in China and Japan (Schein et al., 1994). Among the males in all four countries, there was a high and significant resemblance between the ratings of Men and Managers and a low, often close to zero resemblance between Women and Managers.

Among females, the hypothesis was also confirmed in the UK and Germany (Schein and Mueller, 1992), as well as Japan and China (Schein et al., 1994). In all four country samples there was a reasonably large and significant resemblance between Men and Managers. Across country samples there were differences in the degree of resemblance between Women and Managers, ranging from low to moderate; however, all of the Women–Manager coefficients were significantly smaller than their respective Men–Manager coefficients.

Unlike US female managers and management students, female management students in other countries sex type the management position. The degree of managerial sex typing varied, however, and was usually less than that of their male counterparts. Of note is that the ordering of the size of the resemblance between Women and Managers tended to match that of the ordering of the actual percentages of women in management in each country (see Schein et al., 1994). As suggested by Schein and Mueller (1992) 'the intraclass coefficients derived from the Schein Descriptive Index serve as a barometer of women's views of their opportunities and of their actual participation [in management] as well' (p. 7).

One of the most important hurdles for women in management in all countries has been thought to be the persistent stereotype that associates management with being male. These results provide strong empirical support for that observation, particularly among males. These replications, especially when compared to the US study of management students, reveal a strong and similar pattern of sex typing of the managerial position among male management students internationally.

The similarity in strength of the male perceptions is somewhat disquieting. Regardless of context, there appears to be a devaluation of women's qualifications among male students of management worldwide. Schein et al. (1994) suggest that 'As they become managers and decision makers of the future, these stereotypical attitudes are apt to limit women's access to and promotions within management internationally' (p. 13). These outcomes provide further support for strong equal employment opportunity laws, in all countries, to counteract the negative effects of managerial sex typing on women's career opportunities.

A CLOSER LOOK AT INTERNATIONAL MANAGERIAL SEX TYPING

Is there an international managerial stereotype? While actual requirements and behaviours are undoubtedly different, are there some characteristics perceived to be important to all cultures? How do women fare, compared to men, on these possibly universal requisite management characteristics?

Item data from 6 samples – the recent US corporate (Brenner et al., 1989), and the management student samples from the USA (Schein et al., 1989), the UK and Germany (Schein and Mueller, 1992) and China and Japan (Schein et al., 1994) – were used to establish an international managerial stereotype. For each country sample, the top 15 items rated as most characteristic of successful managers were arrayed. Characteristics found on all 6 country lists or 5 out of the 6 composed the international managerial stereotype. The male samples ($n=1,278$) and the female samples ($n=729$) were examined separately.

For the males, the characteristics meeting the criteria were: Leadership Ability, Ambitious, and Competitive, which were on all 6 managerial lists, and Desires Responsibility, Skilled in Business Matters, Competent, and Analytical Ability, which were on 5 out of the 6 lists of the top managerial

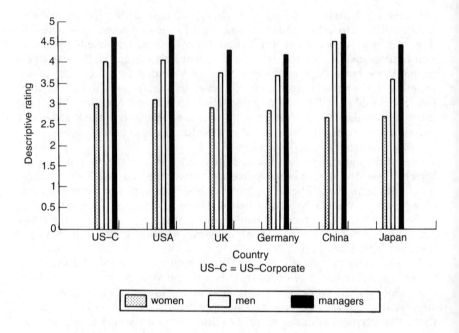

Figure 4.1 Ratings of Women, Men and Managers on Leadership Ability by males in the U.S.A., U.K., Germany, China and Japan.

characteristics. The average ratings of Women and of Men were compared with the average rating of Managers on these 7 items. Women were rated lower than Men (and Managers) on all characteristics in all 6 samples. Across countries, on all items, except Competent, the Women's mean was significantly lower than the Men's. The outcomes for Leadership Ability, as shown in Figure 4.1, illustrate the low Women's ratings and the consistency of views across country samples.

This focus on actual items is not meant as a form of hypothesis testing, as the main analyses do that. However, that women are seen as less likely to possess characteristics perceived internationally as requisite management characteristics, seems to increase the height of the managerial sex typing barrier. Heilman *et al.* (1989), in an extension of their replication study among males, also showed the importance of these same characteristics and women's perceived lack, even as managers. They found that when target terms of 'women managers' and 'men managers' were used, men were still seen as more likely than women to possess the key characteristics of Leadership Ability, Desires Responsibility, Skilled in Business Matters and Analytical Ability. And even when 'successful men managers' and 'successful women managers' were used, men and managers were seen as more likely to have leadership ability than women.

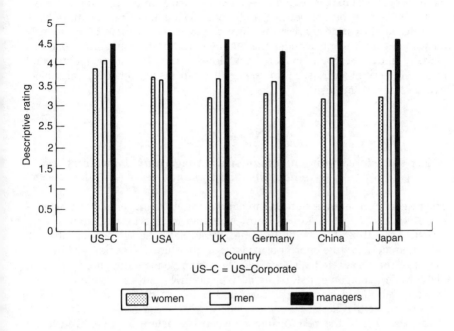

Figure 4.2 Ratings of Women, Men and Managers on Leadership Ability by females
in the U.S.A., U.K., Germany, China and Japan.

Among the females, all 6 female samples placed Leadership Ability and
Competent on the list of top 15 characteristics required of a successful
middle-manager; 5 out of 6 included Skilled in Business Matters, Analytical
Ability, Self-Confident, Desires Responsibility, Prompt and Well Informed. A
set of items similar to the males is not surprising, as most samples exhibited a
very high degree of similarity between males and females on their ratings of
Managers. Also not unexpected was that Women were generally rated lower
than Men, although the differences varied across samples and there were
some instances of Women rated as similar to Men.

Of the 8 items, across country samples, the Women's mean was significantly lower than Men's on 5 items, and there were no differences between
the means of Women and Men on Competency, Prompt, and Well Informed.
Compared to the male responses, the differences between Women and Men
on all 8 items were noticeably smaller than those observed between Women
and Men among the male sample. Figure 4.2, showing the outcomes for
Leadership Ability, illustrates this and highlights the US female managers'
and students' perception of Women as being quite similar to Men, congruent
with their not sex typing the managerial position.

Looking at the international managerial stereotype items illustrates rather
dramatically the unfavourable way in which women are viewed, especially

among males. Male management students in five different countries, and male corporate managers in the USA, view women as much less likely to have leadership ability, be competitive, ambitious, skilled in business matters, have analytical ability or desire responsibility. If one holds this view, as apparently most males do, it is no wonder that women are not in managerial positions globally and in senior managerial positions in the USA. They really don't have 'all the right stuff' (see Stroh *et al.*, 1992) when such stereotypical subjective assessments are used.

CONCLUSION

Sex-role stereotyping and requisite management characteristics: much time, little change

The research on sex-role stereotyping and requisite management characteristics, first done 20 years ago and now extended internationally, allows us to see the strength and inflexibility of the 'think male/think manager' attitude held by males. Despite enormous changes in the status of working women in the USA, the corporate male then and the corporate male now hold the same view. Male management students in five countries, differing politically and economically, hold similar attitudes, and ones not dissimilar from the US corporate executives.

The strength of the relationship between characteristics perceived to be held by men and those perceived as required for managerial success explains why efforts to enhance the status of women in management are so difficult. Underlying the resistance, the foot dragging and the excuses, may be a deeply held attitude of 'for men only', or 'only men are really qualified' to do these jobs. Male sex typing of the managerial job is strong, consistent and pervasive and appears to be a global phenomenon among males (Schein *et al.*, 1994). Neither changes in women's workforce participation, nor cross-cultural differences, seem to affect the view of women as less likely to possess qualities necessary for managerial success.

Twenty years ago in the USA many people believed that as women moved into management, managerial sex typing would diminish. And it did, among women. But men have continued to see women in ways that are not complimentary *vis-à-vis* succeeding in positions of authority and influence. Globally, managerial sex typing exists among men and women. However, women vary cross-culturally in their attitudes. Based on the US data, we would predict that as their participation rate in management improves, they will see men and women as equally likely to be qualified managers. This participation rate, however, can be kept low if the attitudes of male decision-makers, influenced strongly by managerial sex typing, are allowed to go unchecked. As such, legal and structural mechanisms are essential to the change process.

While laws and corporate practices focusing on objective criteria and removing structural barriers are important, it seems time to address ways to change stereotypical attitudes as well. Schein and Davidson (1993), in a replication study in the UK, suggest the need for more research on attitude change during the management education years. Experimental studies to determine effective interventions, done cross-culturally, might lead to important management curriculum applications worldwide.

More research is also needed on the function that maintaining such stereotypical views of women holds for males. Cognitive consistency theories of attitudes might be helpful here in explaining the continued strength of this stereotypical view, despite behavioural evidence to the contrary. As a manifestation of men's attempts to preserve their advantage in the workplace, the need to perceive women as not qualified for traditionally male occupations may well be rooted in sexism (Yoder, 1991) and power issues (Lipman-Bluman, 1984). Rather than focus solely on the glass ceiling, perhaps we also need to learn more about factors contributing to the male manager's need to have a 'protective power shield'.

Finally, research on sex-role stereotyping and requisite management characteristics continues to facilitate the legal and structural changes that are still necessary. Empirically grounded research can be a powerful tool for change, especially in emotionally charged areas such as equal opportunity, and can lay the groundwork for corporate structural changes. As this research, in its historical context, shows, it can also serve as a barometer of attitude change among women and, among men, a watchful measure of what has yet to change.

The pervasiveness of managerial sex typing reflects the global devaluation of women. Embedded in all cultures are traditions, practices and views that impede women's social, political and economic equality. Workplace barriers are one aspect of a whole spectrum of discriminatory practices. Recognizing managerial sex typing as a major barrier to women's opportunities can unite women managers in their change efforts and link these efforts to the broader one of enhancing the rights, freedoms and opportunities of all women globally.

REFERENCES

ANASTASI, A. and FOLEY, J. P., JR (1949) *Differential Psychology*, Macmillan, New York.

ANTAL, A. and IZRAELI, D. (1993) A global comparison of women in management: Women in management in E. A. Fagenson (ed.) *Women in Management: Trends, Issues and Challenges in Managerial Diversity*, Sage, Newbury Park, CA, pp. 52–96.

ANTAL, A. and KREBSBACH-GNATH, C. (1988) Women in management: unused resources in the Federal Republic of Germany, in N. Adler and D. Izraeli (eds) *Women in Management Worldwide*, M. E. Sharpe, Armonk, NY.

BRENNER, O., TOMKIEWICZ, J. and SCHEIN, V. E. (1989) The relationship between sex role stereotypes and requisite management characteristics revisited, *Academy of Management Journal*, Vol. 32, no. 3, pp. 662–9.

BUREAU OF LABOR STATISTICS (1989) Labor force division. Personal communication, February.

DAVIDSON, M. and COOPER, C. (1987) Female managers in Britain – a comparative perspective, *Human Resource Management*, Vol. 26, pp. 217–42.

EPSTEIN, C. (1970) *Women's Place*, University of California Press, Berkeley.

HEILMAN, M. E., BLOCK, C. J., MARTELL, R. F. and SIMON, M. C. (1989) Has anything changed? Current characteristics of men, women and managers, *Journal of Applied Psychology*, Vol. 74, no. 5, pp. 935–42.

HILDEBRANDT, H. and LIU, J. (1988) Chinese women managers: a comparison with their U.S. and Asian counterparts, *Human Resource Management*, Vol. 27, no. 3, pp. 291–314.

LIPMAN-BLUMAN, J. (1984) *Gender Roles and Power*, Prentice Hall, Englewood-Cliffs, NJ.

MACCOBY, E. (ed.) (1966) *The Development of Sex Differences*, Stanford University Press.

MANAGEMENT CENTRE EUROPE (1982) An upward climb for women in Europe, *Management Review*, Vol. 71, no. 9, pp. 56–7.

ROSENKRANTZ, P., VOGEL, S., BEE, H., BROVERMAN, I. and BROVERMAN, D. M. (1968) Sex-role stereotypes and self-concepts in college students, *Journal of Consulting and Clinical Psychology*, Vol. 32, pp. 287–95.

SATO, G. (1990) Role of women in the workplace. Presented at the 1990 American Chamber of Commerce in Japan Employment Practices Conference, 29 November.

SCHEIN, V. E. (1971) The woman industrial psychologist: illusion or reality? *American Psychologist*, Vol. 26, no. 8, pp. 708–12.

SCHEIN, V. E. (1973) The relationship between sex role stereotypes and requisite management characteristics, *Journal of Applied Psychology*, Vol. 57, no. 2, pp. 95–100.

SCHEIN, V. E. (1975) The relationship between sex role stereotypes and requisite management characteristics among female managers, *Journal of Applied Psychology*, Vol. 60, no. 3, pp. 340–4.

SCHEIN, V. E. and DAVIDSON, M. (1993) 'Think manager–think male' – Managerial sex typing among UK business students, *Management Development Review*, Vol. 6, no. 3, pp. 24–8.

SCHEIN, V. E. and MUELLER, R. (1992) Sex role stereotypes and requisite management characteristics: a cross cultural look, *Journal of Organizational Behavior*, Vol. 13, no. 5, pp. 439–47.

SCHEIN, V. E., MUELLER, R. and JACOBSON, C. (1989) The relationship between sex role stereotypes and requisite management characteristics among college students, *Sex Roles*, Vol. 20, no. 1/2, pp. 103–10.

SCHEIN, V. E., MUELLER, R., LITUCHY, T. and LIU, J. (1994) *Think Manager–Think Male: A Global Phenomenon?* Gettysburg College Management Dept. Working Papers. Gettysburg, PA.

STROH, L. K., BRETT, J. M. and REILLY, A. (1992) All the right stuff: a comparison of female and male managers' career progression, *Journal of Applied Psychology*, Vol. 77, no. 3, pp. 251–60.

World of Work (1993) Unequal race to the top, International Labor Organization, February, pp. 6–7.

YODER, J. D. (1991) Rethinking tokenism: looking beyond numbers, *Gender and Society*, Vol. 5, no. 2, pp. 178–92.

PART TWO

Issues in Career Development

CHAPTER 5

Turnover of Female Managers

JEANNE M. BRETT AND LINDA K. STROH

INTRODUCTION

A frequently given explanation for why female managers do not achieve the same degree of career success as male managers is that their turnover rates are higher than those of male managers. Catalyst (1991) reports that human resource managers believe that females are not as committed as males to their careers. Light and Ureta (1992) say that employers equate 'female' with 'quitter'. Other researchers report that promotions and rapid advancement positions are not assigned to females for fear they will quit to marry, have children (Lewis and Park, 1989; Schwartz, 1989), or follow their husbands when they relocate (Markham et al., 1983; Markham and Pleck, 1986). Schwartz (1989) concluded that corporate investment in female managers was not paying off, because too many females leave their organizations. According to this line of reasoning, female managers neither make the necessary investment in an organization to earn career opportunities nor do they merit the investment of the corporation.

In this chapter we review the research on turnover of female managers. We find convincing evidence that female managers do leave their organizations at higher rates than comparable male managers, and so turn this chapter into an investigation of why they do so. We consider three explanations: first, whether female managers are 'bailing out', leaving the workforce to stay at home and take care of their families (Taylor, 1986); second, whether female managers are leaving corporations because of structural and systemic discrimination embedded in organizational policies, practices and culture (Gutek et al., 1990; Rosen and Korabik, 1991); finally, whether female managers are leaving for better career opportunities in organizations that are friendlier to women (Hall, 1990). The chapter reviews the empirical and theoretical literature relevant to each of these explanations for the turnover of managerial women.

TURNOVER RATES

There is substantial evidence from a number of independent sources indicating that female managers leave their organizations at higher rates than male managers. Taylor (1986) reported that 10 years after receiving their

MBA degrees more females than males had dropped out of the workforce. Schwartz (1989) estimated that top performing female managers have turnover rates that are 2½ times those of their male counterparts. Lewis and Park (1989) reported that the percentage of female administrators and professionals in the federal service exiting annually was higher than the percentage of males exiting over the period 1976–86 and that the differences between males and females were particularly acute from 1976 to 1981.

In our own research conducted from 1989 to 1991, we found a 12% difference in turnover rates between female and male managers (Stroh et al., 1993). Fourteen per cent of the male managers but 26% of the female managers left their positions in Fortune 500 organizations during the two years of the study. (Table 5.1 describes the methods of our study.) It is important to note that the male and female managers in the study were comparable. Most had graduate management degrees. All had been offered and accepted a geographical relocation by their Fortune 500 employer during the two years prior to initial data collection. If any group of female managers is likely to exhibit a comparable level of turnover to that of male managers, the female managers in this study surely should; yet, did not.

Table 5.1   **Description of the Stroh et al. (1993) study**

The sample consisted of 615 male and female managers who participated in both a 1989 and 1991 survey. The 1989 sample consisted of 1,029 managers who were transferred in 1987 or 1988 by 20 Fortune 500 corporations. These 20 companies represented 8 industries: pharmaceutical and hospital supplies, communications, consumer products (food), professional and financial services, retailing, hotel management, chemicals, and manufacturing.

Surveys were sent to around 50 randomly selected managers from each organization's list of transferees. The response rate for this portion of the sample was 67%. Because we wished to study issues involving working women, after removing the names, we randomly selected as many as 150 additional managers from each company's list. We sent these managers a letter asking them to participate in the study if they fitted into one of the following categories: dual-earner manager (spouse working), single male manager, or single female manager. A total of 359 additional managers were added to the 1989 sample by this process.

All respondents to the 1989 survey were sent a follow-up survey in 1991. There were 746 managers who responded to the 1991 survey. We were unable to contact 70 managers in 1991. Thus, the overall response rate among those managers we were able to contact was 78%. The analysis sample for this study was 615 managers due to ineligibility (deaths, retirements, 2 requests not to participate further in the study) and missing data.

There were no differences in the 1991 response rate of male and female managers. However, those who did not respond were slightly younger, in 1989, than those who did. They were likely to have fewer children, less organizational tenure and fewer years in the workforce. The common element of difference is that the non-respondents were younger.

BAILING OUT OF THE WORKFORCE FOR FAMILY REASONS

Taylor (1986) suggests that many female managers, even those with MBA degrees from major universities, are bailing out of corporate America to stay home and take care of their families. Schwartz (1989) says:

> Men continue to perceive women as the rearers of their children so they find it understandable, indeed appropriate, that women should renounce their careers to raise families. . . . Not only do they see parenting as fundamentally female, they see a career as fundamentally male. . . . This attitude serves to legitimize a woman's choice to extend maternity leave and even, for those who can afford it, to leave employment altogether for several years.
>
> (*Schwartz, 1989, p. 67*)

Schwartz's (1989) comments suggest, but do not answer, three key questions concerning those female managers who apparently leave the workforce for family reasons: Why do they leave the workforce instead of taking advantage of other options? How long do they stay out? What kinds of jobs do they take when they return? Were there no flexible or part-time options available to these women in their organizations? Are these women out of the workforce an average of 6 months, 12 months, 18 months or longer? Will the new family-leave legislation passed by the US Congress make a significant difference to these women? Are these women using a family interlude to make significant career changes?

The commentators who describe female managers as dropping out of the workforce for family reasons seem to assume that women choose to do so because they want to spend 100% of their time in their family roles. Yet, if they probed a little more deeply into the characteristics of these women's work situation, they might find another explanation. The work–family literature has demonstrated that work tends to be inflexible in its demands, forcing the family to be flexible in response (Bolger *et al.*, 1989). Thus, it may be that at least some of the women managers who 'bail out' of the workforce for family reasons are doing so only because their work environment is not sufficiently flexible to allow them to balance work and family demands.

LESS DEMANDING JOBS – CONSTRUCTING A BALANCE BETWEEN WORK AND FAMILY

Female managers who stay continuously in the workforce, according to Schwartz (1989), can be sorted into two categories: career-primary women and career-and-family women. Most of the latter, Schwartz says, are willing to trade some career growth and compensation for freedom from the constant pressure to work long hours and weekends (Schwartz, 1989, p. 71). Schwartz characterizes employers as taking the position with career-and-family women that if 'you haven't got that motivation, if you want less pressure and greater flexibility, then you can leave and make room for a new generation' (p. 71), presumably of career-primary women and men. When the demands of a female manager's job come into conflict with her role demands as a wife/ mother, some suggest she may leave her organization for another less stressful employment situation (Rosen and Korabik, 1991).

That female managers report higher levels of stress than male managers is well documented. Burke and McKeen (1994) concluded in their review of the stress literature that working women experience more stress than working men, and the sources of that stress are 'related to the expected and actual roles of women in society and to the fact that women still occupy minority status in organizations' (p. 18).

That women act to manage that stress is also documented empirically. Brett and Yogev (1988) found that women restructure their organizational lives to manage family demands more frequently than men. So, it is not inconsistent to project that women are changing jobs and seeking employment that reduces their overall level of stress. These are the women dubbed by *Business Week* (1989) as on the 'mommy track'.

The image conveyed by the 'mommy track' is that the overwhelming stress experienced by these women is due to their family responsibilities. While there is substantial evidence that women in dual-career households carry greater family responsibilities than their husbands (Hochschild, 1989), the intolerable level of stress experienced by those who choose the 'mommy track' may be due not to family but to work. In a study by Higgins *et al.* (1992), work conflict was the most significant predictor of family conflict and of work–family conflict. These authors concluded that because individuals have less control over their work lives than their family lives, it is work, not family, that is the dominant constraint on individuals' lives.

Another study of the stress experienced by male and female managers suggests a different cause of work stress. Davidson and Cooper (1988) rule out the substance of the work as the cause of the extra pressure experienced by women managers. They attribute the heightened stress of female managers to lack of self-confidence and subtle forms of discrimination within organizations (Davidson and Cooper, 1988).

We could find no turnover studies documenting that females are leaving corporate America for less stressful jobs – jobs that provide an easier balance between work and family. There is evidence, however, that females are leaving jobs in corporate America to set up their own companies (Taylor, 1986; Rosen and Korabik, 1990, 1991; Buttner, 1993). According to Buttner (1993), women are using corporate America as their training ground, but when they become frustrated and dissatisfied with the 'glass ceiling', they are launching their own enterprises often competing in the same industries in which they were trained.

Are these female managers motivated to become entrepreneurs to reduce job stress? Presumably, setting up her own company provides the female owner/manager with more control over her time and therefore greater job flexibility. She is also free to develop policies and procedures that do not discriminate against women.

It remains an empirical question whether this entrepreneurial option minimizes the stress at the interface between work and family. Buttner (1993) suggests that these women's motivations are the same as those of male entrepreneurs: independence, autonomy, higher income and the opportunity to be their own bosses. The evidence of entrepreneurial activity by female managers does not rule out the possibility that they are leaving corporate America because of structural and systemic discrimination, or for better career opportunities.

STRUCTURAL AND SYSTEMIC DISCRIMINATION

Davidson and Cooper's research (1988) suggests that structural and systemic discrimination embedded in organizational policies and practices, or lack thereof, may cause higher levels of stress and ultimately higher levels of turnover for female than male managers. Empirical studies are just beginning to link organizational policies and practices to turnover. Gutek *et al.* (1990) estimate that 10% of women quit their jobs because of sexual harassment. Rosen and Korabik (1990) surveyed male and female MBA graduates about their intentions to stay with their current employers. Among the females, office politics, and being in a male-dominated organization were predictors of intentions to leave. Similarly, Miller and Wheeler (1992) reported that women in their study were less satisfied than the men with the recognition they received from their organizations.

If policies and practices that promote subtle or not so subtle forms of discrimination cause females to leave organizations, what evidence is there that female-friendly policies and practices induce females to stay? Ehrlick (1990), writing in *Business Week*, identified female-friendly companies as those in which women held at least 20% of top management positions and at least one or two females reported directly to the chief executive office (CEO). Counter to our expectations that such companies would have policies and practices geared to the concerns of women, there was no consistency among these companies' human resources policies and practices.

Perhaps it is not particular policies or practices that make a company hospitable to female managers but a culture of openness, opportunity and support, that can benefit both male and female managers. In a survey of 76 top-level female managers in the financial industry who were earning on average $171,000 a year, Stroh and Senner (1994) found the two primary reasons given for leaving their current organizations were lack of opportunity for advancement and a male-dominated corporate culture.

A University of Chicago study (Lambert *et al.*, 1993) provides a slightly different perspective on the organizational benefits of policies and practices that are intended to be family responsive. The University of Chicago team undertook a study of additional benefit use and appreciation among the 2,000 employees of Fel-Pro, Inc., a privately held manufacturer and marketer of automotive sealing products and specialty chemicals. This family-held firm provides a vast array of special benefits, some geared to employees, for example income tax preparation, tuition reimbursement, workplace massage, smoke cessation programme; and some to their dependents, for example summer day camp, summer employment, on-site daycare, emergency care for adults, sick childcare. This study did not focus exclusively on managers or females. Indeed, males and females tended to utilize different benefits with different frequencies, for example female employees utilized on-site childcare more than male employees, but the males used sick childcare more than the female employees.

Use and appreciation of these family-friendly benefits distinguished employees with higher performance ratings, lower intended turnover, and fewer disciplinary actions. Thus, the data from the Fel-Pro study, though it did not have a managerial sample, nevertheless suggest that family-friendly benefits policies induce performance and commitment from both male and female employees.

BETTER CAREER OPPORTUNITIES

The dominant reason male managers leave their current organizations is dissatisfaction with their current jobs and organizations, which predicts intentions to leave, which in turn predicts turnover. There are three theoretical models (Mobley, 1977; Price, 1977; Steers and Mowday, 1981) and numerous empirical studies (e.g. Arnold and Feldman, 1982; Michaels and Spector, 1982; Youngblood *et al.*, 1983; Lee and Mowday, 1987; Gerhart, 1990; Huselid and Day, 1991) that propose and confirm these basic relationships.

The glass ceiling literature (Morrison *et al.* 1987) suggests that female managers leave for the same reasons that research has shown that male managers leave. (Most of the turnover research on managerial-level employees has been done on males. This research has not typically focused on the differences between female and male managers (Rosen and Korabik, 1991).)

If female managers' attitudes and intentions predict their turnover, then in order to account for the differential rate of male and female managers' turnover, either (1) the female managers are less satisfied with their jobs and organizations than male managers, or (2) female managers have lower levels of tolerance for dissatisfaction and leave in proportionately higher numbers than males with the same level of satisfaction. Either or both of these explanations could be possible.

The prior discussion of the levels of work stress experienced by female managers, and of the structural and systemic discrimination embedded in organizational policies and practices, provides ready explanations for why female managers may be less satisfied with their jobs and organizations than male managers. The female managers' lower threshold of tolerance for dissatisfaction could be due to either family factors, or lack thereof. If female managers in dual-career relationships are not the primary wage-earners, they may be freer to leave an unsatisfactory employment situation than male managers whose income provides primary support for the family. Alternatively, female managers who do not have families may be freer to leave than male managers who do and who are expected to support them.

We tested these predictions and explanations for differential levels of turnover of male and female managers in the study described in Table 5.1. We found, as expected, that intent predicted turnover for male and female managers ($r = -0.34$, $P \leq 0.01$). Sixty-two per cent of the managers who expected to leave within the subsequent two years did so. Work attitudes, including satisfaction with the job itself, organization loyalty, and self-loyalty (positive), predicted intent to leave for both males and females, and there was a significant interaction between self-loyalty and sex. The self-loyalty index consisted of two items: 'my loyalty is to my own career, not to any particular company' and 'I would be willing to change companies for career advancement'. Female managers were significantly more self-loyal than male managers ($t = -2.26$, $P \leq 0.01$). Both the main effect in the regression equation, indicating the relationship between self-loyalty and intention for male managers ($B = -0.18$, $P \leq 0.01$), and the interaction, indicating the effect for female managers ($B = -0.15$, $P \leq 0.01$) were of similar magnitude, leading us to conclude that the differences here were due to the level of female managers' self-loyalty, not to a difference in threshold.

Other results of this study indicated that contrary to popular stereotypes about why female managers leave, family responsibilities reduced the intentions of both female and male managers to leave their current organizations. Male managers with children intended to stay ($B = 0.09$, $P \leq 0.05$). Presence of children for female managers had no impact on intentions ($B = 0.01$, ns). However, relatively few of the female managers in the study had children (20%). A dual-career relationship increased female managers' intentions to stay ($B = 0.10$, $P \leq 0.05$), but there were no differences between males in dual-career relationships and males in traditional relationships or single males in intentions to stay ($B = 0.07$, ns).

There were also significant differences between male and female managers in the levels of self-reported physiological stress ($t = -4.07$, $P \leq 0.01$). Stress was correlated with turnover intentions ($r = -0.21$, $P \leq 0.01$), but the effect was indirect, and could be completely accounted for by job dissatisfaction and organizational commitment. These results are consistent with the research reviewed above indicating that female managers experience higher levels of stress than males, and that this stress contributes to their turnover.

The data from our study belie the stereotype reported in Catalyst's 1991 survey of chief executive officer (CEO) and human resources (HR) managers. These corporate representatives believed that males leave for career opportunities, and females leave because of family responsibilities and relocation of spouses. Just the opposite, according to our study, both male and female managers leave for career opportunities, but female managers in this study were proportionately more intent on managing their own careers than the males. Family, rather than increasing turnover, reduced it. Female managers in dual-career households were less likely to leave their organizations, as were male managers with children.

The results of our study are consistent with the glass ceiling perspective (Morrison et al., 1987) that female managers lack career opportunities in American corporations. Female managers leave their organizations for the same reasons that male managers leave – dissatisfaction with career opportunities. In our study proportionally more female managers were dissatisfied and intent on managing their own careers. Those who lacked family responsibilities were particularly likely to leave their current organizations.

CONCLUSION

By the mid-1980s, entry-level management positions had become available to women and the focus of those concerned with equality of opportunity for women turned to their career success. Morrison et al. (1987), though studying a sample of female managers nominated by others for having successful careers, nevertheless concluded that female managers were not making it to the top of their organizations. They observed that despite early career successes, female managers were hitting a glass ceiling in middle management.

Our review of the turnover literature suggests that female managers' high rate of turnover is not a legitimate excuse for their failure to reach the top of their organizations. Female managers do leave their organizations at higher rates than male managers. However, their reasons for doing so belie the stereotype held by CEOs and high-level human resources managers (Catalyst, 1991) that they leave for family reasons. The data from a variety of studies suggest that female managers leave their organizations because of dissatisfaction with career opportunities. In our own study, female managers experienced higher levels of stress than male managers – stress that contributed to their lower levels of satisfaction with their jobs and organizations. The female managers were also less optimistic than the male managers that their careers could progress in their current organizations.

Family, rather than stimulating turnover, seems to reduce it, at least for male and female managers in our study, all of whom had relocated for the company in the prior years. Children make male managers less likely to leave their organizations. Dual-career relationships make the female managers less likely, not more likely to leave.

Remarkably, there is no sound research indicating how many female managers leave the workforce to bear and rear children, why they leave, how long they stay out, and what types of jobs they take when they return. Rosen and Korabik's (1990, 1991) study of MBA graduates suggests the type of research design that is needed to answer these questions. We would be surprised if there were significant differences between males and females in the rate of turnover from the first post-MBA job. Subsequently, however, we expect more varied career patterns among the females than the males.

At least three patterns seem likely for female managers: career mobility; career stability; and career and family mix. Career-mobile women would be identified by uninterrupted workforce participation and a relatively high number of employers. Women with this career pattern are likely to have fewer family responsibilities than women in the other categories. These women change companies more rapidly than the women in the other categories and the men in the sample who, we presume, are more likely to be married and have children.

Career-stable women are characterized by uninterrupted workforce participation and longer tenure in fewer companies. When these women have children, they remain in the workforce. We would be particularly interested in why. Do their companies offer supportive policies and practices – either that make being a female manager easier, hence minimizing the work stress typically experienced by women managers, or that facilitate the balancing act between work and family? Were they (the women) the primary wage-earner in their families?

The career–family-mix pattern characterizes those women whose workforce entries and exits have coincided with family events. We would like to know why they chose this option. Did spouse's income make it a viable option for them and not for others? Were they working for companies without supportive policies and practices? Do they use intervals out of the workforce to change the direction of their careers?

Finally, we would like to look into the future. Do these women with different early career patterns continue to follow separate paths, or do they converge? Are the career-mobile women the most likely to reach top management? Are they hired into these top management positions from the external labour market or promoted from within? Do the career-stable women make it to the top of their organizations? If not, why not? Are they hitting a glass ceiling? Are the career–family-mix women most likely to become entrepreneurs?

Even without this needed research, there is sufficient evidence that organizations are losing more than just the 'career and family' female managers, whom Schwartz (1989) represents as expendable. Organizations are also losing the 'career-dominant' female managers to better career opportunities elsewhere. More than other research documenting limited career opportunities for female managers (Morrison *et al.*, 1987; Stroh, Brett and Reilly, 1992), the research on turnover of female managers demonstrates that it is in the employers' own interest to provide better career opportunities for female managers.

The factors that contribute to female managers' intentions to turnover – stress, male-dominated corporate cultures, lack of opportunity – all suggest that it will take more than surface changes, such as career pathing for women, or mentorship programmes, or sexual harassment programmes, to assuage these female managers' dissatisfaction with their work environments. Of course, changing jobs does not guarantee a truly improved work environment either. Contributing to the inter-organizational mobility of the career-dominant female managers may be their ongoing search for a satisfactory job in a female-friendly organization.

REFERENCES

ARNOLD, H. J. and FELDMAN, D. C. (1982) A multivariate analysis of the determinants of job turnover, *Journal of Applied Psychology*, Vol. 67, pp. 350–60.

BOLGER, N., DELONGIS, A., KESSLER, R. C. and WETHINGTON, E. (1989) The contagion of stress across multiple roles, *Journal of Marriage and the Family*, Vol. 51, pp. 175–83.

BRETT, J. M. and YOGEV, S. (1988) Restructuring work for family: how dual-earner couples with children manage, *Journal of Social Behavior and Personality*, Vol. 3, pp. 159–74.

BURKE, R. J. and MCKEEN, C. A. (1994) *Women in Management: Current Research Issues*, Paul Chapman Publishing, London.

Business Week (1989) The mommy track: juggling kids and careers in corporate America takes a controversial turn, *Business Week*, 20 May.

BUTTNER, E. H. (1993) Female entrepreneurs: how far have they come? *Business Horizons*, Vol. 36, pp. 59–65.

CATALYST (1991) *Women in Corporate Management: Results of a Catalyst Survey*, Catalyst, New York, NY.

DAVIDSON, M. and COOPER, C. L. (1988) The pressures on women managers, *Management Decision*, Vol. 25, pp. 57–63.

EHRLICK, E. (1990) Welcome to the women friendly company, *Business Week*, 6 August, pp. 48–55.

GERHART, B. (1990) Voluntary turnover and alternative job opportunities, *Journal of Applied Psychology*, Vol. 75, pp. 467–76.

GUTEK, B. A., COHEN, A. G. and KONRAD, A. M. (1990) Predicting social-sexual behavior at work: a contact hypothesis, *Academy of Management Journal*, Vol. 33, pp. 560–77.

HALL, D. T. (1990) Promoting work/family balance: an organization change approach, *Organizational Dynamics*, Winter, pp. 5–18.

HIGGINS, C., DUXBURY, L. and IRVING, R. (1992) Determinants and consequences of work–family conflict, *Organizational Behavior and Human Decision Processes*, Vol. 51, pp. 51–75.

HOCHSCHILD, A. (1989) *The Second Shift*, Avon Books, New York.

HUSELID, M. A. and DAY, N. E. (1991) Organizational commitment, job involvement, and turnover: a substantive and methodological analysis, *Journal of Applied Psychology*, Vol. 75, pp. 380–1.

LAMBERT, S. J., HOPKINS, K., EASTON, G., WALKER, J., MCWILLIAMS, H., CHUNG, M. S., DIAMOND, V., PULLER, S. and YOUNG, J. (1993) *Added Benefits: The Link between Family-Responsive Policies and Work Performance at Fel-Pro Inc.*, University of Chicago, School of Social Service Administration.

LEE, T. W. and MOWDAY, R. T. (1987) Voluntarily leaving an organization: an empirical investigation of Steers and Mowday's model of turnover, *Academy of Management Journal*, Vol. 30, pp. 721–43.

LEWIS, G. B. and PARK, K. (1989) Turnover rates in federal white-collar employment: are women more likely to quit than men? *American Review of Public Administration*, Vol. 19, pp. 13–28.

LIGHT, A. and URETA, M. (1992) Panel estimates of male and female job turnover behavior: can female nonquitters be identified? *Journal of Labor Economics*, Vol. 10, pp. 156–81.

MARKHAM, W. T., MACKEN, P. O., BONJEAN, C. M. and CORDER, J. (1983) A note on sex, geographic mobility, and career advancement, *Social Forces*, Vol. 61, pp. 1138–46.

MARKHAM, W. T. and PLECK, J. H. (1986) Sex and willingness to move for occupational advancement: some national sample results. *Sociological Quarterly*, Vol. 26, pp. 121–43.

MICHAELS, C. E. and SPECTOR, P. E. (1982) Causes of employee turnover: a test of the Mobley, Griffeth, Hand, and Meglino model, *Journal of Applied Psychology*, Vol. 67, pp. 53–9.

MILLER, J. G. and WHEELER, K. G. (1992) Unraveling the mysteries of gender differences in intentions to leave the organization, *Journal of Organizational Behavior*, Vol. 13, pp. 465–78.

MOBLEY, W. H. (1977) Immediate linkages in the relationship between job satisfaction and employee turnover, *Journal of Applied Psychology*, Vol. 62, pp. 237–40.

MORRISON, A. M., WHITE, R. P., VAN VELSOR, E. and THE CENTER FOR CREATIVE LEADERSHIP (1987) *Breaking the Glass Ceiling: Can Women Reach the Top of America's Largest Corporations?* Addison-Wesley, Reading, MA.

PRICE, J. L. (1977) *The Study of Turnover*, Iowa State University Press, Ames, Iowa.

ROSEN, H. M. and KORABIK, K. (1990) Marital and family correlates of women managers' attrition from organizations, *Journal of Vocational Behavior*, Vol. 37, pp. 104–20.

ROSEN, H. M. and KORABIK, K. (1991) Workplace variables, affective responses, and intention to leave among women managers, *Journal of Occupational Psychology*, Vol. 64, pp. 317–30.

SCHWARTZ, F. N. (1989) Management women and the facts of life, *Harvard Business Review*, Vol. 1, pp. 65–76.

STEERS, R. M. and MOWDAY, R. T. (1981) Employee turnover and post-decision accommodation processes, in L. L. Cummings and B. M. Staw (eds) *Research in Organizational Behavior*, Vol. , pp. 235–81.

STROH, L. K., BRETT, J. M. and REILLY, A. H. (1992) All the right stuff: a comparison of female and male career patterns, *Journal of Applied Psychology*, Vol. 77, pp. 251–60.

STROH, L. K., BRETT, J. M. and REILLY, A. H. (1993) Turned over, or turned off? A comparison of male and female turnover. Presentation to Society of Industrial and Organizational Psychology, San Francisco, April.

STROH, L. K. and SENNER, J. R. (1994) Female top level executives: turnover, career limitations, and attitudes towards the work place, December, *Industrial Relations Research Association Proceedings*.

TAYLOR, A. (1986) Why women managers are bailing out, *Fortune*, Vol. 114, pp. 16–23.

YOUNGBLOOD, S. A., MOBLEY, W. H. and MEGLINO, B. M. (1983) A longitudinal analysis of the turnover process, *Journal of Applied Psychology*, Vol. 68, pp. 507–16.

CHAPTER 6

Career Development Among Managerial and Professional Women[1]

RONALD J. BURKE AND CAROL A. MCKEEN

INTRODUCTION

During the past two decades the dramatic increases in the number of women entering the workforce and pursuing professional and managerial careers has had a major impact on the workforce. Although armed with appropriate education, training and years of experience, managerial and professional women have not made much progress in entering the ranks of senior management. They encounter what some have termed a glass ceiling (Morrison *et al.*, 1987). Because they are now a significant component of the workplace, their recruitment and development is increasingly seen as a bottom-line issue related to corporate success.

Three hypotheses have been advanced in an attempt to understand the underutilization of women at the senior levels of organizations (Burke and McKeen, 1992). The first argues that women are different from men and that this difference is perceived as a deficiency in women when considered against the male organizational norm. Women's attitudes, behaviours, traits, and socialization handicap them in the masculine corporate environment. Research support for this explanation has been limited (Morrison and von Glinow, 1990), and almost all of the evidence shows little or no difference between the traits, abilities, education, and motivations of managerial and professional women and men (Powell, 1990).

A second hypothesis builds on the notion of bias and discrimination by the majority towards the minority. It suggests that managerial and professional women are held back by the bias and stereotypes men have of women (Kanter, 1977). Such bias or discrimination is either sanctioned by the labour market or rewarded by organizations, despite the demonstrated level of job performance of women. As evidence of this (as discussed in Chapter 4), there is widespread agreement that the 'good manager' is seen as male or masculine (Schein, 1973, 1975).

[1] Preparation of this manuscript was supported, in part, by the Faculty of Administrative Studies, York University, the National Centre for Management Research and Development, University of Western Ontario, and the School of Business, Queen's University. Cobi Wolpin provided research assistance in our projects described in this manuscript.

The third hypothesis emphasizes structural and systemic discrimination in organizational policies and practices which affect the treatment of women and which limit their advancement. These policies and practices include women's lack of opportunity and power in organizations, tokenism, lack of mentors and sponsors, and denial of access to developmental opportunities such as challenging assignments. To investigate this hypothesis further, there is a need to understand what policies and practices prevent women from reaching senior management and what factors support the career development of women.

Morrison et al. (1987), in a three-year study of top female executives, identified six factors which contributed to the women's success. These were: help from above, a track record of achievements, a desire to succeed, an ability to manage subordinates, a willingness to take career risks, and an ability to be tough, decisive and demanding. Three derailment factors were common in explaining the failure of some female managers to achieve expected levels. These were: inability to adapt, wanting too much (for oneself or other women) and performance problems.

Furthermore, to be successful, women, more than men, needed help from above, needed to be easy to be with, and to be able to adapt. These factors related to developing good relationships with men in a male-dominated environment. Women, more than men, were also required to take career risks, to be tough, have a strong desire to succeed and to have an impressive presence. These factors could be argued to be necessary to overcome the traditional stereotype of women such as being risk averse, weak and afraid of success. Unfortunately, the narrow band of acceptable behaviour for women contained some contradictions. The most obvious being: take risks but be consistently successful, be tough but easy to get along with, be ambitious but do not expect equal treatment, and take responsibility but be open to the advice of others, that is more senior men. These findings suggest that *additional* criteria for success were applied to women so that women had to have more assets and fewer liabilities than men.

As part of the same study, Morrison et al. (1987) also examined the experiences of women who made it to levels of general management. They identified four critical work experiences: being accepted by their organizations, receiving support and encouragement, being given training and developmental opportunities, and being offered challenging work and visible assignments. In speculating about their future success, they perceived that there were even more constraints and less support now than in lower-level positions. Many reported exhaustion and talked about their futures involving doing something very different from what they were currently doing. In a series of follow-up interviews, Morrison et al. (1992) obtained information from approximately one-third of their original sample and found that although some women had made progress, many were still stuck.

Prior research, including Hall's (1986) publication on career development, does not include any content dealing specifically with the careers of women. The purpose of this chapter is to address that subject, by considering issues relating to the career development of women, and to facilitate the understanding of what initiatives might be undertaken by organizations, what activities and programmes facilitate upward mobility and women's role in these processes.

MODELS OF CAREER DEVELOPMENT

Most researchers have taken the position that general models of career development should fit women as well as men, particularly if women are entering the same occupations and are similar to men in abilities and ambitions. Issues of child-rearing and family have been given little attention and it has been assumed that women would have successful careers by following the male model and by sharing child and home responsibilities with their partners. For dual-career families with children, two people now attempt to do the work of two careers and one homemaker role. Earlier in this century, before the influx of women into the workforce, two people managed one career and one home. Although some work in the home can be purchased by dual-career couples, research by Hochschild (1989) indicates that in such couples, the women do on average 30 extra 24-hour days per year of 'second shift' work, compared to their male partners. Clearly, not all of the traditional homemaker's work can be or is purchased. The dual-career couple has much left to do, and women do the bulk of it.

This difference, as well as findings from literature on the psychology of women, indicates that career development for women may be different from career development for men. For example, work on the early career experiences of MBA graduates by Rosen et al. (1981) found that career motivation and the need for challenging work were similar for men and women, but women had fewer opportunities to share ideas and receive feedback by interacting with their supervisors. Bailyn (1989) found, in a closely matched sample of male and female engineers, that women experienced their careers very differently from men, even though in external aspects they were similar. The women engineers reported less self-confidence and a less integrated view of their work and non-work lives.

This literature, and other developments (Marshall, 1989), suggests the need for a theory of women's career development that is different from men's. Larwood and Gutek (1987) advocate such a theory and list five concerns that need to be added or given particular attention for women: career preparation, career opportunities available in society, the influence of marriage, pregnancy and children, timing and age. Similarly, Gallos (1989) explored the different visions of reality that women bring to work, love and career. She considered women's development from a psychological developmental perspective, as opposed to a cultural or sociological approach.

Gallos (1989) contends that career theories have typically been built on male models of success and work in which there is an assumption of the centrality of work to one's identity and the notion that maturity involves separation from others. For women, attachment to others, not separation, is an important source of both identity and maturity and their development emphasizes the centrality of relationships, attachments and caring. These affect how women view the world around them and how they choose to live their lives. The success of a woman's career complements, rather than replaces, close interpersonal relations. Gallos believes that women express their professional selves over a lifetime, with commitment to accomplishment and a desire for fair treatment and rewards for their efforts, rather than the ongoing organizational affiliation and life choices that put occupational progress first. Phases of development, for women, may not have the linear and predictable character of men's and women may use a broader range of criteria for evaluating their choices than men (Bardwick, 1980).

To overcome the exclusion of family in the male model of career research, Lee (1993) has argued for a new approach to understanding women's careers, which includes the diversity of women's experiences in the workforce and in the family. She proposes six alternative models of women's careers to describe the most common ways women integrate commitment to work and family over the lifespan. Some sequence work and family, one first then the other; others try to combine high commitment to both; still others choose a particular type of work or family situation that makes combining the two easier. She also discusses the costs and benefits of each model for women themselves, the family, organizations and society.

There is also no one 'best' model. Each model has a variety of benefits and costs. An important predictor of satisfaction experienced with any model is the degree of choice and control exercised by a woman in its selection. Multiple patterns can provide satisfaction and fulfilment. It is also important to expand the definition of career, for women, to include work experiences in the context of paid employment and in the family/community.

A few writers have included the broader experiences of women in both home and family spheres and attempted to categorize women's occupational choices and experiences (Daniels and Weingarten, 1982; O'Donnell, 1988; Lee, 1993). These various models of women's career development show great variety and diversity. It is important to appreciate and legitimize the different patterns that characterize women's commitment to occupation and family over the lifespan. The last phrase is critical; one must consider the lifespan perspective because many women change their levels of involvement and participation in employment and family. A cross-sectional design will miss this fact.

WORK EXPERIENCES AND CAREER DEVELOPMENT

The literature on work experiences and career development can be organized within a framework proposed by Morrison (1992). Her model for successful career development includes three elements which interact over time to spur and sustain development. These elements are challenge, recognition and support. This model is based on research with women in managerial practice and is consistent with her earlier work with McCall and Lombardo (McCall et al., 1988), which identified three work experiences with developmental value – specific jobs, other people and hardships. These can be recast as challenge, and presence or absence of recognition and support. The Centre for Creative Leadership has studied the kinds of experiences that develop managers and what makes them developmental. They found that five broad categories of experience had developmental potential (challenging jobs; other people, particularly bosses; hardships; course work; off-the job experiences) but that it was also important for the individual to have learned lessons from them. Learning was made possible, but not guaranteed, by these experiences.

These experiences also fit within Morrison's model with other people forming part of the recognition and support, hardships being part of the challenge, and course work and off-the-job experiences being part challenge and part support.

Morrison defines the components of her model as follows. The *Challenge* of new situations and difficult goals prompts managers to learn the lessons and skills that will help them perform well at higher levels. *Recognition* includes acknowledgement and rewards for achievement and the resources to continue achieving in the form of promotions, salary increases and awards. *Support* involves acceptance and understanding along with values that help managers incorporate their career into rich and rewarding lives. This model assumes that all three elements must be present in the same relative proportions over time – balanced – to permit and sustain development.

Morrison proposes that, for women, an imbalance typically occurs such that the level of challenge exceeds the other two components. Her research shows that aspects of assignments and day-to-day life which constitute challenge are often overlooked, recognition may be slow, and traditional support systems may fall short. Common barriers to advancement (stereotypes, prejudices, male discomfort) contribute to this imbalance, and as a consequence managerial women become exhausted, experience failure and may 'bail out' of this frustrating work situation. Each of the three components of Morrison's model will be used as a framework within which the literature will be discussed.

Challenge

An important method for preparing individuals for executive jobs is to plan a sequence of assignments that provide continued challenge, for example for changing or rotating jobs every year or two. New assignments require the learning of new or better skills, broaden one's perspective, stretch the individual to develop and also serve as 'tests', by which individuals are rewarded, and/or promoted.

Lombardo and Eichinger (1989) listed the 11 most commonly cited challenges (e.g. success and failure were both possible and would be obvious to others; required aggressive individual, take-charge leadership; involved working with new people, a lot of people or both) and conclude that for an experience to be developmental, five or more of these challenges must be present simultaneously. Although job change is the best way of providing these challenges, it is also possible to provide many of these for a manager in her present job in the form of small projects and start-ups, small scope jumps or fix-its, small strategic assignments, course work and coaching assignments, and activities away from work. An organization interested in developing women managers needs to make specific assignments to particular managers, to help them learn from developmental assignments, and to develop feedback mechanisms, so managers can see how effectively they are learning.

An interesting question becomes whether or not managerial and professional women experience the same developmental job demands and learn similar skills from them. One possible explanation for the 'glass ceiling' is that women are afforded different developmental opportunities than men over the course of their careers. McCall *et al.* (1988) and Horgan (1989) suggest that certain types of job assignments and challenging experiences are less available to women. For example, women may be offered staff, not line jobs, and jobs that are not high profile or challenging.

A related explanation for the glass ceiling is that men and women with the same developmental experiences might learn differently from them. This was supported by Ohlott et al. (1990) when they looked at the demands of managerial jobs and factors which may complicate learning from the job. They found that women experienced very different demands from managerial jobs and they had to work harder to prove themselves, but women were also learning about managerial work from a greater variety of sources than were men. Horgan (1989) also suggests that what is learned from a given set of developmental experiences may differ between men and women.

Although some sources of challenge are common to all managers (high stakes, adverse business conditions, dealing with staff members) women may experience additional challenges such as prejudice, isolation or conflict between career and personal life, and may also face higher performance standards, more adverse conditions (resentment and hostility of male staff), more scrutiny and more 'second-shift' work (Hochschild, 1989). Despite these things, limiting challenge is dangerous for the career advancement of women, since giving women less important jobs and not considering them for key assignments blocks their advancement by denying them important business experiences. Morrison advocates not reducing the level of job challenge but reducing demands from other sources – by reducing prejudice, promoting other women, using the same performance standards – and providing commensurate recognition and support so that the critical balance of these three items is retained.

Education, training and development can be conceived of as being either or both challenge and support. To the extent that they may provide technical training, coaching and key assignments they represent challenge and a chance to improve/prove oneself. To the extent that they may involve training geared to women, for example assisting women with issues unique to being women in male-dominated organizations or industries, or providing career pathing or mentoring, they could be viewed as support activities. Some activities, for example mentoring, clearly involve aspects of challenge and support. These two aspects are often referred to as career functions and psychosocial functions. We have chosen to discuss mentoring under Support later in this chapter.

What education, training, and development experiences do managerial and professional women undertake and which of these experiences do they find useful? McKeen and Burke (1991) found that the modal number of training and development activities that managerial and professional women participated in was six (out of a possible 14). The most common activities were orientation programmes, technical training, supervisory coaching, coaching from peers, and receiving key project assignments. The least common activities included advanced management programmes, being sponsored, and career pathing. The least useful activities were orientation programmes, career development programmes, advanced management programmes and networking outside one's organization. Women ranked the most useful of these activities as being sponsored, being mentored, and being involved in the process of career pathing; however, two of these were the least common. Four of the most common activities could be conceptualized as providing challenge and two of the least common activities are those which could be conceptualized as support activities. This supports Morrison's observations that the challenge–recognition–support model for women is often imbalanced by the presence of too little support for the amount of challenge.

Furthermore, professional and managerial women who participated in a greater number of education and developmental activities were more organizationally committed, job satisfied and involved, and had higher career prospects. Thus, training and development seem to be important to women, but it may be useful to frame the various activities and their contribution to the balance in the challenge–recognition–support model.

Recognition

Recognition involves acknowledging and adjusting to the additional challenges faced by women in organizations because they are women. Equal performance by men and women in a male-dominated organization may mean that women have overcome more and this must be recognized. Furthermore, when contemplating a challenge such as a new task or promotion, women may seem less keen because they are aware of the additional challenge of being a woman performing that new task. The reward system must account for this. Morrison concludes that expected rewards fall short for women when one considers additional demands and sacrifices needed. Women are more likely to have the title 'acting' and do the job before getting it than are male colleagues, and receive fewer promotions and benefits and less pay than men (Morrison and von Glinow, 1990). The forms that recognition takes include pay, promotion, perquisites, inclusion in decision, respect and credibility and faith (Morrison, 1992). Statistics which indicate the continuing presence of a glass ceiling are evidence that recognition in the form of promotion has not been forthcoming for women. The necessity for pay equity legislation in Canada (requiring equal pay for work of equal value) is part of the process of recognition in economic terms of the value of women's contribution. Despite such initiatives there is still evidence that professional and managerial women consistently receive less economic recognition (in the form of pay) for the work they perform than do their male colleagues (McKeen and Richardson, 1992).

Other research suggests that women's success is often attributed to luck rather than ability, and it has become the subject of humour that women's contributions in meetings are often unacknowledged and later attributed to men who repeat the messages: 'That's an excellent suggestion, Ms Tuggs, perhaps one of the men would like to make it.' It appears then, that rather than proactively recognizing and rewarding the additional challenge faced by women, many organizations recognize and reward women even less than comparably performing men. The long-standing assertion that being a woman means you have to accomplish twice as much to be considered half as good, gives voice to Morrison's model.

Support

Support is necessary to help women cope with the additional demands, and the absence of acceptance and colleagueship contributes to the isolation and discouragement that women feel (Morrison *et al.*, 1987). Sources of support include features of the work environment such as mentors, sponsors, information feedback and networks as well as organizational and societal supports for dual-career couples.

McKeen and Burke (1991) examined the effects of five experiences on measures of career success and career progress among managerial and professional women. Four of these experiences constituted types of support: (1) support and encouragement by one's organization; (2) training and development opportunities; (3) feeling accepted; (4) an absence of tension from overload and ambiguity from being woman. Women who reported more positive work experiences in these areas also reported greater job and career satisfaction, commitment and career optimism and lower intention to quit. These work experiences were most strongly related to job and career satisfaction and least strongly related to job involvement and future career prospects.

Ohlott *et al.* (1990) developed a model of on-the-job learning, and found that the reinforcement and support of others play a mediating role. Furthermore, they found that women received less support, having as a result to work harder than men.

Morrison *et al.* (1987) identified three levels of pressure reported by managerial and professional women: the demands of the job itself; pressures from their pioneering role (token minority); and strains of family obligations (second-shift work). In addition, to overcome negative stereotypes about women in some areas of corporate performance and yet remain stereotypically feminine enough, women must walk a fine line – not too masculine and not too feminine – in displaying a narrow band of acceptable behaviour.

Research by McDonald and Korabik (1991) on the perception of one of the components of Morrison's model, support, indicates that women, more than men need more psychosocial support to feel as supported in organizations. Taken together these findings suggest that women and men need different kinds and levels of support in the work environment because they face different challenges inside and outside a particular assignment. Moreover, a given level of support may be *perceived* differentially by men and women for reasons we do not yet fully understand.

MENTORS   One of the forms of organizational support is a mentor. The literature on careers suggests that mentors play a crucial role in career development and that they may be even more critical to the career success of women than men (Kanter, 1977; Hennig and Jardim, 1977; Morrison *et al.*, 1987). The literature reports that more women than men who advance to corporate management have mentors, and women who fail to reach these levels cite the absence of mentors as critical to their failure. Persons with mentors have been found to have more organizational policy influence and access to important people and resources (Fagenson, 1989), and higher promotion rates, income and income satisfaction (Dreher and Ash, 1990).

Although mentors are critical to the success of women, there is evidence that there is a smaller supply of mentors available to women than men. Women may have trouble finding mentors because they are *different* from men in more senior positions, they occupy a token status, and there may be potential discomfort in cross-gender relationships. Noe (1988) identified six potential barriers to mentoring relationships involving women. These included lack of contact with potential mentors, high visibility of women as protégés due to their small numbers (tokenism), negative stereotypes making women unattractive as protégés, behavioural differences between men and women, women's use of non-male influence strategies and cultural and organizational biases with respect to cross-gender relationships. Mentor relationships that cross gender lines must be concerned about managing actual closeness and intimacy in the relationship, as well as the perception of those things by others in the organization (Clawson and Kram, 1984). This was highlighted in Bowen's study (1985) which found that resentment of coworkers was a problem in cross-gender mentoring relationships; however, both mentors and protégés felt the positive benefits more than offset the problem. In a study of male mentors and their protégés, Kram (1985) found that female protégés were more likely to experience greater social distance, discomfort and overprotectiveness than male protégés.

In addition to their role in career success, mentoring relationships may have a special role in improving the quality of organizational life for women. The literature suggests that one of the moderating variables which may influence the effect of stress on professional women is mentoring. Mentoring relationships have the potential to alleviate her stress by increasing the protégé's self-confidence, forewarning her about career stress and suggesting ways to deal with it. In addition, female mentors provide unique role models for female protégés because they can more easily relate to the stresses that young women face – discrimination, stereotyping, and family/work interface, and social isolation (Nelson and Quick, 1985).

At the present time there are not sufficient women at senior levels in organizations for them to be able to provide all of the mentoring needs of younger women. Ragins and Cotton (1991) found that women and men do have equal intentions to mentor; however, women perceived more drawbacks to engaging in that role. The drawbacks cited were time and request overload. We must remember that the women, too, exist in organizations in which they may or may not have an appropriate balance of challenge, recognition and support. If they experience the typical imbalance that Morrison anticipates, they will have inadequate support for the amount of challenge. This will influence their perception of the difficulty of the challenge of being a mentor, given their inadequate level of support.

The research suggests the importance of mentoring for women, their relative difficulty in finding mentors, and some of the issues in cross-gender relationships (Ragins, 1989). In addition, it highlights the psychosocial or support aspects of mentoring as being especially important for women. If Morrison is correct about the imbalance in women's lives due to inadequate support, the consideration of the formalization of mentoring relationships for women is warranted. A critical question is whether an organization can create conditions that encourage mentoring. Opinions on this point are divided with some writers arguing that assigned relationships have a low probability of success (Kram, 1985) and others believing that effective mentoring programmes can be created by organizations with proper planning and support (Burke and McKeen, 1989).

NETWORKS An additional source of organizational support may be peer relationships and interpersonal networks. Such networks may also be a source of challenging work and recognition; however, this discussion will focus on their role in support.

It has been suggested that women lack access to informal networks with male colleagues – the 'old boy' network (Ragins and Sundstrom, 1989; Ibarra, 1993). This may result for several reasons. Women may not be aware of informal networks and their importance and potential usefulness, they may not be as skilled as men in building informal networks, and may prefer to communicate with others similar to themselves. Men, being the dominant group, may want to maintain their dominance by excluding women from informal interactions. If women are, in fact, excluded from male networks, they may be missing several ingredients important for career success such as information, resources, support, advice, influence, power, allies, mentors, sponsors and privilege.

Kram and Isabella (1985) examined the role of peer relationships and found they provided a range of developmental supports for personal and professional growth at all career stages. These functions were similar to those obtained from mentors. Although some peer relationships provided only one career function, others provided several career and psychosocial functions. Peer relationships, unlike mentor relationships, were characterized by mutuality with both individuals experienced at being the giver as well as the receiver of various functions.

There have been relatively few studies of women's and men's networks in organizations. Brass (1984, 1985) examined interaction patterns of men and women in one organization, and the effects of these patterns on perceptions of influence and actual promotions. Women were generally rated less influential than men but were similar to men on many other measures. Women and men were not well integrated into one another's networks. Promotions were found to be related to centrality in department, men's and dominant coalition interaction networks. Interestingly, women's networks more closely resembled men's when their immediate work group included both women and men.

Ibarra (1992) used an intergroup perspective to investigate differences in men's and women's access to informal networks at work. Results indicated that men had greater centrality and homophily (relationships with same-sex others) in their network relationships than women. Women's networks were differentiated in that social support was sought from women and instrumental access was sought from men. Men gained centrality through background characteristics such as work experience and professional activities, women gained centrality through control of critical resources. Ties to women took away from women's centrality but added to men's. Women belonging to subgroups with a higher proportion of women had more ties with women but less centrality; however, the gender composition of men's groups did not affect their network patterns.

These studies, taken together with the material reviewed on mentoring, suggest some similarities. Both mentors and peer relationships can facilitate career and personal development. Peer relationships may have some advantages – particularly since a significant number of both women and men have not had mentors – in that they often last longer, are not hierarchical, and involve a two-way helping. In addition, while mentors may be particularly important in the early career stage, peer relationships can be useful at all stages (Kram and Isabella, 1985). It seems clear, however, that managerial and professional women are still less integrated with important organizational networks, and it is these internal networks that influence critical human resource decisions such as promotion and acceptance.

CONCLUSION

What do managerial and professional women want and need?

We undertook two studies of about 250 managerial and professional women in Canada to consider this question. In one case we examined the desirability of 21 different career development opportunities, for example advancement up the professional/technical ladder, a temporary assignment in a different geographical area, more flexible working hours, belonging to a taskforce, company financial support for further academic/professional qualifications, professional career consulting. In the second, we investigated the importance of 19 organizational initiatives or services, for example a good corporate daycare centre, unpaid leaves of absence, a job-sharing programme, a shorter working week, travel policies geared to the needs and convenience of families, family emergency days off.

A similar pattern of findings was observed in both studies. Thus, although some development activities and organizational initiatives were generally rated as more desirable or important than others, there was considerable diversity among the managerial and professional women in the sample. This diversity seemed to depend on two sets of variables. The first consisted of a series of individual demographic characteristics. Managerial women with family responsibilities wanted developmental opportunities and organizational initiatives, characterized by greater flexibility and fewer demands. These women were less interested in developmental activities, geographical moves and career changes. This supports Morrison's belief that women may experience a developmental imbalance such that challenge exceeds available support. Women without family responsibilities were interested in developmental opportunities and organizational initiatives, characterized by greater challenge (visibility, skill development) and geographical mobility. For these women, supports could be conceived of as being adequate to their lives, but challenge was inadequate.

The second set of variables that was associated with this diversity consisted of measures of work outcomes and feeling states. Managerial women interested in lower work demands and greater flexibility were currently dissatisfied with their jobs, less work involved and reporting greater exhaustion and psychosomatic symptomatology. Managerial women interested in greater career development, more challenge and greater depends were more job and career satisfied, more job involved and were optimistic about future career progress. These findings may provide a proxy for the 'cost' to organizations and women of the imbalance of challenge, recognition and support, particularly an imbalance caused by inadequate support.

These findings have implications for both organizations and the managerial and professional women they recruit, hire, utilize and develop. Organizations must realize that managerial and professional women, like men, are not homogeneous. In addition, they must be more sensitive to work and family demands which, together, may be reducing the energy and time available for a single-minded career commitment and in fact *adding to the challenge* faced by women. Consideration must be given to the possibility of alternative career models in which commitment and energy over one's career may follow a different pattern for employees with primary responsibility for family and children. For example, early career commitment when women are single and childless may shift with the as yet unshared burdens of marriage and children, but re-emerge as children become less dependent. Perhaps organizations need to envision a restructured model in which people with primary family/child responsibility contribute later in their lives what others contribute earlier. At the present time these people are women whose life expectancy is several years greater than that of men in North America. This differential longevity would, for example, permit a different career model in which interested women resume and continue career commitment later in their lives than men.

Other initiatives by organizations to rebalance the challenge–recognition–support model must specifically address the needs of women, and remove the barriers which contribute to the imbalance. Women need *active* organizational assistance and support in managing their careers. It has been found (Lee, 1993) that more, and more varied, patterns exist in the careers of women than of men. Women face more choices when it comes to investments in work, investments in family, and the timing of children. Men are influenced by these choices too, but women still experience more dislocation from particular events and usually undertake more second-shift work. Women's choices need to be legitimized and assisted by organizations. It is clear that this second-shift work is not done by free choice in most cases. To say that women choose the 'mommy track' or 'choose' more flexibility over career development activities, is to avoid discussion of the environment in which this choice occurs. We do not know how women would feel about a variety of career development activities if they could make that decision in an environment of at least equally shared second-shift work. If they had the flexibility they wanted/needed and we asked them again about career development activities, how would they respond? What employees bring to the workplace is dramatically influenced by their personal circumstances. Situational characteristics are relevant in attitudes to and energy for work, and we know from the work of Hochschild (1989) and others that the situational characteristics of women with families are dramatically different from those of men. How organizations respond to these different realities will determine how successful they are in assessing what educated women have to offer at various times in their lives. Organizations with long-run views of their relationships with their employees need to consider the present and future realities of their employees' lives and respond creatively and with their employees' input.

Schwartz (1992), based on time spent at three leading US business schools, observed that both women and men students wanted a balanced life, but both groups seemed unrealistic about how long it would take to realize this. She states that women leave the corporate world at higher levels than men because of corporate inflexibility about maternity, the demands of parenting, corrosive working conditions and the separate shifts of men and women. She outlines four areas of action that organizations can undertake to support the performance and advancement of women or, in Morrison's view, provide and rebalance challenge, recognition and support: acknowledge the differences between women and men; provide flexibility to those who need or want it; provide training and development for women so that they can acquire the skills required to succeed; and remove barriers in the corporate environment that exist for women but not for men.

Managerial and professional women need to be aware of and act on the potential sources of dissatisfaction, overload and fragmentation they are experiencing, by making demands on their organization for (temporary) greater flexibility and relief from some of the overload, and negotiating more support from their partners or by buying services. The issue of pay equity is critical to the ability of women to buy the services to do the 'second-shift' work. If access to equal pay and opportunity for advancement are not assured, organizations will lose or underutilize the talents of the capable and educated women who now comprise a significant and vital portion of their workplace.

Our research also suggested the importance for managerial women of stress management and relaxation. Using Morrison's model, this stress can be envisioned as the result of too much challenge for the available levels of recognition and support. Until we effectively restore the balance, organizations and the women in them need to make special efforts to recognize their burden and sustain themselves, while continuing to negotiate for change and balance.

REFERENCES

BAILYN, L. (1989) Understanding individual experience at work: comments on the theory and practice of careers, in M. B. Arthur, D. T. Hall and B. S. Lawrence (eds) *Handbook of Career Theory*, Cambridge University Press, New York, pp. 477–89.

BARDWICK, J. (1980) The seasons of a woman's life, in D. McGuigan (ed.) *Women's Lives: New Theory, Research and Policy*, University of Michigan Center for Continuing Education of Women, Ann Arbor.

BOWEN, D. D. (1985) Were men meant to mentor women? *Training and Development Journal*, Vol. 39, pp. 30–4.

BRASS, D. J. (1984) Being in the right place: a structural analysis of individual influence in an organization, *Administrative Science Quarterly*, Vol. 29, pp. 518–39.

BRASS, D. J. (1985) Men's and women's networks: a study of interaction patterns and influence in an organization, *Academy of Management Journal*, Vol. 32, pp. 662–9.

BURKE, R. J. and MCKEEN, C. A. (1989) Developing formal mentoring programs in organizations, *Business Quarterly*, Winter, pp. 69–76.

BURKE, R. J. and MCKEEN, C. A. (1992) Women in management, in C. L. Cooper and I. T. Robertson (eds) *International Review of Industrial and Organizational Psychology*, John Wiley, New York, pp. 245–83.

CLAWSON, J. G. and KRAM, K. E. (1984) Managing cross-gender mentoring, *Business Horizons*, Vol. 17, pp. 22–32.

DANIELS, P. and WEINGARTEN, K. (1982) *Sooner or Later: The Timing of Parenthood in Adult Times*, Morton, New York.

DREHER, G. F. and ASH, R. A. (1990) A comparative study of mentoring among men and women in managerial, professional and technical positions, *Journal of Applied Psychology*, Vol. 75, pp. 539–46.

FAGENSON, E. A. (1989) The mentor advantage: perceived career/job experiences of proteges versus non-proteges, *Journal of Organizational Behavior*, Vol. 10, pp. 309–20.

GALLOS, J. V. (1989) Exploring women's development: implications for career theory, practice and research, in M. B. Arthur, D. T. Hall and B. S. Lawrence (eds) *Handbook of Career Theory*, Cambridge University Press, New York, pp. 110–132.

HALL, D. T. (1986) *Career Development in Organizations*, Jossey-Bass Publishers, San Francisco.

HENNIG, M. and JARDIM, A. (1977) *The Managerial Woman*, Anchor Press/Doubleday, New York.

HOCHSCHILD, A. (1989) *The Second Shift*, Avon Books, New York.

HORGAN, D. D. (1989) A cognitive learning perspective in women becoming expert managers, *Journal of Business and Psychology*, Vol. 3, pp. 299–313.

IBARRA, H. (1992) Homophily and differential returns: sex differences in network structure and access in an advertising firm, *Administrative Sciences Quarterly*, Vol. 37, pp. 422–47.

IBARRA, H. (1993) Personal networks of women and minorities in management, *Academy of Management Review*, Vol. 18, pp. 56–87.

KANTER, R. M. (1977) *Men and Women of the Corporation*, Basic Books, New York.

KRAM, K. E. (1985) *Mentors in Organizations*, Scott, Foresman, Chicago.

KRAM, K. E. and ISABELLA, L. (1985) Mentoring alternatives: the role of peer relationships in career development, *Academy of Management Journal*, Vol. 28, pp. 110–32.

LARWOOD, L. and GUTEK, B. A. (1987) Working toward a theory of women's career development, in B. A. Gutek and L. Larwood (eds) *Women's Career Development*, Vol. 5, pp. 106–27, Sage, Beverly Hills, CA.

LEE, M. D. (1993) Women's involvement in professional careers and family life: themes and variations, *Business in the Contemporary World*, in press.

LOMBARDO, M. M. and EICHINGER, R. W. (1989) *Eighty-Eight Assignments for Development in Place: Enhancing the Developmental Challenge of Existing Jobs*, Center for Creative Leadership, Greensboro.

MARSHALL, J. (1989) Revisioning career concepts: a feminist invitation, in M. B. Arthur, D. T. Hall and B. S. Lawrence (eds) *Handbook of Career Theory*, Cambridge University Press, New York, pp. 275–91.

MCCALL, M. W., LOMBARDO, M. M. and MORRISON, A. M. (1988) *The Lessons of Experience*, Lexington Books, New York.

MCDONALD, L. M. and KORABIK, K. (1991) Work stress and social support among male and female managers, *Canadian Journal of Administrative Sciences*, Vol. 8, pp. 231–8.

MCKEEN, C. A. and BURKE, R. J. (1991) Work experiences and career success of managerial and professional women: study design and preliminary findings, *Canadian Journal of Administrative Sciences*, Vol. 8, pp. 251–8.

MCKEEN, C. A. and RICHARDSON, A. J. (1992) Women in accounting: still a glass ceiling, *CMA Magazine*, Vol. 66, pp. 22–6.

MORRISON, A. M. (1992) *The New Leaders*, Jossey-Bass Publishers, San Francisco, CA.

MORRISON, A. M. and VON GLINOW, M. A. (1990) Women and minorities in management, *American Psychologist*, Vol. 45, pp. 200–8.

MORRISON, A. M., WHITE, R. P. and VAN VELSOR, E. (1987, 1992) *Breaking the Glass Ceiling*, Addison-Wesley, Reading, Mass.

NELSON, D. L. and QUICK, J. D. (1985) Professional women: are distress and disease inevitable? *Academy of Management Review*, Vol. 10, pp. 206–18.

O'DONNELL, L. N. (1988) *The Unheralded Majority: Contemporary Women as Mothers*, D. L. Heath, Lexington, Mass.

OHLOTT, N., RUDERMAN, M. N. and MCCAULEY, C. D. (1990) Women and men: equal opportunity for development? Paper presented at the Annual Meeting of the Academy of Management, August, San Francisco.

POWELL, G. N. (1990) One more time: Do male and female managers differ? Academy of Management Executive, Vol. 4, no. 3, pp. 68–75.

RAGINS, B. R. (1989) Barriers to mentoring: the female manager's dilemma, *Human Relations*, Vol. 42, pp. 1–22.

RAGINS, B. R. and COTTON, J. C. (1991) Easier said than done: gender differences in perceived barriers to gaining a mentor, *Academy of Management Journal*, Vol. 34, pp. 939–51.

RAGINS, B. R. and SUNDSTROM, E. (1989) Gender and power in organizations: a longitudinal perspective, *Psychological Bulletin*, Vol. 105, pp. 51–88.

ROSEN, B., TEMPLETON, M. E. and KIRCHLINE, K. (1981) The first few years on the job: women in management, *Business Horizons*, Vol. 24, pp. 26–9.

SCHEIN, V. E. (1973) The relationship between sex role stereotypes and requisite management characteristics, *Journal of Applied Psychology*, Vol. 57, no. 2, pp. 95–100.

SCHEIN, V. E. (1975) Relationships between sex role stereotypes and requisite management characteristics among female managers, *Journal of Applied Psychology*, Vol. 60, no. 3, pp. 340–4.

SCHWARTZ, F. N. (1992) *Breaking with Tradition*, Time-Warner Books, New York.

CHAPTER 7

Career Development in Male and Female Managers – Convergence or Collapse?

ROB GOFFEE AND NIGEL NICHOLSON

INTRODUCTION

Increasingly, one reads in the press bleak prognostications about the death of the career as we have known it (*Newsweek*, 1993). But before we bury the concept of career, we should examine the corpse for signs of life, or establish just what it is we are disposing of. As has been argued before (Nicholson and West, 1989), the idea of the career as an orderly cumulative trajectory has been becoming outdated for some time now, though recent trends have accelerated the demise of the traditional concept (Inkson and Coe, 1993). We can either abandon the term in favour of some more neutral expression such as 'work histories', or define career in a way which frees us from normative assumptions, such as Arthur *et al.*'s (1989) 'the evolving sequence of a person's work experiences over time'. Either course firmly locates the career as the property of the person, regardless of its shape. The question we shall seek to address in this chapter is how the enacted career is changing its form for men and women managers in the 1990s.

It is useful, perhaps, to consider first what are the forces which shape careers. Briefly, they are fourfold. First, at the most macro level, are cultural norms and expectations. The significant career event of a change of employer varies dramatically cross-nationally, as a current study by the OECD (reported in the *Economist*, 1993) has shown. The average tenure of workers in Holland, Australia and the USA is no more than 7 years, while in France, Germany and Japan it is over 10 years. Second, is labour market segmentation. Within national economies there exist professional and occupational labour markets with quite distinctive characteristics of high or low mobility, developmental continuity, or future uncertainty. Third, are organizational structures. It is not just the obvious fact that large organizations have greater capacity to engineer lifelong career paths than smaller ones, but that they differ in type. As Sonnenfeld *et al.* (1988) have shown, firms of comparable size have quite different career development characteristics according to their propensity for external versus internal supply flows of personnel, and group versus individual assignment flows. This model leads to a fourfold classification of firms as 'fortresses', 'baseball teams', 'clubs' and 'academies'. Gunz (1989) makes much the same point in describing career paths as possible moves within the three-dimensional space of companies' 'climbing frame' structures. Fourth, careers are the constructs of individual self-determination (Law, 1981). People do not just respond to opportunities, but actively seek experiences of stability and change which meet their needs and perceived interests. It is apparent that these four sets of influences intersect. Structure and agency intertwine via the familiar processes of socialization and adaptation (Nicholson, 1984). In order to understand the changes taking place around us, and predict the future of managerial careers, we need to examine how these influences are affecting men and women differently and similarly.

GENDER AND CAREERS

Most of what we know about managerial career development is based upon the experiences of men. It is their expectations, satisfactions and priorities which have shaped mainstream models and theories. This bias is hardly surprising given the overwhelming dominance of men in managerial positions for much of the 20th century. But since the 1960s increasing numbers of women have been entering the ranks of management. Their arrival has generated a growing body of research into different aspects of female managerial career experience. This work includes the examination of their minority role within male-dominated work organizations (Kanter, 1977; Marshall, 1984; Jagacinski, 1984); sources of stress in and beyond the workplace (Cooper and Davidson, 1982; Davidson and Cooper, 1983); adult development patterns (Gilligan, 1982; Gallos, 1989) and corporate career paths (Larwood and Gutek, 1987). Taken together, these studies provide a body of evidence which can be used as the starting point for comparisons between male and female career experience. But comparison is not straightforward, since rarely are we comparing like with like. Women managers differ from their male collegues in numerous ways (Nicholson and West, 1988; Gutek, 1993). Although there may be some cross-national variations, women managers generally tend to be younger, single and from more middle-class backgrounds. Within organizations they are more numerous in certain sectors, such as services, and functions, such as administration and human resources. Fewer are found in general management and more in specialist positions. Although more highly educated than men they are much less likely to occupy senior managerial positions. Where they do work in jobs which are comparable with their male colleagues they tend to be paid less. Finally, to a greater or lesser extent, women almost always work within organizations dominated by men, either numerically or in effective authority. These biographical, occupational and organizational differences make many 'comparisons' misleading. Few studies have explicitly controlled for such factors.

A further difficulty in comparative work arises from the concepts used to describe and explain career experience. Many of these may carry 'agentic' male values and assumptions (Bakan, 1966; Marshall, 1989), which lay emphasis upon notions of independence, self-assertion, and control. In terms of career theory, this translates into a concern with outward indicators of visible achievement; with job moves as an index of development; status at retirement as a measure of success. The agentic perspective stresses career planning and strategy, the drive to achieve personal goals and the desire for orderly progression. Such an approach, it can be argued, has tended to marginalize and misinterpret the perspectives of many women managers whose experiences cannot easily be mapped in this way (Marshall, 1984). Moreover, as a result of changes in the four forces we identified at the start of this chapter, conventional career concepts are also becoming less helpful in making sense of the career orientations and development patterns of male managers.

THE MALE MANAGERIAL CAREER

As it emerged in the West during the mid-20th century, the conventional managerial career was based around the relatively predictable progression of men through a series of jobs within corporate hierarchies. The criteria for hierarchical advancement were linked to length of service, ability and performance; rewards came in the form of income, status and security. Along with these was a sense of personal achievement which accompanied promotion. Indeed, with work as a central life interest, it was promotion that both conferred and confirmed a sense of personal identity. In the words of one commentator, managers came to 'base their self-conceptions on the assumption that, in due course, they will be what the institution allows persons to be' (Sofer, 1970, p. 36). Career success, through promotion, reaffirmed the value of past accomplishments and maintained the prospects of future development; it became, in effect, synonymous with *personal* development and success.

Men have become used to mapping their career progress on a lifespan timetable, assessing achievement in terms of the linkage of positions and levels with age and experience (Lawrence, 1984; Nicholson, 1993). 'Early' arrival brings additional rewards (Veiga, 1983); delay or blockage, frustration and anxiety. Career theory's normative models describe a biographical stereotype of successive phases of career entry exploration and experiment; early career building, mid-career growth and maintenance, later career evaluation and consolidation (Hall, 1976; Schein, 1978; Super, 1980; Hunt and Collins, 1983; Levinson, 1986). Naturally, writers have hedged this characterization with qualifications and exceptions, around personal, occupational and organizational factors, but left intact the assumption that at least a substantial part of the male managerial career would be characterized by orderly, hierarchical, staged progression.

Whatever value the model had, which is arguable given people's inability to perceive age-grade norms veridically (Lawrence, 1984), its relevance is crumbling before our eyes in the 1990s (Pearson, 1991). Radical corporate restructuring and 'downsizing', driven by competitive pressures (via cost reduction, customer proximation, and business refocusing) are disassembling the corporate 'climbing frames' through which managers, male or female, could ascend via predictable and orderly routes, and reassembling flatter, decentralized models of greater restriction and uncertainty (Kanter, 1983; Ulrich and Lake, 1990). Moreover, within these models managers are becoming increasingly exposed to performance targets which carry career-threatening sanctions if they fail to meet them. These changes, combined with generally increased risks of redundancy, have forced managers to reassess the assumption that their careers will be managed for them by the corporation. Increasingly, they are exhorted to 'manage their own careers'. This may imply seeking development *within* the job rather than through moves between different jobs, especially since companies are characteristically failing to develop alternative non-promotional developmental career paths through their redesigned structures (Hall and Isabella, 1985). It may also mean, paradoxically, contemplating more frequent moves between employers as well as between employment, self-employment and unemployment.

MEN AND WOMEN MANAGERS – A PROCESS OF CONVERGENCE?

Under these circumstances the career experiences of men and women managers are, in some respects, converging. Rapid rates of organizational change make it more difficult for men to plan career routes or, indeed, to sensibly compare 'actual' with 'expected' progress. Career exploration and learning are no longer once-and-for-all early career activities, but have to be engaged, whether willingly or not, by increasing numbers of men at several phases throughout their working lives. For them this may represent a significant change, but women's career experiences have always been rather less 'orderly'. Family and domestic obligations, the priority accorded to husbands' careers and the tendency of employers to assume that working women may have only limited ambitions, are all factors which have contributed to female career paths characterized by interruption and sudden, unanticipated changes in direction (Burke and McKeen, 1993).

This is also beginning to shift male career attitudes towards a greater similarity with women managers. Fewer men now seem to see career success as a central life interest around which other life activities are subordinated (Scase and Goffee, 1989). Perceptions of personal achievement and satisfaction are less strongly determined by career advancement alone. Even among the male managers who continue to view their careers as important and strive for hierarchical promotion, increasing numbers are less prepared to make the kind of sacrifices which could damage private interests and lifestyles and more prepared to incorporate non-work criteria in notions of personal success in a search for greater 'balance' in their lives (Evans and Bartolomé, 1980; Handy, 1989).

Some men may have 'learned' these new attitudes from the growing number of women managers who now work alongside them in the junior and middle layers of many large-scale organizations, though the more potent influence appears to be their disillusionment with evaporating career expectations. This interpretation might place men in distinct contrast to their female colleagues, many of whom – research evidence shows – continue to exhibit very strong career achievement goals, without cleaving to the traditional achievement model (Adler, 1984; Nicholson and West, 1988). Indeed, according to several commentators, as well as women managers themselves, it may be impossible for them to survive without such ambitions.

For their part, women's patterns of lifetime employment are shifting, principally as a function of the increasing volume of time they expect to spend in the labour force (Harmon, 1983). In so far as women's career aspirations are partially formed by their mothers as occupational role models (Tangri, 1972), one can see the potential for increasing numbers of women to resemble men in looking to occupational experience as a source of fulfilment. For working women, there is no evidence that they care less about career advancement (Rynes and Rosen, 1983; Adler, 1984), and moreover, their attitudes resemble those of men more in non-traditional managerial roles than in more traditional (feminized) roles (Moore and Rickel, 1980). This might be taken for the androgenization of women in 'male' roles (Powell, 1988), were it not for the fact that their career expectations and strategies differ, commensurate with the different opportunities and obstacles they face (Nicholson and West, 1988). Here too is some convergence, as male opportunities diminish, and some of the obstacles impeding the entry and advancement of women are removed. Among these, access to suitable mentors to help advance women's careers (as discussed in the previous chapter) has been a major impediment which will lessen as more women rise to positions where they can assist others (Hennig and Jardim, 1977).

ORGANIZATIONAL CHANGE AND THE PSYCHOLOGICAL CONTRACT

The relationship between managers and their employing organization may be usefully conceptualized in terms of the psychological contract (Argyris, 1964; Schein, 1978), denoting the exchange which, either explicitly or implicitly, is negotiated when individuals join, remain with and perform in organizations. Whereas issues relating to pay, working hours and job security may be explicitly negotiated, other expectations may be implicit and may 'involve the person's sense of dignity and worth' (Schein, 1980, p. 23). The psychological contract thus describes mutual expectations between individuals and organizations which are negotiated and renegotiated as work histories unfold. The traditional career model sees this exchange as focusing initially on opportunities for learning and development, subsequently on contribution (often specialized) in return for recognition, and later on security for responsibility. These contracts – effectively a shifting trade of commitment for material and psychological rewards – will vary, as we have suggested, according to factors such as age, experience, career orientation and organizational context.

Despite differences between organizations and industrial sectors, male managers embarked upon their careers with reasonably similar expectations of what might be delivered. Indeed, it was because of their optimism about career progression and the associated improvement in living standards (Gans, 1967; Whyte, 1965) that many were prepared to tolerate the costs that came with it in terms of lifestyles and personal relationships (Bell, 1968; Watson, 1964). As 'organization men', commitment to the corporation was demanded over and above other interests, including their families. If career success required frequent geographical mobility, then wives and children – and the great majority were married with families – were required to adapt and lend emotional support as necessary. In effect, male managers regarded their careers as reasonably safe long-term investments; short-run costs could be defended on the grounds that, in the end, the organization would 'take care' of them. Research evidence suggests a profound gender difference in this contract, but is this now dissolving as a function of the organizational changes which we have described?

In order to understand how the male manager's psychological contract is changing, an expectancy theory-type analysis of the motivational links between effort, performance and outcomes can be applied (Lawler, 1973). The objective measurement of the first element, effort, is frequently a difficult task; for managerial work it is probably impossible. Nevertheless, there are a number of contemporary trends which, combined, suggest pressures for higher levels of work effort on the part of managers. Organizational restructuring is, perhaps, the most important of these. Corporations which 'downsize' and 'delayer' seek, in effect, to do more with less. So-called 'lean' organizations are deliberately attempting to minimize labour costs – through control, typically reduction, of headcount – and to maximize work intensity. Managers have not been immune from these trends, and are now often becoming the main targets (Cascio, 1993). Those who have not lost their jobs in the process frequently report that the price of survival is a higher workload, sustainable only by increasing both work pace and working hours. The load is further exacerbated for those whose jobs have been redesigned in ways which require them to perform tasks for which they have limited technical ability.

Linked to these changes has been an increasing emphasis upon the monitoring and measurement of the second element of expectancy theory, performance. Whereas traditionally managers were able to avoid the kind of work measures and targets which they devised for others, most now find themselves subject to the same disciplines. Indeed, an increasingly significant part of their reward packages are directly tied to such measures. Surveys indicate that men and women managers support the principal of performance assessment as a key determinant of career success (Scase and Goffee, 1989). In practice, however, there are frequently fierce disputes over the manner in which performance is actually measured. Managerial work is typically complex and multidimensional. Few assessments of managerial performance are free of subjective influence, and, in most cases, the selection of, say, five measures will mean the rejection of many more. In addition, of course, the 'agentic' isolation of *individual* performance is exceptionally difficult given that managerial work is, virtually by definition, the achievement of *interdependent* performance. But whether assessment processes are agreed or imposed the message for managers, male and female, is similar; pressures to achieve measurable performance are increasing.

Turning to the third element of the expectancy formulation, the intensification of managerial work is resulting in a range of dysfunctional outcomes, including increased working hours. Recent data indicate that managers in full-time employment in North America, Britain and some other parts of continental Europe are working longer hours and taking less of their holiday entitlements (Scase and Goffee, 1989; Kanter, 1989). Meanwhile there is little to sustain the view that significant reductions are occurring in economies – such as those in the Pacific Rim – where working hours, of (overwhelmingly male) managers and others, have traditionally been higher than in the West. Other indicators of work intensification are rather less direct but might include the reported incidence of psychological and behavioural conditions – such as frustration, tiredness, irritability and so on – which are often linked with high-pressure work environments (Davidson and Cooper, 1983). It is difficult to claim with any confidence, in the absence of reliable comparative research, that these conditions are more commonly experienced now than, say, 20 years ago. What can be said is that the pressures associated with such employment have drawn more attention since the late 1970s and that research studies have repeatedly revealed significant levels of managerial stress. It is also worth adding that those investigations which incorporate the contemporary career reflections of both men and women managers lend tentative support to the idea of intensification. In terms of felt experience, work is perceived to have become 'tougher' both quantitatively and qualitatively (Kanter, 1989; Goffee and Scase, 1992).

If managerial work has become subject to new pressures and more explicitly performance oriented, have there been related changes in positive outcomes or career rewards? Again, comparisons over time are not straightforward, particularly in terms of the assessment of *intrinsic* rewards which derive from such factors as the scope for autonomy, self-fulfilment and personal growth. Survey research purporting to measure such rewards is often neither reliable nor comparable and there are likely to be significant variations according to industrial sector, technology, corporate culture and so on. Shifts in *extrinsic* rewards may be more reliably charted. Here it seems certain that as a result of organizational restructuring two significant rewards are generally less available to managers: job security and promotion, both of which have historically been more important to men than to women, who care more about meaningfulness (Lacy *et al.*, 1983). Few work organizations in the West can now promise young managers a job for life; most cannot even give reasonable assurances that their more experienced managers will survive until normal age of retirement. Nor can those who keep their jobs be guaranteed orderly progress through the corporate hierarchy; the environment is no longer that predictable – and in any event the hierarchy has been progressively flattened! The loss of promotion prospects means, in turn, the loss of steady, incremental increases in status and income on the basis of past achievements. In so far as managerial careers continue to offer rewards – and they do, in terms of salaries, recognition, scope for discretion, personal development and so on – these are becoming more clearly contingent upon current, measurable contribution, however that is assessed.

The expectancy framework therefore leads inexorably to the conclusion that managerial motivation is likely to become more problematic. Effort is emphasized but unmeasurable. Performance is contingent on factors beyond the individual's control, and outcomes are becoming double-edged and unreliable.

COMPARING MEN AND WOMEN

If organizations can no longer deliver expected career rewards to their managers and, at the same time, they intensify work demands and redefine performance then, clearly, the 'rules of the game' are changing. But this process may have a different meaning for men and women since each may have embarked upon their careers with rather different expectations. For some men, typically middle-aged and in mid-career, a considerable readjustment may be required. Denied the sense of job security and steady progression which was implicitly promised at the outset of their careers, they may develop more instrumental and calculative orientations to their work, their careers and, indeed, their employing organizations. These have been described elsewhere as 'reluctant managers . . . cautious about their commitment to employing organisations if only because of the greater risks of career "failure", redundancy and redeployment . . . feelings of psychological well-being can be sustained through limiting the extent of their occupational involvement and corporate attachment' (Scase and Goffee, 1989, pp. 179–80). As we discuss below, this shift in work attitudes may be reflected in, and reinforced by, new patterns of career mobility and in the changing priorities of men in balancing professional and private life.

But it should not be assumed that the career plateau has a similar meaning across different organizational contexts or that lack of promotion prospects evokes the same disappointed reaction amongst all male managers. A variety of coping strategies may allow some to maintain levels of job satisfaction and corporate attachment (Nicholson, 1993). In addition, of course, there are successful senior managers – in middle age and beyond – who have reached the top and for whom career achievement remains a central source of life satisfaction. For these, the organization has 'delivered'; their psychological contract may have been reinforced rather than renegotiated. At the other end of the career spectrum are younger male managers who come to their careers with rather different expectations. For them personal success may be defined through a variety of employment, work and leisure achievements which reflect a desire for autonomy, variety and challenge rather than steady progress through a corporate hierarchy.

The psychological contract for women managers may be shifting in different ways. They, too, may find themselves under pressure – working longer hours and subject to tighter performance measures. In addition, they may perceive a growing discrepancy between their promotion aspirations and the available opportunities (Betz and Fitzgerald, 1987; Scase and Goffee, 1989). But these shifts must be interpreted in the light of the different experiences and priorities of female managers. Women managers have regularly reported the perception that they face additional 'pressures to perform' at work in order to cope with male prejudices, their 'visibility' as a minority and the associated 'dynamics of tokenism' (Kanter, 1977; Davidson and Cooper, 1983). They are also more accustomed to career paths characterized by uncertainty and interruption – linked to pregnancy, childbearing, partners' career moves and so on. Indeed, it may be as a result of this, and the fact that feelings of isolation and loneliness are greater threats to working women than lack of reward, that women have developed work orientations more focused upon the intrinsic rewards of the task at hand rather than any longer-term plan to achieve various 'extrinsic' benefits (Marshall, 1984; Neil and Snizek, 1987). Why develop 'unrealistic' expectations which will inevitably be disappointed (Manhartdt, 1972)? Thus, as Nicholson and West point out, women managers 'have higher growth needs, and are more self-directed and intrinsically motivated in career choices'; by contrast, men are 'more materialistic, status-oriented and goal-directed in their career orientations' (1988, p. 205). Given these differences, it would appear that it is men – particularly in the middle age – rather than women, who are experiencing a substantial shift in their psychological contract. Whilst, then, women managers may have not lacked ambitions, they have never expected to achieve these via the orderly corporate careers anticipated by many men.

MOBILITY PATTERNS AND LIFE PRIORITIES

Empirical research suggests that career mobility patterns for male and female managers have differed. For men, early career phases have been marked by relatively high rates of mobility between organizations as – through a process of trial and error – they explored work options. This has been followed by a period of stability where, with a single employer, they have progressed – in varying degrees – through a hierarchy. In late middle age a secondary peak in mobility has occurred as they became vulnerable to redundancy, early retirement and other forms of involuntary job loss. By contrast, women have tended to move faster between jobs, make more radical switches and keep up a high rate of employer mobility throughout their careers (Nicholson and West, 1988). The distinctive mobility patterns of women managers may be explained by a number of interlinked factors which include their desire to avoid career blockages caused by male prejudice; strong 'inner drives' to experience personal growth; and job changes driven by the relocation of spouses. But whatever the cause, the difference is clear: whereas men have been intent upon finding one organizational home where security, material rewards and status can be achieved, women have maintained a search for development where the journey between organizations stops only upon retiring from employment.

Expressed in this way, the female mobility pattern appears better matched with organizations which are attempting to reduce employee dependence and to refocus career goals. As Nicholson and West (1988) observe, 'The difficulties and dangers that women have to contend with to enter and survive in management have the effect of socialising them to fit this brave and uncertain new world of organisational life better than those men who expect the future to be like the familiar past' (p. 217). But whereas the career expectations of women managers may represent a better match with employer preferences, the fit is not perfect (McKeen and Burke, 1992). Shorter, more intensive career paths with one or several employers do not easily allow 'career breaks' – at least not without disadvantage – for pregnancy and childbearing. Nor do 'lean' organizations with managers working at full stretch offer encouragement for those who would prefer part-time work. It is, perhaps, for these reasons – rather than blatant male prejudice – that the middle echelons of large organizations retain 'female ghettoes', whilst at the top, very few women succeed in breaking through the 'glass ceiling' (Davidson and Cooper, 1992).

In the face of continuing frustration of their career goals women managers have, up until now, responded through more qualifications, more mobility and more ambition. Indeed, they generally remain more optimistic than men about career prospects. But this may not last. There are already signs that, in the face of career barriers which they perceive as male imposed, more women are opting out of corporations and electing to achieve their goals setting up their own businesses (Goffee and Scase, 1985; Carter and Cannon, 1992). Indeed, their propensity for business start-up is increasing at a faster rate than men's.

But how do changes in the psychological contract impact the relative priorities of professional and private life, given the differing family circumstances of men and women managers? The great majority of male managers are married with children; for them the family has traditionally functioned as an important support structure in the pursuit of a career. By contrast, fewer women are married and far fewer have children; for them the family has often been regarded as an obstacle to achievement at work. Many female managers, then, have been prepared to forgo the 'satisfactions' of family life in order to achieve career success.

But a shift in the psychological contract – driven by unfulfilled career expectations and increasing uncertainty – may have resulted in a different relationship between work and family life. Some men may continue to see their careers as a central life interest but may increasingly resist 'negative spillover' from work into family life (Evans and Bartolomé, 1980); certainly more express a concern to separate and protect 'non-work' identities. Such 'good intentions' may fail – evidence suggests that work demands increasingly predominate as more senior managerial positions are achieved – but the shift in publicly expressed aspirations is itself significant. For other men – at middle age and middle levels – there may be the development of a more instrumental orientation to work. This represents a 'rational' renegotiation of the psychological contract; why risk becoming overdependent upon an employing organization when there is little guarantee that such commitment will be reciprocated in terms of job security or career advancement (Goffee and Scase, 1992)? This is likely to be especially painful for the many male managers who persist in believing the future will be like the past in terms of its ability to deliver progressive opportunities (Herriot et al., 1993). Younger male managers, in turn, may protect themselves in advance from such career disappointments by nurturing a life outside employment which provides the skills and emotional satisfactions that work organizations cannot deliver. Unlike the generation above them, these managers may no longer be prepared to sell themselves to the corporation at the expense of their families, their leisure interests and, indeed, their labour market prospects.

Given these shifts, women managers may be better able to locate male partners whose priorities do not prejudice their own career development prospects. Research studies already show that marriage does not, in itself, signal a significant shift in work attitudes or life priorities on their part (Scase and Goffee, 1989). The careful selection of 'sympathetic' partners aware of their career demands and prepared, for example, to defer parenthood and limit family size, has allowed many women managers to maintain their careers as a central life interest. In these cases, the marriage relationship and the associated domestic division of labour is negotiated against a background of well-established career commitments. Of course, research investigations of the existing management population miss those women who, through preference or domestic pressures, have left managerial employment. Nevertheless, it would appear that in the 1990s there is greater scope for women (and men) to combine careers with family responsibilities. A desire for more 'balanced' lifestyles and a greater sharing of domestic responsibilities are social changes which may promote this flexibility. In addition, there may be an increasing awareness that, in the 1990s, two careers represent a better insurance against redundancy and falling living standards than one (Pleck, 1985). In so far as, over time, the career of one partner dominates, this may be determined less by gender and more by ability to stay in employment.

CONCLUSION

Our review has indicated that although, in general, the career development patterns of men and women managers are distinct, there are significant variations within each population. Thus, running across the gender divide are the major sets of influences identified at the start of this chapter, as represented by age, career orientation, family status, organizational setting and economic sector. Shifts in these are producing intergenerational differences for women, as well as men. Younger graduate women in the earlier stages of managerial employment within newly emerging (mixed gender) professional service sectors are likely to experience careers which are quite different from those of women managers a generation above them. Yet we must be careful in making unqualified generalizations concerning the career development experiences of men or women managers. During the 1980s work organizations failed, in different ways, to deliver on their promises to both male and female managers. Whilst, as a result, we can be reasonably sure that the male model of the managerial career is all but redundant, it is less easy to distinguish contemporary patterns which can be clearly differentiated according to gender. In the 1990s organizations are likely to make fewer promises.

It seems clear, then, that 'future research should concentrate upon the *differences* in the work and career experiences of women managers rather than the similarities . . . research needs to specify and contextualize these contrasting experiences and to illustrate the patterns of diversity and change' (Scase and Goffee, 1990, p. 124). Areas worthy of research enquiry might include the comparative assessment of differences within, as well as between the sexes on the four dimensions we have identified as shaping the new landscape of careers: (1) economic and social cultures, whether they are manifest nationally or sectorally, as sources of career norms and values; (2) professional and occupational labour markets as opportunity structures for the portfolio accumulation of portable career assets; (3) organization structures and career management system as sources of career motivation via the psychological contracts they predispose through the presence or absence of threat and uncertainty; and (4) individual intentions and aspirations as they mediate between the world of work and salient facets of the family and non-work life space. The last of these is likely to be an influence of growing relevance. In a society of radically increasing diversity of family structures, working arrangements, household technologies, information media, and recreational opportunities, we can expect to find fewer normative models of life/workstyle adaptation being enacted, and more individualized constructions to solve the problem of how best to live and satisfy one's needs and interests.

REFERENCES

ADLER, N. J. (1984) Women do not want international careers: and other myths about international management, *Organizational Dynamics*, Vol. 13, pp. 66–79.
ARGYRIS, C. (1964) *Integrating the Individual and the Organization*, Wiley, New York.

ARTHUR, M. B., HALL, D. T. and LAWRENCE, B. S. (1989) Generating new directions in career theory, in M. B. Arthur *et al.* (eds) *Handbook of Career Theory*, Cambridge University Press.

BAKAN, D. (1966) *The Duality of Human Existence*, Beacon, Boston.

BELL, C. (1968) *Middle Class Families*, Routledge & Kegan Paul, London.

BETZ, N. E. and FITZGERALD, L. F. (1987) *Career Psychology of Women*, Academic Press, San Diego.

BURKE, R. J. and MCKEEN, C. A. (1993) Career priority patterns among managerial and professional women, *Applied Psychology: An International Review*, Vol. 42, pp. 341–52.

CARTER, S. and CANNON, T. (1992) *Women as Entrepreneurs: A Study of Female Business Owners, Their Motivations, Experiences and Strategies for Success*, Academic Press, London.

CASCIO, W. F. (1993) Downsizing: What do we know? What have we learned? *Academy of Management Executive*, Vol. 7, pp. 95–104.

COOPER, C. L. and DAVIDSON, M. (1982) *High Pressure: Working Lives of Women Managers*, Fontana, London.

DAVIDSON, M. and COOPER, C. (1983) *Stress and the Woman Manager*, Martin Robertson, Oxford.

DAVIDSON, M. J. and COOPER, C. L. (1992) *Shattering the Glass Ceiling: The Woman Manager*, Paul Chapman Publishing, London.

Economist (1993) The Economic Focus: Musical chairs, *The Economist*, 17 July, p. 69.

EVANS, P. and BARTOLOMÉ, F. (1980) *Must Success Cost So Much?* Grant McIntyre, London.

GALLOS, J. V. (1989) Exploring women's development: implications for career theory, practice and research, in M. B. Arthur *et al.* (eds) *Handbook of Career Theory*, Cambridge University Press.

GANS, H. J. (1967) *The Levittowners*, Allen Lane, London.

GILLIGAN, C. (1982) *In a Different Voice*, Harvard University Press, Cambridge, MA.

GOFFEE, R. and SCASE, R. (1985) *Women in Charge*, Allen and Unwin, London.

GOFFEE, R. and SCASE, R. (1992) Organisational change and corporate career, *Human Relations*, Vol. 45, pp. 363–85.

GUNZ, H. (1989) *Careers and Corporate Cultures*, Blackwell, Oxford.

GUTEK, B. A. (1993) Changing the status of women in management, *Applied Psychology: An International Review*, Vol. 42, pp. 301–11.

HALL, D. T. (1976) *Careers in Organizations*, Goodyear, Pacific Palisades, CA.

HALL, D. T. and ISABELLA, L. A. (1985) Downward movement and career development, *Organizational Dynamics*, Vol. 14, pp. 5–23.

HANDY, C. (1989) *The Age of Unreason*, London Business Books, London.

HARMON, L. W. (1983) Testing some models of women's career development. Paper presented at a colloquium at the University of Maryland.

HENNIG, M. and JARDIM, A. (1977) *The Managerial Woman*, Anchor, New York.

HERRIOT, P., GIBSON, G., PEMBERTON, C. and PINDER, R. (1993) Dashed hopes: organizational determinants and personal perceptions of managerial careers, *Journal of Occupational and Organizational Psychology*, Vol. 66, pp. 115–23.

HUNT, J. W. and COLLINS, R. (1983) *Managers in Mid-Career Crisis*, Wellington Lane, Sydney.

INKSON, K. and COE, T. (1993) *Are Career Ladders Disappearing?* Institute of Management, London.

JAGACINSKI, C. M. (1983) Engineering careers: women in a male-dominated field, unpublished manuscript.

KANTER, R. M. (1977) *Men and Women of the Corporation*, Basic Books, New York.

KANTER, R. M. (1983) *The Change Masters*, Allen & Unwin, London.

KANTER, R. M. (1989) *When Giants Learn to Dance*, Simon & Schuster, New York.

LACY, W. B., BOKEMEIER, J. L. and SHEPHERD, J. N. (1983) Job attribute preference and work commitment of men and women in the United States, *Personnel Psychology*, Vol. 36, pp. 315–29.

LARWOOD, L. and GUTEK, B. A. (1987) Working towards a theory of women's career development, in B. A. Gutek and L. Larwood (eds) *Women's Career Development*, Sage, Beverly Hills, CA.

LAW, B. (1981) Careers theory: a third dimension? in A. G. Watts, D. E. Super and J. M. Kidd (eds) *Career Development in Britain*, Hobsons Press, Cambridge.

LAWLER, E. E. (1973) *Motivation in Work Organizations*, Brooks-Cole, Monterey, CA.

LAWRENCE, B. S. (1984) Age grading: the implicit organizational timetable, *Journal of Occupational Behaviour*, Vol. 5, pp. 23–35.

LEVINSON, D. J. (1986) A conception of adult development, *American Psychologist*, Vol. 41, pp. 3–13.

MANHARDT, P. J. (1972) Job orientation of male and female college graduates in business, *Personnel Psychology*, Vol. 25, pp. 361–8.

MARSHALL, J. (1984) *Women Managers: Travellers in a Male World*, Wiley, Chichester.

MARSHALL, J. (1989) Re-visioning career concepts: A feminist invitation, in M. B. Arthur *et al.* (eds) *Handbook of Career Theory*, Cambridge University Press.

MCKEEN, C. A. and BURKE, J. R. (1992) Supporting the career aspirations of managerial women: desired occupational opportunities, *Women in Management Review*, Vol. 7, pp. 16–25.

MOORE, L. M. and RICKEL, A. U. (1980) Characteristics of women in traditional and non-traditional managerial roles, *Personnel Psychology*, Vol. 33, pp. 317–33.

NEIL, C. C. and SNIZEK, W. E. (1987) Work values, job characteristics and gender, *Sociological Perspectives*, Vol. 30, pp. 245–65.

NEWSWEEK (1993) Special report: the world's jobs crisis, *Newsweek*, 14 June.

NICHOLSON, N. (1984) A theory of work role transitions, *Administrative Science Quarterly*, Vol. 29, pp. 172–91.

NICHOLSON, N. (1993) Purgatory or place of safety? The managerial plateau and organizational agegrading, *Human Relations*, Vol. 46, no. 12, pp. 1369–89.

NICHOLSON, N. and WEST, M. A. (1988) *Managerial Job Change: Men and Women in Transition*, Cambridge Univesity Press.

NICHOLSON, N. and WEST, M. A. (1989) Transitions, work histories and careers, in M. B. Arthur *et al.* (eds) *Handbook of Career Theory*, Cambridge University Press.

PEARSON, R. (1991) *The Human Resource: Managing People and Work in the 1990s*, McGraw Hill, London.

PLECK, J. H. (1985) *Working Wives/Working Husbands*, Sage, Beverly Hills, CA.

POWELL, G. N. (1988) *Women and Men in Management*, Sage, Newbury Park, CA.

RYNES, S. and ROSEN, B. (1983) A comparison of male and female reactions to career advancement, *Journal of Vocational Behavior*, Vol. 22, pp. 105–16.

SCASE, R. and GOFFEE, R. (1989) *Reluctant Managers*, Unwin Hyman, London.

SCASE, R. and GOFFEE, R. (1990) Women in management: towards a research agenda, *International Journal of Human Resource Management*, Vol. 1, pp. 107–29.

SCHEIN, E. H. (1978) *Career Dynamics: Matching Individual and Organizational Needs*, Addison-Wesley, Reading, MA.

SCHEIN, E. H. (1980) *Organisational Psychology*, 3rd edn, Prentice Hall, Englewood Cliffs, NJ.

SOFER, C. (1970) *Men in Mid-Career: A Study of British Managers and Technical Specialists*, Cambridge University Press.

SONNENFELD, J. A., PEIPERL, M. A. and KOTTER, J. P. (1988) Strategic determinants of managerial labor markets: a career systems view, *Human Resource Management*, Vol. 27, pp. 369–88.

SUPER, D. E. (1980) A life-span life-space approach to career development, *Journal of Vocational Behavior*, Vol. 26, pp. 182–96.

TANGRI, S. S. (1972) Occupational role innovation among college women, *Journal of Social Issues*, Vol. 28, pp. 177–99.

ULRICH, D. and LAKE, D. (1990) *Organizational Capability*, Wiley, New York.

VEIGA, J. F. (1983) Mobility influences during managerial career stages, *Academy of Management Journal*, Vol. 26, pp. 64–85.

WATSON, W. (1964) Social mobility and social class in industrial communities, in M. Gluckman and E. Devond (eds) *Closed System and Open Minds*, Oliver & Boyd, London.

WHYTE, W. H. (1965) *The Organization Man*, Penguin, Harmondsworth.

CHAPTER 8

Gender Bias in the Selection and Assessment of Women in Management

BEVERLY ALIMO-METCALFE

INTRODUCTION

One approach to understanding the underrepresentation of women in management, and in particular the paucity of women in senior management, is to scrutinize the assessment processes used by organizations.

Entry into an organization and movement through the hierarchy can be seen as a series of boundary passages (Schein, E. 1973) at which individuals are judged with respect to their appropriateness to 'fit' into the organization and to perform certain roles. They are assessed either overtly or covertly, explicitly or implicitly, in discrete events or ongoing activities, using formal or informal methods, adopting standardized and/or non-standardized techniques (Nieva and Gutek, 1980; Ragins and Sundstrom, 1989; Alimo-Metcalfe, 1993). As a result, decisions are made with respect to selection, job placement, promotion, access to developmental and training opportunities, and particular career tracks. Consequences are, therefore, both immediate and long term with respect to career development.

Despite legislation on sex discrimination and equal opportunities in the USA and UK, and affirmative action in the USA, there is little evidence that much has improved (Hansard Society, 1990; Hirsh and Jackson, 1990; Equal Opportunities Commission, 1991; US Department of Labor, 1991; Fagenson, 1993; Davidson and Cooper, 1993) and it may even be getting worse (Institute of Management, 1994). In fact, as assessment techniques become more complex and 'sophisticated', the problems of identifying particular bias with respect to gender becomes potentially more subtle and, consequently, far more difficult either to notice or challenge (Alimo-Metcalfe, 1993).

Since the literature on gender bias suggests that the sources are so ubiquitous (e.g. Nieva and Gutek, 1980; Wallston and O'Leary, 1981; Ragins and Sundstrom, 1989) there is a need to focus, in a systematic fashion, on some of the factors relating to the selection and assessment of women in management. In this chapter, some of the US and UK literature will be reviewed with respect to each of the major stages of an assessment procedure, namely: the identification of the *criteria* for management against which the assessment will be based; the *method or technique* adopted for gathering the data which constitute the basis of the assessment decision; and the *assessors' judgements* of women's performance.

THE CRITERIA OF EFFECTIVE MANAGEMENT

There is no evidence in the UK that women in management are less academic-
ally qualified than men (e.g. Davidson and Cooper, 1984), and in fact one
major study (Alban Metcalfe and Nicholson, 1984) found that women were
better educationally qualified. Several US studies have found that equally
qualified women are extended fewer job offers, receive lower salaries, and are
seen as less desirable for managerial positions (e.g. Dipboye et al., 1975; Terborg, 1977; Dubno, 1985; Madden, 1985; Rosenbaum, 1985).

Whilst educational qualifications might reasonably constitute pre-
requisites for managerial selection, clearly other criteria are being adopted to
judge suitability. These criteria, such as knowledge, skills, and personal
qualities and traits, form the bedrock of the assessment process.

WHAT MAKES AN EFFECTIVE MANAGER?

Whether it be for selection, or deciding on promotion, the process of identifying criteria for an effective manager usually takes the form of a job and/or
person analysis. Wright et al. (1990) state that 'Information gleaned from job
analysis is utilised in virtually every human resource practice, including performance appraisal, training and development, compensation, and selection'
(in Levine et al., 1983, p. 299). It is clearly therefore the starting point for the
current examination of potential gender bias.

A variety of job analysis techniques are commonly adopted by organizations. These include: gathering data from interviews and other verbal reports
of current post incumbents or their managers and colleagues; or a more
structured form of interviewing called the Critical Incident Technique
(Flanagan, 1954). A development of the Critical Incident Technique called the
Behaviorally Anchored Rating Scale (Smith and Kendall, 1963) produces behavioural scales. The Repertory Grid Technique (Kelly, 1955) is another technique of eliciting data, but it differs importantly from the others in that it
attempts to eliminate or at least reduce, the influence of the interviewer in
determining the dimensions or criteria on which effectiveness or lack of effectiveness is judged.

There are two major aspects of this activity which are of direct importance
to the subject of this chapter. The first is, what are the popular or pervasive
views of effective management; and the second is, do women and men describe effective managerial styles in the same way?

There is, without doubt, substantial gender bias in the literature on models
of management. What a manager does, management qualities, skills, knowledge and experience, and other associated topics are based on solidly male
foundations (e.g. Schein, V. 1973, 1975, 1978; Massengill and Di Marco, 1979;
Powell and Butterfield, 1979; Marshall, 1984). Apparently little has changed in
the 1990s (Padgett, 1990; Jacobson and Jacques, 1990; Schein's Chapter 4 in
this book), and indeed the reverse may be true, with superficial change mask-
ing the need for radical changes (Calas and Smircich, 1993).

It is only since the early 1980s that a female perspective has been introduced into research on management. Gilligan (1982) and Marshall (1984) and
other feminist scholars (e.g. Harding, 1986; Weedon, 1987; Calas and Jacques,

1988; Calas and Smircich, 1988, 1992), rather than comparing women to the male norm of management, have offered 'The Women's Voice Perspective', asking 'what might be learned from the positive contributions of the uniquely female experience?' (Jacobson and Jacques, 1990, p. 2).

Even now, there are few general management books that include this last perspective in the subject matter. Such a perspective remains hidden and peripheral to mainline management education and discourse, probably as a result of being defined, not as 'advances in management research', but as feminist studies in management. The reality is, therefore, that models, principles, and skills of management as bodies of knowledge have changed little with respect to the influence of women's thinking and behaviour since the early 1970s.

Most reviews of the literature (Denmark, 1977; Bartol, 1978; Dobbins and Platz, 1986) and a large field study (Donnell and Hall, 1980) have concluded that, generally speaking, there are no gender differences in leadership style. However, some studies have found differences. Jago and Vroom (1982) reported that women adopted a more participative style in decision-making than men. A British study by Ferrario (1990), which is described more fully in Chapter 8, also found differences in female and male managers' self-reports of preferred managerial style. More women than men preferred the team management style.

One of the most recent US studies of gender and management style, conducted by Rosener (1990), found that in a sample of female and male leaders, men were more likely to report adopting the 'transactional' leadership style, which relies on the power of position and formal authority, whereas women were more likely to report adopting a 'transformational leadership' style, which encourages participation, power and information sharing, and enhancing people's self-worth.

The relevance of the above findings to the process of assessment is crucial with respect to understanding one of the major and ubiquitous sources of gender bias in selection and assessment of women in management, namely, what is believed to constitute managerial effectiveness. If what constitutes the current body of 'received wisdom' with respect to what is effective managerial behaviour, is so completely male, and furthermore, if the senior managers from whom one is eliciting examples of effective managerial behaviour are male, then every aspect of the assessment process will be permeated by this androcentrism. This includes the dimensions against which individuals will be assessed; the behavioural indicators of effectiveness and non-effectiveness which form part of the selection interview; the selection of psychometric instruments which may be used in the assessment process; the design of the assessment centre, including the exercises which constitute its content, and the behavioural guidelines or checklists which assessors use when observing and assessing the performance of candidates.

Given the above, it is perhaps not surprising that in a recent study investigating the possibility of gender bias in job analysis, in which the repertory grid interview technique was employed (which is non-directional in nature) (Sparrow and Rigg, 1993), it was found that when a small sample of male and female managers were asked to describe the qualities required of male and female incumbents of their job, very different profiles emerged. The 'feminine job' regarded characteristics relating to team management, people orientation, participation, etc. as central; whereas the 'masculine job' regarded vision, entrepreneurship, forcefulness, being detached and having an analytic and systematic approach as important.

In a study currently being conducted by the author, also using the repertory grid interview technique, between senior female and male public-sector managers, qualitatively different constructs of managerial effectiveness are emerging (Alimo-Metcalfe, 1994b).

Whilst the study had not been completed, there are indications that the 'models of management' described by women and men are extraordinarily different.

The implications that these data might have for subsequent stages of the assessment process are considerable.

THE SECOND STAGE OF ASSESSMENT: SELECTING THE PREDICTOR OR TECHNIQUE

Choice of a particular assessment technique depends on a variety of factors, including, importantly: (a) the purpose for the assessment, and (b) the variables being measured.

Focusing on assessment for selection or promotion, a wide variety of techniques is used by organizations, ranging from selection/employment interviews, through cognitive tests and personality instruments, to assessment centre methodologies. Taking each of these in turn, I would like to examine the potential sources of gender bias with respect to their design, and use.

THE SELECTION/EMPLOYMENT INTERVIEW

Despite its unrivalled reputation as a highly unreliable technique with low predictive validity, the selection/employment interview remains the most common selection process used by organizations for management selection (Hunter and Hunter, 1984; Robertson and Makin, 1986; Robertson and Iles, 1988; Smith and Abrahamsen, 1992). Interviews can be regarded as a social judgement process which is highly subjective and therefore easily susceptible to bias and prejudices. Not surprisingly, they have been found to have an adverse impact on women when presenting themselves for 'out of role' jobs. Clear evidence exists that similarly qualified and experienced women receive lower evaluations than men in managerial selection situations (e.g. Rosen and Jerdee, 1974; Cohen and Bunker, 1975), particularly when they are regarded as physically attractive (Heilman and Saruwatari, 1979; Iles and Robertson, 1988), and when the job involves supervising male subordinates (Rose and Andiappan, 1978). Prejudice would appear to be equally true for male and female interviewers (Dipboye et al., 1975, 1977). The reason for this has been explained in terms of sex-role stereotyping and role incongruence (Nieva and Gutek, 1980; Wallston and O'Leary, 1981; Glick et al., 1988).

A study by Glick et al. (1988), which was designed to test the hypothesis that 'discrimination against women and men who applied for stereotypically "masculine" and "feminine" jobs, respectively, could be reduced by providing individual information suggesting that the applicant was an exception to his or her gender stereotype and possessed traits usually associated with the opposite gender', found that whilst 'individualising information eliminated sex-typed personality inferences about male and female applicants' and affected applicants' perceived job suitability . . . sex discrimination was not eliminated' (p. 178). Male applicants were still preferred for the traditionally male job, and female applicants were favoured for the traditionally female job.

These findings may rather depressingly support Webster's (1982) conclusions that, whilst training can improve interviewers' questioning, it had no effect on the quality of judgements made.

USE OF PSYCHOMETRICS IN SELECTION AND ASSESSMENT

Organizations are increasingly employing psychometric instruments. The most commonly used in the UK are forms of critical reasoning, and personality measures (Robertson and Makin, 1986; Smith and Abrahamsen, 1992).

Standardized tests are regarded as offering reliable and 'objective' information of an individual's ability or potential, which, if carefully selected to relate to job-relevant dimensions, may be deemed as offering non-gender-biased data. In fact, it may be argued that the sources of bias are so subtle, that the bias becomes insidious and extremely difficult to challenge.

Webb (1987) states

> it is well established, but worth restating, that measures of individual abilities are not neutral with respect to all social categories, but are normative. They contain evaluative judgements about what should count as 'skills' and 'abilities' and what test items measure these. They are likely to be modelled on the perceived traits of current job occupants, which means that atypical applicants are disadvantaged.
>
> (Rose and Rose, 1979, p. 4)

Women in management clearly constitute one such group.

Tests are constructed from items which are identified within a particular population and then piloted on a similar population. From this, norms are produced which are again based on the sample population. It becomes increasingly clear that the derivation of items, the scales that they produce, and the norms against which the scores are interpreted, are highly likely to be substantially male biased with respect to a managerial population. Mottram (1987) makes the point that few test manuals include adequate information as to how the test was constructed, the characteristics of the population sampled, and whether they were validated, bearing in mind potential sex differences. He adds 'There are often practical problems in assembling separate norm tables for men and women, but the test user needs to know just what sort of yard stick is being provided, especially when there are differences in average scores between the sexes on one or more parts of the test' (Mottram, 1987, p. 6). Even if these norm tables were available to users, one cannot presume that many would have the knowledge, the interest or the experience in employing their judicious use with a view to safeguarding against potential gender bias in score interpretation.

Differences have been found in scores obtained by women and men on a variety of psychometric instruments, including cognitive ability tests.

COGNITIVE ABILITY TESTS

Intelligence tests are increasingly used in managerial selection, usually as part of an assessment centre procedure, although they are also used regularly to augment the selection interview.

The construct of intelligence is socially defined and not surprisingly, therefore, has changed over time. Webb states that, contrary perhaps to public opinion,

> The construction of test items can be manipulated so as to favour one group over another [and that this] has long been known in the sphere of intelligence testing. . . . The IQ debate continues, but there is adequate work to substantiate the argument that the construction of such tests can be manipulated to reproduce, or to undermine, socially approved results for the distribution of intelligence according to class, gender and ethnicity (Block, 1976; Walker, 1981; Gardner, 1983).
>
> (Webb, 1987, p. 19)

She also goes on to quote Rose (1976, p. 119) as saying, 'in early versions of the tests, males and females scored differently on certain items (the females scored higher). The tests were modified . . . Which measures the biological "reality", the test with, or without, the differential scoring items?'

Large organizations may develop their own test or even a battery of tests, for selection of applicants to a particular occupation, or a particular level in the organization. The British Civil Service is one of the few organizations which has developed and validated its own tests, and furthermore, has monitored the results obtained by female and male applicants. When it found that only 29% of its 'fast track' entrants were women, despite the fact that roughly equal numbers of females and males were applying, it investigated the distributions of scores. It was found that women were more likely to score around the middle range, with greater proportion of men scoring at the extremes of highest and lowest scores (OMCS, 1988). If the threshold level of acceptable scores is in the upper-middle range and above, this will lead to fewer women qualifying. If, in addition, there is no evidence that obtaining a particularly high score in a particular test directly and significantly correlates with subsequent performance in a job, then application of such a technique of selection constitutes indirect discrimination (Equal Opportunities Commission, 1988).

PERSONALITY MEASUREMENT

One of the earliest and major areas of leadership research over the last 50 or so years has focused on personality.

Personality questionnaires, like cognitive tests, are becoming more commonly used in managerial selection (e.g. Muchinsky, 1986; Robertson and Iles, 1988; Smith and Abrahamsen, 1992). This is in spite of an ongoing debate as to the strength of the predictive validity of personality measurements, which is generally regarded as relatively low (around 0.2 or lower), but currently the subject of meta-analytic reviews, themselves hotly debated (e.g. Pesonnel Management, 1991; Tett et al., 1993; Kinder and Robertson, 1993).

There are several aspects with respect to their design, construction, interpretation, and general application that are a matter of concern with respect to potential gender bias.

Personality questionnaires are constructed on the basis of identifying items which reflect dimensions which exist in the body of literature relating to personality theory. As stated earlier, most of the research in pre-1980s' psychology has derived from studies of men, conducted by men, in response to questions proposed by men, and the data analysed from a male perspective (Jacobson and Jacques, 1990). Many, if not most, 'classic' theories of personality were created in this manner.

Achievement motivation is one such aspect of personality research which forms a key concept in organizational behaviour, and which is used as a dimension of suitability for managerial and other professional occupations (McClelland et al., 1953). Yet the research on which it was derived was conducted widely on exclusively male managers. It is particularly interesting to note that when researchers attempted to replicate McClelland's formative work on achievement motivation using women as subjects (Veroff et al., 1953), the women responded in ways which were interpreted as their being less motivated than men. However, Betz and Fitzgerald (1987) note 'Interestingly, the researchers did not seem to think it important that under relaxed conditions, females actually scored higher than males in the amount of achievement imagery in their TAT's' (p. 137, quoted in Jacobson and Jacques, 1990, pp. 8–9).

Perhaps more importantly, scholars have critically examined the construct of achievement motivation and found it to be multidimensional (Helmreich and Spence, 1978), and defined and valued differently by females and males (Sutherland and Veroff, 1985, cited in Jacobson and Jacques, 1990, p. 11).

Gilligan (1982) cogently summarizes the concerns with respect to the effects of potential gender bias:

> McClelland (1975) reports that 'psychologists have found sex differences in their studies from the moment they started doing empirical research [p. 81]'. But because it is difficult to say 'different' without saying 'better' or 'worse', and because there has been a tendency to construct a single scale of measurement, and because that scale has been derived and standardized on the basis of men's observations and interpretations of research data predominantly or exclusively drawn from studies of males, psychologists have tended, in McClelland's words, 'to regard male behaviour as the "norm" and female behaviour was some kind of deviation from that norm [p. 81].' Thus, when women do not conform to the standards of psychological expectation, the conclusion has been that something is wrong with the women.
>
> (Gilligan, 1982, pp. 90–1)

ASSESSMENT CENTRES

There has been a significant growth in the use of assessment centres by organizations (Robertson and Makin, 1986; Gaugler et al., 1987).

The popularity of the assessment centre lies in its relatively high levels of predictive validity, when compared with other predictors such as interviews, and psychometrics (Thornton and Byham, 1982; Gaugler *et al.*, 1987; Herriot, 1989). Because of their high costs they tend to be used for 'special' assessments, such as senior management selection, or for allocating places to 'high fliers' for fast-track career development programmes.

The assessment centre comprises all stages of the assessment process. It differs from other methods of assessment in a variety of ways, including the fact that a number of individuals are assessed at the same time; it collects data on a range of behavioural activities, ranging from group problem-solving tasks, to psychometrics and interviews. Several assessors evaluate each participant during the course of the centre. Whilst assessment centres can vary in length from 8 hours to 5 days, the average length is probably around 1½ to 2 days (Thornton and Byham, 1982).

My concerns are several, but before describing them it should also be added that no studies have found direct evidence to support my contentions of potential gender bias.

Several studies have found no sex difference in assessment centre ratings (e.g. Bray, 1971; and review by Thornton and Byham, 1982). Others have found either higher ratings for women (Walsh *et al.*, 1987) or examples of when women were rated higher on some dimensions, and men higher on others (Howard and Bray, 1988, cited in Baisden and Koonce, 1993). Gaugler *et al.* (1987) found evidence of assessment centres having higher validity for women (cited in Baisden and Koonce, 1993). However, Alimo-Metcalfe (in preparation) has re-examined these studies and suggested that the data can be interpreted as providing evidence of different forms of validity of assessment centres for women and men. Briefly stated, they suggest sources of lower *concurrent* validity, but higher predictive validity, for women.

Why then should I entertain concerns as to their fairness? In fact these comments relate more to the design of the centres.

POSSIBLE SOURCES OF GENDER BIAS IN ASSESSMENT CENTRE METHODOLOGY

The first stage of the assessment centre design is the identification of criteria or dimensions being assessed. Sources of potential gender bias at this stage were discussed earlier. In an assessment centre, assessors are trained in behavioural observation techniques since they will be rating candidates whilst observing their performance in a variety of activities. Often the assessors are given 'behavioural frameworks' or 'guidelines' which contain specific examples of above-average, average, and below-average behavioural indicators. If these indicators have emerged from sampling a totally male or predominately male group, and if there is evidence that there are gender differences in interactive and management style, then clearly these offer potential sources of gender bias. Brief reference has already been made to these studies.

Of particular importance to the situation of the assessment centre, are findings from other studies relating to gender and managerial style. Callan (1993), for example, has stated,

> In contrast to male managers, it is agreed that female managers can often bring a high relationship approach to managing (Statham, 1987; Russell *et al.*, 1988),

which includes a willingness to listen, to seek participation, a wish for disclosure and greater concern about maintaining good interpersonal relationships.

(Callan, 1993, p. 13)

Statham (1987), in her study of female and male bosses of secretaries, concluded that 'sex-differentiated management models may well exist, that women may use a more task-engrossed and person-invested style, while men may use a more image-engrossed and autonomy-invested style' (p. 425). (Rosener's (1990) study of sex differences in preferred leadership style has already been cited.)

Fagenson, in her book *Women in Management* (1993), states

Evidence suggesting that women managers have a transformational, democratic, and/or 'web' rather than hierarchical style of leadership, and more satisfied subordinates than men managers has raised questions about the appropriateness and effectiveness of a masculine military model of management in corporate settings (Bass, 1991; Eagly and Johnson, 1990; Loden, 1985; Rosener, 1990).

(Fagenson, 1993, p. 5)

Deborah Tannen's book (1990), on the differences in the way women and men communicate, highlights the subtleties of gender differences in verbal interaction, which one suspects have yet to be absorbed into the established 'body of knowledge' (see also Chapter 11). These data support the view that the sorts of behaviours regarded as 'effective' in assessment centres being used to identify potential for senior management, may be heavily biased towards the male way of dealing with situations. The result may be, then, that if women handle situations differently, their behaviours are either ignored, or allocated relatively low scores.

Since candidates in assessment centres perform tasks in groups, we should also note possible sources of gender bias in relation to group dynamics. Evidence exists that women are less likely to emerge as leaders in leaderless groups (Strodbeck and Mann, 1956; Megargee, 1969; Piliavin and Martin, 1978).

It would not be unreasonable to presume that candidates attending assessment centres for senior management positions were predominantly male. This means that those who do attend are typically performing in unbalanced sex-ratio groups (that is unequal numbers of females and males). Kanter (1977b) stated in some of her earlier work, that being in a numerical minority inhibits that member's performance in a group situation, particularly one without a history of working together. A study by Finigan (1982) obtained results that confirmed this for three sex-ratio situations: male-dominant groups, female-dominant groups, and those in which there were equal numbers of both sexes. However, underachievement was particularly pronounced for females in male-dominant groups. This was found to be due, in part, to males controlling the input of women to discussion.

A further aspect of gender and performance on tasks needs to be considered in the context of the assessment centre. Gender research has highlighted the importance of the fact that not all tasks are gender neutral (Carbonell, 1984). Moreover, women are found to play a more active role in female tasks (Carbonell, 1984) and are perceived as more capable (Nieva and Gutek, 1980).

Since the assessment centre is specifically designed to replicate 'real-life' managerial situations, which are clearly male gendered (Kanter, 1977a; Ragins and Sundstrom, 1989), how can one assume that this will not affect the performance of females?

GENDER AND THE EVALUATION OF ONGOING PERFORMANCE: PERFORMANCE APPRAISAL

Findings relating to gender bias in managerial performance evaluation have produced varying results. On occasions, studies have found that men receive higher evaluations (e.g. Rosen and Jerdee, 1973; Dipboye *et al.*, 1977; Cohen *et al.*, 1978), others that women receive higher evaluations (Abramson *et al.*, 1977; Pulakos and Wexley, 1983; Peters *et al.*, 1984). Some studies have found no differences in the evaluation of females and males (e.g. Moses and Boehm, 1975; Hall and Hall, 1976; Lee and Alvares, 1977; Tsui and Gutek, 1984).

The assessment of performance is an ubiquitous activity in organizations and in the past was generally located in the performance appraisal process. Research on gender effects in performance appraisal is of particular value because it is conducted in organizational as opposed to laboratory settings, and rather than being based on the oft-used student population, it involves 'real' managers. Judgements made in appraisals can have immediate and far-reaching implications for the individual. They can, for example, involve decisions relating to training and development opportunities and career development; in some organizations they are used as a basis for promotion and pay. Their impact is potentially considerable.

As with other studies on performance evaluation, findings in relation to gender bias have been mixed. In one study for example (Mobley, 1982) it was concluded that bias favoured women. In other studies no sex effect was found (Hall and Hall, 1976; Griffeth and Bedeian, 1989) although they were not forming part of a general appraisal discussion. However, in a national study of 1,600 managers in the British National Health Service (NHS) (Institute of Health Services Management, 1991; Alimo-Metcalfe, 1992), it was found that in a subsample of the most senior managers, twice as many males as females obtained the highest performance-related pay (PRP) rating, whereas twice as many women as men were given the lower rating. Ratings were also given on occasions to managers not subject to PRP; however, not all who were rated for performance were told their rating. Analyses showed that of those who did not know, they were significantly more likely to be women. Since not knowing one's rating means that you cannot challenge it, women were clearly more disadvantaged.

A study of telecommunications executives (Society of Telecom Executives, 1992) found a very similar pattern with respect to significant differences between PRP ratings given to women and men. More ominously, the study found that comparing the PRP paid to individuals with the same appraisal marking, women received lower amounts on average. Not surprisingly, the authors of the report conclude that 'There is prima facie evidence that appraisals and the PRP (performance related pay process) arrangements have operated in a way that discriminates against women' (p. 3).

If this is the case, then it may be that the organizations are contravening an EU Equal Pay Directive which states: 'The quality of work carried out by a worker may not be used as a criterion for pay increments where its application shows itself to be systematically unfavourable to women' (extract from 1989 Danfoss Ruling).

Some studies have revealed a more insidious and hidden bias operating against women. For example, a study by Gupta et al. (1980) reported that whilst there were no sex differences amongst performance ratings, women received fewer promotions than men. Similar data were obtained by Williams and Walker (1985) who collected data in the British Civil Service, which rates not only overall performance but also promotability and long-term potential.

Evidence has also been found of bias favouring men in discretionary pay in several British organizations, including: universities (Association of University Teachers, 1991); a large insurance company (cited in Society of Telecom Executives, 1992); and the Civil Service (First Division Association, 1992). A study of merit pay in four organizations in the UK (Bevan and Thompson, 1992) concluded that '[gender] bias may enter the appraisal and merit pay process at a myriad of points' (p. x), including managers (of both sexes) valuing different attributes in men than they do in women, which in many cases reinforce gender stereotypes.

Sex differences have been found in the way in which appraisals have been conducted. Corby (1982, 1983) highlighted the different quality of appraisals for women and men in the British Civil Service. Whilst the men, generally speaking, received critical feedback, the women were far more likely to receive innocuous, non-specific criticism, if indeed they received any. Harlan and Weiss (1982), in a field study of 100 managers also found that women were less likely to receive critical feedback, but also formal objectives and incentives to improve. Corby interprets the lack of critical feedback to women as suggesting the discomfort that male bosses felt in relation to female subordinates. She adds that since the quality of information exchanged in the appraisal was crucial for developmental purposes, and indeed is used, whether explicitly or implicity, for the purposes of making recommendations for promotion, it is a process not to be overlooked when investigating organizational procedures in women's career development. She in fact found that women were promoted far less frequently than men, and furthermore, that they were more likely than men to be assigned 'to narrow or restricted areas of work or to particular locations based on pre-conceived assumptions about the capabilities, characteristics, domestic circumstances and interests of women' (Corby, 1983, p. 30).

In the author's investigation of appraisal in the NHS, it was found that women managers experienced greater difficulties with respect to: talking freely about what they wanted to discuss; discussing their relationship with their appraiser (their manager); giving feedback to their appraiser; and identifying their areas of strength. Despite these findings, women were significantly more positive about the motivational effects of the appraisal, and of its benefit to the organization, and specifically in helping to create a team atmosphere and leading to greater openness and trust in the organization (Alimo-Metcalfe, 1992, and in press). Despite, and perhaps because of these findings, I find the data disquieting. There are several reasons for this, including the sense of women's disempowerment as reflected in their lack of influence on the agenda of the appraisal discussion, and their apparent acceptance of inferior treatment. Moreover, this appears to be within the context of evidence of gender bias in performance evaluation. The picture is also particularly depressing for women since the NHS is the third largest employer in the world and certainly the largest employer of women in Europe. Almost 80% of its employees are female, that is almost one million. Representation of women in senior management (about 18%) reflects the dismal and common picture of a preponderance at junior levels, and a significant minority in senior and top management (Equal Opportunities Commission, 1991).

The findings of gender bias in performance appraisal are of particular concern for women in the UK, given the unprecedented interest of organizations in Britain in introducing PRP. The British government has its introduction into public-sector organizations high on its agenda (Thompson, 1992) and it is in these organizations where a substantial proportion of women in paid employment are located (Equal Opportunities Commission, 1991; Davidson and Cooper, 1993).

One way of attempting to minimize gender bias in evaluative performance appraisals, and of improving the quality of feedback in developmental appraisals, would be to adopt Hazucha's suggestion (1992) that those people evaluating or appraising be required to provide specific observation of behaviours to substantiate their judgements.

CONCLUSION

This chapter has argued that as organizations purportedly attempt to increase the 'fairness' and 'objectivity' of assessment processes by adopting more 'sophisticated' forms of assessment, they may in fact be increasing the effect of gender bias. Furthermore, as the techniques of assessment become more complex, sources of bias are far less obvious and hence less likely to be challenged.

REFERENCES

ABRAMSON, P. R., GOLDBERG, P. A., GREENBERG, J. H. and ABRAMSON, L. M. (1977) The talking platypus phenomenon: competency ratings as a function of sex and professional status, *Psychology of Women Quarterly*, Vol. 2, pp. 114–24.

ALBAN METCALFE, B. and NICHOLSON, N. (1984) *The Career Development of British Managers*, British Institute of Management Foundation, London.

ALIMO-METCALFE, B. (1992) Gender and appraisal: findings from a national survey of managers in the British health service. Paper presented at the Global Research Conference on Women in Management, October 21–23, Carleton University, Ottawa, Canada.

ALIMO-METCALFE, B. (1993) Different gender-different rules: assessment of women in management, in P. Barrar and C. L. Cooper (eds) *Managing Organizations in 1992: Strategic Responses*, Routledge, London.

ALIMO-METCALFE, B. (1994a) The gender discrimination of leadership assessment. Paper presented at the 22nd International Congress on the Assessment Center Method, April 26–29, San Francisco, CA.

ALIMO-METCALFE, B. (1994b) Using the repertory grid to investigate female and male constructs of leadership. Paper presented at the 23rd International Congress of Applied Psychology, July 17–22, Madrid.

ASSOCIATION OF UNIVERSITY TEACHERS (1991) *Pay in Universities*, AUT, London.

BAISDEN, H. E. and KOONCE, B. (1993) Understanding gender differences in assessment center performance. Paper presented to the International Assessment Center Congress, 29 March–1 April, Atlanta, GA.

BARTOL, K. M. (1978) The sex structuring of organisations: a search for possible causes, *Academy of Management Review*, Vol. 3, pp. 805–15.

BASS, B. (1991) Debate: is it time to stop talking about gender differences? *Harvard Business Review*, Jan–Feb, pp. 151–3.

BETZ, N. E. and FITZGERALD, L. F. (1987) *The Career Psychology of Women*, Academic Press, Florida.

BEVAN, S. and THOMPSON, M. (1992) *Merit Pay, Performance Appraisal and Attitudes to Women's Work*, Institute of Manpower Studies, Report No. 234, IMS, Sussex.

BLOCK, J. H. (1976) Issues, problems, and pitfalls in assessing sex differences, *Merill-Palmer Quarterly*, Vol. 22, pp. 283–308.

BRAY, D. W. (1971) The assessment center: opportunities for women, *Personnel Magazine*, Vol. 48, pp. 30–44.

CALAS, M. B. and JACQUES, R. (1988) Diversity or conformity? Research by women on women in organisations. Paper presented at the 7th Annual Conference on Women in Organisations, Long Beach, CA.

CALAS, M. B. and SMIRCICH, L. (1988) Reading leadership as a form of cultural analysis, in J. G. Hunt *et al.* (eds) *Emerging Leadership Vistas*, Lexington Books.

CALAS, M. B. and SMIRCICH, L. (1989) Using the 'F' word: feminist theories and the social consequences of organizational research, in A. J. Mills and P. Tancred (eds) *Gendering Organizational Analysis*, Sage, London.

CALAS, M. B. and SMIRCICH, L. (1993) Dangerous liaisons: the 'feminine-in-management' meets globalization, *Business Horizons*, special issue on women and work, March/April.

CALLAN, V. J. (1993) Subordinate–manager communication in different sex dyads: consequences for job satisfaction, *Journal of Occupational and Organizational Psychology*, Vol. 66, no. 1, pp. 13–27.

CARBONELL, J. L. (1984) Sex roles and leadership revisited, *Journal of Applied Psychology*, Vol. 69, pp. 44–9.

COHEN, S. L. and BUNKER, K. A. (1975) Subtle effects of sex-role stereotypes on recruiters' living decisions, *Journal of Applied Psychology*, Vol. 60, pp. 566–72.

COHEN, S. L., BUNKER, K. A., BURTON, A. L. and MCMANUS, P. D. (1978) Reactions of male subordinates to the sex-role congruency of immediate supervision, *Sex Roles*, Vol. 4, pp. 297–311.

CORBY, S. (1982) *Equal Opportunities for Women in the Civil Service*, HMSO, London.

CORBY, S. (1983) Women in the Civil Service: looking back or held back? *Personnel Management*, February, pp. 28–31.

DANFOSS RULING (1989) Extract from ruling of the Court of Justice of the European Communities, 17 October, on the interpretation of the meaning of EEC Equal Pay Directive 75/117.

DAVIDSON, M. J. and COOPER, C. L. (eds) (1993) *European Women in Business and Management*, Paul Chapman Publishing, London.

DENMARK, F. L. (1977) Styles of leadership, *Psychology of Women Quarterly*, Vol. 2, pp. 99–113.

DIPBOYE, R. L., ARVEY, R. D. and TERPSTRA, D. E. (1977) Sex and physical attractiveness of raters and applicants as determinations of résumé evaluations, *Journal of Applied Psychology*, Vol. 62, pp. 288–94.

DIPBOYE, R. L., FROMKIN, H. L. and WIBACK, K. (1975) Relative importance of applicant's sex, attractiveness, and scholastic standing in evaluation of job applicant résumés, *Journal of Applied Psychology*, Vol. 60, pp. 39–43.

DOBBINS, G. H. and PLATZ, S. J. (1986) Sex differences in leadership: how real are they? *Academy of Management Review*, Vol. 11, pp. 118–27.

DONNELL, S. M. and HALL, J. (1980) Men and women as managers: a significant case of no significant difference, *Organizational Dynamics*, Vol. 8, pp. 60–77.

DUBNO, P. (1985) Attitudes towards women executives: a longitudinal approach, *Academy of Management Journal*, Vol. 28, pp. 235–9.

EAGLY, A. and JOHNSON, B. T. (1990) Gender and leadership style: a meta-analysis, *Psychological Bulletin*, Vol. 108, pp. 233–56.

EQUAL OPPORTUNITIES COMMISSION (1988) *Avoiding Sex Bias in Selection Testing: Guidance for Employers*, EOC, Manchester.

EQUAL OPPORTUNITIES COMMISSION (1991) *Women and Men in Britain 1991*, HMSO, London.

FAGENSON, E. A. (ed.) (1993) *Women in Management: Trends, Issues, and Challenges in Managing Diversity*, Sage, London.

FERRARIO, M. (1990) Leadership style of British men and women managers. Unpublished MSc Dissertation, University of Manchester, Faculty of Management Sciences.

FINIGAN, M. (1982) The effects of token representation on participants in small decision-making groups, *Economic and Industrial Democracy*, Vol. 3, pp. 531–50.

FIRST DIVISION ASSOCIATION (1992) *FDA News*, January.

FLANAGAN, J. C. (1954) The critical incident technique, *Psychological Bulletin*, Vol. 51, pp. 327–58.

GARDNER, H. (1983) *Frames of Mind*, Paladin, London.

GAUGLER, B. B., ROSENTHAL, D. B., THORNTON, G. C. and BENTSON, C. (1987) Meta-analysis of assessment center validity, *Journal of Applied Psychology*, Vol. 72, no. 3, pp. 493–511.

GILLIGAN, C. (1982) *In a Different Voice: Psychological Theory and Women's Development*, Harvard University Press.

GLICK, P., ZION, C. and NELSON, C. (1988) What mediates sex discrimination in living decisions? *Journal of Personality and Social Psychology*, Vol. 55, no. 2, pp. 178–86.

GRIFFETH, R. W. and BEDEIAN, A. G. (1989) Employee performance evaluations: effects of ratee age, rater age, and ratee gender, *Journal of Organizational Behavior*, Vol. 10, pp. 83–90.

GUPTA, N., BEEHR, T. A. and JENKINS, G. D. (1980) The relationship between employee gender and supervisor-subordinate cross-ratings, *Proceedings of the Academy of Management*, Vol. 40, pp. 396–400.

HALL, F. S. and HALL, D. T. (1976) Effects of job incumbents' race and sex on evaluation of managerial performance, *Academy of Management Journal*, Vol. 19, pp. 478–81.

HANSARD SOCIETY (1990) *Women At the Top*, The Hansard Society for Parliamentary Government, London.

HARDING, S. (1986) *The Science Question in Feminism*, Cornell University Press, Ithaca.

HARLAN, A. and WEISS, C. L. (1982) Sex differences in factors affecting managerial career advancement, in P. A. Wallace (ed.) *Women in the Workplace*, Auburn House, Boston, MA.

HAZUCHA, J. F. (1992) *Women in Management: Not Enough Ado . . . About Something*, Personnel Decisions, Inc., Minneapolis, MN.

HEILMAN, M. E. and SARUWATARI, L. R. (1979) When beauty is beastly: the effects of appearance and sex on evaluations of job applicants for managerial and non-managerial jobs, *Organizational Behavior and Human Performance*, Vol. 23, pp. 360–72.

HELMREICH, R. L. and SPENCE, J. T. (1978) *The Work and Family Orientation Questionnaire: An Objective Instrument to Assess Components of Achievement Motivation and Attitudes Towards Family and Career*, JSAS Catalog of Selected Documents in Psychology, Vol. 8, no. 35.

HERRIOT, P. L. (1989) *Assessment and Selection in Organisations*, Wiley, London.

HIRSH, W. and JACKSON, C. (1990) *Women into Management: Issues Influencing the Entry of Women into Managerial Jobs*, IMS Report No. 158, Institute of Manpower Studies, University of Sussex, Brighton.

HOWARD, A. and BRAY, D. W. (1988) *Managerial Lives in Transition*, Guilford, New York.

HUNTER, J. E. and HUNTER, R. (1984) Validity and utility of alternative predictors, *Psychological Bulletin*, Vol. 96, pp. 72–98.

ILES, P. A. and ROBERTSON, I. T. (1988) Getting in, getting on, and looking good: physical attractiveness, gender and selection decisions, *Guidance and Assessment Review*, Vol. 4, no. 3, pp. 6–8.

INSTITUTE OF HEALTH SERVICES MANAGEMENT (1991) *Individual Performance Review in the NHS*, Institute of Health Services Management, NHS Training Directorate, London.

INSTITUTE OF MANAGEMENT/REMUNERATION ECONOMICS (1994) *National Management Salary Survey*, Institute of Management/Remuneration Economics, London.

JACOBSON, S.W. and JACQUES, R. (1990) Of knowers, knowing, and the known: a gender framework for revisioning organizational and management scholarship. Paper presented at the Academy of Management Annual Meeting, San Francisco, 10–12 August.

JAGO, A. G. and VROOM, V. H. (1982) Sex differences in the incidence and evaluation of participative leader behaviour, *Journal of Applied Psychology*, Vol. 67, pp. 776–83.

KANTER, R. M. (1977a) *Men and Women of the Corporation*, Basic Books, New York.

KANTER, R. M. (1977b) Some effects of proportions on group life: skewed sex ratios and responses to token women, *American Journal of Sociology*, Vol. 82, pp. 965–90.

KELLY, G. (1955) *The Psychology of Personal Constructs*, Vol. 1, Norton, New York.

KINDER, A. J. and ROBERTSON, I.T. (1993) Letter to *The Psychologist*, March, p. 117.

LEE, D. M. and ALVARES, K. (1977) Effects of sex on descriptions and evaluations of supervisory behavior in a simulated industrial setting, *Journal of Applied Psychology*, Vol. 62, pp. 405–10.

LEVINE, E. L., ASH, R. A., HALL, H. and SISTRUNCK, F. (1983) Evaluation of job analysis methods by experienced job analysts, *Academy of Management Journal*, Vol. 26, pp. 339–48.

LODEN, M. (1985) *Feminine Leadership or How to Succeed in Business Without Being One of the Boys*, Times Books, New York.

MADDEN, J. F. (1985) The persistence of pay differentials: the economics of sex discrimination, in L. L. Larwood, A. H. Stromberg and B. A. Gutek (eds) *Women and Work, Vol. 1: An Annual Review*, Sage, Beverly Hills, CA.

MARSHALL, J. (1984) *Women Managers: Travellers in a Male World*, Wiley, Chichester.

MASSENGILL, D. and DIMARCO, N. (1979) Sex role stereotypes and requisite management characteristics, *Sex Roles*, Vol. 5, pp. 561–80.

MCCLELLAND, D. C., ATKINSON, J. W., CLARK, R. A. and LOWELL. E. L. (1953) *The Achievement Motive*, Appleton, New York.

MEGARGEE, E. I. (1969) Influence of sex roles in the manifestation of leadership, *Journal of Applied Psychology*, Vol. 53, pp. 317–82.

MOBLEY, W. H. (1982) Supervision and employee race and sex effects on performance appraisals: a field study of adverse impact and generalizability, *Academy of Management Journal*, Vol. 25, pp. 598–606.

MOSES, J. L. and BOEHM, V. R. (1975) Relationship of assessment centre performance to management progress of women, *Journal of Applied Psychology*, Vol. 60, pp. 527–9.

MOTTRAM, R. (1987) Problems for the test user in avoiding sex bias, *The Occupational Psychologist. Special Issue: Gender Issues in Occupational Psychology*, Vol. 3, pp. 6–7.

MUCHINSKY, P. M. (1986) Personnel selection methods, in C. L. Cooper and I. T. Robertson (eds) *International Review of Industrial and Organizational Psychology*, Wiley, Chichester.

NIEVA, V. F. and GUTEK, B. A. (1980) Sex effects of evaluation, *Academy of Management Review*, Vol. 5, no. 2, pp. 267–76.

OMCS (1988) *Equal Opportunities for Women in the Civil Service*. Progress Report 1984–1987. Cabinet Office, Office for the Minister for the Civil Service, London.

PADGETT, D. L. (1990) Gender and general research on leadership: visions and vitality. Paper presented at the Academy of Management Annual Meeting, San Francisco, 10–12 August.

Personnel Management (1991) Personality tests: the great debate, *Personnel Management*, September, pp. 38–42.

PETERS, L. H., O'CONNOR, E. J., WEEKLY, J., POOYAN, A., FRANK, B. and ERENKRANTZ, B. (1984) Sex bias and managerial evaluations: a replication and extension, *Journal of Applied Psychology*, Vol. 69, pp. 349–52.

PILIAVIN, J. A. and MARTIN, R. R. (1978) The effect of the sex composition of groups on style of social interaction, *Sex Roles*, Vol. 4, no. 2, pp. 281–96.

POWELL, G. N. and BUTTERFIELD, D. A. (1979) The 'good manager': masculine or androgynous? *Academy of Management Journal*, Vol. 22, pp. 395–403.

PULAKOS, E. D. and WEXLEY, K. N. (1983) The relationship among perceptual similarity, sex and performance ratings in manager–subordinate dyads, *Academy of Management Journal*, Vol. 26, pp. 129–39.

RAGINS, B. R. and SUNDSTROM, E. (1989) Gender and power in organizations: a longitudinal perspective, *Psychological Bulletin*, Vol. 105, no. 1, pp. 51–88.

ROBERTSON, I. T. and ILES, P. A. (1988) Approaches to managerial selection, in C. L. Cooper and I. Robertson (eds) *International Review of Industrial and Organizational Psychology*, John Wiley, London.

ROBERTSON, I. T. and MAKIN, P. J. (1986) Management selection in Britain. A survey and critique, *Journal of Occupational Psychology*, Vol. 59, no. 1, pp. 45–57.

ROSE, G. L. and ANDIAPPAN, P. (1978) Sex effects on managerial living decisions, *Academy of Management Journal*, Vol. 21, pp. 104–12.

ROSE, S. (1976) Scientific racism and ideology: the IQ racket from Galton to Jensen, in S. Rose and H. Rose (eds) *The Political Economy of Science*, Macmillan, London.

ROSE, S. and ROSE, H. (1979) *The Political Economy of Science*, Macmillan, Basingstoke.

ROSEN, B. and JERDEE, T. H. (1974) Influence of sex-role stereotypes on personnel decisions, *Journal of Applied Psychology*, Vol. 59, pp. 9–14.

ROSENBAUM, J. E. (1985) Persistence and change in pay in inequalities: implications for job evaluation and comparable worth, in L. L. Larwood, A. H. Stromberg and B. A. Gutek (eds) *Women and Work. Vol. 1: An Annual Review*, Sage, Beverly Hills, CA.

ROSENER, J. (1990) Ways women lead, *Harvard Business Review*, November/December, pp. 119–25.

RUSSELL, J. E. A., RUSH, M. C. and HERD, A. M. (1988) An exploration of women's expectations of effective male and female leadership, *Sex Roles*, Vol. 18, nos. 5/6, pp. 279–87.

SCHEIN, E. H. (1973) Personal change through interpersonal relationships, in W. G. Bennis, D. E. Berlew, E. H. Schein and F. I. Steel (eds) *Interpersonal Dynamics*, 3rd edn, Dorsey, Homewood, IL.

SCHEIN, V. E. (1973) The relationship between sex-role stereotypes and requisite management characteristics, *Journal of Applied Psychology*, Vol. 57, no. 2, pp. 95–100.

SCHEIN, V. E. (1975) Relationships between sex role stereotypes and requisite management characteristics among female managers, *Journal of Applied Psychology*, Vol. 60, no. 3, pp. 340–4.

SCHEIN, V. E. (1978) Sex role stereotyping, ability and performance. Prior research and new directions, *Personnel Psychology*, Vol. 31, pp. 259–68.

SMITH, M. and ABRAHAMSEN, M. (1992) Patterns of selection in six countries, *The Psychologist*, Vol. 5, no. 5, May, pp. 205–7.

SMITH, P. C. and KENDALL, L. M. (1963) Retranslation of expectations, *Journal of Applied Psychology*, Vol. 47, no. 2, pp. 149–55.

SOCIETY OF TELECOM EXECUTIVES (1992) *Stressing Performance*, STE Research, London.

SPARROW, J. and RIGG, C. (1993) Job analysis: selecting for the masculine approach to management, *Selection and Development Review*. Published by the British Psychological Society, Vol. 9, no. 2, April, pp. 5–8.

STATHAM, A. (1987) The gender model revisited: differences in the management styles of men and women, *Sex Roles*, Vol. 16, nos. 7–8, pp. 409–29.

STRODBECK, F. L. and MANN, R. D. (1956) Sex role differentiation in jury deliberation, *Sociometry*, Vol. 19, no. 1, pp. 3–11.

SUTHERLAND, E. and VEROFF, J. (1985) Achievement, motivation and sex roles, in V. E. O'Leary, R. K. Unger and B. S. Wallston (eds) *Women, Gender and Social Psychology*, Erlbaum, Hillsdale, NJ.

TANNEN, D. (1990) *You Just Don't Understand: Women and Men in Conversation*, William Morrow & Co.

TERBORG, J. R. (1977) Women in management: a research review, *Journal of Applied Psychology*, Vol. 62, pp. 647–64.

TETT, R. P., JACKSON, D. N. and ROTHSTEIN, M. (1993) Personality measures as predictors of job performance: a meta-analytic review, *Personnel Psychology*, Vol. 44, pp. 703–42.

THOMPSON, M. (1992) *Pay and Performance: The Employer Experience*, Institute of Manpower Studies, Report No. 218, IMS, Brighton, Sussex.

THORNTON, G. C. and BYHAM, W. C. (1982) *Assessment Centers and Managerial Performance*, Academic Press, London.

TSUI, A. S. and GUTEK, B. A. (1984) A role set analysis of gender differences in performance, affective relationships, and career success of industrial middle managers, *Academy of Management Journal*, Vol. 27, pp. 619–35.

US DEPARTMENT OF LABOR (1991) *A Report on the Glass Ceiling Initiative*, Government Printing Office, Washington DC.

VEROFF, J., WILSON, S. and ATKINSON, J. W. (1953) The achievement motive in high-school and college-age women, *Journal of Abnormal and Social Psychology*, Vol. 48, pp. 108–19.

WALKER, B. (1981) Psychology and feminism: if you can't beat them join them, in D. Spender (ed.) *Men's Studies Modified*, Pergamon, Oxford.

WALLSTON, B. S. and O'LEARY, V. E. (1981) Sex makes a difference: differential perceptions of women and men, in L. Whitter (ed.) *Reviewing Personality and Social Psychology*, Vol. 2, pp. 9–41, Sage, Beverly Hills, CA.

WALSH, J. P., WEINBERG, R. M. and FAIRFIELD, M. L. (1987) The effects of gender on assessment centre evaluations, *Journal of Occupational Psychology*, Vol. 60, pp. 305–9.

WEBB, J. (1987) Gendering selection psychology, *The Occupational Psychologist*, Special Issue: *Gender Issues in Occupational Psychology*, Vol. 3, December, pp. 4–5.

WEBSTER, E. C. (1982) *The Employment Interview: A Social Judgement Process*, SIP Publications, Schomberg, Ontario.

WEEDON, C. (1987) *Feminist Practice and Post Structuralist Theory*, Basil Blackwell, Oxford.

WILLIAMS, R. S. and WALKER, J. (1985) Sex differences in performance rating: a research note, *Journal of Occupational Psychology*, Vol. 58, pp. 331–7.

WRIGHT, P. M., ANDERSON, C., TOLZMAN, K. and HELTON, T. (1990) An examination of the relationships between employee performance and job analysis ratings, *Academy of Management Best Paper Proceedings 1990*, pp. 299–303, Washington, DC.

CHAPTER 9

Women as Managerial Leaders

MARGARET FERRARIO

INTRODUCTION

The focus of the following discussion is on women and managerial leadership. Due to complex and fast-changing environments, organizations need managers to be effective leaders, to effect and respond to change, and achieve the desired results through others. During the course of this chapter leaders and managers are treated as synonyms so that reference to female leaders means women holding a formal position of leadership in an organization, that is managers.

The subject of women in managerial leadership has dominated management research over the last 20 years. Most of this has been conducted in the USA, but as more women enter management, studies on women as leaders have been conducted in the UK, Scandinavia, Japan and Australia. A review of the research suggests that there have been three major themes in the study of women leaders. Firstly, a body of research was initiated which aimed to examine gender differences in leadership. Much of this research was person oriented, that is sex differences were examined by comparisons of self-report measures of personal characteristics, typically leadership style. There is also a large body of research which takes into account the situational context and explains possible gender differences as a function of the organizational context. A second theme in the research to some extent plays down the differences/similarities issue and focuses on the special contribution women managers can bring to an organization and highlights their effectiveness as managerial leaders. The third underlying theme which has pervaded the research on women in management is the barriers and negative attitudes women face to attain managerial positions and progress through the organizational hierarchy. Current research tends to place less emphasis on the differences/similarities of women leaders compared to men and more on identifying the factors inhibiting their progress. Research is now concerned with helping to break down the barriers women managers face in order to promote more women into leadership positions and improve the quality of their working life.

GENDER DIFFERENCES AND MANAGERIAL LEADERSHIP

Much of the early research on women as managerial leaders was concerned with the extent to which there are gender differences between male and female managers. This was examined from both a person-centred and an organization-centred approach. The person-centred view attempts to determine if women's career progression is due to factors that are internal to women. The organization-centred approach takes the perspective that women's underrepresentation is due to the difficulties faced in the context of the organization.

Person-centred research

Much of the early research on women managers concentrated on assessing whether women possessed the qualities commonly assumed to be characteristic of managers. Studies focused on areas such as personality, motivation to manage, personal attributes and skills, and leadership style. More recently, 'competencies' of women managers have been assessed.

PERSONALITY   Examination of personality traits of women managers have found no evidence of any dissimilarity to men. Four personality traits often measured are dominance, responsibility, achievement and self-assurance (Miller, 1976; Donnell and Hall, 1980; Brenner, 1982; Steinberg and Shapiro, 1982). The majority of studies show that when education and level in the organization are controlled, there is generally no difference between men and women managers (Brenner, 1982). Despite the evidence to show that men and women managers have few personality differences, many studies have shown that there is widespread belief that women do not possess the personality traits required for successful managers (e.g. Schein, 1973; Rosen and Jerdee, 1978; Massengill and DiMarco, 1979).

MOTIVATION TO MANAGE   It has been argued that there are three components of personality which have an influence on managerial success through their impact on motivational processes; they are locus of control, self-efficacy and need for achievement (Porter and Lawler, 1968). An in-depth study of 48 successful British women managers (White et al., 1992) found that they had an internal locus of control, that is they had a strong belief in their own ability to control the direction of their careers. Bandura (1977) claims that self-efficacy influences choice of behaviour. White et al. (1992) found that women managers possessed high self-efficacy and the majority stated that tenacity and perseverence had been major determinants of their success. These women managers also rated highly on the need for achievement, often cited as an indicator of successful managers. Furthermore, 'the motivations of successful women were found to be very similar to those of male high flyers' (Cox and Cooper, 1988, p. 221). The findings of an American study by Harlan and Weiss (1982) suggest that the motivation to manage may be influenced by the organizational context. They compared two organizations, one in which women comprised 19% of all managers, and the other only 6%. In the 6% organization, self-report measures showed a lower motivation to manage compared to men, in addition to lower self-esteem. However, in the organization where women encompassed 19% of the managers, there was no gender difference. They concluded that where women were in a small minority group, they tended to lower their goals to conform with the organizational climate and be more realistic regarding their expectations.

ATTRIBUTES AND SKILLS   There is little evidence to suggest women differ from men in various personal attributes. For example, women have been found to be similar to men in potential managerial capability (Bass et al., 1971), co-operation and competition (Lirtzman and Wahba, 1972) and problem-solving (Matthews, 1972). Blackstone and Weinreich-Haste (1980) found that any sex differences in cognition have been overstated and had no physiological basis. Moreover, studies reveal that there are more differences within each sex than between sexes. Reviews of the literature on comparisons of men and women managers conclude that women possess the necessary qualifications and skills for management and professional positions (Herbert and Yost, 1979). As highlighted by Davidson and Cooper (1992), many studies have shown that women managers are more likely to possess higher qualifications compared to their male counterparts (Alban-Metcalfe and Nicholson, 1984; Davidson and Cooper, 1987; Nicholson and West, 1988; Ferrario, 1990; Coe, 1992).

LEADERSHIP STYLE   Much of the research on gender differences and leadership style used self-report measures and dominated leadership research from the 1960s to the 1980s. The evidence is conflicting and inconsistent. Conclusions about leadership style and gender differences have largely been based on laboratory experiments using American student populations. Demonstrating sex differences in the leadership styles of actual managers has proven more difficult. Several studies have demonstrated that men and women differ in leadership behaviours and effectiveness (e.g. Petty and Lee, 1975; Bartol and Butterfield, 1976). Other studies, conducted in American public service organizations, have found no significant difference in leadership styles of men and women (Day and Stogdill, 1972; Bartol and Wortman, 1976; Osborn and Vicars, 1976). A survey of Greek firms also revealed no significant differences in leadership style, nor in subordinate satisfaction, between employees with male and female managers (Bourantas and Papalexandris, 1990).

In a review of the literature, Marshall (1984) found that studies which revealed differences between men and women's leadership style were usually those in which women managers scored higher on the supporting dimensions of leadership (e.g. Brenner and Vinacke, 1979; Davidson and Cooper, 1983, 1984). A study by Ferrario and Davidson (1991), which looked at a range of style, demographic, situational and sex-role self-report measures, found that British women managers scored significantly higher on both people- and task-oriented dimensions than did male managers. The majority of the female sample had a more 'team' management style. In contrast, significantly more men were identified as 'laissez-faire', which is characterized by less leader involvement in both people- and task-oriented activities. However, the data also revealed that these sex differences may be the result of individuals holding different sex-role identities which may be correlated with, but not rigidly determined by, sex. Other researchers have argued that true insight into sex-role behaviour requires a use of psychological sex rather than biological sex as an independent variable (e.g. Putnam, 1982).

COMPETENCIES   Critics of previous leadership research have claimed that studies were based on a simplistic view of leadership (that is task- vs people-orientation). There is a current trend in leadership theory which emphasizes a range of managerial competencies. Quinn et al. (1990) devised a competing values framework to guide managers on the competencies required of them. According to this theory there are four management models (rational goal theory; human relations theory; open systems model; and internal process theory). It was argued that these models both complement and contradict each other. Managers have to take a holistic view and make complex decisions in a dynamic system which is constantly evolving. Quinn et al. (1990) argued that the 'master' manager must possess the necessary competencies to read environmental cues. A recent Australian study by Vilkinas and Cartan (1993) administered Quinn et al.'s questionnaire (1990) in order to measure men and women managers' perception of the presence of certain managerial roles and their related competencies used. The results of the study indicated no significant differences in the competencies which male and female managers display, nor in the managerial roles they exhibit.

Organization-centred research

The inconsistent findings of sex of leader and leadership style or effectiveness have been difficult for researchers to explain. There was a general consensus that leadership style was not just a function of sex differences (e.g. Chapman and Luthans, 1975). There was the further problem of causality. The assumption in the previous research cited tends to be that factors intrinsic to the person influence various outcomes, for example job satisfaction, group performance. However, research has shown the need to look at the context in which leader and subordinates are active (Kerr et al., 1974; Schriesheim and Murphy, 1976; Bass, 1981). Many critics of the person-centred approach, particularly style theories, stated that an understanding of leadership effectiveness, as related to variables such as gender, required an analysis of situational demands (e.g. Korman, 1966). Researchers began to concentrate on studies of women managers in the context of the organization. Evaluation of women managers compared to men was undertaken from an appreciation of the organizational context. Much of the research suggests that women managers' style or behaviour may be strongly influenced through belonging to a minority group. There is, therefore, pressure either to adopt their male colleagues' management style or to display a more 'feminine' relations-oriented style and become victims of occupational segregation by being relegated to people-handling staff functions such as personnel or retailing. The lack of female mentors at senior executive level may also have an influence on women managers' style and behaviour.

WOMEN MANAGERS AS A MINORITY GROUP   Kanter (1977) has described the impact of the structural determinants of behaviour in organizations, such as the structure of opportunity (high or low), the structure of power (high or low) and the proportional distribution of people of different categories. Kanter (1977) chose the term 'tokens' for the underrepresented members of women senior managers. She observed that token women in a large organization were highly visible and subject to greater performance pressures than their male counterparts. Also, because differences between 'token' women managers and men managers tend to be exaggerated, women in this situation may conform to their male colleagues' style of management to reduce their 'visibility' (Powell, 1988). According to Marshall (1984) the dominant majority focuses on maintaining its position of power and keeping the subdominant group in place by labelling this group substandard and assigning appropriate social roles. The subdominant or minority group's main concern is to cope by accommodation or adjustment to the dominant group's goals in order to survive. Thus, in management, 'women, being lower status members, are expected to provide encouragement and support; men who already have high status, have more opportunities to make task contributions, have more influence, and receive more expressions of acceptance' (Gregory, 1990, p. 258).

OCCUPATIONAL SEGREGATION Assumptions about appropriate behaviours for women managers have some parallels in the kinds of functions to which they are assigned in organizations. Evidence of occupational segregation confirms that women are most likely to become managers in traditionally female occupations assigned to people-handling staff functions deemed more appropriate to their 'emotional tuning' and more developed interpersonal skills. Many studies have revealed that the majority of women managers are to be found in service occupations or specialist functions which include retailing, catering and personnel (Alban-Metcalfe and Nicholson, 1984; Lockwood and Knowles, 1984; Martin and Roberts, 1984; Coe, 1992). Studies have revealed that women managers' job preferences may be influenced partly by the existing sex ratios of the job. In a study of Japanese women managers, Lam (1992) found that the unattractiveness of managerial jobs to women was 'a self-reinforcing cycle in which the lack of representation of women in turn attracts very few women' (Lam, 1992, p. 204). There were also strong cultural pressures characterized by male resistance to women's entry into managerial roles so as not to disrupt the traditional hierarchical relationships between the sexes.

Furthermore, studies around the world have consistently shown that there are very few women attaining senior executive roles. In an examination of women's membership of the British Institute of Directors, Hammond and Holton (1993) found that at the most senior levels in both the public and the private sector very few women were represented. Furthermore, there is no woman chief executive listed in Britain's top 100 companies encompassed in *The Times* 1,000 (Allen, 1991).

SUPPORT FROM SUPERIORS A recurring pattern in the literature is the importance of support from superiors, especially for women managers. Heller (1982) found, from interviews with men and women leaders, that the women received their greatest support from their superior. This was in contrast to the men whose bosses were their greatest critics. The notion that a supportive boss is crucial to the success of women in management was also found in Hennig and Jardim's (1977) study of 25 successful women executives. These women typically entered the organization at the level of secretary or administrative assistant, became attached to a particular boss and were promoted through the organizational hierarchy with them. These women attributed their success largely to the support of their superior. Kanter (1977) also observed that encouragement of a male 'sponsor' was critical in promotions of women managers.

According to Levinson (1978) a 'mentor' or sponsor who guides one's career through early adulthood is almost essential to success. It is, therefore, possible that mentors may be influential on both men's and women's developing leadership style. The bulk of the research on the role of mentors as an aid to women's career development has revealed some interesting findings. For example, Arnold and Davidson (1990) found that both male and female managers reported their mentors were instrumental in gaining access to the formal network of power relations within their organizations. Several studies in the UK and the USA have found that to succeed in a trade union career, women have needed the support both of other women in leadership and of senior male leaders in a sponsorship role (Gray, 1988; Ledwith et al., 1990). Some studies suggest that it is particularly important for women managers to be mentored by other women. For example, Fitt and Newton (1981) found that male mentors were less likely to perceive women as competent and deferred establishing relationships with women protégés until they had a proven track record. A major problem for women leaders is the lack of female mentors, particularly at senior management level (McKeen and Burke, 1989; Arnold and Davidson, 1990).

WOMEN AS EFFECTIVE LEADERS

Following a large amount of research involved in assessing whether gender differences existed, there was a shift in emphasis from gender/leadership comparisons towards the special contribution women can bring as managers. Many writers on women and leadership attempted to minimize the differences between men and women to promote equal opportunities. In the 'special contribution' approach men and women are assumed to be capable of making different and equally valuable contributions to organizations (e.g. Calvert and Ramsey, 1992). As Billing and Alvesson (1989) point out, this perspective was a result of a broad societal trend: 'Changes in society and in organisations are making traditional leadership patterns obsolete and are forcing people to consider non-traditional styles of behaviour which, it is assumed, makes it possible for women to fit in better even in leadership positions' (Billing and Alvesson, 1989, p. 72). The traditional 'male managerial model' (aggressive, competitive, rational, and firm) of effective leadership gradually began to disappear from the management textbooks. Changes in competition and technology were demanding a different style. As organizations changed, so did the need for different theories of leadership and skills which included good communication, participation and teamwork traditionally associated with a 'female' style of management. The literature also shows that women may have a different attitude to power conducive to a good working environment. Furthermore, research evaluated the effectiveness of women entrepreneurs as their numbers increased significantly worldwide over the last decade.

Toward a more flexible style of managerial leadership

Managing flexibility became the hallmark of the successful contemporary manager and the concept of 'androgyny' became popular. In the late 1980s there was a growing acknowledgement of the benefits of both 'female' and 'male' managerial styles – the 'androgynous' manager, where each style is considered appropriate under different circumstances (Blanchard and Sargent, 1984). All men and women have a mixture of both masculine (task-oriented and instrumental) and feminine (person-oriented and expressive) personality characteristics. Individuals who are androgynous have many masculine and many feminine traits. According to Bem (1975) they are able to respond more effectively than either masculine or feminine individuals to a wide variety of situations.

Korabik and Ayman (1989) interviewed 30 women managers in Canada and also administered the Bem Sex-Role Inventory. They found that the androgynous women managers were rated more highly by their superiors in overall effectiveness than those characterized as masculine or feminine. Korabik and Ayman (1989) assert that although androgyny is an effective style in our fast-paced society, it may be even more important for women than for men because 'the traditional feminine role entails many attitudes and behaviours (e.g. passivity and dependence) which are incompatible with those seen as managerial (assertive, rational and logical)' (Korabik and Ayman, 1989).

Critics of 'flexible' leadership may argue that it contains the seeds of further stereotyping. Significantly more research would need to be carried out to evaluate its effectiveness and impact on women managers. However, this philosophy may serve as a useful vehicle for women's entry into managerial positions. For example, Antal and Krebsbach-Gnath (1993) state that in the last 10 years there has been an increase of women managers in Germany and they suggest one of the factors promoting more women into management is the influence of the management literature and company seminars calling for more flexible styles of management. Some authors have commented that women possess flexibility in leadership, a greater ability to be empathetic and to create a more productive work climate (e.g. Rosener, 1990). Indeed, the leadership literature suggests some organizations actively look for certain new leadership approaches which are associated with women, such as good interpersonal skills.

Some research in the 1980s on women as leaders confirmed that women possess the skills required by progressive organizations. An American study (Jago and Vroom, 1982) which used both male and female students and managers found that both female students and managers displayed a more participative leadership style. Moreover, the data also revealed that 'the intended behaviour of women is in greater agreement with the prescriptions of a normative model of decision-making, a measure that has been found to be predictive of economic and attitudinal measures of actual leader effectiveness (Vroom and Jago, 1978; Margerison and Glube, 1978)' (Jago and Vroom, 1982, p. 781). Marshall (1984) conducted interviews with 30 British women managers and found they had a distinctive style of management which displayed more understanding and sympathy for others and that their relations-oriented style was due to their having access to more varied 'softer' techniques in personal relationships. Similarly, research by Davidson and Cooper (1983, 1984) on differences between British male and female managers also revealed women managers' 'relations-oriented' style.

Women's attitude to power

Many female writers, such as Grant (1988), claim women often have a different attitude to power compared with men. Whilst men see power as an ability to control, Grant (1988) suggests women tend to view power as a capacity stemming from and directed towards the entire community. Therefore, women's view of power is less individualistic and more relational. Many other studies have highlighted women managers' attitude to power. For example, White *et al.* (1992) classified their sample of successful British women managers as 'wise politicians'. Their political style fell into one of two categories – either 'team coaches' or 'visionaries', both of which operate on a system of personal or unshared meaning and were able to think beyond existing paradigms. According to White *et al.* (1992) this 'may give them the ability to challenge the normative nature of power, and to think beyond the constraints allocated to women in society and organizational settings' (p. 223).

In a well-publicized US leadership survey by Rosener (1990) male respondents described themselves in ways that characterize what management experts call 'transactional' leadership. This means they perceive job performance as a series of transactions with subordinates 'exchanging rewards for services rendered or punishment for inadequate performance' (Rosener, 1990, p. 120). Women managers described themselves as 'transformational' leaders which are characterized by encouragement of participation, sharing of power and information, enhancing others' self-worth and energizing others. It has been argued that women can enhance organizations by changing the style of leadership (Loden, 1985); they could exercise power in a more constructive way, utilize human resources more effectively, encourage creativity and change the hierarchical structures (Grant, 1988).

The increase in women entrepreneurs

There has been a large increase in the number of women entering self-employment, together with an increase in studies comparing men and women entrepreneurs. The growth of women entrepreneurs has been evident particularly in the USA where women own 30% of sole proprietorships and partnerships (Fagenson and Jackson, 1993). In the UK women comprise at least 25% of the self-employed population (Alimo-Metcalfe and Wedderburn-Tate, 1993). In Japan, where there are more cultural barriers to attaining managerial positions, there are 2½ million women who run their own businesses (Women's Bureau, 1989). There are various reasons why women are prepared to run their own business including inequality of career prospects or inflexibility of organizations in accommodating domestic responsibilities. A Spanish study carried out by the Women's Institute in 1989, which involved 105 in-depth interviews, found that the motives of the majority of women were, in order of importance: 'personal and professional fulfilment, motives related to improved well-being, the desire to obtain a salary, and, finally, purely business motives' (Fernandez, 1993).

Studies have shown, however, that, as in organizations, women are more likely to experience disadvantages than men in the form of, for example, negative attitudes from agencies and commercial sources of advice and lack of morale and support from partners for domestic responsibilities. In spite of the disadvantages, research suggests that women are just as successful as men. Kalleberg and Leicht (1991) conducted a three-year study on 411 companies in the USA and found that in spite of the barriers women encounter in terms of law codes and the structures of economic and financial institutions, women's businesses were just as successful as the men's. They also found that the determinants of survival and success operated in much the same way for both sexes.

BARRIERS TO WOMEN IN MANAGERIAL POSITIONS

There is currently a shift of emphasis on evaluating women managers compared to men. As Marshall (1984) states, research which takes a comparative male–female approach is in danger of comparing women's experience or behaviour against a traditional 'male' standard. If the male stereotype and experience is equated to the successful manager, then women are considered unsuitable if they differ. Overall, the results from the majority of the research suggest that, in general, there are basically no significant differences in the way in which men and women manage. Indeed, there are quite a number of studies which show ways women can be effective in organizations. Despite the evidence, women are still not attaining a comparable proportion of managerial jobs to their male counterparts, especially at the senior level.

This would suggest that research should be directed toward understanding the barriers to women's progress and the conditions under which they work in organizations. There has been a large variety of studies on the barriers women face in organizations compared to their male counterparts which illustrates that many women are denied the same opportunities as men in the career context and therefore not given the same experience and career development. Barriers can be both formal and informal. Formal barriers include a lack of targets to promote higher female participation in training, a lack of flexible working arrangements and childcare benefits and provision for dual-earner households. However, much of the research suggests that it is the informal barriers which hinder women's career development. These include sex-role stereotyping, negative attitudes and exclusion from male managerial groups. A recent report by the British Institute of Management (1992) found that the main barrier to women in management is that of male attitudes. The report recommends that a policy targeted only at the formal barriers, for example special training, crèche facilities, 'is unlikely to succeed in its aim of increasing the proportion of women in management, if it is implemented in a predominantly male culture' (Coe, 1992).

Existence of sex-role stereotypes

A large number of studies have provided widespread evidence of stereotyped thinking about women and strongly suggest that sexual discrimination reduces women's opportunities for attaining management positions. Stereotypes do not only influence recruitment and selection to a particular position; they also affect ongoing career development and performance evaluation. For example, in the USA, over 80% of women CEOs claimed stereotyping and preconceptions of women managers were the main reasons for women's inability to gain top jobs within their organization (Fagenson and Jackson, 1993).

Schein (1973) found that the 'successful manager = man'. Fifteen years later Brenner et al. (1989) replicated the study to examine the link between sex-role stereotyping and perceived requisite management characteristics. They found that female managers viewed successful managers as possessing characteristics, attitudes and temperaments that are ascribed to both men and women in general. Disturbingly, the male managers still adhered to a male managerial stereotype: 'that male managers have not changed their attitudes over the last 15 years is a message to corporate leaders and legislators as to the importance of maintaining affirmative action pressures' (Brenner et al., 1989, p. 668) (see Chapter 4 for details).

In a replicated study, Heilman et al. (1989) also found that male managers persist in viewing women in general as far more deficient in the attributes necessary for success as a manager than men in general. A more recent study by Baack et al. (1993) also found that managers harboured more stereotypes than females. Men and women managers were given lists of general skill clusters (see Boyatziz, 1982) necessary for leader advancement to the top. It was found that men and women managers generally agreed on the skills most needed by both male and female managers for advancement. However, both male and female respondents perceived women as more emotional and less committed. It was also found that managers in general perceived males as having a significantly greater need than female managers to develop skills in enhancing customer relations.

The myths surrounding gender stereotypes and requisite managerial characteristics may disappear as more women enter managerial positions. Studies of managers and non-managers have indicated more acceptance of women as managers over time. This may be due to the occupational socialization process. Some research has shown that the 'attitudinal gap' decreases due to occupational socialization (Gomez-Mejia, 1983).

Attitudes to women managers

The results of some studies (Rosen and Jerdee, 1974; Schein, 1975) indicate that, in general, male and female managers hold similar and often negative attitudes toward women in management positions. Further, successful managers are perceived to possess those characteristics, temperaments and attitudes more commonly ascribed to men than to women. In addition, studies have been made of males and females in training groups (e.g. Jago and Vroom, 1982). Men and women were given decision-making tasks. Yet, even though women in the training groups used more appropriate decision-making methods than did males, they were evaluated less favourably by peers in their groups.

Negative attitudes toward women as managers are pervasive in the management literature. In Japan, a hostile corporate climate is seen as the major barrier to the relatively few Japanese women able to secure managerial positions. Attitudes towards managerial posts for women also vary sharply by industry, with support for women's advancement being more common from the service and retail businesses than manufacturing (Steinhoff and Tanaka, 1993). An Indian study by Gulhati (1989) also found male managers rated women negatively as managers, yet female managers perceived themselves as being as capable as men in management positions.

Exclusion from male groups

Women managers in token positions can be subjected to isolation imposed by male colleagues. It has been argued that the historical dominance of men within the public sphere and in the field of management and organizational life, has brought about a tradition of 'male' standards, assumptions and rules which alienate women. In a review of personal networks of women and minorities in management, Ibarra (1993) found that one of the most frequently reported problems experienced by both women and racial minorities is the limited access to or exclusion from informal interaction networks (Kanter, 1977; Fernandez, 1981; O'Leary and Ickovics, 1992). Exclusion from the 'old boy' network can also perpetuate male customs, traditions and negative attitudes towards women. However, there is evidence of a growing movement encouraging women to form networking groups which originated in the USA and is growing in momentum in the UK. These female networks help combat isolation and form their own social support (Davidson and Cooper, 1992).

THE IMPACT OF BARRIERS ON WOMEN MANAGERS

The research on the barriers women face compared to their male counterparts has uncovered some disturbing effects on women experiencing difficulties within organizations. Detrimental effects include occupational stress (Davidson and Cooper, 1980); discrimination (Snizek and Neil, 1992); lower salaries (Terrell, 1992); role conflict (Hennig and Jardim, 1979); blocked promotion and career development; and balancing work and home responsibilities (Davidson and Cooper, 1983; Scase and Goffee (1989). The pressures on women as managerial leaders is a cause for concern. Regardless of whether or not women managers differ from their male colleagues it is important to consider the prospect of an increasing number of women managers entering organizations. Therefore, it is important to consider the conditions and quality of working life to reduce unnecessary and avoidable pressures on women managers (Billing and Alvesson, 1989).

CONCLUSION

The research on women as managerial leaders has taken many different forms from person-centred to organization-centred. Many research studies have examined gender and leadership to highlight either differences or similarities between men and women. Yet, as critics suggest, 'each approach has tended to be labelled as heresy when viewed through the eyes of the other' (Adler, 1993, p. 9). Viewing women managers as different to men may imply they are an inferior group (Calvert and Ramsey, 1992). Recognition of difference may suggest that there is one appropriate way to manage. Alternatively, Adler (1993) suggests that to focus on similarities between men and women managers is to neglect a female manager's uniqueness in terms of contribution to the organization.

In general, the research on women managers working within organizations and as entrepreneurs over the last 20 years has shown that women are as effective as men as managerial leaders. As more women now enter managerial positions, particularly in the Western world, there is a growing consensus that current research approaches should concentrate on examining the organizational context, biases and stereotyping which presently exclude women from attaining management positions. In spite of the evidence to the contrary, women managers in the 1990s are still subjected to negative attitudes and sex-role stereotyping which hampers career development.

Findings from the research on men and women managers is that whilst it is no longer productive to look at ways women managers may differ from their male colleagues, it is important to conduct more research on the negative perceptions and attitudes which contribute to the underrecruitment of women to management positions. In order to eliminate discriminatory evaluation, future research should investigate the processes through which negative perceptions bias women as managerial leaders. More research in this area would contribute to our understanding of the problems and barriers women encounter and how these might be overcome. Furthermore, most of the research on women as managers has been conducted in the USA and the UK. Cross-cultural studies of women as leaders have been sparse as have those on minority groups such as blacks and Asians. This research is needed in order to conduct comparisons on factors such as demographics, occupational segregation and discrimination.

There have been numerous studies comparing men and women in positions of leadership. A criticism of much of the research is that the measures used have been self-report. Some critics suggest that men and women have a tendency to stereotype their personal behaviour as much as they stereotype the behaviour of others (Epstein, 1991). There has been insufficient research to study men and women managers in organizational settings. A worthwhile approach in studying women as managers would be to examine the factors required for success and effectiveness in the organizational context. This has been reiterated by Gregory (1990) who claims research 'should be both organisation- and individual-focused, with the latter taking the perspective of helping the woman manager to cope with the alien culture of the organisation' (p. 263). This view favours action-oriented research which goes beyond assessment of a situation and implements a course of action to remedy a problem, for example strategies to minimize bias in the promotion process. More emphasis is being placed on ethnographic research, in which research is conducted within the organization (e.g. Sheppard and Fothergill, 1984). This is a more holistic approach which examines the differing perspectives of men and women managers and their experience of organizational life.

REFERENCES

ADLER, N. J. (1993) Competitive frontiers: women managers in the triad', *International Studies of Management and Organisation*, Vol. 23, no. 2, pp. 3–23.

ALBAN METCALFE, B. M. and NICHOLSON, N. (1984) *The Career Development of British Managers*, British Institute of Management Foundation, London.

ALIMO-METCALFE, B. M. and WEDDERBURN-TATE, C. (1993) Women in business and management – the United Kingdom, in M. J. Davidson and C. L. Cooper (eds) *European Women in Business and Management*, Paul Chapman, London.

ALLEN, M. (1991) *The Times 1000, 1991–1992*, Times Books, London.

ANTAL, A. B. and KREBSBACH-GNATH, C. (1993) Women in management in Germany: East, West and Reunited, *International Studies of Management and Organisation*, Vol. 23, no. 2, pp. 49–69.

ARNOLD, V. and DAVIDSON, M. J. (1990) Adopt a mentor – the new way ahead for women managers? *Women in Management Review and Abstracts*, Vol. 5, no. 1, pp. 10–18.

BAACK, J., CARR-RUFFINO, N. and PELLETIER, M. (1993) Making it to the top: specific leadership skills – a comparison of male and female perceptions of skills needed by women and men managers, *Women in Management Review*, Vol. 8, no. 2, pp. 17–23.

BANDURA, A. (1977) *Social Learning Theory*, Prentice Hall, Englewood Cliffs, NJ.

BARTOL, K. M. and BUTTERFIELD, D. A. (1976) Sex effects in evaluating leaders', *Journal of Applied Psychology*, Vol. 61, pp. 446–54.

BARTOL, K. M. and WORTMAN, M. S. (1976) Sex effects in leader behaviour, self-descriptions and job satisfaction in a hospital, *Personnel Psychology*, Vol. 28, 533–47.

BASS, B. M. (ed.) (1981) *Stogdill's Handbook of Leadership: A Survey of Theory and Research*, Free Press, NY.

BASS, B. M., KRUSELL, J. and ALEXANDER, R. (1971) Male managers' attitudes towards working women, *American Behavioural Scientist*, Vol. 15, pp. 221–36.

BEM, S. L. (1975) Sex role adaptability: one consequence of psychological androgyny, *Journal of Consulting and Clinical Psychology*, Vol. 31, pp. 634–43.

BILLING, DUE Y. and ALVESSON, M. (1989) Four ways of looking at women and leadership, *Scandinavian Journal of Management*, Vol. 5, no. 1, pp. 63–80.

BLACKSTONE, T. and WEINREICH-HASTE, H. (1980) Why are there so few women scientists and engineers? *New Society*, Vol. 51, pp. 383–5.

BLANCHARD, K. H. and SARGENT, A. G. (1984) The one minute manager is an androgynous manager, *Training and Development Journal*, May, Vol. 38, no. 5, p. 85.

BOURANTAS, D. and PAPALEXANDRIS, N. (1990) Sex differences in leadership, *Journal of Managerial Psychology*, Vol. 5, no. 5, pp. 7–10.

BOYATZIZ, R. E. (1982) *The Competent Manager: A Model for Effective Performance*, John Wiley & Sons, NY.

BRENNER, O. C. (1982) Relationship of education to sex, managerial status, and the managerial stereotype, *Journal of Applied Psychology*, Vol. 67, pp. 380–8.

BRENNER, O. C., TOMKIEWICZ, J. and SCHEIN, V. E. (1989) The relationship between sex role stereotypes and requisite management characteristics, *Academy of Management Journal*, Vol. 32, pp. 662–9.

BRENNER, O. C. and VINACKE, W. E. (1979) Accommodative and exploitative behaviour of males versus females and managers versus nonmanagers as measured by the test of strategy, *Social Psychology Quarterly*, Vol. 42, no. 3, pp. 289–93.

CALVERT, L. M. and RAMSEY, V. (1992) Bringing women's voice to research on women in management: a feminist perspective, *Journal of Management Inquiry*, Vol. 1, no. 1, pp. 79–88.

CHAPMAN, T. and LUTHANS, F. (1975) The female leadership dilemma, *Public Personnel Management*, Vol. 4, pp. 173–9.

COE, T. (1992) *The Key to the Men's Club: Opening the Doors to Women in Management*. A British Institute of Management Report, BIM, London.

COX, C. and COOPER, C. L. (1988) *High Flyers*, Basil Blackwell, Oxford.

DAVIDSON, M. J. and COOPER, C. L. (1980) The extra pressures on women executives, *Personnel Management*, Vol. 12, no. 6, pp. 48–51.

DAVIDSON, M. J. and COOPER, C. L. (1983) *Stress and the Woman Manager*, Martin Robertson, London.

DAVIDSON, M. J. and COOPER, C. L. (1984) Occupational stress in female managers: a comparative study, *Journal of Management Studies*, Vol. 21, no. 2, pp. 185–205.

DAVIDSON, M. J. and COOPER, C. L. (1987) Female managers in Britain: a comparative perspective, *Human Resources Management*, Vol. 26, no. 2, pp. 217–42.
DAVIDSON, M. J. and COOPER, C. L. (1992) *Shattering the Glass Ceiling: The Woman Manager*, Paul Chapman, London.
DAY, D. R. and STOGDILL, R. M. (1972) Leader behaviour of male and female supervisors: a comparative study, *Personnel Psychology*, Vol. 25, pp. 353–60.
DONNELL, S. M. and HALL, J. (1980) Men and women as managers: a significant case of no significant difference, *Organizational Dynamics*, Spring, pp. 60–77.
EPSTEIN, C. F. (1991) Ways men and women lead, *Harvard Business Review*, Jan/Feb, pp. 150–1.
FAGENSON, E. A. and JACKSON, J. J. (1993) The status of women managers in the United States, *International Studies of Management and Organisation*, Vol. 23, no. 2, pp. 93–112.
FERNANDEZ, J. P. (1981) *Racism and Sexism in Corporate Life*, Heath, Lexington, MA.
FERNANDEZ, M. V. (1993) Women in business and management – Spain, in M. J. Davidson and C. L. Cooper (eds) *European Women in Business and Management*, Paul Chapman, London.
FERRARIO, M. (1990) Leadership styles of British men and women managers. Unpublished dissertation, University of Manchester, Institute of Science and Technology.
FERRARIO, M. and DAVIDSON, M. J. (1991) Gender and management styles: a comparative study. Paper presented at the British Academy of Management Conference, University of Bath.
FITT, L. W. and NEWTON, D. A. (1981) When the mentor is a man and the protege a woman, *Harvard Business Review*, Vol, 59, no. 2, pp. 3–4.
GOMEZ-MEJIA, L. R. (1983) Sex differences during occupational socialization, *Academy of Management Journal*, Vol. 26 (September), pp. 492–9.
GRANT, J. (1988) Women as managers: what can they offer to organizations? *Organizational Dynamics*, Winter, pp. 56–63.
GRAY, L. (1988) Women in union leadership roles, *Interface*, Vol. 17, no. 3, pp. 7–9.
GREGORY, A. (1990) Are women different and why are women thought to be different? Theoretical and methodological perspectives, *Journal of Business Ethics*, Vol. 9, pp. 257–66.
GULHATI, K. (1989) Attitudes toward women managers: a comparison of attitudes of male and female managers in India. Management research papers, Templeton College, Oxford.
HAMMOND, V. and HOLTON, V. (1993) The scenario for women managers in Britain in the 1990s, *International Studies of Management and Organisation*, Vol. 23, no. 2, pp. 71–91.
HARLAN, A. and WEISS, C. L. (1982) Sex differences in factors affecting managerial career advancement, in P. A. Wallace (ed.) *Women in the Workplace*, Auburn House, Boston, pp. 59–100.
HEILMAN, M. E., BLOCK, C. J., MARTELL, R. F. and SIMON, M. C. (1989) Has anything changed? Current characterizations of men, women, and managers, *Journal of Applied Psychology*, Vol. 74, no. 6, pp. 935–42.
HELLER, T. (1982) *Women and Men as Leaders: In Business Education and Service Organisations*, Praeger, NY.
HENNIG, M. G. and JARDIM, A. (1978) *The Managerial Woman*, Marion Boyars, London.
HERBERT, S. G. and YOST, E. B. (1979) Women as effective managers: a strategic model for overcoming the barriers, *Human Resource Management*, Vol. 7, pp. 18–25.
IBARRA, H. (1993) Personal networks of women and minorities in management: a conceptual framework, *Academy of Management Review*, Vol. 18, no. 1, pp. 56–87.
JAGO, A. G. and VROOM, V. H. (1982) Sex differences in the incidence and evaluation of participative leader behaviour, *Journal of Applied Psychology*, Vol. 67, pp. 776–83.
KALLEBERG, A. L. and LEICHT, K. T. (1991) Gender and organizational performance: determinants of small business survival and success, *Academy of Management Journal*, Vol. 34, no. 1, pp. 136–61.
KANTER, R. M. (1977) *Men and Women of the Corporation*, Basic Books, NY.
KERR, S., SCHRIESHEIM, C. A., MURPHY, C. J. and STOGDILL, R. M. (1974) Toward a contingency theory of leadership based upon the consideration and initiating structure literature, *Organisational Behaviour and Human Performance*, Vol. 12, pp. 62–82.
KORABIK, K. and AYMAN, R. (1989) Should women managers have to act like men? *Journal of Management Development*, Vol. 8, no. 6, pp. 23–31.
KORMAN, A. K. (1966) Consideration, initiating structure and organisational criteria, *Personnel Psychology*, Vol. 18, pp. 349–60.

LAM, A. C. L. (1992) *Women and Japanese Management: Discrimination and Reform*, Routledge, London and New York.

LEDWITH, S. *et al.* (1990) The making of women trade union leaders, *Industrial Relations Review and Report (London)*, 25 April, pp. 3–4.

LEVINSON, D. J. (1978) *The Seasons of a Man's Life*, Ballantine, NY.

LIRTZMAN, S. and WAHBA, M. (1972) Determinants of coalitional behaviour of men and women: sex roles or situational requirements? *Journal of Applied Psychology*, Vol. 56, pp. 406–11.

LOCKWOOD, B. and KNOWLES, W. (1984) Women at work in Great Britain, in M. J. Davidson and C. L. Cooper (eds) *Women at Work: An International Survey*, Wiley, Chichester.

LODEN, M. (1985) *Feminine Leadership or How to Succeed in Business Without Being One of the Boys*, Times Books, New York.

MCKEEN, C. A. and BURKE, R. J. (1989) Mentor relationships in organisations: issues, strategies and prospects for women, *Journal of Management Development*, Vol. 8, no. 6, pp. 33–43.

MARGERISON, C. and GLUBE, R. (1978) Leadership decision-making: an empirical test of the Vroom and Yetton model. *Journal of Management Studies*, Vol. 16, pp. 45–55.

MARSHALL, J. (1984) *Women Managers: Travellers in a Male World*, Wiley, Chichester.

MARTIN, J. and ROBERTS, C. (1984) *Women and Employment: A Lifetime Perspective*, Office of Population Consensus and Surveys, HMSO, London.

MASSENGILL, D. and DIMARCO, N. (1979) Sex-role stereotypes and requisite management characteristics: a current replication, *Sex Roles*, Vol. 5, pp. 561–70.

MATTHEWS, E. (1972) Employment implications of psychological characteristics of men and women, in M. E. Katzell and W. C. Byham (eds) *Women in the Work Force*, Behavioural Publications, NY.

MILLER, J. B. (1976) *Toward a New Psychology of Women*, Beacon Press, Boston.

NICHOLSON, N. and WEST, M. (1988) *Managerial Job Change: Men and Women in Transition*, Cambridge University Press.

O'LEARY, V. E. and ICKOVICS, J. R. (1992) Cracking the glass ceiling: overcoming isolation and alienation, in U.Sekeran and F. Leong (eds) *Womanpower: Managing in Times of Demographic Turbulence*, Sage, Beverly Hills, CA, pp. 7–30.

OSBORN, R. M. and VICARS, W. M. (1976) Sex stereotypes: an artifact in leader behaviour and subordinate satisfaction analysis, *Academy of Management Journal*, Vol. 19, pp. 439–49.

PETTY, M. M. and LEE, G. K. (1975) Moderating effects of sex of supervisor and subordinate on relationships between supervisory behaviour and subordinate satisfaction, *Journal of Applied Psychology*, Vol. 60, pp. 624–8.

PORTER, L. W. and LAWLER, E. E. (1968) *Managerial Attitudes and Performance*, Irwin, Homewood, IL.

POWELL, G. N. (1988) *Women and Men in Management*, Sage, Newbury Park, CA.

PUTNAM, L. L. (1982) In search of gender: a critique of communication and sex-roles research, *Women's Studies in Communication*, Vol. 5, pp. 1–9.

QUINN, R. E., FAERMAN, S. R., THOMPSON, M. P. and MCGRATH, M. R. (1990) *Becoming a Master Manager: A Competency Framework*, John Wiley & Sons, Toronto.

ROSEN, B. and JERDEE, T. H. (1974) Effects on applicant's sex difficulty of job on evaluations of candidates for managerial positions, *Journal of Applied Psychology*, Vol. 59, pp. 511–12.

ROSEN, B. and JERDEE, T. H. (1978) Perceived sex differences in managerially relevant characteristics, *Sex Roles*, Vol. 4, pp. 837–43.

ROSENER, J. B. (1990) Ways women lead, *Harvard Business Review*, Nov/Dec, pp. 119–25.

SCASE, R. and GOFFEE, R. (1989) *Reluctant Managers: Their Work and Life Style*, Unwin Hyman, London.

SCHEIN, V. E. (1973) The relationship between sex role stereotypes and requisite management characteristics, *Journal of Applied Psychology*, Vol. 57, pp. 95–100.

SCHEIN, V. E. (1975) The relationship between sex role stereotypes and requisite management characteristics among female managers, *Journal of Applied Psychology*, Vol. 60, pp. 340–4.

SCHRIESHEIM, C. A. and MURPHY, J. (1976) Relationships between leader behaviour and subordinate satisfaction and performance, a test of some situational moderators, *Journal of Applied Psychology*, Vol. 61, pp. 634–41.

SHEPPARD, D. and FOTHERGILL, P. (1984) Image and self-image of women in organisations. Paper presented at the Canadian Research Institute for the Advancement of Women, Montreal.

SNIZEK, W. E. and NEIL, C. C. (1992) Job characteristics, gender stereotypes and perceived gender discrimination in the workplace, *Organization Studies*, Vol. 13, no. 3, pp. 403–27.

STEINBERG, R. and SHAPIRO, S. (1982) Sex differences in personality traits of female and male master of business administration students, *Journal of Applied Psychology*, Vol. 67, pp. 306–10.

STEINHOFF, P. G. and TANAKA, K. (1993) Women managers in Japan, *International Studies of Management and Organisation*, Vol. 23, no. 2, pp. 25–48.

TERRELL, K. (1992) Female–male earnings differentials and occupational structure, *International Labour Review*, Vol. 131, no. 4, pp. 387–404.

VILKINAS, T. and CARTAN, G. (1993) Competencies of Australian women in management, *Women in Management Review*, Vol. 8, no. 3, pp. 31–5.

VROOM, V. H. and JAGO, A. G. (1978) On the validity of the Vroom–Yetton model, *Journal of Applied Psychology*, Vol. 63, pp. 151–62.

WHITE, B., COX, C. and COOPER, C. L. (1992) *Women's Career Development: A Study of High Flyers*, Blackwell, Oxford.

WOMEN'S BUREAU (1989) *The Actual Condition of Women Workers*, Printing Office, Ministry of Finance, Tokyo.

WOMEN'S INSTITUTE (1989) *Female Business Activity*, Women's Institute, Madrid.

PART THREE

Gender and Relationships at Work

CHAPTER 10

The Social Construction of Relationships among Professional Women at Work

ROBIN J. ELY

INTRODUCTION

Work relationships among women have received minimal attention from researchers interested in women and work (Gurin, 1987; O'Leary, 1988). Yet, it has been well documented that many women openly recognize the importance of other women in their lives and often find strength through their connections with women in both private (Booth, 1972; Bell, 1981; Brehm, 1985; Belle, 1987) and work spheres (Brass, 1985; Kram, 1986; McPherson and Smith-Lovin, 1987; Ibarra, 1992). In the limited, mostly popular literature that does investigate the character of women's same-sex relationships at work, there is a pervasive finding/belief that women are competitive and often work to undermine each other (Briles, 1987; Madden, 1987). At the same time, many feminists have attempted to dispel these beliefs and alternatively define the politics of gender to reflect solidarity and mutual support among women. Contradictory themes in the gender difference literature have supported both perspectives: on the other hand, portrayals of women as insecure, over-controlling, and unable to engage in 'team play' (e.g. Hennig and Jardim, 1977) have reinforced a view of women's relationships as competitive; on the other hand, more recent portrayals of women as relationship oriented, participatory, non-hierarchical, and interested in sharing power and information (e.g. Helgesen, 1990; Rosener, 1990) have reinforced a view of women's relationships as mutually supportive.

Proponents of both perspectives rely on women's sex-role socialization to explain the personality traits and behaviour patterns they attribute to women, largely ignoring the sociocultural contexts within which women work. This focus on sex-role socialization tends to overlook individual, group, and situational differences that exist among women. it also supports constraining (often negative) stereotypes about women (Ryan, 1971; Caplan and Nelson, 1973; Riger and Galligan, 1980) and their capacity to work productively with one another.

This chapter explores an alternative view of gender in organizational life in an effort to construct a more coherent, contextual understanding of relationships among professional women at work. This view emphasizes the socially constructed nature of gender and highlights the organizational processes through which gender distinctions emerge and become salient for groups or individuals (Wharton, 1992). In particular, this chapter explores how women's proportional representation in positions of power shapes the role gender plays in the work lives of professional women, and how this, in turn, influences the kinds of relationships they establish with other women at work. As such, this work explicates the link between organizational characteristics at the macro-level and individuals' organizational experiences at the micro-level.

To date, researchers interested in the effects of sex composition on women's workplace experiences have tended to focus on the dynamics of tokenism in work groups, originally documented by Kanter (1977). This work has been based on the assumption that the negative effects that accrue to individuals in underrepresented groups will be vastly reduced or eliminated once balanced representation is achieved. Little attention has been paid, however, to where in the organization's hierarchy the balances and imbalances occur. This chapter questions whether parity in the representation of professional men and women lower down in the hierarchy is, in fact, a sufficient condition for alleviating the negative effects of tokenism, or whether the real problem lies in the inadequate representation of women in positions of organizational power. In particular, whereas Kanter attributed the difficulties professional women encounter in their relationships with other women to their token status, this chapter proposes that in the absence of women at higher levels, these difficulties will persist for professional women lower down in the organization, despite balanced representation at those levels.

Central to this inquiry is the development of a framework for understanding the psychological processes through which organizational structures influence individuals. Following Wharton's (1992) lead, this chapter uses social identity theory (Turner, 1975, 1982, 1984, 1985; Tajfel, 1978, 1982; Tajfel and Turner, 1985) and its recent organizational applications (Ashforth and Mael, 1989; Kramer, 1991) to help make this link. Social identity theory offers a way to conceptualize the meaning and significance individuals attach to their identity group memberships. Of particular interest here are: (1) how the distribution of power between men and women in organizations influences the meaning and significance women attach to their gender group membership; (2) how women's assessment of their gender group influences the gender roles they enact at work; and (3) how these factors combine to influence women's workplace relationships.

Results from a study of the work lives and relationships of 30 randomly selected white women attorneys employed as associates in US law firms further illustrate and provide empirical support for the ideas advanced in this chapter.[1] Half of the participants in this study were from four firms with at least 15% women partners (that is, 'sex-integrated' firms) and half were from four firms with at least one but typically not more than 5% women partners (that is, 'male-dominated' firms). The study employed a triangulation of

---

[1] This work was conceived and executed with an explicit interest in the experiences of white professional women in predominantly white organizations. All but one woman in the sample offered that they either were, or wished to be, in a relationship with a man, suggesting that the sample was largely heterosexual. I have noted those portions of the theoretical framing and results of this study that may be especially bound by the racial and sexual identities of this particular class of women.

methods, including both quantitative and qualitative analyses of interview and questionnaire data, to compare women's experiences in the two types of firms. In all firms included in the study, women constituted between 38 and 50% of the associates. Thus, in Kanter's terms, the peer groups of all participants were 'balanced' or nearly balanced with respect to the representation of women and men.[2]

SOCIAL IDENTITY AND THE ORGANIZATION

The usefulness of social identity theory for this project lies in its attempt to capture how individuals' identity group memberships, such as their sex, shape their perspectives and experiences in different settings. Rather than assuming that distinctions based on sex are always activated and are activated in psychologically similar ways for all women, social identity theory approaches gender distinctions as socially constructed, the meaning, significance, and consequences of which vary for individuals across settings (Wharton, 1992). Central to the theory are the social psychological mechanisms by which members of various groups carve out and attach value to their group identities in relation to one another – identities which shape in significant ways not only one's self-concept, but one's relationships to others both within and outside of one's group as well.

According to this perspective, 'identity' represents 'the location of an individual in social space' (Gecas et al., 1973, p. 477). Identity has a personal component derived from idiosyncratic characteristics (such as personality, physical, and intellectual traits) and a social component derived from salient group memberships (such as sex, race, class, and nationality) (Ashforth and Mael, 1989). In addition to processes of self-categorization, the social component of identity involves the attachment of value to particular social categories (Pettigrew, 1986). As such, 'an individual's knowledge of his or her memberships in social groups together with the emotional significance of that knowledge' constitute social identity (Turner and Giles, 1981, p. 24).

Organizations are important determinants of these aspects of social identity in contemporary society (Wharton, 1992). In particular, organizational characteristics, such as levels of segregation/integration and discrimination/equity, are likely to structure members' identification with groups by shaping the relative value attached to groups. As such, organizations are powerful social systems that can deny or offer opportunities for growth and advancement to groups that are oppressed in the larger society. In this way, organizations can assist in either reinforcing or dismantling a group's oppression, with consequences for the psychological as well as economic well-being of individual group members.

Accordingly, the emotional significance to women of their gender may be shaped at least in part by the extent to which power differentials are constructed along sex lines: the degree of correlation between membership in sex and hierarchical groups may communicate to organization members that what is female is good, bad, or indifferent, and thus can reinforce perceptions of the adequacy or inadequacy of women as a group (Alderfer, 1987). As

[2] For full descriptions of this study and its results, see Ely (1990, 1993, 1994).

such, organizations where women are underrepresented in positions of power and authority may communicate to women a basic incompatibility between membership in their gender group and membership in more powerful organizational groups. Sexism, more likely evident in such work environments, may further reinforce the stigma associated with being female. Thus, the organization may reflect and sustain women's oppressed status in the larger society. Under these circumstances, women may be more likely to perceive women, and characteristics typically associated with women, as devalued. Organizations where women are more adequately represented in positions of power may be less sexist and may encourage women to redefine previously negatively valued characteristics in a more positive direction, or create new dimensions on which to assume positive distinctiveness.

As reported in Ely (1993), interview and survey data collected from women law associates supported these hypotheses. Compared to women in firms with a relatively high proportion of women partners (that is, sex-integrated firms), women in firms with a relatively low proportion of women partners, (that is, male-dominated firms) reported more experiences of sexism at work and were more likely to perceive characteristics they had ascribed to women as a liability in their firms. Interviews with these women revealed the kinds of messages they received to this effect. For example, partners communicated their values by rewarding certain behaviours. One participant described a woman colleague who was given a 'set of brass balls to put on her desk because she had become much more aggressive, the way she needed to become, in the way she negotiated for clients'. Other women looked to the (few) women partners for cues about what kinds of behaviours their firms valued. For example, another participant observed, 'The women who are going to become partners here, who are going to be important partners here, are going to be women who act pretty much like men.' Another described the more successful women in her firm as women 'whose femaleness is not noticed all the time' and who are 'modelling more on men'.

These perspectives lie in sharp contrast to those offered by women in sex-integrated firms. As expected, these women perceived less sexism in their work environments and rated characteristics they had ascribed to women as more compatible with success in their firms. Many linked this perception to the presence of a significant number of women in their partnerships. For example, one woman recalled the year when her firm promoted several women into the partnership as a 'kind of turning point'. She no longer felt there was 'some sort of quota', and described a subsequent 'relaxation' among women associates, 'one less thing to worry about' as they anticipated their reviews for entry into the partnership. Similarly, another explained that 'because of [the women partners'] success, we're perceived as having the ability to be successful'. For these associates, as for many women from the more sex-integrated firms, the entry of women into the partnership indicated the very real possibility that they too could become partners, and that neither their sex nor their gender, per se, would pose a barrier. Indeed, as expected, women in these firms were more likely than their counterparts in male-dominated firms to describe both stereotypically masculine characteristics, such as aggressiveness, and stereotypically feminine characteristics, such as sensitivity, as valued by their firms.

These findings suggest that organizations with relatively few women in positions of power are experienced as less hospitable to women and less accepting of attitudes, values, and behaviours typically associated with women. These organizations are likely to foster in women a set of adaptive strategies, explored in the next section, which may, in turn, interfere in the development of constructive work relationships.

INDIVIDUAL RESPONSES TO GROUP DEVALUATION

According to Tajfel (1978), members of devalued groups engage in a range of strategies designed to reverse the negative perceptions of their group or of themselves as members of their group. The starker the reality of disparities between groups, the greater the need for members of the low-status group to achieve positive distinction relative to other group members or to dissociate from the group altogether. Again, organizations may play an important role in determining both the particular strategy an individual chooses to employ and its effectiveness. In organizations where there appear to be few opportunities for women to advance, professional women striving to succeed may engage, either consciously or unconsciously, in strategies designed to differentiate themselves from women as a group and identify instead with men (Kanter, 1977). Attempts to differentiate stem from the fear of becoming too identified with women – a fear of being inextricably linked to the fate of women as a group. Such attempts are often predicated on a woman's conscious or unconscious belief in women's 'inferiority' relative to men. The extent to which a woman internalizes such beliefs is the extent to which 'internalized sexism' shapes her gender identity.

Male colleagues become the reference group for professional women adopting this orientation. Accordingly, women's strategies for enhancing their own position relative to other women in the organization involve compliance with gender roles defined in deference to men's preferences, thereby reinforcing men's dominant position. Two such roles include the seductress/sex object role and the masculine role.

Women cast in the seductress/sex object role rely on sexual attractiveness and flirtation as a way of gaining acceptance in the eyes of their more powerful male colleagues. As MacKinnon (1979, p. 174) has argued, the economic realities of women's lives, resulting from women's generally inferior position in the workplace, may place demands on them to 'market sexual attractiveness to men, who tend to hold the economic power and position to enforce their predilections'. Indeed, Gutek (1985) has shown that sexuality tends to be more prominent and more problematic for women in work settings where men are numerically dominant. In these settings, private sphere relations between men and women, defined in sexual terms, are more likely to 'spill over' into relationships at work. Similarly, Kanter (1977) has described the role of the seductress/sex object as one of the few available to token women for whom opportunities to advance are limited. Both Gutek and Kanter have suggested that women's sexuality will become less salient as the number of professional women in organizations increases. The argument advanced here proposes that until their numbers increase in *senior* positions, this role will persist as a strategy for women seeking to advance.[3]

An alternative strategy for women is to enact a masculine role, adopting values and behaviours traditionally associated with men. This assimilationist strategy has been well documented in the popular and scholarly literatures (Kanter, 1977; Gutek, 1985; Briles, 1987; Coppolino and Seath, 1987). Again, both Gutek (1985) and Kanter (1977) link this strategy to pressures women experience in work environments where men are numerically dominant. According to Gutek, a high percentage of one sex in a job category leads to the expectation that people in that job should behave in a manner consistent with the gender role of the numerically dominant sex. Aspects of the gender role for the numerically dominant sex spill over into the work role. Thus, people in men's jobs are often expected to 'act like men' to be perceived as good workers. Kanter has argued similarly that in these circumstances token women aspiring to advance to more powerful positions may act like men in an effort to gain acceptance by the gate-keepers of those positions. Again, the argument advanced in this chapter is that, despite balanced representation among professional men and women lower down in the organization, women will continue to enact this role in organizations where stark imbalances exist in positions of power.[4]

Gender identity may be less problematic for women in organizations that appear not to restrict women's access to senior positions. Because women in these organizations are less likely to experience their gender as a barrier to promotion, they may feel less constrained by traditional gender role prescriptions and perceive a wider range of behaviours as acceptable within their work roles.

Evidence reported in Ely (1993, 1994) showed, as expected, that women in male-dominated firms were more likely to comply with gender roles defined on what they perceived to be men's terms. Compared to women in sex-integrated firms, these women were more likely to report sexual behaviour, such as flirtation, as a strategy in which women engaged in order to advance in their organizations. One woman explained:

> Some of the guys – especially the ones that got there because they have this lust for power – love it when women flirt with them. Part of the accoutrement of the power is having women love you. And if you don't act like you really love them, I think you suffer. . . . You're not in that little group, and that can work against you.

[3] Work by Hurtado (1989) suggests that this strategy may be more available to white women than to women of colour, due to differences in the relational positions of these groups to the source of power and privilege in predominantly white organizations, white men. Whereas white women's subordination is achieved by white men's seduction, she argues, the subordination of women of colour is achieved by white men's rejection. Thus, 'the avenues of advancement . . . that are open to white women who conform to prescribed standards of middle-class femininity are not even a theoretical possibility for most women of color' (Hurtado, 1989, p. 843). Lesbian women, who may find men's sexual attention less engaging than heterosexual women, may also be less likely to employ this stratety.

[4] The research cited here documents the use of this strategy by white women; it is unclear how racial or sexual identity may affect the viability of this strategy for other groups of women.

Although none of the women interviewed for this study described themselves as relying on this strategy to advance, women in male-dominated firms provided numerous such accounts of other women. For example, women partners were described variously as 'very flirtatious', 'pandering to men', and having 'brown-nosed' the partners 'by using disgustingly typically feminine wiles'. In addition, more women in these firms reported rumours of woman partners having had affairs with powerful men. None the less, most agreed that women were ultimately likely to be the losers if they were to go too far beyond flirtation. As one participant explained, 'You have to be a good sport, but the Virgin Mary too.'

Even more common were accounts by women in male-dominated firms of how they had learned to conform to a more 'masculine' or 'male' image in order to succeed in their firms. As one woman explained, she found it necessary to approach her work 'in sort of a male mould. . . . I can't really rely on or develop those attributes that are considered sort of feminine. . . . Those attributes just don't mesh well [here].'

Again, as with the more sexualized approach, taking this strategy too far was also likely to fail. One participant explained:

> There's nothing men hate more – especially men in power – than a woman is [too much] like a man. It's a very negative thing. There was a very well-qualified woman who was interviewing at our firm for a position. She had years of experience in the exact practice area that we were recruiting for, but when she showed up on the doorstep . . . people hated her. Men and women alike said, 'She's too mannish.' She had this very deep voice, she was very asexual in her dress, and she didn't get the job.

Some women in male-dominated firms were able to forge neither a sexualized nor a masculinized gender identity at work. For most of these women, gender identity was simply problematic and often a source of either low self-esteem, job dissatisfaction, or both. As one such participant explained:

> What I always have trouble with in my own case is: Am I different because I'm a woman? And I think in my own case . . . the answer [is] not that they are really discriminating against me because I'm a woman, but because I'm a woman, I just really don't have the qualities that lead to success in that firm. I'm very unaggressive. I hate controversy. I like to please – I very much would like to please. And I hate litigation. I hate conflict. I really don't thrive in that kind of situation, and I also don't thrive on pressure. And that's something that [I've been criticized for] in my formal evaluation. I think that's partly because of my socialization.

Whether women complied with a sexualized or a masculinized image of female gender in their efforts to advance, or whether they simply resigned themselves to failure, women's struggles with their gender identity in these firms were shaped in large measure by the devaluation of women in systems where male preferences prevailed.

By contrast, women in sex-integrated firms drew on both traditionally masculine, as well as traditionally feminine images when describing themselves. Moreover, these women portrayed their femininity in positive, rather than negative, terms, and were more likely to report that they felt free to express their individuality at work (Ely, 1993). One representative woman, who emphasized her more 'masculine' qualities of 'aggressiveness' and 'forthrightness', also commented that 'the times when I'm most successful are when I am most feminine', referring to her capacity to relate empathically to clients. Another woman felt she was 'in with a group of people who appreciate the qualities that I think of as feminine', for example, her capacity to be 'creative in different ways'. A third described initially having had a difficult time developing a personal relationship with the men in the partnership, but noted learning more recently that 'part of it is bringing your own personality in. I don't think you can just leave your personality at home and try to fit into the sort of grey-bearded stereotype. I'm not going to grow a grey beard.'

These comments suggest that gender identity for these women was less problematic than for women associates in the male-dominated firms. Able to view themselves as viable candidates for partnership without particular attention to gender role prescriptions, women from sex-integrated firms were concerned with traditional conceptions of appropriate gender behaviour at work, and more capable of exhibiting a range of characteristics within their work role.

Organizational structures that reinforce women's inferior status encourage women to enact gender roles that, ironically, serve to reinforce men's dominance. Though these strategies may lead to success for a few, women's warnings against being too sexual or too mannish attest to the ambiguity of these roles and the difficulty women are likely to encounter as they negotiate the fine line between successful and unsuccessful enactment of them. Moreover, to the extent that women internalize the organization's message that women are less worthy than men, these roles can come to represent disdain for oneself and for one's group. As explored in the next section, efforts to build supportive alliances with other women under these conditions are unlikely.

IMPLICATIONS FOR WOMEN'S WORK RELATIONSHIPS

Subtly and not-so-subtly enforced reliance on men's definitions of acceptable gender role behaviour, together with a structured dependency on men's evaluations for advancement, reinforce for women that '[i]nteraction with women is . . . a lesser form of relating on every level' (Barry, 1979, p. 18). In this vein, Lipman-Bluman has argued that women's historical dependence on powerful men makes it more difficult for women to turn to each other for support:

> The pragmatic recognition that males controlled economic, political, educational, occupational, legal, and social resources created a situation in which men identified with and sought help from other men. Women, recognizing the existential validity of the situation, also turned to men for help and protection. By now, it is practically a psychological truism that individuals identify with other individuals whom they perceive to be the controllers of resources in any given situation. . . . This uneven array of resources systematically made men more interesting to women, women less interesting and useful to other women, and women fairly often unnecessary and/or burdensome to men. The disparity of resources made it apparent that men were the most valued social beings.
>
> (*Lipman-Bluman, 1976, pp. 17–18*)

Kanter (1977) has suggested that women may perceive links to other women as not only less useful, but actually detrimental, to their careers. If women seeking to advance in the organization perceive their gender as a barrier to upward mobility, their subsequent efforts to create psychological distance between themselves and women as a group are likely to translate into more distant interpersonal relationships as well. Kanter reported that men often initiated and reinforced this tendency by setting up invidious comparisons between women, where one was characterized as superior, and the other as inferior – exaggerating traits in both cases. The 'successful' woman, relieved to be so judged, was reluctant then to enter an alliance with the identified failure for fear of jeopardizing her own acceptance. Instead, she had an interest in maintaining the distance by reinforcing the perceived differences in their capabilities (for example, by comparing herself favourably to the other in front of her senior colleagues). Although Kanter predicted that with larger numbers of women supportive alliances would be more likely to develop based on emotionally positive experiences of identification, the perspective advanced here suggests that this outcome may be further contingent on the degree to which women are represented in positions of organizational power.

It follows that under conditions where resources and opportunities are perceived to be scarce for women, relationships between women may also be more competitive. Indeed, Keller and Moglen (1987) have suggested that women often tend to compare themselves with one another, rather than with men, in their assessments of whether and how they will make it to the top. A perception that only one or two women will succeed may promote rivalries among women, pitting them specifically against one another. By contrast, if women in firms with higher proportions of senior women experience their working environment as less hostile and their gender group membership as a less salient criterion for evaluation and comparison, it may be easier for them to identify with women peers as sources of support, rather than as competitors for limited resources.

Consistent with these hypotheses, women law associates in male-dominated firms encountered more problems with and were more critical of their women peers compared to women in sex-integrated firms (Ely, 1994). In particular, these women characterized fewer of their relationships with women peers as supportive and more of these relationships as competitive in ways that impeded their ability to work together.

When describing the competitiveness they experienced in relation to other women, women in male-dominated firms often focused on feelings of envy or jealousy. The following excerpts provide examples of this from three women:

> It's very complicated because some of it is very rational and you can identify what you have to do to get certain places, and some of it is just green-eyed monster stuff. Sometimes I just feel envious of her political connections, and I do these irrational things like wishing I could do everything she can do.

> With women, it's like being jealous over a man . . . [whereas] I feel that if I'm being competitive with a man, it's just good clean fun. I really want to kick his ass. I just don't feel that kind of malicious aspect to it that I do with [a woman].

> [Competition with women has] more of a personal element [compared to men]. I'm jealous of her looks. . . . And she's very self-confident and I'm jealous about that also.

Another participant from a male-dominated firm offered the following description of competitiveness in one of her relationships with a woman associate who was slightly senior to her:

It both helps and hurts. It cuts both ways. It helps because I think it makes her feel protective of me against the outside world. It becomes a sort of sisterly or familial relationship. The way it hurts is both of us say things to each other that we would never say to other lawyers in a similar situation. . . . There are just things that make the atmosphere tense. On the one hand, she uses me for ideas and she cultivates my thinking on my own. But then, when she wants to be the boss [because she has had more years of experience], she just wants me to turn it off. . . . And it's terrible. You feel like all of a sudden your dignity has been taken away from you. And that's a problem. She just doesn't like to give up that little power. And then I've hurt her feelings several times, too, because she's very sensitive about the fact that I'm bright and I'm her friend. She seems threatened by my intelligence or by the fact that I might be competent too.

According to this account, in order for each woman to express her competence, the other was required to give up a piece of herself: 'dignity' on the part of the participant, 'power' on the part of her colleague.

This account, like those above, suggests that women in male-dominated firms had difficulty perceiving their work accomplishments and competencies as independent of one another. In each, one's strengths, for example political connections, self-confidence, dignity or power, fostered in the other feelings of inadequacy or insecurity, or, at the very least, a sense that there could be only one winner – as in a competition 'over a man'. Indeed, in male-dominated firms, this construction of competition as zero-sum was a consistent theme in women's more troubled accounts of competition.

Other accounts women gave in their interviews show how perceptions of limited access to senior positions may have fostered these kinds of competitive experiences. For example, one woman made the following observation:

It's a divide and conquer strategy on the part of men. . . . I can see it starting to happen in terms of the women who are thinking about how the men perceive them vis-à-vis the other women, and thinking that we can't all quite make it – that being a woman is going to be a factor in their decision, so what kind of woman do they want? It's very subtle. . . . And I'm very concerned about that because I think that means we're going to modify our own self-concepts and the way we treat each other. I'm not so sure that isn't going to be somewhat painful.

Two other participants described this dynamic in action. They had observed women being especially critical of other women, and questioned whether this was a strategy they might be using to gain a comparative advantage:

She does little things to me that I think are not fair. She will jokingly sort of disparage me in front of the partner. . . . And she's laughing the whole time and I don't know if she's trying to sabotage me, or if she really doesn't know [what she's doing].

Some people say she destroys people whom she sees as a threat to her. . . . She's done things that subtly may be undermining so that [another woman and I] are less of a threat. [For example,] she has characterized [a woman peer] to the partners as 'fru-fru' – too feminine, too emotional, organized but maybe not the highest calibre brain. . . . A little bit like she is too flirty.

Other women's accounts suggested that senior men sometimes fuel women's competitive feelings by drawing comparisons between them. Indeed, women in male-dominated firms reported more situations in which the behaviour of powerful men exacerbated tension in their relationships with other women (Ely, 1990) For example when relating a particularly painful experience of competitiveness, one woman described an event where a male partner compared her disfavourably to her female colleague in public. 'He played us off one another,' she explained.

Similarly positioning a senior male in her account of a competitive relationship, another participant from a male-dominated firm described 'a rivalry' between a woman colleague and herself, generated by their shared dependence on a male partner for whom they were both working. She criticized her co-worker as a woman who 'exudes a lot of sexuality' and resented the attention she received from this partner and others when she flirted with them:

> That's one of the reasons I initially started to dislike her. With all the men, she's constantly fixing their ties and stuff, which I resent. And it's funny, because they don't seem to brush her away. They sort of seem to strut a little bit, puff up a little bit, like they like the attention. . . . I know that I won't benefit from that at all, because I can't do that.

The repeated references to sexuality in these excerpts – the comparison drawn above between competition with women and 'being jealous over a man', the competitiveness generated from jealousy over another woman's looks, and the criticisms that other women associates are 'too flirty' or too sexual – suggest the variety of ways in which issues of sexuality were a source of disturbance in peer relationships among women in male-dominated firms. Indeed, results showed that, compared to women in sex-integrated firms, these women were more critical of their peers for inappropriately expressing sexuality at work and, more generally, for the image of women they portayed (Ely, 1994).

By contrast, women in sex-integrated firms were more likely to characterize relationships with women peers as supportive and less likely to experience distress in these relationships as a result of competitive feelings. They were also less critical of their women peers.

A story one participant told exemplifies the way competition and support were expressed in these relationships. She and her friend were both eligible for early promotion to the same partnership slot. The participant was not chosen. The competitive feelings that ensued were channelled productively, however, into a win–win resolution. While this woman felt hurt at not being chosen and described feelings of competitiveness with her colleague, she was able to compare their strengths and weaknesses, and the differences between them in the kinds of work they each preferred to do. On this basis, she was able to recognize, or at least rationalize, the decision as a just one. After her colleague was promoted, they worked together to gain an understanding of why the interviewee had not been chosen to fill the position. As a partner, her colleague was now privy to information that could help the interviewee understand and reverse the perceptions that had kept her from receiving the partnership offer. By sharing this information, her colleague made the interviewee's future candidacy for partnership much more viable.

In this incident, these women recognized the structural realities of competitiveness in their relationship with each other. Moreover, they seemed able to use this understanding to turn a potentially threatening situation with another woman, where a zero-sum orientation might have been dysfunctional both for the relationship and for the work, into shared gain through mutual support, that is, positive-sum outcomes.

These findings suggest that underlying women's different experiences with competition may be differences in the meaning women attribute to their gender identity. If being female provides a basis for shared understanding with other women, without necessarily representing a threat to women's well-being, then gender identity can provide the capacity for empathy and support among group members in much the way women in sex-integrated firms found support through their connections with women peers. If, however, being female signals a threat to one's well-being, then the fear of one's fate as inextricably linked to that of other women precludes the development of such relationships. Clinical research suggests that under these circumstances, a woman may lose a sense of herself as a fully separate entity (Lindenbaum, 1987), that is, she may become 'over-identified' with other women. This situation ironically may call for excessive efforts to differentiate from the other in an attempt to establish oneself as separate. This may explain a woman's dual tendency in male-dominated firms to construct the other's strength as evidence of her own weakness and, at the same time, to defend against this construction by denigrating the other to enhance herself. According to Lindenbaum (1987), excessive differentiation in the over-identified pair presents serious problems for the relationship:

> When the internal representation of one's self is merged with the [other] . . . the experience of 'felt difference' evokes a deep sense of abandonment and, depending on the pathological extent of the merger, a perceived loss of self. . . . Envy, a destructive affect, emerges to defend against this loss. It is a desperate attempt to eradicate the separateness, the experience of 'felt difference', by spoiling what the other has, or by taking it back for one's self. Aspects of this experience can be so toxic that they often remain unconscious.
>
> (Lindenbaum, 1987, p. 200)

Thus, envy is the emotion that emerges at the point of differentiation in the over-identified pair. In male-dominated firms, it was competition fuelled by envy that created problems.

By contrast, women in sex-integrated firms seemed able to use gender identity as a source of connection and support in their peer relationships. As such, competition was a more constructive experience for women in these firms. According to Lindenbaum (1987, p. 203), this form of competition 'requires two people, each of whom has a sufficiently separate identity to risk measuring her self against the separate identity of the other'. In these circumstances, competition is expressed

> as a kind of relatedness in which two women who are separate selves motivate each other toward some heightened capacity without fearing damage to one's

self, the other, or the relationship. The partners are separate and connected in a competitive process. The process itself can encourage a separateness that is relational rather than reactive, a sense both of the ongoing presence of an other and of a self that is separate and whole.

(Lindenbaum, 1987, p. 207)

CONCLUSION

The theory and research presented in this chapter provide an alternative to the contradictory accounts of women's relationships supported by different theories of women's sex-role socialization. By considering the differentiated representation of women across levels of the organization's hierarchy, this work moves beyond the literature on tokenism and highlights the distribution of power within organizations as an important influence on the social construction of women's relationships. In particular, the degree to which men and women are perceived to share equally in, or have equal access to, positions of power may influence the relative value professional women attach to their gender at work. This in turn shapes the gender roles women enact and helps to structure the nature of their relationships.

In male-dominated firms, where promotions have been reserved largely for men, women may perceive their gender group membership as less valued. In their efforts to advance, women are encouraged to enact gender roles that comport with men's preferences, thereby reinforcing men's dominance. By limiting the range of acceptable behaviour for women to a narrow, ambiguously defined, and potentially demeaning set of gender roles, organizations make it difficult for women to find positive bases for identifying with each other. Instead, women's inadequacies become focal. This further reinforces women's inferior status, leading them to become hypercritical of one another and to compete all the more defensively for a comparative advantage over other women.

In sex-integrated firms, where promotion appears less tied to either sex or gender, women may define their gender in more positive terms, feel less restricted to particular gender roles, and find gender to be a positive source of identification with other women. Women in these firms are better able to manage their competitive feelings in productive ways and to build relationships of support. These kinds of relationships are more likely to grow out of conditions that allow women to compete legitimately with one another for promotion – conditions structured in part by women's greater representation at senior levels.

Until organizations change the negative messages they send about women's relative worth, or until women recognize the pitfalls of their organizations and resist the often unconscious and subtle ways they internalize such messages, women's relationships with one another are bound to be problematic. Common expectations among women that they should support one another, and their disappointment when they do not, often lead women to criticize their women colleagues and to feel bad about themselves. Women must recognize that to develop these connections with women in organizations that remain hostile to women, they must first reckon with the male-dominated structures within which they work and make more conscious, deliberate, and informed choices about who they are.

REFERENCES

ALDERFER, C. P. (1987) An intergroup perspective on group dynamics, in J. Lorsch (ed.) *Handbook of Organizational Behavior*, Prentice-Hall, Englewood Cliffs, NJ.

ASHFORTH, B. E. and MAEL, F. (1989) Social identity theory and the organization, *Academy of Management Review*, Vol. 14, pp. 20–39.

BARRY, K. (1979) *Female Sexual Slavery*, Prentice-Hall, Englewood Cliffs, NJ.

BELL, R. (1981) Friendships of women and men, *Psychology of Women Quarterly*, Vol. 5, pp. 402–17.

BELLE, D. (1987) Gender differences in the social moderators of stress, in R. Barnett, L. Biener and G. Baruch (eds) *Gender and Stress*, Free Press, New York.

BOOTH, T. (1972) Sex and social participation, *American Sociological Review*, Vol. 37, pp. 183–92.

BRASS, D. J. (1985) Men's and women's networks: a study of interaction patterns and influence in an organization, *Academy of Management Journal*, Vol. 28, pp. 327–43.

BREHM, S. (1985) *Intimate Relationships*, Random House, New York.

BRILES, J. (1987) *Woman to Woman: From Sabotage to Support*, New Horizon Press, Far Hills, New Jersey.

CAPLAN, N. and NELSON, S. (1973) On being useful: the nature and consequences of psychological research on social problems, *American Psychologist*, Vol. 28. pp. 199–211.

COPPOLINO, Y. and SEATH, C. B. (1987) Women managers: fitting the mould or moulding the fit, *Equal Opportunities International*, Vol. 6, no. 3, pp. 4–10.

ELY, R. J. (1990) The role of men in relationships among professional women at work, *Best Papers Proceedings*, Academy of Management.

ELY, R. J. (1993) The power in demography: Women's social constructions of gender identity at work. Working Paper Series, John F. Kennedy School of Government, Cambridge, Mass.

ELY, R. J. (1994) Organizational demographics and the dynamics of relationships among professional women, *Administrative Science Quarterly*, forthcoming.

GECAS, V., THOMAS, D. L. and WEIGERT, A. J. (1973) Social identities in Anglo and Latin adolescents, *Social Forces*, Vol. 51, pp. 477–84.

GURIN, P. (1987) The political implications of women's status, in F. J. Crosby (ed.) *Spouse, Parent, Worker*, Yale University Press, New Haven.

GUTEK, B. A. (1985) *Sex and the Workplace*, Jossey-Bass, San Francisco.

HELGESEN, S. (1990) *The Female Advantage: Women's Ways of Leadership*, Doubleday, New York.

HENNIG, M. and JARDIM, A. (1977) *The Managerial Woman*, Pocket Books, New York.

HURTADO, A. (1989) Relating to privilege: seduction and rejection in the subordination of white women and women of color, *Signs: Journal of Women in Culture and Society*, Vol. 14, no. 4, pp. 833–55.

IBARRA, H. (1992) Homophily and differential returns: sex differences in network structure and access in an advertising firm, *Administrative Science Quarterly*, Vol. 37, pp. 422–47.

KANTER, R. M. (1977) *Men and Women of the Corporation*, Basic Books, New York.

KELLER, E. F. and MOGLEN, H. (1987) Competition: a problem for academic women, in V. Miner and H. E. Longino (eds) *Competition: A Feminist Taboo?* The Feminist Press, New York.

KRAM, K. E. (1986) *Mentoring at Work: Developmental Relationships in Organizational Life*, Scott, Foresman, Glenview, IL.

KRAMER, R. M. (1991) Intergroup relations and organization dilemmas: the role of categorization processes, *Research in Organizational Behavior*, Vol. 13, pp. 191–228.

LINDENBAUM, J. P. (1987) The shattering of an illusion: the problem of competition in lesbian relationships, in V. Miner and H. E. Longino (eds) *Competition: A Feminist Taboo?* The Feminist Press, New York.

LIPMAN-BLUMAN, J. (1976) Toward a homosocial theory of sex roles: an explanation of the sex segregation of social interaction, in M. Blaxall and B. Reagon (eds) *Women and the Workplace*, University of Chicago Press.

MACKINNON, K. (1979) *Sexual Harassment of Working Women*, Yale University Press, New Haven.

MADDEN, T. R. (1987) *Women Versus Women: The Uncivil Business War*, AMACOM, New York.

MCPHERSON, J. M. and SMITH-LOVIN, L. (1987) Homophily in voluntary organizations: status distance and the composition of face-to-face groups, *American Sociological Review*, Vol. 54, pp. 365–81.

O'LEARY, V. E. (1988) Women's relationships with women in the workplace, in B. Gutek, A. H. Stromberg and L. Larwood (eds) *Women and Work: An Annual Review*, Vol. 3, Sage, Newbury Park, CA.

PETTIGREW, T. F. (1986) The intergroup contact hypothesis reconsidered, in M. Hewstone and R. Brown (eds) *Contact and Conflict in Intergroup Encounters*, Basil Blackwell, New York.

RIGER, S. and GALLIGAN, P. (1980) Women in management: an exploration of competing paradigms, *American Psychologist*, Vol. 35, pp. 902–10.

ROSENER, J. (1990) Ways women lead, *Harvard Business Review*, November–December, pp. 119–25.

RYAN, W. (1971) *Blaming the Victim*, Vintage Books, New York.

TAJFEL, H. (1978) Socialization categorization, social identity and social comparison, in H. Tajfel (ed.) *Differentiation between Social Groups*, Academic Press, New York.

TAJFEL, H. (1982) *Social Identity and Intergroup Relations*, Cambridge University Press.

TAJFEL, H. and TURNER, J. C. (1985) The social identity theory of intergroup behavior, in S. Worchel and W. G. Austin (eds) *Psychology of Intergroup Relations*, Nelson-Hall, Chicago.

TURNER, J. C. (1975) Social comparison and social identity: some prospects for intergroup behaviour, *European Journal of Social Psychology*, Vol. 5, pp. 5–34.

TURNER, J. C. (1982) Towards a cognitive redefinition of the social group, in H. Tajfel (ed.) *op. cit.*

TURNER, J. C. (1984) Social identification and psychological group formation, in H. Tajfel (ed.) *The Social Dimension: European Developments in Social Psychology*, Vol. 2, pp. 518–38.

TURNER, J. C. (1985) Social categorization and the self-concept: a social cognitive theory of group behavior, in E. J. Lawler (ed.) *Advances in Group Processes*, Vol. 2, JAI Press, Greenwich, Connecticut.

TURNER, J. C. and GILES, H. (1981) *Intergroup Behavior*, Basil Blackwell, New York.

WHARTON, A. S. (1992) The social construction of gender and race in organizations: a social identity and group mobilization perspective, *Research in the Sociology of Organizations*, Vol. 10, pp. 55–84.

CHAPTER 11

Gender Differences in Communication and Behaviour in Organizations

SUSAN SCHICK CASE

INTRODUCTION

In 1984 when completing my first large research study on gender and language, I had a conversation with my nine-year-old daughter, Stephanie, about science and what scientists do. I wanted her to know that science was more than the earth science and simple natural biology she was being exposed to at school. So I began telling her about my research on language. I told her that as a scientist, I was trying to find out if men and women talked the same way.

She immediately said, 'Of course they don't, because they are different.' I proceeded to tell her that the results of my study (Case, 1985) showed that they, indeed, had different ways of talking. Then she asked me, 'Do girls and boys talk differently?' Instead of answering, I asked her what she thought. Without hesitation, she said, 'They do,' and gave an example. 'Girls would say, "Boys are kind of bad." ' I asked her if they'd always say it that way. She responded: 'No, they might also say, "Boys are sort of bad." But boys wouldn't talk that way. Boys would say, "Boys are bad!" When they talk, they talk strong.'

I found her answer intriguing and asked why girls would say 'kind of' and 'sort of'. Her reply was: 'It's fairer, Mom. Boys aren't bad all the time. So since they are bad only sometimes, "sort of" and "kind of" is fairer in telling the truth. Boys though seem to talk in strong ways.' Although at the time I had spent three years on this topic, my daughter captured the essence of an important difference in both her example and explanation.

This chapter explores systematic differences in the way men and women use language in their interactions in organizations and how this communication reflects and expresses cultural views of gender. As we will see, language plays critical roles in creating and perpetuating gendered identities and social patterns in interaction. Since the early 1970s, scholars have studied speech communities. In these communities people share understandings about goals of communication, strategies for enacting these goals, and ways of interpreting communication (Labov, 1972).

When travelling from an English-speaking to a non-English-speaking culture it is easy to know you are entering a different communication culture because the language used differs from the language that you use. It is less apparent, though, when people use the same language, but in different ways to achieve different goals. Harvard psychologist Carol Gilligan (1982) recognized this problem, saying that 'men and women may speak different languages that they assume are the same . . . creating misunderstandings which impede communication and limit the potential for cooperation and care in relationships' (p. 173). Studies of gender and communication (Kramarae', 1981; Case, 1988, 1990, 1993a, 1993b; Coates, 1989; Coates and Cameron, 1989; Tannen, 1990) have convincingly shown that men and women embody two distinct speech communities operating from very dissimilar assumptions about the goals and strategies of communication.

Much managerial behaviour occurs through linguistic activity. Kanter (1977) found that managers spent anywhere from one-third to one-half of their work day consumed by meetings with other organizational members, not including 'time with secretaries, on the telephone, or in routine communication around the office' (p. 56). Inclusion of telephone calls accounted for another 20% of the manager's day. Kanter's review of related research suggested that from 50% to 93% of a manager's total time was spent in social intercourse. Yet organizational analysis of behaviour has paid almost no attention to how people actually speak (Mintzberg, 1973; Gronn, 1983; Levine *et al.*, 1984). Since the language people use and the associations they make reveal how they see and interact with their world, the experiences of women, and their increasing presence in the workforce, mandate understanding their cultural perspective, respecting their differences where they exist, and seeing the value in this different voice (Case, 1993b).

Over the years I have sat in meetings and been continuously struck by how differently men and women describe and frame problems. As I thought more about it, it is not surprising that there are different perceptions, beliefs, behaviours, and ways of describing experience because as men and women, they have had different experiences growing up. I have also been aware of the organizational invisibility of many women and their words. It is a common practice in meetings for a woman manager's words to be 'ignored' only to be taken up by men, minutes later, and accorded approval.

Understanding gender differences in the language typically used by men and women in organizations is a way to understand better the enactment of relationships between them when they work together. Since language is a verbal indicator of the social structure of society, it is the way we convey thoughts to each other about how we see the world, and reflects our attitudes towards each other. Differences in managerial talk occur partly as a function of differing socialization experiences of men and women (Case, 1988, 1990, 1993a), and partly as a function of differing equations of power held by each (Case, 1993b). Communication is not just a way to transmit organizational information, it is also an important means of establishing and maintaining relationships with other people.

In this chapter we explore how men and women typically communicate. Before we look at general differences in this area, it is important to point out the enormous diversity in style and practices within each gender group. Most women and men have at their disposal a variety of conversational and speech skills, any of which they may draw upon, depending on the situation, their purposes, the roles they are playing, and the context. All the generalizations about patterns of behaviour that we will be making should not replace our own awareness of the basic variability in language among women and among men. Nevertheless, there are some important gender patterns. It is these generalizable differences about gendered speech communities that are discussed.

Maltz and Borker (1982) state that men and women 'come from different sociolinguistic subcultures, having learned to do different things with words in a conversation, so that when they attempt to carry on conversations with one another, even if both parties are attempting to treat one another as equals, cultural miscommunication results' (p. 200). Because men and women tend to be socialized into distinct speech communities, they learn different rules about the purposes of communication and the ways to indicate support, interest, and involvement. Because women and men have dissimilar rules for talk, they often misread each others' meanings and misunderstand each others' motives. This leads to frustration and tension between people. Understanding each style is a foundation for better understanding between people in organizations. Learning to use aspects of different styles allows people to be more flexible and effective in their interactions.

In order to understand gender differences in communication, it is helpful to explore how gendered speech communities are created through childhood socialization practices. It is through peer interactions that children learn both to talk and to interpret each others' communication. They learn how to make intentions known with words, and how to respond to others' words. They learn codes to show interest and codes for involvement with others (Tannen, 1990). It is through continual interacting with one another that the rules of communication are learned.

In a classic study by Maltz and Borker (1982), insight into the importance of children's play in shaping patterns of communication was first supported. They noticed that children almost always play in sex-segregated groups, and that they tend to play different types of games. Girls play games like house and school, whereas boys play games like football and baseball. It is in these sex-segregated peer group games that distinct understandings of communication and the rules by which it operates are formed. During this period 'members of each sex are training, self-consciously to differentiate their behaviour from that of the other sex and to exaggerate that difference' (p. 203). Men and women thus acquire different rules for communication that impact their behaviours in organizations.

GIRLS' GAMES

Girls tend to play their games in very small groups or in pairs. Their favourite games, like house and school, do not have clear-cut goals, rules or roles. Unlike a triple play in baseball, there is no triple play in playing house. Girls have to talk to each other to decide what they are doing in their game and what roles each person will take. There is no external structure to guide the play. In order to play school, girls have to discuss first who will be the teacher and who will be the student. Through this discussion girls develop the rules and roles for their games. What is important in girls' games is the process of interaction, since there are no external goals. If the game is to work, girls have to work out their problems through talk and co-operation with one another. Disputes have to be negotiated since there are no rules that can be applied. It is from these games that girls learn the normative communication patterns of their speech communities. The world of girls is clearly one of co-operation and equality of power with a heavy emotional investment in pair friendships. Girls must learn to read relationships and situations sensitively. According to Maltz and Borker, girls' games teach three basic communication rules:

(1) To create and maintain relationships of closeness and equality, use collab-orative, co-operative talk. The heart of relationships is the process of communication, not the content.
(2) Avoid criticism as much as possible but, if necessary, do it gently. Never exclude others, outdo them, or put them down.
(3) Pay attention to relationships with others, interpreting accurately and responding sensitively to others' feelings.[1]

In the relatively leaderless groups characteristic of girls, Maltz and Borker (1982) argue, 'There is a basic contradiction in the structure of girls' social relationships. Friends are supposed to be equal and everyone is supposed to get along, but in reality they always don't. Conflict must be resolved, but a girl cannot assert social power or superiority as an individual to resolve it . . .' (p. 12). Bossiness is bad because it denies equality, so 'girls learn to direct things without seeming bossy, or they learn to not direct' (p. 13). 'What girls learn to do with speech is cope with the contradiction created by an ideology of equality and cooperation and a social reality that includes dif-ference and conflict' (p. 12). Girls mediate, submerge, transform, and some-times resolve conflict and contradiction through talk.

From these rules it is easy to see that girls' games stress co-operation, collaboration and sensitivity to others' feelings which reinforce other aspects of feminine socialization. Girls learn that their worth depends on being good people. This means to be sensitive, inclusive, and co-operative. Girls' interac-tion purpose is not to achieve some outcome, but rather the goal is the communication process itself. The structure and strategies for friendly inter-actions among women show considerable continuity with findings about girls' interactions (Treicher and Kramarae, 1983). Women's general orienta-tion is interactional, relational, participatory, and collaborative.

BOYS' GAMES

When we look at boys' games, we find a very different pattern. Boys live and play in a world where hierarchy and dominance are primary, with friendship centering around physical activity and competition. This pattern leads to distinctive understandings of communication. Boys' games usually involve large groups instead of small groups or pairs. A baseball team is composed of 9 individuals; a football team, 11. most of the games that boys play are

---

[1] Goodwin (1980) states that the non-hierarchical framework of black urban girls she has studied 'provides ground for rather intricate processes of alliance formation between equals against some other party' (p. 172). This work suggests that black girls use some of the same kind of collaborative talk also heard among white females.

competitive games with clear goals. Unlike girls' games, they are organized by rules and roles that indicate who does what and how the game is to be played. There is no need to talk about how to play the game because the play is structured by standard goals, rules and roles of how to play. The only talk ever needed is around strategies to reach the goals.

In boys' games, individual status depends on standing out in the game, in being better than other players, in dominating the action. From these games, boys learn how to interact in their speech communities. In particular, they learn three rules:

(1) Use communication to assert yourself, your ideas, and to achieve something.
(2) Use communication to attract and maintain an audience.
(3) Use communication to take the focus from others and get it yourself. In competing for the 'talk stage', make sure others do not gain more attention than you.

The emphasis in these rules is on competition and individuality, as well as doing something to accomplish a goal. Boys learn that they have to do things to be valued as team members. Boys use words to attain and maintain dominance, to gain and keep an audience, and to assert identity. One can see the undercurrent here of masculinity's emphasis on being invulnerable and guarded. If others are the competition, then you can't let them know too much about yourself and your weaknesses. Intensely close, personal relationships are unlikely to be formed in such groups.

The basic rules of communication that adult women and men use are refined and elaborated versions of the very same ones evident in the childhood games of both boys and girls. Women's speech is interactional, engaging others and building on others' contributions, progressively developing an overall conversation. It is a communication style centering around intimacy, emphasizing connection and efforts to minimize difference. Men's speech is characterized by arguing and verbal posturing. It is a communication style centering on independence, emphasizing differentiation, status, and control (Tannen, 1990, p. 26). Communication between men and women can be like cross-cultural communication with women and men typically engaging in distinctive styles of communication with different purposes, rules, and understandings of how to interpret talk (Kramarae, 1981; Treicher and Kramarae, 1983; Bates, 1988; Tannen, 1990).

In the section that follows, features of women's and men's speech that have been identified by a number of researchers will be discussed. Through this discussion, some of the complications that arise when men and women operate by different rules in conversations with each other will be evident. Each sex wrongly interprets cues according to its own rules.

WOMEN'S SPEECH

Communication is one of the primary ways that women establish and maintain relationships with one another. The purpose of conversation is to share things about themselves and to learn about others. Human relationships are central in women's lives (Gilligan, 1982; Schaef, 1985). And for women, talk is the essence of relationships. Conversations can be viewed as negotiations of hierarchies of friendship for closeness (Tannen, 1990, p. 25). Consistent with this primary goal, women's speech tends to display identifiable features that foster connections, support, closeness, and understanding.

Equality between people is generally important in women's communication (Aries, 1976, 1987). Women's orientation to conversation is as a co-operative enterprise, mutually constructed for common interest (McConnell-Ginet, 1982). The goal is often to maintain friendship and good social relationships. To achieve symmetry, women often match experiences to indicate that 'You're not alone in how you feel.' Typical ways to communicate equality would be by saying, 'The same thing has happened to me. I know how you feel', 'I've felt the same way' or 'I've done that too.' To show fairness, modesty, and respectfulness there is a more equal distribution of talk time, a form of conversational generosity (Coates, 1989).

High-status women work to raise the status of less experienced women by doing away with power differences and establishing more closeness and equal rank with them through conversation (Jenkins and Kramer, 1978; Ellis, 1982; Astin and Leland, 1991). They do this by drawing other women out, allowing power gestures by lower-ranked women, and refraining from power gestures like correction, reproach, or criticism, instead giving non-critical hearing responses. The patterns of activity and dominance in women's conversations change from meeting to meeting.

Growing out of the desire for equality is a participatory mode of interaction in which communicators respond to and build on each others' ideas in the process of conversation (Edelsky, 1981; Kramarae, 1981; Belk et al., 1988; Fitzpatrick, 1988; Gayle and Preiss, 1991; De Francisco, 1992). Rather than a turn-taking structure in which you tell your ideas and then I'll tell my ideas, women's speech more characteristically follows an interactive pattern in which different voices weave together to create conversations. The floor for women involves solidarity, simultaneity, and collaboration (Helgesen, 1990; Rosener, 1990; Astin and Leland, 1991; Cantor and Bernay, 1992). Women use it to break down barriers and establish equality. Women frequently use over-laps and simultaneous speech where more than one speaker speaks at the same time (Treicher and Kramarae, 1983; Tannen, 1990). This tends to happen in more interaction-oriented talk, especially where the listener is enthusiastic (Coates, 1989).

In simultaneous speech, co-conversations are occurring which involve asking questions and making comments, signalling active involvement and the co-creation of a joint text. Participants absorb more than one message at a time; simultaneous speech does not threaten comprehension. It allows multilayered development of topics. There is no competition for turns. Speakers do not become upset when others join in. It is a joint effort with speakers concerned that they contribute to a jointly negotiated whole. Topic shifts are gradual rather than abrupt. Conversations between women in informal contexts show that co-operativeness is not a myth (Coates, 1989). Women display a fuller range of their abilities in such informal, collaborative ventures. In contrast, when the floor involves hierarchical interactions where turn-takers stand out and floors are won and lost, women do not assert themselves as effectively.

Showing support for others is also important in women's speech (Jourard, 1971a, 1971b; Schegloff, 1972; Cosby, 1973; Derlega and Chaikin, 1976; Fisherman, 1978, 1983; Spender, 1980, 1989; Kramarae, 1981; Maltz and Borker,

1982; Case, 1988, 1990, 1993a, 1993b; Rosener, 1990; Tannen, 1990; De Francisco, 1991; Dindia and Allen, 1991). It is demonstrated by the expression of understanding and sympathy with a friend's situation or feelings. 'I really feel for you' or 'I think you did the right thing' are communicative clues that women understand and support how another person feels. In studies of women's consciousness-raising groups (Jenkins and Kramer, 1978; Ellis, 1982), little emphasis was found on dominance and hierarchy. Instead there was an orientation toward collaboration and support with groups actively discouraging the establishment of leaders.

Minimal responses, such as 'mm hmm' or 'uh huh', inserted throughout streams of talk to indicate attention and interest, are used by women as support work (Maltz and Borker, 1982; Fishman, 1983; Aries, 1987; Coates, 1989). They do not interrupt the flow of talk and are devices to produce jointly a conversational text (Coates, 1989). For women this usually means, 'Continue, I'm listening', whereas for men it means 'I agree' and is used at the end of statements (Fishman, 1983). Henley and Kramarae (1991) suggest that this may explain women's more frequent use of this form of talk, men's confusion when women give positive minimal responses to them, then later discover that they do not agree with what had been said, and women's complaint that men are not listening enough when women talk.

Related to these first two features is women's typical attention to the relationship level of communication (Andrews, 1987; Tannen, 1990). The relationship level of talk focuses on feelings and the relationship between communicators rather than on the content of the messages. Language is used for conversational exchange. Its role is often to patch up strained areas so participants can devote themselves to the general well-being of each other. Women use collaborative conflict avoidance strategies as peacemakers in relationships when there is conflict (Belk et al., 1988; Fitzpatrick, 1988; Gayle and Preiss, 1991; De Francisco, 1992). Great care is taken not to force others to lose face. In conversations between women, it is common to hear probing questions for greater understanding of feelings and perceptions surrounding the subject of talk (Tannen, 1990). 'Tell me more about what happened' and 'How did you feel when it occurred?' are probes that help a listener understand a speaker's perspective. Women address their remarks to individuals in the group 90% of the time with their remarks personal and direct (Aries, 1976, 1987). The content of talk is dealt with, but usually not without serious attention to the feelings that are involved.

Conversational 'maintenance work' (Fishman, 1978) is a fourth feature of women's speech style. This involves efforts to sustain conversation by inviting others to speak and by prompting them to elaborate on their experiences. Women acknowledge previous utterances and try to connect with them. They jointly build on an idea using individual contributions for progressive development of meaning. Individual authority may be seen as disruptive. Women's talk has explicit rules for the acknowledgement of what has been said by the previous speaker and requiring that a connection be made to it, whereas men have no such rules to follow and some male strategies call for ignoring it (Schegloff, 1972; Fishman, 1978, 1983; Spender, 1980, 1989; Kramarae, 1981; Aries, 1982; Maltz and Borker, 1982; Kollock et al., 1985; Aries, 1987; Robinson and Smith-Lovin, 1990; Tannen, 1990; De Francisco, 1991; Henley and Kramarae, 1991). As part of this maintenance work women ask questions that initiate topics for others: 'Tell me about your meeting', 'What was your trip to Brazil like?' This sort of communication opens the conversational door and maintains interaction. Where women see questions as part of conversational maintenance, men see them as information requests (Henley and Kramarae, 1991).

Responsiveness is a fifth quality of women's talk (Tannen, 1990). For most women, the language of conversation is primarily a language of rapport: a way of establishing connections and negotiating relationships. Emphasis is placed on displaying similarities and matching experiences. As women do this they get people to work together by saying 'Tell me more' or 'That's really interesting', nodding and using eye contact to signal they are interested; giving more listening responses; asking questions such as 'What did you mean?' and responding positively and enthusiastically during the conversation. Tannen called this 'rapport talk' (pp. 76, 77). Really talking requires careful listening. To women it means reciprocal drawing out of each others' ideas and meanings (Goldberger et al., 1987). Responsiveness reflects learned tendencies to care about others and to make them feel valued and included (Lakoff, 1975). Since talk for women is not about information but about interaction, it is constructed in ways that allow symmetry in relationships between and among others.

A sixth quality of women's speech is tentativeness which leaves open the door for others to respond and express their opinions. This may be expressed in a number of forms. Sometimes women qualify statements by saying, 'I'm probably not the best judge of this, but . . .' In other situations they use verbal hedges such as 'I kind of feel you may be overreacting.' Another way to keep talk provisional is to tag a question on to a statement that invites another to respond: 'That was an interesting suggestion, wasn't it?'

Lakoff (1975) noted that women used more hedges, qualifiers and tag questions than men. She claimed they represented lack of confidence and uncertainty as a result of women's socialization into subordinate roles and low self-esteem. However, alternative explanations of women's tentative style of speaking have been suggested. Both McMillan et al. (1977), studying mixed-sex discussion groups of college students, and Fishman (1980), studying heterosexual couples talking at home, found that women used tags to elicit responses from uncommunicative male conversational partners. Holmes (1984) found that women used tags to express solidarity by facilitating the addressee's contribution to discourse. Coates (1989) found that not only do tags invite others to speak and facilitate their entering the discourse, but that they also check for the taken-for-grantedness of what is being said and signal, if there is no response, that the speaker has the support of the group. Hedges, in contrast, respect the face needs of all participants in a conversation. Through a hedge, the speaker shows that she does not want to offend the addressee by assuming agreement (Coates, 1989). They assist in the negotiation of sensitive topics since the speaker does not take a hard line. Some research shows that people in leadership and facilitation roles use tags and hedges to sustain interaction (Johnson, 1980; Holmes, 1984).

People outside of women's speech community may misinterpret women's use of this form of communication, seeing it as uncertainty and deference. But rather than reflecting powerlessness, the use of hedges, qualifiers and tag questions may express women's desire to keep conversations open and to include others. It is easier to jump into a conversation that has not been sealed shut with firm statements. A tentative style of speaking becomes an enabling device that supports women's general desire to create equality and include others.

A final feature of women's talk is a personal, concrete style (Cosby, 1973; Derlega and Chaikin, 1976; Case, 1988, 1990, 1993a, 1993b; De Francisco, 1991; Rosener, 1990; Tannen, 1990; Dindia and Allen, 1991). Typical of women's conversations are details about experiences, personal disclosures, and anecdotes (Jourard, 1971a, 1971b; Case, 1988, 1990, 1993b; Tannen, 1990; Dindia and Allen, 1991). These are valued forms of communication. Women often reason from personal experience. In my own work, women used personal experiences rather than authority 89% of the time when they tried to convince others of their point of view. Men used proof from authority, appealing to objectivity 91% of the time (Case, 1985, 1988, 1990). The forms of speech women used cultivated a personal tone in their communication, facilitating feelings of closeness by connecting communicators' lives. Thus, the personal characteristics of much of women's interaction is another device to sustain interpersonal closeness.

MEN'S SPEECH

In masculine speech communities the goals of talk involve exerting control, preserving independence, and enhancing status. Conversation is an arena for proving oneself and negotiating prestige. This leads to two general tendencies in men's communication. First, men use talk to establish and defend their personal status and their ideas. This is done by asserting themselves and/or by challenging others. Second, when they want to support another, they typically do this by respecting the other's independence and avoiding condescending communication (Tannen, 1990). As we review features of masculine talk, these tendencies should become more clear.

Men often speak to exhibit knowledge, skill, or ability in order to establish their own status and value. They give opinions, suggestions, task information, and tell people what to do (Strodtbeck and Mann, 1956; Bales, 1970; Kramarae et al., 1983; Tannen, 1990). They tend to make their remarks to the group as a whole, not to individuals (Aries, 1976), a tendency that has been viewed as an exercise of power in a group (Bales, 1970). Equally typical is the tendency to avoid disclosing personal information that might make a man appear weak or vulnerable (Derlega and Chaikin, 1976; Morgan, 1976; Kramarae, 1981; Tannen, 1990; Dindia and Allen, 1991). For instance, if someone expresses a concern about a problem with a colleague, a man might say 'The way you should handle that is . . .' or 'You ought to just tell him . . .' This illustrates the tendency to give advice that Tannen reports is common in men's speech.

On the relationship level of communication, giving advice does two things. First, it focuses on instrumental activity – what another should do – and does not acknowledge feelings. Second, it expresses superiority and maintains control. It says 'I know what you should do' or 'I would know how to handle that.' Since talk for men is a means to preserve independence and negotiate and maintain status in a hierarchical social order, this is done by exhibiting their skill and knowledge (Tannen, 1990). They hear problems as requests for solutions and respond by giving advice, acting as experts, and lecturing their audience, rather than sympathizing or sharing problems. Tannen called this 'report talk' (p. 76). As men do their report talking, they give fewer listener responses, make authoritative statements rather than ask questions, and challenge rather than agree (pp. 127–30). Between men, advice giving seems understood as a give and take, but it may be interpreted as unfeeling and condescending by women whose rules for communication differ. If women want advice, they ask for it.

A second feature of men's talk is instrumentality – the use of speech to solve problems. Efforts focus on getting information, discovering facts, and suggesting solutions. Between men this is comfortable since both speakers have typically been socialized to value instrumentality. However, conversations between women and men are often derailed since there is no agreement on what an informational, instrumental focus means. When a man focuses on the content level of meaning after a woman has disclosed a problem, she may feel he is disregarding her emotions and concerns. He, on the other hand, may be trying to support her in the way he has learned to show support – suggesting ways to solve the problem.

A third feature of men's communication is conversational dominance. Despite jokes about women's talkativeness, research indicates that in most contexts men dominate the conversation. One of the most widely used indicators of dominance is the amount of interaction initiated by individuals. To take up time speaking is an exercise of power. Compared with girls and women, in mixed-sex groups, at public gatherings, in classrooms, and in many other contexts, boys and men, regardless of their status, spend more time talking than women (Soskin and John, 1963; Argyle et al., 1968; Bernard, 1972; Hilpert et al., 1975; Swacker, 1975; Thorne and Henley, 1975; Eakins and Eakins, 1978; Spender, 1980; Maltz and Borker, 1982; Treicher and Kramarae, 1983; Case, 1988, 1990, 1993b; Mulac, 1989; Tannen, 1990; Henley and Kramarae, 1991), and for longer periods of time (Thorne and Henley, 1975; Eakins and Eakins, 1978; Spender, 1980; Aries, 1987; Mulac, 1989). Male experts also talk longer than women with similar expertise (Swacker, 1975; Treicher and Kramarae, 1983; Case, 1988, 1990, 1993b). In keeping with this pattern, men initiate more interactions than women (Kalcik, 1975; Spender, 1980; Aries, 1982; Crawford and Chaffin, 1987; Case, 1988, 1990, 1993b). Spender (1980) found that in mixed groups women initiate only 34% of the interactions. This is important because those who talk the most in groups tend to become the leaders.

Men also engage in other verbal behaviour that sustains conversational dominance. They may divert conversations by using what another has said as a jump-off point for their own topics (Zimmerman and West, 1975, 1978; Eakins and Eakins, 1978; Treicher and Kramarae, 1983; Case, 1988, 1990, 1993a). This is an effective strategy since men's topics are more often pursued after they have been brought up (Fishman, 1978, 1983; Tannen, 1990; De Francisco, 1991).

Or they may interrupt others while they are talking. While both sexes engage in interruptions, most research suggests that men do it more frequently (Argyle et al., 1968; Zimmerman and West, 1975, 1978; Eakins and Eakins, 1978; West, 1982, 1984; Bohn and Stutman, 1983; West and Zimmerman, 1983; Case, 1988, 1990, 1993b; Robinson and Smith-Lovin, 1990; Tannen, 1990). For example, Zimmerman and West (1975) recorded 31 segments of conversation in public places and private residences. In same-sex conversations interruptions were equally divided between the two speakers, whereas in cross-sex conversations 96% of all interruptions were by men. In a study of mixed-sex managerial groups (Case, 1988) 73% of the interruptions were by males. In our 1990 study of academic women and men in mixed groups, 32 interruptions were made by men to 1 interruption by a woman. Men are more likely to interrupt women than other men (Zimmerman and West, 1975, 1978; Eakins and Eakins, 1978; Treicher and Kramarae, 1983; West and Zimmerman, 1983; Case, 1988, 1990, 1993b), and women are more likely than men to allow interruption of their talk. In our study of managerial conversation, 79% of the women allowed interruptions in contrast to 21% of the men (Case, 1988).

Not only do men seem to interrupt more than women, but they do so for different reasons. Men use interruptions to control conversations by challenging other speakers' ideas or taking the talk stage from them by changing the topic. These forms of topic control are attempts to dominate a conversation and impose one's ideas on others. This is a means of 'doing power'. The intent is oneupmanship (Maltz and Borker, 1982; Case, 1985, 1988, 1990, 1993b; Henley and Kramarae, 1991). Men are willing to engage in open argument and conflict in public settings with other men (Goodwin, 1980; Maltz and Borker, 1982; Treicher and Kramarae, 1983; Tannen, 1990; Gayle and Preiss, 1991). For many women, they find that their speaking options get functionally closed down in such conversations.

When women interrupt, they are more likely to interrupt other women than they are to interrupt men (Treicher and Kramarae, 1983; Kollock et al., 1985; Orcutt and Harvey, 1985). They rarely interrupt to change the topic. When women interrupt other women they are more likely to be rapport building by elaborating on the other's theme, using overlap speech in a supportive way which builds on another's utterance, or asking interruptive questions for clarification of what the speaker was saying in order to understand. Their purpose in interrupting appears to be a way to indicate interest, show support, encourage elaboration, and to respond (Treicher and Kramarae, 1983; Kollock et al., 1985; Orcutt and Harvey, 1985; Aries, 1987; Tannen, 1990). In general, the more powerful person in an interaction interrupts more (Rogers et al., 1975; West and Zimmerman, 1978; Courtright et al., 1979; Kollock et al., 1985).

A fourth feature of men's communication style is a tendency to express themselves in assertive, absolute ways. Compared with women, their language is typically more authoritative, direct, and forceful (Eakins and Eakins, 1978; Case, 1988, 1990, 1993a, 1993b; Tannen, 1990). Men's speech tends to show personal confidence rather than uncertainty. Tentative speech such as hedges and disclosures are used less frequently by men than by women (Kollock et al., 1985). This is consistent with gender socialization in which men learn to use talk to assert themselves and to take and hold on to positions. However, when another person does not share that understanding of communication, speech that is directive and absolute may appear to close the conversation off and leave no room for others to speak.

Fifth, men's speech tends not to be highly responsive to others, especially on the relationship level of communication. Both men and women give what are called 'minimal response cues', which are verbalizations such as 'yeah' or 'right' or 'mm hmm'. In interaction with women, who demonstrate interest vigorously, men's use of minimum response cues inhibits conversation because they are perceived as indicating lack of involvement (Fishman, 1978, 1980). Another way that men's conversation is generally less relationally responsive than women's is lack of expressed empathy and lack of self-disclosures. In cross-gender conflict situations, men often use unilateral conflict avoidance strategies of withdrawal, efforts to get women to be 'less emotional' and efforts to avoid sensitive topics getting on the floor (Kramarae, 1981; Barnes and Buss, 1985; Belk *et al.*, 1988; Fitzpatrick, 1988; De Francisco, 1991). Within the rules of men's speech communities, sympathy or empathy of any sort is a sign of condescension; and revealing personal problems is seen as making one vulnerable. Yet women's speech rules count empathy, sympathy, and disclosure as demonstrations of equality and support. This creates potential for misunderstanding between men and women.

Finally, compared with women, men communicate more abstractly. They frequently speak in general terms removed from concrete experiences and distanced from personal feelings (Treicher and Kramarae, 1983; Schaef, 1985). They tend to speak in a linear manner, moving sequentially through points. Talk is straightforward, without many details. Women, on the other hand, use more detailed, less linear speech, embedding information within the context of the people involved and the events that occurred, so that the listener can become a part of the situation. This appears unfocused and rambling to men. The abstract style of men's speech reflects the public and impersonal contexts in which they often operate and the less personal emphasis in their speech communities. Within public environments, norms for speaking call for theoretical, conceptual, and general thought and communication. Men are not inclined toward self-revelation of personal information about thoughts, feelings, and experiences (Morgan, 1976; Kramarae, 1981; Tannen, 1990; Dindia and Allen, 1991). Yet within more personal relationships or teams, abstract talk can create barriers to knowing others well enough to work together effectively.

DOES IT MATTER?

The patterns described above, that women use conversation primarily to negotiate and express a relationship interactionally, whereas men use conversation as display, can translate into very different communication behaviours at work between men and women (Case, 1993a, 1993b). Thus, joke telling, boasting, ribbing, and other forms of ritualized verbal aggression, in which it is expected to perform verbally and to one-up someone else and earn admiration from those observing, are commonly found in informal male conversation. As an observer it is like watching a game of verbal ping pong. For males, getting and holding the floor is of prime importance, while for females getting the floor is not particularly problematic. What is a problem for women is getting people engaged and keeping them engaged – maintaining the conversation and the interaction (Maltz and Borker, 1982, p. 209). Personal sharing to achieve closeness is much more common in all-female groups. In same-sex groups members share implicit assumptions about how to proceed, carrying out both task and support-related functions; whereas in mixed-sex groups, the rules are less clear cut. More awkward silences and hesitations occur (Aries, 1987).

Since men like hierarchy, they accept what the boss says, and will pull rank when they have to. Since women are less comfortable with hierarchy, they use language to achieve rapport. They want their way, as the men do, but want everyone to agree. Pulling tank is not a comfortable strategy for them. Men boast of achievements at work to establish their place in the hierarchy, whereas women keep their achievements private because boasting violates their egalitarian norms. Not only do women not boast, but they often put themselves down. This is a way to get information out without boasting, but men take this modesty as a lack of self-confidence.

Another area where differences occur involves speaking out. Men like speaking up at meetings. They often jockey for a position in a large group. Women prefer talking one-on-one and use their language to maintain intimacy. Men see this as a waste of time, but women find that friendly relations pay off for them in loyalty and smooth business relations. They want to be friends with co-workers. If they feel their co-workers are strangers, they feel distant, alienated, and uncomfortable. Men also like to tell people what to do. They give orders. Women in high-status positions know they have power, so they bend over backwards not to be bossy. Instead of giving direct orders, they often use indirectness such as, 'Do you think you can give me the report by tomorrow instead of Monday?' Men frequently accuse women of being manipulative because they try to get people to do things without making demands. To women, it's just not being bossy.

Conflict is inevitable in organizations. Men see it as both necessary and an impersonal part of their social relations. They are openly competitive. Women temper competition and try to avoid conflict through problem-solving, since they take it more personally and view it more negatively and disruptively than men (Maltz and Borker, 1982).[2] Women, unlike men, are more apt to make decisions by consensus. Men are more apt to make unilateral decisions and enforce them.

Organizations typically foster interaction patterns that are more compatible with men's established interaction patterns than with women's. For example, the male form of interaction in committee meetings is a turn-taking form. Getting the floor is a form of symbolic domination, establishing power and position in the hierarchy. Men usually play a dominant role, controlling the interaction, talking more, and frequently violating rules of polite turn-taking. Women are more likely to talk less, seek permission to speak, and take more responsibility for encouraging and supporting other speakers. This division of labour often has women nurturing the conversation by working to keep it going and by obeying the rules implicit in polite interactions. Men freely violate the rules without repercussions and further dominate the conversation by using a disproportionate amount of time. Women are more comfortable with a more open, collaborative, accessible floor, where individual

---

[2] Ethnicity makes a difference in conflict approach or avoidance. Women who are of Eastern European Jewish background, Italian, Greek, and Arabic are more likely to see arguments as positive and a way to show closeness. Such women may not avoid conflict (Tannen, 1991). Women from these cultures are viewed more negatively in the USA than men from these cultures. These women are perceived as too aggressive because they are being judged by 'typical' standards for women.

contributions are used as touchstones for the progressive development of group meaning, and where the exercise of individual authority may be seen as disruptive.

Patterns of interaction for mixed-sex conversations make no allowances for such differences. Changes in the structure and labour demographics of work organizations will not revolutionize women's experience in a 'man's world' unless the interactions which sustain those structural arrangements are simultaneously transformed (Goffman, 1976). The dynamics of women's interaction patterns must be recognized, valued as legitimate, and incorporated into the structure of organizations so that women have real opportunities for equality (Case, 1993b).

There is a more subtle way that differences in goals and purposes for talk affect the co-operation between the sexes and tend to work against shared meaning. Barbara Bates (1988) discusses three such kinds of language that characterize the life of large organizations. Military language focuses on hierarchy and images of conflict with an enemy; athletic language mixes connotations of war with those of teamwork and camaraderie among participants; and sexual language serves a variety of functions, reinforcing the notion of dominance equalling sexual control and providing release through jokes among male colleagues. Many women in work situations with men are ill-equipped to interpret military, athletic and sexual language in ways that do not leave them either isolated as females or compromised as workers.

Terms borrowed from combat have become part of the everyday vocabulary of members of organizations: Clients are 'targeted' by the sales 'force', powerful people are referred to as 'big guns' and workers are put on the 'front lines' or 'in the trenches' to see how they react 'under fire'. This language of war suggests that a parallel kind of activity occurs in organizational life (p. 157). The language of athletics is even more widespread. Sports talk is a major form of small talk used to create comfort and demonstrate expertise in conversations between colleagues. Sports teams portray the world of work as a continual game or a context in which 'our' team is trying to beat 'their' team (p. 157). A troubling feature of sexual language and anecdotes on the job is that they often place non-participant members in difficult situations. A woman who hears a demeaning joke about another woman or women in general has no easy exit from the situation. If she is silent, she will be seen as judging her male colleagues or lacking a sense of humour. If she laughs, her male co-workers may think of her as 'one of us' for the moment, but she may leave upset at her own collusion with a damaging stereotype. The situation for men is similar. If they don't express enjoyment of or participate in sex talk, they may be stereotyped as 'wimps'. This distances them from the informal power structure in the organization and thus may decrease their chances for achievement reserved for consistent 'team players' (p. 158).

The military symbols prominent in most large organizations, and the preference by many men to conduct business in exclusively male communication settings, produce a subtle separation which many women are unwilling or unable to fight. Sexual jokes and casual talk about sports reinforce male-to-male friendships and leave the lone woman or women in a group without a comfortable way to join the conversation. While organization theories suggest a more open climate for workers, the language of organizational culture can say to the new sex on the block, 'You're welcome to come in for a while, if you'll play the game our way' (Bates, 1988, p. 166).

Consequences of such differences are enormous. Maltz and Borker (1982) focus on male and female miscommunication, pointing out that differences in verbal strategies and different interpretations of the same strategies lead to misunderstanding and misinterpretation. Their analysis though does not question who benefits from such differences. At this time women's conversational goals are devalued in interactions with men where they are regularly talked over and at. Cross-cultural explanations are not sufficient to explain why men's preferences typically receive priority (Graddol and Swann, 1989; Henley and Kramarae, 1991; De Francisco, 1992). Men's interactional styles in organizations currently work to their advantage in dominating the talk, influence and decision-making in groups. Hierarchies determine whose version of a communication situation will prevail; whose speech style will be the one required to learn the communication style, and interpret the meaning of the other; whose language style will be seen as deviant, irrational, inferior; and who will be required to imitate the others' style in order to fit into society. In most organizations, men's preferences set the communication norms. Women do more accommodating of their communication style.

Some existing research suggests that each sex becomes more restricted and less flexible in the kinds of messages they send when both sexes are present in a group (Aries, 1985, 1987). However, other studies show that gender differences in the sex composition of groups lead to less stereotypical behaviour by some men when they are in the presence of the other sex. They disagree less (Piliavin and Martin, 1978), use more supportive statements (Bohn and Stutman, 1983), and address more interaction to individuals rather than to the group as a whole (Aries, 1976). Also, themes of aggression and competition are less prevalent in mixed groups than in all-male groups. Although men may initiate more interaction than women in mixed-sex groups, women strongly influence the situation, as males communication behaviour comes closer to a female pattern. These studies suggest that the presence of women increases the frequency of supportive, personal interaction and decreases competitiveness in men, allowing them more variation in their interpersonal styles. The results are not as clear concerning whether female behaviour in mixed groups becomes more sex-role stereotypic with women becoming less likely to take initiative in stating their opinions (McMillan et al., 1977; Aries, 1985; Case, 1988, 1990, 1993b) or less sex-role stereotypic (Piliavin and Martin, 1978; Case, 1993a) than in all-female groups.

Gender differences in communication must not be overdrawn. There are no absolutes across situations. The characteristics described are not possessed exclusively by either sex, but are used by the sexes with different frequencies (Bodine, 1975; Case, 1988, 1990, 1993a, 1993b). Gender arrangements and patterns of similarity and differences may vary not only by sex, but by situation, race, social class, education, religion, or subculture. Cross-sex misunderstandings may interact with racial, ethnic, age, class, and sexual preference groups. The patterns described by Maltz and Borker (1982), Case (1985, 1988, 1990, 1993a), and Tannen (1990), as well as many other researchers, describe primarily the dominant white/anglo, middle- and upper-class culture and cannot be taken as indicative of all communication. Communication is a complex interaction. Contextual factors such as the situation, environmental context, and relationship of the participants must also be taken into account.

The view of communication cultures presented here does not presume that early experience or what people learn from peer groups is beyond changing. When people learn to interpret each others' rules, they are less likely to misread motives. When people are able to combine the skills and strengths they associate with each other, they are then able to be more flexible in interactions in their organizations, adapt flexibility to varying communication environments, and develop flexibility in their own communication behaviour. In our own work (Case, 1993a) evidence is provided that people can use a style of speech that is simultaneously assertive and supportive in language behaviour, although not at the same time, with the same words.

CONCLUSION

It is clear that the different sexes use certain characteristics of speech more frequently and in sharply distinctive ways, although the speech of all women and all men is not homogeneous. It is a pitfall to believe that a given speech form is intrinsically strong or weak, and that for people in management to be effective they must talk and act like men (Bennis, 1984). In fact, there may be organizational and personal costs to attempts to shape all managers into imitators of traditional organizational males, honing in on the rational, analytic, and competitive, at the expense of traditional relation-oriented skills such as understanding, listening, awareness of others' feelings, and collaboration (Case, 1988).

Until recently, the kinds of skills believed necessary for managers were identified with a masculine pattern of communication: giving directions, controlling emotion, and dominating interpersonal situations. Images of competence have begun to expand. Rather than try to change speech patterns, women can capitalize on the strengths of some of the differences that emerge from their feminine heritage that are clearly suited for current organizational realities.

In a study of what was important for MBAs on first jobs and 5 and then 10 years later, Louis (1990) found that they were unprepared for a range of people management abilities which became increasingly important over time. Building effective relationships laterally and with superiors and subordinates, to work in groups as both a team member and leader, to be able to interpret work group values, to be able to influence without formal authority both interpersonally and in groups, to increase participative decision-making capabilities, and to be able to work in flexible networks instead of hierarchical organizations were seen as vital. Also important was understanding the prevalence of ambiguity, and interdependence of tasks. Men in management are now hearing in many *Fortune* 500 companies that leadership and supervision require sensitivity, active listening, encouragement, and praise of subordinates, and opening oneself to team problem-solving rather than acting as the sole leader (Yukl, 1994).

Porter and McKibbin (1988), in an AACSB-commissioned study on university, corporation and graduate perspectives on management education, also stressed the need for managers to develop their people skills around lateral relationships, participative decision-making, interpersonal skills and leadership skills. Also needed were an increased understanding of the impact of globalization, the external regulatory environment, and broadened education to help managers understand the impact of managerial decisions on other organizational factors besides the 'bottom line'. Additional criticism of MBAs' inabilities to work with people has come from executives of *Fortune*, 1000 companies (Opinion Research Corporation, 1989).

Boyatzis (1982) studied characteristics of managers that were related to effective and superior performance. Of the 19 abilities he identified, 12 focused on people skills concerning aspects of leadership, human resource management, directing subordinates, or focusing on others.

The decline of America's economic and political power requires a new kind of leadership befitting an age of interdependent global enterprise, instant communication, and ecological limits. The workplace is being radically altered. Companies are casting aside old values, downsizing, and replacing bureaucratic formal structures that emphasize chain-of-command to become leaner organizations with a focus on innovation and fast-paced information exchange (Naisbitt and Aburdene, 1986; American Management Association, 1989).

Fortune magazine describes emerging management practices to meet the demands of today's world because of a confluence of changing values and economic necessity. Flexible networks will replace hierarchical organizations. Workers will be encouraged to make decisions on their own. Group learning will replace orders from the top. Global thinking will replace national perspectives. Creativity and intuition will join quantitative analysis for informed decision-making. Love and caring will be legitimate workplace motivators. Mental and spiritual enhancement of participants will replace or augment the profit motive (Rose, 1990).

Ford Motor Company, seeking a phrase to express the essence of its managerial revolution, adopted a motto: 'No more heroes!' Nancy Badore, director of its executive development center, is responsible for training the company's top 2,000 managers worldwide in the 'new culture' values. The reinvented corporation is 'an environment for nurturing personal growth', a place in which 'top-down authoritarianism is yielding to a networking style, and where everyone is a resource for everyone else' (Naisbitt and Aburdene, 1986, p. 72).

Based on current organizational realities, the information economy, global competition, deregulation, the heavy legal context in which business must operate, and the demands of the team approach, female values of inclusion and connection are emerging as valued leadership qualities. The trend today is toward training managers to be consultative rather than directive, open rather than controlled, and egalitarian rather than dominant in their interpersonal relations with workers.

Certain features of women's speech (indirectness, mitigation of criticism, solicitation of others' ideas, mutual sharing) allow alternative ideas to be expressed and permit an examination of differing value positions. These features influence the performance and goal attainment of the organization as a whole as well as helping development of complex and novel decisions that require pulling together perspectives and information from many different groups. Women's speech is compatible with leadership activity for today's organization. The organizing principle for business has shifted from a command and control style of management used by men to the facilitating, orchestrating leadership style of women (Naisbitt and Aburdene, 1990).

The problem with celebrating gender-based language differences at this time is that they do not carry connotations of 'different, but equal'. There are strengths of both sexes' traditional styles. Wide variations should be allowed in fitting the behaviours to the circumstance. Because men have historically dominated institutional life, masculine forms of communication are the standard in most work environments. Defining men and masculine patterns as normative leads to perceptions that women and feminine styles are not just different, but inferior. Thus men and men's attributes and activities serve as the standard against which the virtues of all human attributes and activities are measured. Leadership has typically been linked with masculine models of communication – assertion, independence, competitiveness, and confidence. Deference, inclusivity, collaboration, and co-operation, prioritized in women's speech communities, have been linked with subordinate roles rather than leadership.

People within organizations carry ideas about how male and female leaders or non-leaders are supposed to act and talk. They have definite evaluative attitudes about which sex is 'better' or 'superior' for any of the reported differences. Similar behaviour is reacted to differently depending on whether these behaviours are exhibited by men or women (Condry and Condry, 1976; Morley, 1976; Eichler, 1980; Kelly et al., 1980; Macke et al., 1980; Nieva and Gutek, 1981; Morrison et al., 1987; Case, 1993a).

Both sexes are capable of making changes in their personal constructs to meet changed goals. Organizations are becoming communities where sharing information is key and the rules of hierarchy are coming undone. But women who try to be more self-affirming can be surprised to find that they have stumbled into an interpersonal battlefield (Johnson and Goodchild, 1976; Fulmer, 1977; Astin and Leland, 1991). Men who try to soften their communication styles and listen more carefully may find they are no longer viewed as able to act decisively. On the other hand, women who exhibit participative and democratic behaviours are judged much more positively by their subordinates than men are (Guido-Di Brito et al., 1986). Behaviours in line with gender-role expectations are evaluated more positively (Merton, 1972; Franzwa, 1974; Deaux, 1976; Eakins and Eakins, 1978; Epstein, 1981; Nieva and Gutek, 1981); those that are not are evaluated negatively (Merton, 1972; McClelland, 1975; Goldberg, 1975; Eagly, 1978; Hollander and Julian, 1978; Epstein, 1981; Spence, 1981; Case, 1993a). Again, the risk of change coexists with the need for change.

A major management function is to detect potential problems and respond before they become major problems. Good listening is an active process of making sense out of what is heard, although it is often an unrecognized process. Listening is important in gathering information about managerial decisions and making people feel that their ideas and beliefs are of value. Listening is perhaps the prototypical female skill. Studies on gender differences in the use of language have repeatedly suggested men speak more than women, while women do more listening.

The women I studied were better active listeners than their male counterparts (Case, 1988, 1990), with the exception of wide-verbal-repertoire males who were excellent active listeners (Case, 1993a). They rephrased ideas, asked for clarification, and used qualifiers and modal construction in idea genera-tion. They learned from what was said and what was not said. It is far more common in an interaction to let one's mind wander, to think about what to say next, and when to jump in with an idea. Most men in the group showed the latter characteristic by cutting off others to make their points and by changing the topic of conversation. They were concerned with powers over others. The quality of women's listening was different – more intense, thoughtful, and attentive. Women valued listening as a way of making others feel comfortable, important, and as a means of encouraging others to find their own voices and grow.

In my research both women's speech and wide-verbal-repertoire speech permitted the examination of differing value positions through supportive listening, sensitivity to others' needs, and mutual sharing of emotions and personal knowledge. These seemed to be styles driven by a vision of end values, not by a particular method and means to get there. They would appear to be appropriate styles when response to change is needed, when coping with ambiguous situations, when problems require a long-range perspective, and when a variety of values need to be understood. The speech used by women helped consensus to be reached by competing groups, in-creased the interaction and the empowerment of others, and was generally a co-operative style which fostered participation and communication rather than domination.

Women's speech characteristics displayed a type of power, the 'power to', or empowerment (Bates, 1988, p. 380). This more recent view of power in-volves the ability to accomplish goals and to help others achieve their goals as well. It flourishes in a climate of equality more than in an environment struc-tured as a hierarchy. As people accomplish goals, their self-esteem increases. This increases in personal affirmation are a central resource for organizations.

In Astin and Leland's (1991) cross-generational study of social change in-volving 77 women leaders, they found that all demonstrated a leadership style based on empowerment and collective action to initiate and sustain change. By working closely with others and empowering them to act on their own, they demonstrated how collaborative, non-hierarchical forms of leader-ship help promote new thinking and new ideas. Virtually all the women in the study conceived of leadership as a process of 'working with people and through people' (p. 157). This way of understanding power has become more visible in recent years. It means 'becoming powerful to accomplish your own goals and spreading the power you possess so that other people become able to accomplish their goals as well' (Bates, 1988, p. 39).

Communication skills such as supportiveness, attentiveness, and collabora-tion enhance morale and productivity in work settings (Helgesen, 1990). Women leaders use collaborative, participative communication that enables others, reflecting how their speech communities taught them to interact (Aries, 1987; Helgesen, 1990; Rosener, 1990). Men, in general, engage in more directive, unilateral communication to exercise leadership, which is consis-tent with their learned view of talk as a way to assert self and achieve status (Eagly and Karau, 1991). There are different 'tones' to men's and women's leadership. Empowering co-operative approaches are crucial models for leadership in the 21st century, and involve new ways of communicating. Both sexes can develop communication skills that advance leadership as they find themselves in positions requiring abilities not emphasized in their earlier socialization.

REFERENCES

AMERICAN MANAGEMENT ASSOCIATION (1989) *Survey on Downsizing and Outplacement*, Washington, DC.

ANDREWS, P. H. (1987) Gender differences in persuasive communication and attribution of success and failure, *Human Communication Research*, Vol. 13, no. 3, pp. 372–85.

ARGYLE, M., LALLIJEE, M. and COOK, M. (1968) The effects of visibility on interaction in a dyad, *Human Relations*, Vol. 2, pp. 3–17.

ARIES, E. (1976) Interaction patterns and themes of male, female, and mixed groups, *Small Group Behavior*, Vol. 7, no. 1, pp. 7–18.

ARIES, E. (1982) Verbal and nonverbal behavior in single-sex and mixed-sex groups: are traditional sex-roles changing? *Psychology Reports*, Vol. 51, pp. 127–34.

ARIES, E. (1985) Male female interpersonal styles in all male, all female, and mixed groups, in A. Sargent (ed.) *Beyond Sex Roles*, 2nd edn, West, St. Paul, MN.

ARIES, E. (1987) Gender and communication, in P. Shaver and C. Hendrick (eds) *Sex and Gender, Vol. 7. Review of Personality and Social Psychology*, Sage, Newbury Park, CA.

ASTIN, H. S. and LELAND, C. (1991) *Women of Influence, Women of Vision: A Cross-Generational Study of Leaders and Social Change*, Jossey-Bass Publishers, San Francisco.

BALES, R. F. (1970) *Personality and Interpersonal Behavior*, Holt, Rinehart & Winston, New York.

BARNES, H. L. and BUSS, D. M. (1985) Sex differences in the interpersonal behavior of married couples, *Journal of Personality and Social Psychology*, Vol. 48, pp. 654–61.

BATES, B. (1988) *Communication and the Sexes*, Harper & Row, NY.

BELK, S., GARCIA-FALCONI, R., HERNANDEZ-SANCHEZ, J. and SNELL, W. (1988) Avoidance strategy use in the intimate relations of women and men from Mexico and the United States, *Psychology of Women Quarterly*, Vol. 12, pp. 165–74.

BENNIS, W. G. (1984) False grit, in D. Kolb, I. Rubin and J. McIntyre (eds) *Organizational Psychology: Readings on Human Behavior in Organizations*, Prentice-Hall, Englewood Cliffs, NJ (reprinted from *Savvy Magazine*, June 1980).

BERNARD, J. (1972) *The Sex Game*, Atheneum, New York.

BODINE, A. (1975) Sex differentiation in language, in B. Thorne and N. Henley (eds) *Language and Sex: Difference and Dominance*, Newbury House Publications, Rowley, MA.

BOHN, E. and STUTMAN, R. (1983) Sex-role differences in the relational control dimension of dyadic interaction, *Women's Studies in Communication*, Vol. 6, pp. 96–104.

BOYATZIS, R. (1982) *The Competent Manager: A Model for Effective Performance*, John Wiley & Sons, New York.

CANTOR, D. W. and BERNAY, T. (1992) *Women in Power: The Secrets of Leadership*, Houghton Mifflin Company, Boston.

CASE, S. S. (1985) A sociolinguistic analysis of the language of gender relations, deviance and influence in managerial groups. Unpublished doctoral dissertation, State University of New York at Buffalo.

CASE, S. S. (1988) Cultural differences, not deficiencies: an analysis of managerial women's language, in L. Larwood and S. Rose (eds) *Women's Careers: Pathways and Pitfalls*, Praeger Publishing, NY.

CASE, S. S. (1990) Communication styles in higher education, in L. Welch (ed.) *Women in Higher Education: Changes and Challenges*, Praeger Publishing, NY.

CASE, S. S. (1993a) Wide-verbal-repertoire speech: gender, language, and managerial influence, *Women's Studies International Forum*, Vol. 16, no. 3, pp. 271–90.

CASE, S. S. (1993b) The collaborative advantage: the usefulness of women's language to contemporary business problems, *Business and the Contemporary World*, Vol. 5, no. 3, pp. 81–105.

COATES, J. (1989) Gossip revisited: language in all-female groups, in J. Coates and D. Cameron (eds) *Women in Their Speech Communities*, Longman, London.

COATES, J. and CAMERON, D. (1989) *Women in Their Speech Communities*, Longman, London.

CONDRY, J. and CONDRY, S. (1976) Sex differences: a study of the eye of the beholder, *Child Development*, Vol. 47, pp. 812–19.

COSBY, P. C. (1973) Self-disclosure: a literature review, *Psychological Bulletin*, Vol. 79, pp. 73–91.

COURTRIGHT, J. A., MILLAR, F. E. and ROGERS-MILLAR, L. E. (1979) Domineeringness and dominance: replication and expansion, *Communication Monographs*, Vol. 46, pp. 179–92.

CRAWFORD, M. and CHAFFIN, R. (1987) Effects of gender and topic on speech style, *Journal of Psycholinguistic Research*, Vol. 16, no. 1, pp. 83–9.

DEAUX, K. (1976) *The Behavior of Men and Women*, Brooks/Cole, Belmont, CA.

DE FRANCISCO, V. (1991) Difference or dominance: a critique of two theoretical attempts to explain gender-based communication barriers. Presented at Gender and Language Parasession of 5th Annual International Conference on Pragmatics and Language Learning, University of Illinois, Urbana.

DE FRANCISCO, V. (1992) Deborah Tannen (1990) You just don't understand. Women and men in conversation. Review. *Language in Society*.

DERLEGA, W. J. and CHAIKIN, A. L. (1976) Norms affecting self-disclosure in men and women, *Journal of Consulting and Clinical Psychology*, Vol. 44, no. 3, pp. 376–80.

DINDIA, K. and ALLEN, M. (1991) Sex differences in self-disclosure: a meta-analysis. Presented at the 14th Annual Communication, Language and Gender Conference, Marquette University, Milwaukee, Wisconsin.

EAGLY, A. H. (1978) Sex differences in influenceability, *Psychological Bulletin*, Vol. 85, pp. 86–116.

EAGLY, A. H. and KARAU, S. J. (1991) Gender and the emergence of leaders: a meta-analysis, *Journal of Personality and Social Psychology*, Vol. 60, pp. 687–710.

EAKINS, B. and EAKINS, G. (1978) *Sex Differences in Human Communication*, Houghton Mifflin, Boston.

EDELSKY, C. (1981) Who's got the floor? *Language in Society*, Vol. 10, pp. 383–421.

EICHLER, M. (1980) *The Double Standard: A Feminist Critique of Feminist Social Science*, St Martin's Press, New York.

ELLIS, D. G. (1982) Relational stability and change in women's consciousness-raising groups, *Women's Studies in Communication*, Vol. 5, pp. 77–87.

EPSTEIN, C. F. (1981) Outsiders within, in C. F. Epstein, *Women in Law*, Basic Books, New York.

FISHMAN, P. M. (1978) What do couples talk about when they're alone, in D. Butterf and E. C. Epstein (eds), *Women's Language Style*, Department of English, University of Akron, Akron, Ohio.

FISHMAN, P. M. (1980) Conversational insecurity, in H. Giles, W. Robinson and P. Smith (eds) *Language: Social Psychological Perspectives*, Pergamon Press, New York.

FISHMAN, P. M. (1983) Interaction: the work women do, in B. Thorne, C. Kramarae and N. Henley (eds) *Language, Gender and Society*, Newbury House, Rowley, MA.

FITZPATRICK, M. A. (1988) *Between Husbands and Wives. Communication in Marriage*, Sage, Newbury Park, CA.

FRANZWA, H. (1974) Place in semantic space. Address to the Speech Communication Association Convention, Chicago.

FULMER, R. M. (1977) *Practical Human Relations*, Richard D. Irwin, Homewood, IL.

GAYLE, B. M. and PREISS, R. W. (1991) Gender and the use of conflict styles. Presented at the 14th Annual Communication, Language, and Gender Conference, Marquette University, Milwaukee, Wisconsin.

GILLIGAN, C. (1982) *In a Different Voice*, Harvard University Press, Cambridge, MA.

GOFFMAN, E. (1976) Gender display, *Studies in the Anthropology of Visual Communication*, Vol. 3, pp. 69–77.

GOLDBERG, P. (1975) Are women prejudiced against women? in C. S. Rothschild (ed.) *Toward a Sociology of Women*, Xerox College Publishing, Lexington, MA (reprinted from *Trans-Action*, April 1968).

GOLDBERGER, M., CLINCHY, B., BELENKY, M. and TARULE, J. (1987) Women's ways of knowing: on gaining voice, in P. Shaver and C. Hendrick (eds) *Sex and Gender*, Vol. 7. *Review of Personality and Social Psychology*, Sage, Newbury Park, CA.

GOODWIN, M. H. (1980) Directive-response speech sequences in girls' and boys' task activities, in S. McConnell-Ginet, R. Borker and N. Furman (eds) *Women and Language in Literature and Society*, Praeger, New York.

GRADDOL, D. and SWANN, J. (1989) *Gender Voices*, Basil Blackwell, Oxford.

GRONN, P. C. (1983) Talk as the work: the accomplishment of school administration, *Administrative Science Quarterly*, Vol. 28, pp. 1–21.

GUIDO-DI BRITO, F., CARPENTER, D. and DI-BRITO, W. (1986) Women in leadership and management: review of the literature, 1985 update, *NASPA Journal*, Vol. 23, no. 3, pp. 22–31.

HELGESEN, S. (1990) *Female Advantage: Women's Ways of Leadership*, Doubleday, New York.

HENLEY, N. and KRAMARAE, C. (1991) Gender, power, and miscommunication, in N. Coupeland, H. Giles and J. Wiemann (eds) *Miscommunication and Problematic Talk*, Sage, Newbury Park, CA.

HILPERT, F., KRAMER, C. and CLARK, R. A. (1975) Participant's perception of self and partner in mixed-sex dyads, *Central States Speech Journal*, Vol. 26, pp. 52–6.

HOLLANDER, E. P. and JULIAN, J. W. (1978) A further look at leader legitimacy, influence, and innovation, in L. Berkowitz (ed.) *Group Processes*, Academic Press, New York.

HOLMES, J. (1984) Women's language: a functional approach, *General Linguistics*, Vol. 24, pp. 149–78.

JENKINS, L. and KRAMER, C. (1978) Small group process: learning from women, *Women's Studies International Quarterly*, Vol. 1, pp. 67–84.

JOHNSON, J. L. (1980) Questions and role responsibility in four professional meetings, *Anthropological Linguistics*, Vol. 22, pp. 66–76.

JOHNSON, P. B. and GOODCHILD, J. D. (1976) How women get their way, *Psychology Today*, Vol. 10, no. 5, pp. 69–70.

JOURARD, S. M. (1971a) *Self-Disclosure: An Experimental Analysis of the Transparent Self*, Wiley, New York.

JOURARD, S. M. (1971b) *The Transparent Self*, 2nd edn, Van Nostrand, Princeton, NJ.

KALCIK, S. (1975) '. . . like Ann's gynecologist or the time I was almost raped': personal narratives in women's rap groups, *Journal of American Folklore*, Vol. 88, pp. 3–11.

KANTER, R. M. (1977) *Men and Women of the Corporation*, Basic Books, New York.

KELLY, J., KERN, J., KIRKLEY, B., PATTERSON, J. and KEANE, T. (1980) Reactions to assertive versus unassertive behavior: differential effects for males and females, and implications for assertiveness training, *Behavior Therapy*, Vol. 11, pp. 670–82.

KOLLOCK, P., BLUMSTEIN, P. and SCHWARTZ, P. (1985) Sex and power in interaction: conversational privileges and duties, *American Sociology Review*, Vol. 50, pp. 34–46.

KRAMARAE, C. (1981) *Women and Men Speaking*, Newbury House Publications, Rowley, MA.

KRAMARAE, C., SCHULZ, M. and O'BARR, W. (eds) (1983) *Language and Power*, Sage, Beverly Hills, CA.

LABOV, W. (1972) *Sociolinguistic Patterns*, University of Pennsylvania Press, Philadelphia.

LAKOFF, R. (1975) *Language and Women's Place*, Harper & Row, New York.

LEVINE, V., DONNELSON, A., GIORA, D. and SIMS, K. P., JR (1984) Scripts and speech acts in administrative behavior: the interplay of necessity, chance, and free will, *Educational Administration Quarterly*, Vol. 19, pp. 93–110.

LOUIS, M. R. (1990) The gap in management education, *The Magazine of the Graduate Management Admission Council*, Vol. VI, no. 3, pp. 1–12.

MACKE, A. S. and RICHARDSON, L. W. with J. COOK (1980) *Sex-Typed Teaching Styles of University. Professors and Study Reactions*, The Ohio State Univ. Research Foundation, Columbus, OH.

MALTZ, D. and BORKER, R. (1982) A cultural approach to male–female miscommunication, in J. Gumperz (ed.) *Handbook of Language and Social Psychology*, John Wiley, London.

MCCLELLAND, D. C. (1975) *Power: The Inner Experience*, Irvington, New York.

MCCONNELL-GINET, S. (1982) The origins of sexist language in discourse. Unpublished paper.

MCMILLAN, J. R., CLIFTON, A. K., MCGRATH, D. and GALE, W. S. (1977) Women's language: uncertainty or interpersonal sensitivity and emotionality? *Sex Roles*, Vol. 3, pp. 545–59.

MERTON, R. K. (1972) Insiders and outsiders, *American Journal of Sociology*, Vol. 78, pp. 9–47.

MINTZBERG, H. (1973) *The Nature of Managerial Work*, Harper & Row, New York.

MORGAN, B. S. (1976) Intimacy of disclosure topics and sex differences in self-disclosure, *Sex Roles*, Vol. 2, no. 2, pp. 161–6.

MORLEY, E. (1976) Women's thinking and talking (Case 9-477-055), *International Case Clearing House*, Graduate School of Business, Harvard University.

MORRISON, A., WHITE, R. and VAN VELSOR, E. (1987) *Breaking the Glass Ceiling*, Addison-Wesley, Reading, MA.

MULAC, A. (1989) Men's and women's talk in same-gender and mixed-gender dyads: power or polemic? *Journal of Language and Social Psychology*, Vol. 8, nos. 3–4.

NAISBITT, J. and ABURDENE, P. (1986) *Reinventing the Corporation*, Warner Books, New York.

NAISBITT, J. and ABURDENE, P. (1990) *Megatrends 2000 – Ten New Directions for the 1990s*, William Morrow, New York.

NIEVA, V. and GUTEK, B. (1981) *Women and Work. Vol. 1*, Praeger, New York.

OPINION RESEARCH CORPORATION (1989) Business executives see newly hired managers as poorly prepared in key skills, *ORC Issue Watch*, Princeton, NJ.

ORCUTT, J. and HARVEY, L. (1985) Deviance, rule-breaking and male dominance in conversation, *Symbolic Interaction*, Vol. 8, no. 1, pp. 15–32.

PILIAVIN, J. A. and MARTIN, R. R. (1978) The effects of the sex composition of groups on style of social interaction, *Sex Roles*, Vol. 4, pp. 281–96.

PORTER, L. and MCKIBBIN, L. (1988) *Management Education and Development: Drift or Thrust into the 21st Century?* McGraw-Hill, New York.

ROBINSON, D. T. and SMITH-LOVIN, L. (1990) Timing of interruptions in group discussions, in E. Lawler, B. Markovsky, C. Ridgeway, and H. Walker (eds) *Advances in Group Processes: Theory and Research (Vol. 11)*, JAI Press, Greenwich, CT.

ROGERS, W., JONES, T. and STANLEY, E. (1975) Effects of dominance tendencies on floor holding and interruption behavior in dyadic interaction, *Communication Research*, Vol. 1, pp. 113–22.

ROSE, F. (1990) A new age for business? *Fortune*, Vol. 8, October, pp. 156–64.

ROSENER, J. (1990) Ways women lead, *Harvard Business Review*, Nov/Dec, pp. 119–25.

SCHAEF, A. W. (1985) *Women's Reality: An Emerging Female System in a White Male Society*, 2nd edn, Winston Press, Minneapolis.

SCHEGLOFF, E. (1972) Sequencing in conversational openings, in J. Gumperz and D. Hymes (eds) *Directions in Sociolinguistics: The Ethnography of Communications*, Holt, Rinehart & Winston, New York.

SOSKIN, W. and JOHN, V. (1963) The study of spontaneous talk, in R. Barker (ed.) *The Stream of Behavior*, Appleton-Century-Crofts, New York.

SPENCE, J. T. (1981) Changing conceptions of men and women: a psychologist's perspective, in E. Langland and W. Gove (eds) *A Feminist Perspective in the Academy: The Difference It Makes*, University of Chicago Press.

SPENDER, D. (1980) *Man Made Language*, Routledge & Kegan Paul, London.

SPENDER, D. (1989) *The Writing or the Sex? Or Why You Don't Have to Read Women's Writing to Know it's No Good*, Pergamon Press, New York.

STRODTBECK, F. L. and MANN, R. B. (1956) Sex-role differentiation in jury deliberations, *Sociometry*, Vol. 19, pp. 3–11.

SWACKER, M. (1975) The sex of the speaker as a sociolinguistic variable, in B. Thorne and N. Henley (eds) *Language and Sex: Difference and Dominance*, Newbury House Publications, Rowley, MA.

TANNEN, D. (1990) *You Just Don't Understand: Women and Men in Conversation*, William Morrow & Co., New York.

TANNEN, D. (1991) Personal conversation. University of Illinois, Urbana, IL.

THORNE, B. and HENLEY, N. (1975) Difference and dominance: an overview of language, gender, and society, in B. Thorne and N. Henley (eds) *Language and Sex: Difference and Dominance*, Newbury House Publications, Rowley, MA.

TREICHER, P. and KRAMARAE, C. (1983) Women's talk in the ivory tower, *Communication Quarterly*, Vol. 31, no. 2, pp. 118–32.

WEST, C. (1982) Why can't a woman be more like a man? An interactional note on organizational game-playing for managerial women, *Work and Occupations*, Vol. 9, no. 1, pp. 5–29.

WEST, C. (1984) When the doctor is a lady, *Symbolic Interaction*, Vol. 7, no. 1, pp. 87–106.

WEST, C. and ZIMMERMAN, D. (1983) Small insults: a study of interruptions in cross sex conversations between unacquainted persons, in B. Thorne, C. Kramarae and N. Henley (eds) *op. cit.*

YUKL, G. (1994) *Leadership in Organizations*, 3rd edn, Prentice Hall, Englewood Cliffs, NJ.

ZIMMERMAN, D. and WEST, C. (1975) Sex roles, interruptions, and silences in conversations, in B. Thorne and N. Henley (eds) *Language and Sex: Difference and Dominance*, Newbury House, Rowley, MA.

ZIMMERMAN, D. and WEST, C. (1978) Male–female differences in patterns of interruption and responses to interruption in two-party conversations. Paper read at 9th World Congress of Sociology, Sweden.

CHAPTER 12

Women and Sexual Harassment: Work and Well-Being in US Organizations

JEANETTE N. CLEVELAND

INTRODUCTION

Sexual harassment is not a new phenomenon at work nor is it infrequent. In 1992 over 10,000 sexual harassment complaints were filed with the US Equal Employment Opportunity Commission (EEOC) (*Newsweek*, 1992). Further, there is evidence that fewer than 5% of sexual harassment targets report their experiences to authorities (Livingston, 1982; Fitzgerald *et al.*, 1988; Fitzgerald and Shullman, 1993) and even fewer file formal complaints, which suggests that the number of incidents of sexual harassment far exceeds 10,000 per year. Although no one is immune from sexual harassment in the workplace, the clear majority of perpetrators of sexual harassment are men and the clear majority of targets are women (Gutek, 1985; US Merit Systems Protection Board, 1981, 1988). There is some disagreement about what behaviours constitute sexual harassment, but there is clear consensus that sexual harassment carries personal, social, and organizational consequences. Much of the research on sexual harassment is conducted in the USA although other countries, including the UK (Davidson and Cooper, 1992; Gay, 1991) have recognized this problem. In the present chapter I will review the literature on sexual harassment, focusing primarily on the US academic and organization-based research.

The chapter is organized into five sections. First, the history, definition, and the incidence of sexual harassment are discussed. The first wave of research on sexual harassment in the USA focused on the definition of sexual harassment and the extent to which women encountered such behaviour at work and in educational settings (Gutek, 1993). The second section of the chapter reviews numerous potential explanations for sexual harassment. The third section reviews both personal and situational or organizational correlates of sexual harassment. Finally, there is evidence that sexual harassment has a significant effect on the health, well-being, and work productivity of targets and presumably perpetrators as well. The fourth section of this chapter reviews research on the consequences of sexual harassment. I will provide suggestions in section five on individual and organizational strategies that can be implemented to address sexual harassment, both in terms of preventing such behaviour and in terms of addressing its consequences.

BRIEF HISTORY AND DEFINITION OF SEXUAL HARASSMENT

Women's participation in American organizations has increased significantly since the Second World War (Morrison and von Glinow, 1990); together with their increased presence in the workforce, there have been increased experiences of gender discrimination and sexual harassment. The number of women in managerial, executive and administrative positions has doubled in only 20 years (Reskin and Ross, 1990; US Department of Labor, 1993; Martin, 1993). Despite these gains, however, women continue to occupy predominantly lower-level positions, and are often segregated into a limited number of jobs. Further, they are often excluded from career ladders leading to top management and are often targets of sexual harassment (Baron et al., 1986). Women managers tend to occupy lower-level management positions and have little power or authority over others, especially men (Bergmann, 1986; Boyd et al., 1990; US Department of Labor, 1991).

Myths and misconceptions abound about sexual harassment. Sexual harassment is not something that women ask for, nor are nice women or women in managerial positions with some formal position of power immune (Evans, 1978; Biaggio et al., 1990). Sexual harassment is not an individual problem, but rather an organizational one. Sexual harassment in the workplace is not a compliment nor is it fun, trivial or a figment of a woman's imagination. Sexual harassment can be described in behavioural terms. Although not everyone agrees on the range or variety of behaviours that constitute sexual harassment, most people agree on a subset of such behaviours. Further, sexual harassment has real individual and organizational consequences for both the harasser, the target of harassment and, potentially, bystanders involved in the harassment situation.

Legal and research history of sexual harassment

Until 1976 there was no legal term to identify sexual harassment in the USA. Although in the USA, there are few explicit laws that prohibit sexual harassment (Somers, 1982), students can find some protection under Title IX of the Education Amendment of 1972 and employees in organizations under Title VII of the Civil Rights Acts of 1964 and 1992. In the UK sexual harassment is also regarded as discrimination under the Sex Discrimination Act 1975 (Alimo-Metcalfe and Wedderburn-Tate, 1993).

In the USA the case Meritor Savings Bank FSC v. Vinson (1986) established two legal definitions or facets of sexual harassment. The first is quid pro quo which involves demands for sexual favours in return for a job-related outcome. This form of harassment involves an unwanted imposition of sexual requirements in the context of unequal power (MacKinnon, 1979). The second facet of sexual harassment involves a hostile work environment where sexual attention is persistent and unwelcome, although the threat of actual loss of job or job benefits is not necessarily present. A hostile work environment is difficult to define. In Robinson v. Jacksonville Shipyards (1988), the court clarified the standard for determining the reasonableness of a hostile work environment claim, and a woman did not have to demonstrate that she had suffered psychologically or mentally. In *Ellison* v. *Brady* (1991), the court ruled that what reasonably constituted sexual harassment differed for men and women and that such differences should be taken into account. Here, the court departed from a gender-neutral, reasonable-person standard and assumed that men and women differ on what behaviours are perceived as sexual harassment. In fact, there is consistent and considerable evidence that men and women do differ in their perceptions of what behaviours constitute sexual harassment (Fitzgerald and Shullman, 1993). Numerous researchers have advocated that the courts need to adopt a reasonable-*woman* standard to replace a more gender-neutral reasonable-*person* standard (Gohmann and Thacker, 1992).

What is sexual harassment?

Fitzgerald (1990) identifies two types of definitions of sexual harassment. Type I involves a general description of the nature of behaviour and possibly the nature of the relationships of the person involved. An example of a Type I definition is the one developed by EEOC:

> Unwelcome sexual advances, request for sexual favors, and other verbal or physical conduct of a sexual nature constitute sexual harassment when (1) submission to such conduct is made explicitly or implicitly a term or condition of an individual's employment, (2) submission to or rejection of such conduct by an individual is used as a basis for employment decisions affecting such individual, or (3) such conduct has the purpose or effect of substantially interfering with an individual's work performance or creating an intimidating, hostile, or offensive working environment.
>
> *(EEOC, 1980, p. 33)*

Numbers 1 and 2 of this definition reflect *quid pro quo* sexual harassment while number 3 introduces the hostile work environment as constituting sexual harassment. MacKinnon's (1979) legal definition is probably one of the most influential non-regulatory Type I definitions,

> sexual harassment . . . refers to the unwanted imposition of sexual requirements in the context of a relationship of unequal power. Central to the concept is the use of power derived from one social sphere to lower benefits or impose deprivations in another . . . when one is sexual, the other material the cumulative sanction is particularly potent.
>
> *(MacKinnon, 1979, p. 1)*

Type II definitions are more concrete and specific. According to the Office of Human Resources (1991), sexual harassment can be divided into three categories: verbal, that is whistling, catcalls, telling sexual jokes or stories, asking about sexual fantasies, and so forth; non-verbal, that is looking a person up and down, staring at someone, blocking a person's path, following the person, giving personal gifts, displaying sexually suggestive visuals, making facial expressions such as winking, throwing kisses, and so forth; and physical, that is giving a massage around the neck or shoulders, touching a person's clothing, hair or body, hanging around a person, hugging, kissing, patting or stroking, touching, and so forth (Office of Human Resources, 1991; US Customs Service, 1992).

An alternative approach to defining sexual harassment comes from empirical research on the topic (Fitzgerald, 1990). Specifically, researchers have asked students and employees to identify those behaviours that they perceive or believe reflect sexual harassment. The most complete efforts of this kind were conducted by Till (1980) and Fitzgerald and Shullman (1985). Till (1980) asked a national sample of college students to describe sexual harassment experiences that they had encountered and developed five categories of sexual harassment. The categories vary in degree of severity and include: (1) generalized sexist remarks and behaviours that are designed to degrade and insult, (2) inappropriate and offensive but essentially sanction-free sexual advances where there is no penalty attached to the woman's response, (3) solicitation of sexual activity or other sex-related behaviour by promise of reward, (4) coercion of sexual activity by threat of punishment (*quid pro quo*), and (5) sexual crimes and misdemeanours. Fitzgerald and Shullman (1985) also obtained input from college students and conceptually derived a five-factor scale of sexual harassment that is consistent with Till's five categories. The Fitzgerald and Shullman (1985) scale includes: (1) gender harassment (e.g. sexist remarks and jokes), (2) seductive behaviour (e.g. inappropriate sexual advances), (3) sexual bribery (e.g. solicitation with promise of reward), (4) sexual coercion, (e.g. sexual harassment with threat of punishment), and (5) sexual imposition (e.g. fondling, assault).

Fitzgerald and Shullman (1993) note that over 50 articles in the last 10 years have attempted to define sexual harassment. Although it has been defined conceptually, empirically, and legally, there continues to be some disagreement on what behaviours constitute sexual harassment. One reason for this lack of consensus is that research shows consistent gender differences in the perceptions of sexual harassment. Furthermore, perceptions of sexual harassment are influenced by the severity of the behaviour, the characteristics of the harasser, and characteristics of the target.

Incidence of sexually harassing behaviour and perpetrators

According to national surveys of US Federal employees, one out of four workers reported experiencing sexual harassment on the job over a two-year period (US Merit Systems Protection Board, 1981). Although male employees did report experiencing sexual harassment (15%), women were far more likely to report experiencing such behaviours (42%). Numerous studies on the frequency of sexual harassment on university campuses show that 10 to 92% of the respondents in studies report experiencing sexual harassment (Collins and Blodgett, 1981; Sandler, 1981; LaFontaine and Tredeau, 1986; Graverholz, 1989). In the US Navy, 42% of the enlisted women and 26% of the women offenders reported that they had been sexually harassed in a one-year survey period while on duty, on base or on ship (Culbertson *et al.*, 1992). Fitzgerald *et al.* (1988) found that although 51 to 76% respondents reported experiences of sexual harassment, only 3% reported it to an official. Similarly, Stephenson *et al.* (1989) found that 59% of undergraduate students reported experiencing sexual harassment but only 3% reported it to an official. In the UK, Davidson and Cooper (1992) found that 59% of women reported sexual harassment at work. Similar to the USA, there is evidence of severe underreporting of sexual harassment in the UK. Kingsmill (1989) quotes a 1989 survey by a London School of Economics student which reported that only 25% of sexual harassment incidents were reported, while in Davidson and Cooper (1992), only 14% of the employees reported incidences through formal means.

Women are the most frequent target of sexual harassment while men are the most frequent harasser or perpetrator (Ryan and Kenig, 1991). In addition, many harassing experiences reported by women occurred repeatedly, often lasting longer than a week and many longer than 6 months (US Merit Systems Protection Board, 1981). The women tend to be younger than their harasser (Gutek and Dunwoody, 1988; Fain and Anderton, 1987). Single or divorced women and women with a higher level of education report more sexual harassment experiences (Fain and Anderton, 1987; Martin, 1978). Finally, women in non-traditional jobs, including male-dominated management jobs, experience more sexual harassment (Gutek, 1985; Coles, 1986; Gutek and Dunwoody, 1987).

The most frequent harasser is a woman's peer or co-worker, followed by a superior (US Merit Systems Protection Board, 1981; Gutek, 1985). However, more severe forms of sexual harassment are perceived to be initiated by one's superior. The most commonly experienced harassment includes unwanted sexual teasing, jokes, remarks, questions, unwanted sexual looks, staring, gestures and unwanted sexual whistles, calls, hoots and yells. That is, the more frequent forms of sexual harassment appear to fall into the gender harassment or seduction categories developed by Fitzgerald and Shullman (1993). The more severe forms of sexual harassment are less often reported and are more likely to be initiated by the superior.

Tangri et al. (1982) found that women and men in non-traditional fields experience more sexual harassment. Ryan and Kenig (1991), on the other hand, found that women in traditional areas were more likely to experience sexual harassment. Lach and Gwartney-Gibbs (1993) suggest that women in traditional and non-traditional jobs experience different types of sexual harassment. For women in traditional jobs, sexual harassment is characterized as a threat of losing one's job. It begins with subtle compliments, hints for dates and jokes. Carothers and Crull (1984) found that when women refuse these advances in traditional jobs, the result is work sabotage, reprimands and potentially job loss.

On the other hand, women in non-traditional jobs (including managerial jobs) are more likely to experience sexual harassment as a sexually demeaning work environment including hostile and threatening sexual comments, accompanied by non-sexual acts designed to let the woman know she is an outsider (Lach and Gwartney-Gibbs, 1993). Gutek and Cohen (1987) reported that women in non-traditional jobs report more of all kinds of sexual harassment than any other group of women. Tangri et al. (1982) found that these women are as likely to be harassed by their peers as their supervisors. One interpretation of these findings is that sexual harassment appears to be a form of retaliation against women for threatening male economic and social power (Lach and Gwartney-Gibbs, 1993). Lee (1993) also indicated that women managers may experience sexual harassment from subordinates and superiors, as well as peers (Clarke, 1986). Clarke (1986) discovered that women managers were most likely to encounter a hostile work environment inflicted by co-workers, clients and subordinates. That is, for the female manager harassment is likely to occur on or regarding business trips, entertaining clients, and at social functions.

EXPLANATIONS OF SEXUAL HARASSMENT

The first wave of research on sexual harassment focused on the two areas just reviewed in this chapter: (1) the definition of sexual harassment, and (2) its frequency (Gutek and Dunwoody, 1987; Gutek, 1993). A second wave in research reflects an attempt to explain or understand why sexual harassment occurs in organizations. Each of the explanations identifies varying determinants of sexual harassment behaviour and, as such, has significantly different implications for what method or techniques can address or eliminate it.

Biological, organizational and sociocultural models

Tangri et al. (1982) derived three models to explain sexual harassment and assessed them using a sample of 20,083 Federal employees. The models included the natural/biological model, the organizational model, and the sociocultural model. The natural/biological model suggested that sexual harassment is a result of a natural sexual attraction between people. One version of this explanation asserts that sexual harassment is a natural outcome of stronger male sex drives. That is, men have stronger sex drives than women and, therefore, will more frequently initiate sexual contact. A key feature of this explanation is that sexual harassment may be an outcome of a natural process, and that men do not intend to harass. This model is similar to the individual differences model proposed by Nieva and Gutek (1981). The organizational model, on the other hand, states that sexual harassment results from the 'opportunity structures created by organizational climate, hierarchy, and specific authority relations' (Tangri et al., 1982, p. 35). That is, physical, structural, and normative features of organizations provide the opportunity for men to harass women. For example, often men and women are differentially distributed in positions of authority with men in positions of greater power. This appears to be true at all levels of the organization and across virtually all functional units. Nieva and Gutek's (1981) structural institutional and intergroup model is consistent with the organizational model and maintains that sexual harassment is the result of structures within the organization that provide the opportunity for people in higher positions to use their authority to influence lower-status employees to engage in sexual interactions.

The sociocultural model suggests that power differences between men and women, supported by society at large, lead to the harassment of women at work. Men are rewarded for being assertive sexually while women are rewarded, both socially and economically (Gutek, 1985), for being more compliant and passive. The sociocultural model is compatible with aspects of the sex-role and intergroup explanations proposed by Nieva and Gutek (1981).

Little empirical evidence has been found to support the natural/biological or individual deficit explanations of sexual harassment (Tangri et al., 1982). Partial support was found for the organizational model, although some predictions were not supported. Using data of the US Merit Systems Protection

Board, partial support was found for the sociocultural model. Tangri *et al.* (1982) concluded that each of the models provided some useful information about the reasons for sexual harassment but none provides a full explanation.

Sex-role spillover model

To address some of the weaknesses in several of these models, Gutek and Morasch (1982) developed the sex-role spillover model in which characteristics from each of the major models were integrated. Sex-role spillover occurs when gender-based roles inappropriate to work carry over into the workplace. For example, men or women are sometimes expected to behave at work in ways that are consistent with a traditionally masculine or feminine stereotype, that is, women expected to be nurturant or men expected to be dominant in a mixed-group discussion. One aspect of sex-role spillover that is particularly relevant to sex harassment is the stereotype of female as sex object.

The sex-role spillover model combines aspects of structural institutional, the sex-role and the intergroup explanations proposed by Nieva and Gutek (1981) as well as aspects of Tangri *et al.*'s (1982) organizational model and sociocultural model. However, it focuses on specific workplace characteristics rather than on individual characteristics or general societal issues (Gutek, 1985). Gutek (1985) found empirical support for the sex-role spillover model of sexual harassment. She hypothesized and found that women in male-dominated jobs were more likely to report sexual overtures than other women (74% in non-traditional jobs *vs* 50% women in total sample).

Individual differences and sexual harassment

One line of research in this area has attempted to identify the individual characteristics that distinguish men who sexually harass from men who do not (Pryor, 1987). The little information available on sexual harassers has generally come from the descriptions obtained from victims (targets) themselves. Sexual harassers tend to be married, older than their target, the same race as their target, and are more likely to be a co-worker than a supervisor. Pryor (1987) has developed a scale designed to assess the sexual harassment proclivities of men. He found that men scoring high on the survey designed to assess one's likelihood to sexually harass (LSH) were more likely to hold adversarial beliefs, to have difficulty assuming the perspective of others, to have high rape propensities, and to behave in sexually exploitative ways when their motives could be somewhat hidden by situational excuses.

Consistent with the search for individual differences variables associated with sexual harassment is the 'bad apples' argument in the ethical decision-making literature (Trevino and Youngblood, 1990). The 'bad apples' argument suggests that unethical behaviour in organizations is the result of a few corrupt or unsavoury individuals (Simpson, 1987) who lack some personal quality such as moral character. Individual variables that have been associated with ethical behaviour include locus of control, economic value orientation, political value orientation, Machiavellianism, and cognitive moral development (Hegarty and Sims, 1978, 1979; Trevino *et al.*, 1985). To date, however, the empirical research on sexual harassment has not identified clear or stark differences between males who engage in sexual harassment and those who do not. The current profile of a typical sexual harasser is nearly identical to the profile of a typical male worker. There is a need for future research to determine whether there are psychological or social-psychological correlates.

Power and sexual harassment

It is widely believed that the concept of power is central to understanding sexual harassment (Collins and Blodgett, 1981; DiTomaso, 1989). A feminist perspective on sexual harassment emphasizes a power relationship, male over female, and the potential for economic coercion that threatens women's economic livelihood. Further, the harassment of women reflects women's status in society and asserts their sex role over their work role (Gutek, 1985). From a legal perspective, sexual harassment reflects an unequal power relationship that is exploitative (e.g. *quid pro quo*). It reflects an abuse of power rather than a sexual issue (Dziech and Weiner, 1984). From an organizational perspective, sexual harassment is the improper use of power to obtain sexual gratification. It is coercive, exploitative, and women are treated as sex objects (Gutek, 1985; DiTomaso, 1989). Although these numerous perspectives on sexual harassment include power as a determinant, there is little empirical information or theoretical articulation on how power leads to or contributes to sexual harassment.

Cleveland and Kerst (1993) developed a model depicting how societal, organizational and individual power characteristics are involved in sexual harassment. They indicate that power plays a key role in sexual harassment, although its role may be more clearly visible in some forms of harassment – supervisory *quid pro quo* – than in others – peer or subordinate hostile work environment. Cleveland and Kerst (1993) discuss three levels of power that come together at work to provide the conditions for sexual harassment: societal, organizational, and interpersonal or personal power. Both societal and organizational power sources provide the bases for specific work conditions in an organization that may enhance or inhibit sexual harassment. For example, men hold higher-status positions while women are more likely to hold positions that lack power (Kanter, 1977). Individuals who occupy a higher-status position are expected or believed to be within their rights to make demands of those in lower-status positions. Sexual harassment may be viewed by those with high power as simply an extension of that right. Informally, and perhaps most important to individuals in management positions, there is evidence that informal power structures among colleagues or co-workers exclude women. Kanter (1977) found that managers acquire power through networks with others including peers, subordinates, and mentors. Men have greater ease and opportunity to develop these networks that are central and critical to the organization (Brass, 1985). Therefore, formally a male and female manager may have equal power (through these organizational positions) but, often informally, the man has access to greater opportunity, resources and rewards than does the woman.

Both the societal and organizational bases of power set the conditions of the work environment, which, in turn, interacts with the interpersonal or personal power of men and women. Given that women are less likely to occupy positions where they have the opportunity to exercise power, it is not surprising that women are less likely to be perceived as having power or to use the most effective tactics for exercising the power they have. Moreover, women's power strategies may actually perpetuate the perceptions of powerlessness. Thus, societal, organizational and personal factors combine to affect the perceptions of women as relatively powerless in the workplace, which increases the likelihood of sex harassment.

Sexual harassment by supervisor, co-workers, and subordinates

Depending upon the source of harassment, different power issues may be involved. The presence of formal power differences is fairly obvious when the harasser involves the supervisor. Supervisors have the capacity to distribute rewards or punishments and they evaluate the performance of subordinates and make decisions regarding promotions and pay increases. Initial conceptualizations of sexual harassment, both the legal and feminist perspectives, clearly had the supervisor in mind as the perpetrator. Sexual harassment by a supervisor is particularly harmful to the individual and the organization by virtue of the position of power he holds. Supervisors are instrumental in the formation of work climate and establishing the norms for acceptable and unacceptable behaviour.

Co-workers are the most frequent perpetrators of sexual harassment in organizations although they tend to engage in less severe forms. Although this finding is cited as evidence that power differences cannot fully explain sexual harassment, Cleveland and Kerst (1993) discuss how informal power differences among men and women occupying the same or similar jobs can create conditions for harassment. Carothers and Crull (1984) state that male workers are overtly hostile toward women who challenge or compete with them for jobs – especially high-status, male-dominated occupations with high pay and benefits. There is accumulating evidence that a woman who occupies that same position as a man simply does not have the same level of authority or power (Kanter, 1977; Ragins and Sundstrom, 1989). Women are typically given less decision-making discretion and less latitude for exercising power (by their largely male supervisors) than their male co-workers (Wolf and Fligstein, 1979). Further, women are not perceived to have legitimate power or to hold positions of specialty in areas that are central or critical. Male co-workers might employ sexual harassment in a goal-directed manner to acquire and maintain more informal power than their female co-workers.

Co-workers can exercise power by providing or withholding information, co-operation and support. There is evidence that men feel uncomfortable or may be unwilling to work as equals with women (Pleck, 1976). As well, men threatened by female co-workers may believe that an increase in power for women translates to a decrease in power for men (DiTomaso, 1989). One strategy to acquire or increase power would be to highlight a woman's sex role – her womanness or sexuality – over her gender role and thereby remind her, and others in the work group as well, that she is a member of an outgroup. Over time the outgroup member receives less challenging work assignments and eventually may be less well informed than co-workers in the supervisor's ingroup. According to Cleveland and Kerst (1993), because working well with one's co-workers is a requirement in many managerial positions, co-workers can, in fact, accrue formal power bases and demand sexual favours from a woman in return for co-worker support and favourable peer feedback to the supervisor. In addition, co-worker sexual harassment tends to be less severe in form. Because people have more difficulty labelling less severe forms of sexual harassment, a woman co-worker may have a difficult time gaining support for an allegation of co-worker harassment. Other co-workers and the supervisor may rally more around the better-networked male harasser than the female target.

'Contrapower harassment' is the term coined by Benson (1984) to describe sexual harassment that occurs when the target has formal power over the perpetrator. Similar to co-worker harassment, subordinate harassment can occur when the male has informal power resources to rely on that the target has not. Consider the example where a female manager is the sole or near lone woman in a functional area. The subordinates may be quite aware that although she occupies the supervisory position, the woman has little real access to resources and collegial support. She may be viewed as occupying the position solely to satisfy affirmative action requirements. The goal of the harassment in contrapower harassment is to devalue the woman's work role by highlighting her sexuality or gender role – her helplessness, incompetence, passivity. There is an attempt to acquire or enhance one's own power by denigrating another through sexist comments or gender harassment (Graverholz, 1989).

Formal position power may enable a supervisor to engage in sexual harassment. That is, supervisors can harass because they have the formal authority to request favours from a less powerful subordinate. On the other hand, sexual harassment by a peer or subordinate may provide a mechanism to gain power or to minimize power differentials between employees or between the supervisors and employee. Therefore, depending upon the position of the harasser, the mechanism for linking power to sexual harassment may differ, although it is a central construct in understanding harassment by all their groups (Cleveland and Kerst, 1993).

CORRELATES OF SEXUAL HARASSMENT: INDIVIDUAL AND ORGANIZATIONAL

Who is harassed and who does the harassing? One of the major issues with this question is that the responses are largely based on self-report data obtained either from women who have experienced harassment directly or from male and female subjects in studies designed to assess perceptions of sexual harassment.

Target characteristics

There is no profile of the typical person who encounters or experiences sexual harassment. Research *does* indicate that targets of sexual harassment are likely to be women, younger, single or divorced, have a higher education and tend to have less traditional jobs. However, all women are vulnerable (Lach and Gwartney-Gibbs, 1993).

People differ in the extent to which they 'see' or perceive that a behaviour constitutes harassment. One of the most consistent and robust research findings in this area is that women tend to label more behaviours as sexual harassment than do men (Collins and Blodgett, 1981; Powell, 1986; Gutek and Dunwoody, 1987). Consistently, behaviour initiated by a supervisor or someone with power is likely to be viewed as harassment (Reilly *et al.*, 1982; Fitzgerald, 1990). The more explicit or severe the harassing behaviours (e.g. joking or teasing *vs* physical contact, forced kissing), the more likely the behaviour will be labelled as sexual harassment by both men and women. Further, gender differences in perceptions tend to diminish as the severity of behaviour increases.

Gutek and Dunwoody (1987) also indicate that the interpersonal relationship (prior interaction) influences the perceptions of harassment. Gruber and Bjorn (1986) found that women with lower self-esteem or low life satisfaction were found to respond more passively to harassment than women with higher esteem. This suggests that lower self-esteem women may be particularly vulnerable. Being 'feminine', including passive, nurturant and submissive, may increase a woman's likelihood of being a target (Quina, 1990). Women with high self-esteem and traditional sex-role attitudes tend to be most tolerant and least aware of potential harm that sexual harassment can have on its targets (Malovich and Stake, 1990).

Harasser characteristics

There has been limited success in developing a profile of the sexual harasser, due to lack of replication of results; the statement that 'Harassers are similar to the average man' continues to hold true (Fitzgerald and Weitzman, 1990). Harassers are likely to be older than their targets and married. Moreover, the typical harasser is a male co-worker who has likely harassed other women at work (US Merit Systems Protection Board, 1981; Gutek, 1985). The finding that harassers tend to be married suggests that harassment is not a romantic or personal interest exchange but may serve a more 'pragmatic purpose' (Fitzgerald and Weitzman, 1990, p. 131).

Powell (1986) found that men higher in masculinity tended to rate fewer behaviours as sexual harassment. On the other hand, women higher in masculinity tended to view more behaviours as sexual harassment. Consistent with this finding, Dziech and Weiner (1984) and Pryor (1987) found that sexual harassers, and men likely to harass, hold more extreme versions of our cultural stereotype of masculinity as the dominance of men over women. Men who emphasize male social and sexual dominance and who are insensitive to other people's perspectives are likely to initiate severe sexual harassing behaviour (Pryor, 1987). Pryor and Stroller (1992) found that social power and sexuality are linked in the mind of men with a high likelihood to sexual harassment. Bargh and Raymond (1992) also provided evidence of a dominance-sexuality link. These findings are partially consistent with the feminist view that sexual harassment is not solely sexual, but is also an expression of power (DeAngelis, 1991; Pryor *et al.*, 1993).

However, personal characteristics of the harasser and the target are only one aspect of sexual harassment. Research has yet to consistently find stable individual difference variables that describe a typical perpetrator. (For exception, see Perry (1983) who found that harassers have reputations for being sexually exploitative, suggesting a more stable trait.) That is, the profile of organizational sexual harassers or 'bad apples' has continued to elude researchers. However, it is difficult to draw conclusions from research on harassers who actually go on trial because they represent probably fewer than 40% of harassment incidences (Pryor *et al.*, 1993).

Organizational correlates

Organizations that are more sexualized create the conditions that are conducive to sexual harassment (Gutek, 1985; Haavio-Mannila *et al.*, 1988; Tangri *et al.*, 1982). Women in organizations that support, allow or accept sexual harassment are more likely to report such incidences (Lach and Gwartney-Gibbs, 1993). Indeed, LaVite (1991) has found evidence of a Person × Situation interaction. A male who scores high in terms of likelihood to sexually harass is more likely to engage in harassment in situations where the local norms, however transmitted, are permissive.

Other important situational factors include sex ratio within a job, sex-role spillover, and the number of males with a high likelihood to sexually harass in a work group (Larwood and Gutek, 1984; Lafontaine and Tredeau, 1986; Pryor *et al.*, 1993). Women in male-dominated jobs are highly visible and are often viewed as the spokesperson for all women. Furthermore, they are found to be more frequent objects of sexual harassment than women in mixed or traditionally female jobs (Schneider, 1982; Lafontaine and Tredeau, 1986). One reason that male-dominated sex ratio can increase a woman's likelihood of harassment is due to sex-role spillover. A woman's minority status may highlight the incongruity between one's sex role and one's work role.

Rules and norms that managers apply to subordinates, and management power styles, work habits, and dress all contribute to perceptions of the permissiveness of the organizational climate to sexual harassment. When upper levels of management condone such behaviour, they send a message throughout the whole organization (Larwood and Gutek, 1984). On the other hand, if an organization is rated high on support for equal employment, it is likely to be rated as lower in incidences of sexual harassment (Lafontaine and Tredeau, 1986).

CONSEQUENCES OF SEXUAL HARASSMENT FOR EMPLOYEES AND THE ORGANIZATION

Most research on the consequences of sexual harassment has very appropriately focused on the emotional–psychological, physical and work-related outcomes for the target of harassment. However, sexual harassment affects not only the target, but also the effectiveness of the organization, the harasser, and bystanders or persons who were not harassed directly, but observed the harassment. We know very little about how the harassing behaviour, if not punished or halted, affects the harasser's perceptions of the target, other potential targets, and his work performance and relations. There is also little empirical information on the reactions and productivity of harassment observers or bystanders.

Outcomes for the target

One of the most common emotional or psychological outcomes of sexual harassment is general tension and anger (Crull, 1982). Silverman (1976) found that 78% of women who were harassed reported that they suffered emotionally. Loy and Stewart (1984), in a telephone survey of 550 individuals who had been harassed found that 75% experienced stress. Gutek (1985; Jensen and Gutek, 1982) found that 40% of women felt disgust, 30% anger, anxiety or hurt and some experienced depression, sadness or guilt (less than 10%). In the classic US Merit Systems Protection Board (1981) survey, 21–82% of the women reported that their emotional or physical condition worsened after the harassment. Sexual harassment adversely affects self-esteem (Gruber and Bjorn, 1986) and self-confidence (Benson and Thomson, 1982), as well as the woman's relationships with other men (Gutek, 1985).

Targets of harassment also engage in self-blame (Jensen and Gutek, 1982, e.g. 'I should have bolted the door'). There is fear of retaliation and beliefs that the incident or behaviours will not be perceived by others as serious (Koss, 1990). Gutek and Koss (1993) suggest that the emotional and psychological outcomes of sexual harassment resemble symptoms of post-traumatic stress disorder (Koss, 1990). Further, they cite oral testimony before US Congress (Kilpatrick, 1992) indicating that women who suffered from post-traumatic stress disorder (PTSD) and depression were more likely to have experienced sexual harassment. In general, the emotional and psychological outcomes for women who have reported sexual harassment include tension and anxiety, uncontrolled and persistent anger, feelings of fear, alienation, helplessness, sadness and depression, and unwarranted feelings of guilt or self-blame (Terpstra and Baker, 1991).

Physical ailments often accompany psychological problems. Crull (1982) found that 62% of targets of sexual harassment who sought assistance at the Working Women's Institute reported physical symptoms including nausea, headaches, tiredness, gastrointestinal problems, jaw tightness, teeth grinding, binge eating, inability to sleep, loss of appetite, weight loss and crying spells (Sandler, 1981; Loy and Stewart, 1984; Gutek, 1985). Sexual harassment increases one's stress level. Matteson and Ivancevich (1987) suggest that approximately 50–70% of physical illnesses are associated with elevated stress. Such illnesses would include heart disease, ulcers and stomach and kidney diseases. Although there are self-report data on physical symptoms associated with sexual harassment, more research is needed on actual physical outcomes of harassment.

Although not based on controlled studies, there is clear evidence that sexual harassment can significantly and adversely affect a woman's career. Harassment can lead to negative interpersonal relations at work (DiTomaso,

1989; Culbertson *et al.*, 1992). It can lead an enabler or harasser to form alliances with male co-workers (Schneider, 1982; Gutek, 1985) and can isolate the target. Students report dropping courses and changing majors as a result of sexual harassment (Fitzgerald *et al.*, 1988). Over a two-year period, 36,000 US Federal employees quit their jobs, transferred or were reassigned or fired due to sexual harassment (US Merit Systems Protection Board, 1988). Generally, 1 in 10 women reported they left their jobs due to sexual harassment (Gutek *et al.*, 1980; US Merit Systems Protection Board, 1981). Culbertson *et al.* (1992) found that sexual harassment adversely affected women's job satisfaction including women's satisfaction with their co-workers and their supervisor (O'Farrell and Harlan, 1982).

The impact of sexual harassment on the target's performance on the job is less clear. Renick (1980) reported that harassed employees tend to be more accident prone and to take more sick leave. Based on self-report data, 10% of both male and female targets reported a decrease in work performance (US Merit Systems Protection Board, 1981, 1988). According to Gutek and Koss (1993), sexual harassment may have an indirect effect on performance. Harassment denies women access to informal social networks and to feedback necessary to perform their work successfully (Martin, 1978, 1980). Access to informal networks and performance feedback may be especially important for managerial and executive women who rely extensively on such avenues of information (Murphy and Cleveland, 1991; Cleveland and Kerst, 1993). Benson and Thomson (1982) asserted that long-term effects of sexual harassment include decreased career and organizational commitment.

Outcomes for harasser

Few studies have specifically identified the consequences of engaging in sexual harassment for the harasser. Davidson and Earnshaw (1990) reported that in the UK the most common punishment for the harasser was an official or non-official warning. The next most likely outcome was no action at all. More than half (54%) of the personnel directors surveyed indicated that the harasser never faced dismissal, while the target had a greater likelihood of transfer. It seems likely that similar consequences, or lack thereof, occur in US organizations and university settings.

Kipnis (1990) describes a process that suggests that unchallenged harassment may actually encourage subsequent harassment. Specifically Kipnis states that the successful exercise of power or influence over another can have metamorphic effects on both the power-holder (harasser) and the social relationship between the more and less powerful. The metamorphic effect can lead a power-holder to change his self-evaluation and increase his view of his own worth (Cleveland and Kerst, 1993). Because the power-holder or harasser often does not receive feedback, especially negative feedback, about his behaviour, he will believe that he is better and that generally accepted rules, laws or values do not apply to him (Kipnis, 1990), that is, the harasser will perceive virtually no sanctions to his behaviour. Perhaps an even more problematic consequence of the metamorphic effect is the likelihood that successful influence strategies (sexual harassment) will be followed by the harasser's devaluation of the less powerful target. Subsequent behaviour of the harasser includes increasing social distance (Kipnis, 1990), thereby increasing the ease of exercising the control of others in a negative manner. As psychological and social distance between the harasser and target grows (as a result of the metamorphic effect), the perceived barriers to these behaviours diminish and sexual harassment continues. More research is needed to understand the harasser's perspective on his or her behaviour.

Bystander or observer outcomes of sexual harassment

Co-workers may actually exacerbate problems associated with harassment. Loy and Steward (1984) found that co-workers tend to ignore or isolate people who have been sexually harassed or to perceive them as trouble-makers (MacKinnon, 1979). They do not want to associate with targets, in part because of the risks in reporting sexual harassment. These risks include fear of retaliation, from both supervisor and co-worker, fear of challenging an individual with organizational authority, and the fear of not being taken seriously. The latter risk is especially an issue for women in male-dominated jobs such as management. A woman's co-workers are likely to be mostly men. Given that there are consistent gender differences in the perception of what behaviours constitute harassment, disagreements between a female target and her male co-workers are likely. We know little about the conditions under which an observer of a harassing exchange will say or do something or the characteristics of the bystander who will intervene. Does the observation of a sexually harassing incident have a quieting effect on the co-worker? Under what conditions would a bystander support the target or confront the harasser? These are empirical questions that have yet to be addressed.

Organizational outcomes

In 1980 the EEOC published guidelines on sexual harassment. In 1981 only 29% of organizations surveyed had policies regarding sexual harassment, compared to 97% of organizations surveyed in 1987 (Bureau of National Affairs, 1987). However, often these policies indicate that the first step in the reporting process is to report the incident to one's supervisor and yet up to 50% of harassment cases involve the supervisor (Gutek, 1985). Also, there has been virtually no evaluation of the effectiveness of their procedures or policies in addressing harassment at work. According to Collins and Blodgett (1981), many managers in the USA believe that the seriousness and frequency of sexual harassment is overrated (two-thirds of men and half of women surveyed agreed with the statement that sexual harassment was exaggerated). Gutek (1985) found that fewer than 5% of her respondents stated that sexual harassment was a major problem. In the UK, only 65 of the 100 personnel directors surveyed believed sexual harassment was a serious management issue (Davidson and Earnshaw, 1990). Gutek and Koss (1993) report that there is little information on the direct or indirect costs of sexual harassment to the organization; much of the information is speculative or anecdotal. It appears that a general organizational outcome of sexual harassment is that management may be more likely to see the trouble caused by complaints of sexual harassment than to be aware of the effects of sexual harassment itself (Gutek and Koss, 1993).

STRATEGIES FOR REDUCING SEXUAL HARASSMENT: INDIVIDUAL AND ORGANIZATIONAL RESPONSES

There are a number of reactions that both the target and the organization can have to sexual harassment. Some responses are most likely among targets and they may vary in terms of their effectiveness in stopping the harassment and in their consequences, that is, co-worker isolation, target being discharged. One characteristic of this literature, however, is that there are few studies that empirically assess the effectiveness of specific individual or organizational responses.

Individual reactions and coping strategies

Targets or recipients of sexual harassment are slow to acknowledge and respond to incidences of harassment. One of the most frequent reactions is to ignore the behaviour (US Merit Systems Protection Board, 1981) or to avoid the harasser (Fitzgerald et al., 1988; Culbertson et al., 1992; Fitzgerald and Shullman, 1993), although few find these approaches useful. The most effective actions appear to be direct and informal, such as telling the harasser to stop (US Merit Systems Protection Board, 1981). Only a very small percentage of targets report the experience to their supervisors (Culbertson et al., 1992) and even fewer filed a formal grievance. Few individuals discuss their experiences with others (US Merit Systems Protection Board, 1981, 1988) and most women ignore the behaviour or do nothing.

Although more research is needed on the relative effectiveness of responses to sexual harassment, there are studies examining the perceptions of what strategies affect sexual harassment. For example, respondents to the US Merit Systems Protection Board survey (1988) were asked what reactions made things better. Responses that were perceived to be effective by most female employees included asking or telling the person to stop (61%), avoiding the person (45%), threatening to tell the supervisor (55%), reporting the behaviour to the supervisor or other official (49%), transferring, disciplining or giving the harasser a poor performance rating (48%), or making a joke of the behaviour (40%).

There are a variety of reasons why women are reluctant to discuss or report these incidents. Often, women are blamed for the harassment. Collins and Blodgett (1981) stated that there is some disagreement even among women about whether they should be able to handle it themselves. Men more than women believe that women should be able to handle sexual harassment ('It is her problem' – not an organizational problem). Women also fear that the harassment will reflect negatively on their character. Further, there is evidence cited earlier in this chapter indicating that women who do speak out are often ignored by co-workers or discredited. Livingston (1982) found that in some cases, more active coping strategies such as speaking out can lead to increased stress. Women also feel that nothing will be done even if they do speak out (Sandler, 1981). For example, in the US Navy the most common negative reaction by women who did report the sexual harassment was, 'I was humiliated in front of others' (33% of enlisted women and 34% of officers, Culbertson *et al.*, 1992).

Gruber and Bjorn (1986) suggest three reasons why individuals tend to use an indirect method so frequently. First, indirect methods allow women to handle the situation without significant disruption of the work setting or of relations with others (Collins and Blodgett, 1981; Gutek, 1985). Second, women may perceive direct methods such as confronting the harasser or filing a complaint as more risky. A woman may generate a more hostile work environment if she forces a person or the organization to deal with the sexual harassment incident (DiTomaso, 1989). Finally, Gruber and Bjorn (1986) state that some forms of sexual harassment, especially less severe, more frequently occurring forms, are ambiguous. Therefore, it may be difficult to distinguish sexual harassment from behaviour that reflects a combination of sexual attraction and offensive behaviour.

Organizational responses and interventions

Interventions to deter sexual harassment are difficult to develop because there is not agreement regarding the behaviours that constitute sexual harassment (Pryor and Day, 1988). Certainly, women perceive more sexual harassment than men, especially in ambiguous cases (Benson and Thompson, 1982). Livingston (1982) recommends that employer actions include issuing a policy statement which identifies the employer's commitment to deter sexual harassment. The statement needs to include a definition of unacceptable behaviour, the explicit statement that the organization disapproves of such behaviour, the detrimental effects of the behaviour, and an indication of the corrective or disciplinary actions to be taken. The policy statement should establish grievance procedures and, in general, educate employees about the importance and impact of sexual harassment. Although most US organizations currently have sexual harassment policies (Bureau of National Affairs, 1987), many of these policies indicate that the first step in reporting an incident is to one's supervisor who is often the harasser (Gutek, 1985; US Customs Service, 1992). Organizations also recomment that the target confront the offender directly if possible, to make it clear that they are not interested or that the behaviour is unacceptable. Other organizations provide checklists for employers to assess the appropriateness of their behaviours. The Office of Human Resources of the US Fish and Wildlife Service provides the following checklist: Does the behaviour help or hinder in the accomplishment or work or mission? Does the behaviour offend or hurt other members of the work group who are exposed to it? Can the behaviour send out signals that may invite sexually harassing behaviour on the part of others? Can the behaviour be interpreted as intentionally harmful or harassing?

Biaggio *et al.* (1990) suggest a number of interventions. First, key employees in the organization can be targeted to attend workshops or training on sexual harassment. Employees can be informed about organizational policy. The training should be interactive and experiential. Participants should have the opportunity to respond to simulations, role play, and videos. Second, new employer orientations can be used to disseminate information and heighten awareness about what is acceptable and unacceptable through guidelines and organizational policies. Finally, for educational purposes memos with sexist comments can be circulated throughout a department or organization to exemplify unacceptable behaviour. Organization interventions have been limited in scope (i.e. information dissemination, awareness heightening) and success has rarely been addressed. This is one area that is waiting for good research efforts.

CONCLUSION

What we know and what we do not know: future research needs

Women are increasingly entering male-dominated managerial occupations. However, as the research data show, women continue to be segregated into lower, less central or critical areas of management, and given fewer resources and authority than their male counterparts. Sexual harassment is reported to be one method for maintaining women's less favourable economic and occupational status within organizations. However, except for a few notable studies (see Gutek, 1985, and US Merit Systems Protection Board, 1981, 1988), much of the sexual harassment research has utilized non-managerial and student populations. Research needs in this area can be categorized into five areas: construct articulation, target research needs, harasser research needs, organizational research needs, and more general research issues.

Fitzgerald and Shullman (1993), who themselves have been pioneers in the development of scales that empirically define sexual harassment, stress the need for conceptual clarity of the construct of sexual harassment. They state that the legal distinction between quid pro quo and hostile work environment is not sensitive enough. Sexual harassment is a multidimensional construct and in order to understand the harassment context, researchers need to look jointly at target, harasser and organizational characteristics. They suggest that the type and extent of sexual harassment in the workplace are functions of target, perpetrator (harasser) and organizational factors. It is likely that different factors or combinations of these three variables lead to gender harassment as opposed to more severe forms of sexual harassment. As I noted earlier in this chapter, it is also likely that different explanations of sexual harassment may be more accurate or appropriate for one form of harassment than for another. Moreover, we know less about the extent and forms of sexual harassment that women managers encounter and that minority managers experience.

Although past research on harassers has not yielded a set of traits or characteristics that could be used to predict who is likely or not likely to harass, there should be continued research in this area. As the definitions of sexual harassment become more sophisticated and somewhat more complex, researchers may be better equipped to identify personal or social factors that will enhance the success of identifying individuals who are likely to engage in sexually harassing behaviours. However, I will stress that I am not advocating solely a 'bad apples' approach to sexual harassment. In fact, I strongly urge that researchers use the Harasser × Organization interaction as the unit of analysis. That is, we need to know what combinations of personal and organization characteristics come together to lead to sexual harassment. The incest and sexual assault literatures may be useful sources of insight, and theory developed in these areas may lead to more successful prediction of who harasses at work. Surely, individuals who engage in harassment at work do not confine such behaviours to the work domain.

Depending upon the specific harassment behaviours that are displayed, there has been little research on what interventions can address (effectively) such behaviours. There is little information on the interventions designed to address harasser behaviour directly. Are different interventions needed depending upon the severity of the harassment or other harassment features? Would interventions include some combination of individual or group therapy, as well as training programmes designed by the organization, that is information dissemination, awareness heightening, education of organizational factors involved in harassment, and so forth?

A third area of future research is identified by Gutek and Koss (1993). They urge that more research is needed in following targets or victims over time to assess psychological distress, somatic effects and work changes resulting from harassment. There is a need for measures that assess such responses to sexual harassment and these measures – like those used by Fitzgerald and Brock (1992) – should include person variables, event variables, organizational variables and environmental variables.

Perhaps the area that is in most urgent need of future research includes organizational response and interventions to sexual harassment (Fitzgerald and Shullman, 1993). There has been little attention given to the actual responses organizations make and how these responses address or exacerbate or perpetuate the problems associated with the harassment incidents. Do organizational policies inhibit the reporting of harassment? Does the initial organizational response contribute to co-worker or supervisor retaliation toward the target?

As Fitzgerald and Shullman indicate, the lack of a consensual definition of sexual harassment contributes to the difficulty in identifying training needs, goals and behavioural objectives or outcomes of a training intervention. Lack of behavioural objectives, such as individual skill building, contributes to an ambiguity in how to evaluate training effectiveness. Also, consistent with some explanations of sexual harassment, the most appropriate intervention may involve an organization development (OD) intervention to alter norms and values of the organization, as well as alter organizational hierarchy and culture, roles within the organization, and so forth (Fitzgerald and Shullman, 1993). There has been little articulation regarding what OD strategies might be useful in addressing power issues, communication problems, and supervisor–subordinate and co-worker to co-worker interpersonal issues as they apply to a sexual harassment situation. Therefore, future research should focus on identifying training techniques that would be useful for individual skill-building and OD interventions that can be implemented to address contextual problems that are associated with the occurrence of sexual harassment. It may be that programmes such as diversity training may have inadvertent outcomes such as decreasing the hostile work environment for women managers in organizations.

Finally, sexual harassment is a human resource issue, not exclusively a woman's issue, and it is a phenomenon that occurs outside the USA.

Organizational climate or culture, organizational rewards, supervisory rewards and support/co-worker relations all comprise the fabric of an organization that is either productive or unproductive. Management, historically, has been concerned about identifying the patterns of these factors, that are associated with satisfaction and high-performing employees. A work setting that is not hostile, personally and sexually, for either men or women, is a part of this organizational fabric. Both sex discrimination and sexual harassment are human resource factors that are a part of organizational life that contributes to the dissatisfaction and decreased productivity of a significant group of employees. Managing human resources involves managing the quality of work lives of both women and men. Therefore, sexual harassment is a legitimate human resource issue and should not be trivialized or marginalized.

Much of the research cited in this chapter was collected in the USA and the UK. There is a need for future collaborative research regarding sexual harassment issues in other countries. In a recent book on European management women, only 1 country (the UK) out of 11 (UK, Ireland, Denmark, Netherlands, Germany, France, Belgium, Greece, Italy, Portugal, and Spain) (Davidson and Cooper, 1993) mentioned sexual harassment as an issue for female managers. It may be that in these countries such issues as gaining access to management continue to pose the most significant problems. However, future research may be proactive and anticipate that once women gain access, they will encounter problems similar to women in the USA. If they do not or have not, then it would be beneficial to know what factors distinguish the situations that face women in Europe from the factors that face US women managers.

REFERENCES

ALIMO-METCALFE, B. and WEDDERBURN-TATE, C. (1993) Women in business and management – the United Kingdom, in M. S. Davidson and C. L. Cooper (eds) *European Women in Business and Management*, pp. 16–42, Paul Chapman, London.

BARGH, J. and RAYMOND, P. (1992) Automatic power–sex association in men likely to be sexual harassers. Paper presented at the meeting of the Society for Experimental Social Psychology, San Antonio.

BARON, J. N., DAVIS-BLAKE, A. and BIELBY, W. T. (1986) The structure of opportunity: how promotion ladders vary within and among organizations, *Administrative Science Quarterly*, Vol. 31, pp. 248–73.

BENSON, D. J. and THOMSON, G. E. (1982) Sexual harassment on a university campus: the confluence of authority relations, sexual interest, and gender stratification, *Social Problems*, Vol. 29, pp. 236–51.

BENSON, K. (1984) Comment on Crocker: an analysis of university definitions of sexual harassment, *Signs*, Vol. 9, pp. 377–97.

BERGMANN, B. R. (1986) *The Economic Emergence of Women*, Basic Books, New York.

BIAGGIO, M. K., WATTS, D. and BROWNELL, A. (1990) Addressing sexual harassment: strategies for prevention and change, in M. A. Paludi (ed.) *Ivory Power: Sexual Harassment on Campus*, State University of New York Press, Albany, NY, pp. 213–30.

BOYD, N., MULVIHILL, M. and MILES, J. (1990) *Patriarchy and Postindustrialism: Women and Power in the Service Economy*. Departmental Working Paper, 90–1, Carleton University, Department of Sociology and Anthropology, Ottawa.

BRASS, D. J. (1985) Men's and women's networks: a study of informal interaction patterns and influence in an organization, *Academy of Management Journal*, Vol. 28, pp. 327–43.

BUREAU OF NATIONAL AFFAIRS (1987) *Sexual Harassment: Employer Policies and Problems,* June, Washington, DC.

CAROTHERS, S. C. and CRULL, P. (1984) Contrasting sexual harassment in female- and male-dominated occupations, in K. B. Sacks and D. Remy (eds) *My Troubles are Going to have Trouble with Me: Every Day Trials and Triumphs of Women Workers,* Rutgers University Press, New Brunswick, NJ, pp. 219–27.

CLARKE, L. W. (1986) Women supervisors experience sexual harassment too, *Supervisory Management,* Vol. 31, pp. 35–6.

CLEVELAND, J. N. and KERST, M. E. (1993) Sexual harassment and perceptions of power: an under-articulated relationship, *Journal of Vocational Behavior,* Vol. 42, pp. 49–67.

COLES, F. S. (1986) Forced to quit: sexual harassment complaints and agency response, *Sex Roles,* Vol. 14, pp. 81–95.

COLLINS, E. G. C. and BLODGETT, T. B. (1981) Sexual harassment: some see it . . . some won't, *Harvard Business Review,* Vol. 59, pp. 77–94.

CRULL, P. (1982) Stress effects of sexual harassment on the job: implications for counseling, *American Journal of Orthopsychiatry,* Vol. 52, pp. 539–44.

CULBERTSON, A. L., ROSENFELD, P., BOOTH-KEWLEY, S. and MAGNUSSON, P. (1992) Assessment of sexual harassment in the Navy: results of the 1989 Navy-wide survey. Navy Personnel Research and Development Center, San Diego, CA.

DAVIDSON, M. J. and COOPER, C. L. (1992) *Shattering the Glass Ceiling,* Paul Chapman, London.

DAVIDSON, M. J. and COOPER, C. L. (1993) *European Women in Business and Management,* Paul Chapman, London.

DAVIDSON, M. J. and EARNSHAW, J. (1990) Policies, practices and attitudes towards sexual harassment in UK organizations, *Personnel Review,* Vol. 19, pp. 23–7.

DEANGELIS, T. (1991) Sexual harassment common, complex, *American Psychological Association Monitor,* Vol. 22, pp. 29–30.

DITOMASO, N. (1989) Sexuality in the workplace: discrimination and harassment, in J. Hearn, D. L. Sheppard, P. Tancred-Sheriff and G. Burrell (eds) *The Sexuality of Organization,* Sage, Newbury Park, CA, pp. 71–90.

DZIECH, B. W. and WEINER, J. (1984) *The Lecherous Professor,* Beacon Press, Boston.

Ellison v. *Brady* (1991) 54 FEP Cases 1347, USCA, 9th Circ.

EQUAL EMPLOYMENT OPPORTUNITY COMMISSION (1990) Guidelines on discrimination on basis of sex (29 CFR Part 1604, *Federal Register 45 (219).*

EVANS, L. J. (1978) Sexual harassment: women's hidden occupational hazard, in J. R. Chapman and M. Gates (eds) *The Victimization of Women,* Sage, Beverly Hills, pp. 203–23.

FAIN, T. C. and ANDERTON, D. L. (1987) Sexual harassment: organizational context and diffuse status, *Sex Roles,* Vol. 17, pp. 291–311.

FITZGERALD, L. F. (1990) Sexual harassment: the definition and measurement of a construct, in M. A. Paludi (ed.) *Ivory Power: Sexual Harassment on Campus,* State University of New York Press, Albany, NY, pp. 21–44.

FITZGERALD, L. F. and BROCK, K. F. (1992) Women's responses to victimization: validation of an objective inventory to assess strategies for responding to sexual harassment, unpublished manuscript.

FITZGERALD, L. F. and SHULLMAN, S. L. (1985) The development and validation of an objectively scored measure of sexual harassment. Paper presented to the annual meeting of the American Psychological Association, Los Angeles.

FITZGERALD, L. F. and SHULLMAN, S. L. (1993) Sexual harassment: a research analysis and agenda for the 1990s, *Journal of Vocational Behavior,* Vol. 42, pp. 5–27.

FITZGERALD, L. F., SHULLMAN, S. L., BAILEY, N., RICHARDS, M., SWECKER, J., GOLD, V., OMEROD, M. and WEITZMAN, L. (1988) The incidence and dimensions of sexual harassment in academia and the workplace, *Journal of Vocational Behavior,* Vol. 32, pp. 152–75.

FITZGERALD, L. F. and WEITZMAN, L. M. (1990) Men who harass: speculation and data, in M. A. Paludi (ed.) *Ivory Power: Sexual Harassment on Campus,* State University of New York Press, Albany, New York, pp. 125–40.

GAY, V. (1991) Sexual harassment: legal issues, past and future developments, in M. J. Davidson and J. Earnshaw (eds) *Vulnerable Workers: Psychosocial and Legal Issues,* John Wiley, Chichester, pp. 203–21.

GOHMANN, S. F. and THACKER, R. A. (1992) Definition and emotional effects of sexual harassment: does the 'reasonable woman' differ from the 'reasonable man'. Paper presented at the Academy of Management Conference, Las Vegas, NV.

GRAVERHOLZ, E. (1989) Sexual harassment of women professors by students: exploring the dynamics of power, authority and gender in a university setting, Sex Roles, Vol. 21, pp. 789–801.

GRUBER, J. E. and BJORN, L. (1986) Women's responses to sexual harassment: an analysis of sociocultural, organizational, and personal resource models, Social Science Quarterly, Vol. 67, pp. 814–26.

GUTEK, B. A. (1985) Sex and the Workplace, Jossey Bass, San Francisco, CA.

GUTEK, B. A. (1993) Personal communication. Society for Industrial and Organizational Psychology, San Francisco, CA.

GUTEK, B. A. and COHEN, A. G. (1987) Sex ratios, sex-role spillover, and sex at work: a comparison of men's and women's experiences, Human Relations, Vol. 40, pp. 97–115.

GUTEK, B. A. and DUNWOODY, V. (1987) Understanding sex in the workplace, in A. H. Stromberg, L. Larwood and B. A. Gutek (eds) Women and Work: An Annual Review, 2, Sage, Beverly Hills, CA, pp. 249–70.

GUTEK, B. A. and KOSS, M. P. (1993) Changed women and changed organizations: consequences of and coping with sexual harassment, Journal of Vocational Behavior, Vol. 42, pp. 28–48.

GUTEK, B. A. and MORASCH, B. (1982) Sex-ratios, sex-role spillover and sexual harassment of women at work, Journal of Social Issues, Vol. 38, pp. 55–74.

GUTEK, B. A., NAKAMURA, C. Y., GAHART, M., HANDSCHUMACHER, I. and RUSSELL, D. (1980) Sexuality in the workplace, Basic and Applied Social Psychology, Vol. 1, pp. 255–65.

HAAVIO-MANNILA, E., KAUPINEN-TOROPAINEN, K. and KANDOLIN, I. (1988) The effects of sex composition of the workplace on friendship, romance, and sex at work, in B. A. Gutek, A. H. Stromberg and L. Larwood (eds) Women and Work, 3, Sage, Beverly Hills, CA.

HEGARTY, W. H. and SIMS, H. P., JR (1978) Some determinants of unethical decision behavior: An experiment, Journal of Applied Psychology, Vol. 63, pp. 451–57.

HEGARTY, W. H. and SIMS, H. P., JR (1979) Organizational philosophy, policies and objectives related to unethical decision behavior: a laboratory experiment, Journal of Applied Psychology, Vol. 64, pp. 331–8.

JENSEN, I. W. and GUTEK, B. A. (1982) Attributions and assignment of responsibility of sexual harassment, Journal of Social Issues, Vol. 38, pp. 121–36.

KANTER, R. M. (1977) Men and Women of the Corporation, Basic Books, New York.

KILPATRICK, D. G. (1992) Treatment and counseling needs of women veterans who were raped, otherwise sexually assaulted, or sexually harassed during military service. Testimony before the US Senate committee on Veterans' Affairs, 30 June.

KINGSMILL, D. (1989) What is sexual harassment? Sunday Times, 23 April.

KIPNIS, D. (1990) Technology and Power, Springer-Verlag, New York/Berlin.

KOSS, M. P. (1990) Changed lives: the psychological impact of sexual harassment, in M. Paludi (ed.) Ivory Power: Sexual Harassment on Campus, State University of New York Press, Albany, NY, pp. 73–92.

LACH, D. H. and GWARTNEY-GIBBS, P. A. (1993) Sociological perspectives on sexual harassment and workplace dispute resolution, Journal of Vocational Behavior, Vol. 42, pp. 102–15.

LAFONTAINE, E. and TREDEAU, L. (1986) The frequency, sources, and correlates of sexual harassment among women in traditional male occupations, Sex Roles, Vol. 15, pp. 433–42.

LARWOOD, L. and GUTEK, B. A. (1984) Women at work in the USA, in M. J. Davidson and C. L. Cooper (eds) Working Women: An International Survey, John Wiley, Chichester, pp. 237–67.

LAVITE, C. (1991) The interaction between situational factors and individual predispositions in the likelihood to sexually harass. Unpublished master's thesis, Illinois State University.

LEE, B. A. (1993) The legal and political realities for women managers: the barriers, the opportunities, and the horizon ahead, in E. A. Fagenson (ed.) Women in Management: Trends, Issues and Challenges in Managerial Diversity, Sage, Newbury Park, CA, pp. 246–73.

LIVINGSTON, J. A. (1982) Responses to sexual harassment on the job: legal, organizational, and individual actions, *Journal of Social Issues*, Vol. 38, pp. 5–22.

LOY, P. H. and STEWART, L. P. (1984) The extent and effects of sexual harassment on working women, *Sociological Focus*, Vol. 17, pp. 31–43.

MACKINNON, C. A. (1979) *Sexual Harassment of Working Women*, Yale, New Haven, CT.

MALOVICH, N. J. and STAKE, J. E. (1990) Sexual harassment on campus: individual differences in attitudes and beliefs, *Psychology of Women Quarterly*, Vol. 14, pp. 63–81.

MARTIN, P. Y. (1993) Feminist practice in organizations: implications for management, in E. A. Fagenson (ed.) *Women in Management: Trends, Issues, and Challenges in Managerial Diversity*, Sage, Newbury Park, CA, pp. 274–96.

MARTIN, S. (1978) Sexual politics in the workplace: the interactional world of policewomen, *Symbolic Interaction*, Vol. 1, pp. 55–60.

MARTIN, S. (1980) *Breaking and Entering: Policewomen on Patrol*, University of California Press, Berkeley.

MATTESON, M. T. and IVANCEVICH, J. M. (1987) *Work Stress: Effective Human Resources and Management Strategies*, Jossey-Bass, San Francisco.

Meritor Savings Bank FSC v. Vinson (1986) 477 US 57, 106 S. Ct, 2399.

MORRISON, A. M. and VON GLINOW, M. (1990) Women and minorities in management, *American Psychologist*, Vol. 45, pp. 200–8.

MURPHY, K. R. and CLEVELAND, J. N. (1991) *Performance Appraisal: An Organizational Perspective*, Allyn & Bacon, Needham Heights, MA.

Newsweek (1992) Did America 'get it'?, 28 December, pp. 20–2.

NIEVA, V. F. and GUTEK, B. A. (1981) *Women and Work: A Psychological Perspective*, Praeger, New York.

O'FARRELL, B. and HARLAN, S. L. (1982) Craftworkers and clerks: the effects of male coworker hostility on women's satisfaction with nontraditional jobs, *Social Problems*, Vol. 29, pp. 252–64.

OFFICE OF HUMAN RESOURCES (1991) *Sexual Harassment is Illegal*, US Fish and Wildlife Service, Washington, DC.

PERRY, S. (1983) Sexual harassment on the campuses: deciding on where to draw the line, *Chronicle of Higher Education*, 26 March, pp. 21–2.

PLECK, J. H. (1976) Male threat from female competence, *Journal of Consulting and Clinical Psychology*, Vol. 44, pp. 608–13.

POWELL, G. N. (1986) Effects of sex-role identity and sex on definitions of sexual harassment, *Sex Roles*, Vol. 14, pp. 9–14.

PRYOR, J. B. (1987) Sexual harassment proclivities in men, *Sex Roles*, Vol. 17, pp. 269–90.

PRYOR, J. B. and DAY, J. D. (1988) Interpretations of sexual harassment: an attributional analysis, *Sex Roles*, Vol. 18, pp. 405–17.

PRYOR, J. B., LAVITE, C. M. and STROLLER, L. M. (1993) A social psychological analysis of sexual harassment: the person/situation interaction, *Journal of Vocational Behavior*, Vol. 42, pp. 68–83.

PRYOR, J. B. and STROLLER, L. M. (1992) Sexual cognition processes in men who are high in the likelihood to sexually harass. Unpublished manuscript, Illinois State University.

QUINA, K. (1990) The victimization of women, in M. Paludi (ed.) *Ivory Power: Sexual Harassment on Campus*, State University of New York Press, Albany, NY.

RAGINS, B. R. and SUNDSTROM, E. (1989) Gender and power in organizations: a longitudinal perspective, *Psychological Bulletin*, Vol. 105, pp. 51–88.

REILLY, T., CARPENTER, S., DULL, V. and BARTLETT, K. (1982) The factorial survey: an approach to defining sexual harassment on campus, *Journal of Social Issues*, Vol. 38, pp. 99–110.

RENICK, J. (1980) Sexual harassment at work: why it happens, what to do about it, *Personnel Journal*, August, pp. 658–62.

RESKIN, B. and ROSS, C. R. (1990) *Job Segregation, Authority, and Earnings among Women and Men Managers*, University of Illinois, Department of Sociology, Champagne/Urbana.

Robinson v. Jacksonville Shipyards (1988) 54 FEP Cases DC Fla.

RYAN, J. and KENIG, S. (1991) Risk and ideology in sexual harassment, *Sociological Inquiry*, Vol. 61, pp. 231–41.

SANDLER, B. R. (1981) Sexual harassment: a hidden problem, *Educational Record*, Vol. 62, pp. 52–7.

SCHNEIDER, B. E. (1982) Consciousness about sexual harassment among heterosexual and lesbian women workers, *Journal of Social Issues*, Vol. 38, pp. 75–98.

SILVERMAN, D. (1976–1977) Sexual harassment: working women's dilemma, *Quest: A Feminist Quarterly*, Vol. 3, pp. 15–24.

SIMPSON, J. C. (1987) Wall Street's courting of MBAs proceeds apace despite scandals, *Wall Street Journal*, Section 2, p. 1.

SOMERS, A. (1982) Sexual harassment in academe: legal issues and definitions, *Journal of Social Issues*, Vol. 38, pp. 23–32.

STEPHENSON, H., WATKINS, J., WALLACE, J., SCHWERIN, M. T. and VAUX, A. (1989) *Survey of Sexual Harassment at Southern Illinois University.* Technical Report, Applied Research Consultants, Department of Psychology, Southern Illinois University, Carbondale.

TANGRI, S. S., BURT, M. R. and JOHNSON, L. V. (1982) Sexual harassment at work: three explanatory models, *Journal of Social Issues*, Vol. 38, pp. 33–54.

TERPSTRA, D. E. and BAKER, D. D. (1991) Sexual harassment at work: the psychosocial issues, in M. J. Davidson and J. Earnshaw (eds) *Vulnerable Workers: Psychosocial and Legal Issues*, John Wiley, Chichester, pp. 179–201.

TILL, F. (1980) *Sexual Harassment: A Report on the Sexual Harassment of Students*, National Advisory Council on Women's Educational Programs, Washington, DC.

TREVINO, L. K., SUTTON, C. D. and WOODMAN, R. W. (1985) Effects of cognitive moral development and reinforcement contingencies on ethical decision-making: An experiment. Paper presented at the 45th Annual Meeting of the Academy of Management, San Diego, CA, August.

TREVINO, L. K. and YOUNGBLOOD, S. A. (1990) Bad apples in bad barrels: A causal analysis of ethical decision-making behavior, *Journal of Applied Psychology*, Vol. 75, pp. 378–85.

US CUSTOMS SERVICE, TREASURY (1992) *Dealing with Sexual Harassment*, Washington, DC.

US DEPARTMENT OF LABOR (1991) *A Report on the Glass Ceiling Initiative*, Government Printing Office, Washington, DC.

US DEPARTMENT OF LABOR (1993) *Employment and Earnings*, Government Printing Office, Washington, DC, January.

US MERIT SYSTEMS PROTECTION BOARD (1981) *Sexual Harassment in the Federal Workplace: Is it a Problem?* United States Government Printing Office, Washington, DC.

US MERIT SYSTEMS PROTECTION BOARD (1988) *Sexual Harassment in the Federal Government: An Update*, United States Government Printing Office, Washington, DC.

WOLF, W. C. and FLIGSTEIN, N. D. (1979) Sex and authority in the workplace: the causes of sexual inequality, *American Sociological Review*, Vol. 44, pp. 235–52.

CHAPTER 13

Changing Men and Changing Managements: Social Change, Social Research and Social Action

JEFF HEARN

INTRODUCTION

The topic of men and management is an obvious one yet strangely unfamiliar. While management, and particularly top management, remains dominated by men, this fact continues to avoid critical attention in most of the research on management. And yet of course men are there, in the research, writing and publication, but usually implicitly so. It is generally taken for granted that it is men who are managers, or who are at least the dominant group, both socially and numerically, in management. While the women-in-management debate is well established, its establishment in this way is itself a response to male norms in management. The women-in-management literature has explored some of the reasons for women's position in relation to management, blocks to entry and promotion, and possible strategies for women in seeking to enter or rise in management. Its focus has been on the plight of women and what, with certain limits, women can do about it, particularly within organizations. Far less attention has been given to how these problems stem from the power of men, and the intense associations that persist between the power of men and the power of management (Kanter, 1977; Bradley, 1986; Hearn, 1989, 1992a, 1992b). Without changing men, it is difficult to change managements in certain fundamental ways; and without changing managements, it is difficult to change men in equally fundamental ways.

While it is remarkable how little the problem of men/managements is explored, this needs to be addressed in order to increase women in management, and to transform from something oppressive to something empowering. The problem is well known: men's behaviour in management is often oppressive and there are too many men in management. These two aspects are probably linked; they are probably two sides of the same coin. Naming men as men (Hanmer, 1990; Collinson and Hearn, 1994b) has clear and subversive implications not just for management, but for our understandings of men, work, leadership, and organizations too. These are some of the issues addressed in this chapter. In the first section I explore some of the changes and challenges to men that have occurred in recent years. This is followed by a review of recent research on the relationship of men and management. Finally, I turn to the practical issues of changing management and changing men in management.

CHANGING MEN

The most fundamental challenge to men, and thus to men in management, has come from feminism. From the late 1960s and early 1970s, there has been a wide variety of feminist analysis of men – seeing men as a gender class, as dominant yet potential allies, as unchanging, as capable of change. Feminism has, then, provided a very powerful set of critiques of men. While there are many varieties of feminism most would seem to include these kinds of elements: the priority of women's experience, of action by women for women; the recognition of sisterhood and shared oppression as women; the need to reduce the power of men; the linking of theory and practice, the personal and the political, the public and the private (see e.g. Delmar, 1986).

Increasingly, links have also been made between struggles around sexism and those around racism, ageism, heterosexism, and other oppressions. The challenge of feminism is thus more than just a question of who performs formal management roles – it is a more total challenge, rather more than a paradigm shift. Management processes are but one part of a system of power and authority relations, both within and outside organizations. Feminist theory and practice is centrally concerned with questions of power, and the ways in which management and leadership relate to the power of gender in society. This involves critical attention to men's domination of both formal management, and the structure of power, especially the hierarchical structure of power, within organizations (Wells, 1973) – not just positions of power, but also the currency of power, by which domination is maintained. The process of management, what counts as management, the means to legitimacy in management are male dominated in most organizations. Preferences for men generally equal preferences for power, and vice versa (Kanter, 1977). In contrast, a feminist view of power, that is, of the potential of power, may reconceptualize it from 'power over' to 'empowerment', 'power to' and 'power for' (Carroll, 1984); management and leadership can thus become a mutual and reciprocal process of coalition building, using 'culturally diverse leadership models that empower women' (National Women's Studies Association, 1988).

A different kind of critique has been produced from gay liberation and gay scholarships, from the process of men loving and desiring men. This also contradicts the dominant ideologies and practices of men, men's power and thus men's management.

These two critiques, feminist and gay, do not necessarily coincide – indeed they may themselves diverge, or even contradict. However, both have assisted in making men and masculinity, and indeed management, problematic. Men and masculinity are no longer just natural; men are no longer born leaders or 'born managers'. It is now clear that phrases like 'he's a good manager of men', 'he leads his troops well', 'he excels in man management' are themselves problematic: men managers are socially constructed.

These kinds of challenges to men operate at different levels: personally (both intra- and interpersonally), politically, socially, theoretically. They have brought a wide range of responses from men – hostility, indifference, sometimes willingness to change. One particularly interesting and relevant set of changes and responses has come from men in political contexts, attempting to develop pro-feminist, anti-sexist ways of being men in men's groups, networks, campaigns, writing, and so on. From the beginnings of the modern Women's Movement in the 1960s, some have seen the need for men to review drastically their power and their masculinity. From the late 1960s, at least small numbers of men have developed men's groups, partly as a response to the demands, both public and private, of women and the Women's Movement. Looking at this story, or stories (Rowan, 1987; Hearn, 1987; Segal, 1990), what is interesting is how many of the issues that were being raised by or for men in the 1970s in political contexts are now being taken more seriously in some working, professional, and indeed managerial contexts. For example, a 1970s list of commitments produced by a men's anti-sexist collective covers the following areas:

- commitment to the (anti-sexist men's) group;
- consciousness-raising done rigorously;
- support for the Women's Liberation Movement;
- support for Gay Liberation;
- sharing childcare;
- learning from gay and feminist culture;
- action on our own behalf;
- propaganda and outreach programmes (linked to action);
- link-ups with other Men Against Sexism groups;
- enunciation of violence (physical, emotional and verbal)

(Commitments Collective, n.d.)

Other challenges come from more academic and more theoretical work on men. Recent critical studies on men have focused on such issues as the relationship between commonalities and differences between men, men's lives and biogaphies and sources of men's power. Understandings of men's power are now complicated in the sense that power may be reproduced structurally, institutionally, through socialization, interpersonally and intrapersonally through psychodynamic processes. The simultaneous operation of these forms of power makes for a more complex set of policies on changing men, and male managements. Men in managements need to understand in the light of more general critical studies on men, particularly in relation to the diversity of masculinities.

A major contribution to the theorizing of 'masculinities' rather than just 'masculinity' has been made by Carrigan et al. (1985). They show how masculinity is not one thing, but operates in diverse ways in different situations, including organizational settings, and that furthermore it entails power relations between different forms. Thus hegemonic masculinity/ies, for example white, heterosexual, dominant, malestream, powerful etc., may themselves dominate non-hegemonic masculinities, for example black, gay, subordinate, counter, less powerful etc. Masculinities are as much about relations between men as they are about relations of men to women. These themes have been explored further by a variety of writers (e.g. Connell, 1987; Brod, 1987; Segal, 1990; Morgan, 1991; Hearn, 1992b).

Thus rather than talking just of a monolithic, or even a hegemonic, masculinity, it is now recognized that it is more accurate to refer to a wide range of particular masculinities. These may be defined in relation to particular social locations, social divisions, and social differences; organizations are of central importance in this process. They might be defined in relation to such constructions as age, appearance, bodily facility, care, economic class, ethnicity, fatherhood and relations to biological reproduction, leisure, marital and kinship status, mentality, occupation, religion, sexuality, size, violence (Hearn and Collinson, 1990, 1994; Collinson and Hearn, 1994b).

An important issue is how the gender class of men interrelates with this diversity of masculinities in organizations and managements. In simple terms, masculinities of men in gendered organizations and managements might be understood as ideologies or ideological representations of the gender class of men. A more complex position is that experiences of men's gender class may be in contradiction with the diverse experiences of masculinities as men in gendered organizations and managements. The relationship of men as a gender class and the diversity of masculinities also involves a number of paradoxes. For example, one of the ways in which men's power as a gender class may be maintained is through the construction of a false monolith of men/masculinity ('organization man', 'bureaucratic man', 'the manager') that excludes the diversity of men's experiences and masculinities. In an apparently very different way, men's collective power may also be maintained through the division of men by economic class, ethnicity and other forms of hierarchical domination of men by men in organizations, and indeed elsewhere. Furthermore, diverse particular masculinities are themselves means of constructing differences along other social dimensions or, more accurately, particular masculinities and particular other social differences, mutually reinforce each other and occur simultaneously. Gendered organizations thus become sites for such diversifications and differentiations, as well as for the exertion of the collective power and interests of men.

MEN, MASCULINITIES AND MANAGEMENTS

This brings us to the need for much more explicit attention to the relationship of men and management in gendered organizations. It is truly amazing how men's domination of management has not become a serious topic of concern in management theory and management thought. Even theories that address the gender structure of labour markets and men's domination there have usually not produced analyses which deconstruct the categories of men and masculinity along with the exploration of the tensions, alliances and inconsistences to be found in management. Indeed, rather than exploring masculinities and management, they have tended to focus on the examination of women's experience of employment and/or trade union practices. Thus the feminist insight of the deconstruction of 'men' and 'masculinity' has not been generally evident in the deconstruction of management. These comments obviously are even more applicable in mainstream/malestream management theory and indeed management ideology and practice. There are innumerable ways in which management, both in theory and practice, implicate 'men' and 'masculinities' – in dominant models of management, styles of management, the language of management (often militaristic or sporting), management culture, managerialism, and so on (Hearn, 1989).

What we call 'management', both as the actual practice of managers, and as theory – management theory – can be understood to a large extent as a series of instances of what certain men do. It is within a general male-dominated social context that dominant and traditional forms of management have developed, characteristically performed or assumed to be performed by men. Management has traditionally implied maleness, and maleness has often carried with it managerial and leadership qualities, sometimes inherently, that women are assumed by men to lack.

DOMINANT MODELS

These patterns are clear if we consider briefly some dominant models of management, taken for convenience from Weber's three ideal types of authority (Weber, 1964). First, consider the father, the basis of the social system known as patriarchy. The crucial feature of this kind of authority is, as Weber recognizes, that it is traditionally taken for granted as a socially accepted status given to the traditional role not the individual. The 'father figure' remains a strong model of leadership in many organizations. Secondly, let us turn to the management of individual 'great men' (Bass, 1981). Management is here understood as one product of qualities possessed by 'the great and the good', notably the quality of charisma. Such models have been liberally transferred from the male military leader, with his eye for the 'killing', to other organizational situations (Weick, 1979). Thirdly, leadership may be seen as part of rational-legal authority within bureaucratic organizations, typically inhabited by male bureaucrats. More explicit commentaries on 'bureaucratic man' (Kohn, 1971), 'organization man' (Whyte, 1956), and 'corporation man' (Jay, 1972) are implicitly talking about the management and men, and the organizational contexts within which men are supposed to manage.

It can hardly be surprising that much management theory has developed as male theory, that is theories about the world from a male point of view. For example, leadership traits and masculine traits have often showed a remarkable coincidence in terms of such qualities as 'dominance', 'initiative', 'persistence', 'ambition', 'self-confidence', 'emotional control' (Bass, 1981, Chapter 4). Interrelations of 'masculinity' and 'leadership' take many forms, including basic assumptions about what each is in the first place. Within traditional associations of 'masculinity' and 'leadership', there is a complementary association of 'femininity' and 'non-leadership', or 'followship'. In some organizations, men's managerial roles have a spatial dimension, including direction of women into and in boundary roles considered by them as non-leadership roles. Ironically, boundary roles may demand considerable initiative and sometimes considerable autonomy (Miles, 1980), qualities that might elsewhere be labelled as those of management. Alternatively, men's management may be seen as adaptability, even though a major feature of women's dual or triple roles, as paid workers, mothers, carers of parents and others, is adaptability, the ability to do several things at once.

METAPHORS AND LANGUAGE

Assumption of maleness and references to the world of men recur in the theory and practice of leadership. F. W. Taylor wrote of the 'management of men', and urged managers to base their practice on baseball (1947, p. 46). Metaphors from sport and the military remain particularly popular. Dubin's (1979) survey of metaphors of leadership includes 'batting a thousand' and 'the lone ranger'. Texts on leadership persist in talking of 'men' when they mean 'managers' or 'leaders': for example, Peters and Waterman (1982) write of 'Man Waiting for Motivation'; Handy (1978) talks of the Gods of Management, though one of them is Athena. Such assumptions are deeply entrenched in thinking and language; the language of management and leadership often equates with the language of masculinity; leaders are often 'he', just as 'chairs' often remain 'men'.

MASCULINE MANAGEMENT AND FEMININE MANAGEMENT

Another way in which assumptions about maleness and masculinity impinge on management theory and practice is in terms of different types and styles of management. The contrast between instrumental leadership and socio-emotional leadership can be seen as: a contrast between 'male' or more 'masculine' styles of management and 'female' and more 'feminine' styles of men's management; or a contrast between men's management and women's management. For example, Jago and Vroom (1980) found that women in their study tended to be significantly more participative in their management style than men. On the other hand, Korabik (1980) concluded that sex role orientation was a better predictor of managers' behaviour than their sex. Accordingly, a strong male sex role orientation emphasized initiation, while those with a female orientation were higher on consideration. Such contrasts recur throughout management and organization theory – for example between transactional and transformational leadership (Burns, 1978); between Theory X and Theory Y (McGregor, 1968).

While Theory Y and other relatively participative styles of management may typically be thought of as more 'feminine', it is important to consider that these can also be used by men in some organizational contexts as a means of reasserting male bonding in teams, groups, work units, and so on. More subtly, some managements, whether authoritarian or democratic, may use men's social bonding tendency to ease the task of management – men may participate in their own exploitation, through 'self-management', or task groups.

PERCEPTIONS OF MASCULINITY AND MANAGEMENT

A slightly different approach is found in studies which connect not observation or self-perception but others' perceptions of managers or assumptions about 'successful' leaders, with masculinity and femininity. This moves the discussion from what men do or do not do as managers to how managers are perceived, by women and by men. Rosen and Jerdee (1974) found that the effectiveness of certain supervising behaviours was rated differentially as a function of the sex of the leader. Somewhat similarly, Schein's (1973) studies of successful middle-managers found that other managers, women and men, tended to perceive them as possessing characteristics, attitudes and temperaments more commonly ascribed to men than women (see Chapter 4). Interestingly, the less experience men have had of working with women, the harder they think a transition to women in management might be (Bowman *et al.*, 1965).

MASCULINE PSYCHODYNAMICS AND MANAGEMENT

Some commentators have developed psychodynamic analyses of management and leadership. Adorno *et al.* (1950) specified the 'authoritarian personality', and its relation to the rigid masculinity of 'pseudo-masculinity'; and McClelland (1961) the 'achievement motive', almost exclusively of 'boys', 'sons' and 'men'. More recently, Mant (1983) has outlined a psychodynamic approach to leader types, drawing on the work of Bion and Melanie Klein. The fundamental distinction made by Mant is between the 'binary' or 'raider' type, which is psychologically dominated by fight/flight experiences, in which if A wins B loses, and vice versa; and the 'ternary' or 'builder' type, which is psychologically dominated by dependence experiences, in which relations, including conflicts, between A and B are understood in terms of some external value or ideal. Parallels can be drawn with Weber's (1964) 'instrumental rationality' and 'value rationality', and Argyris's (1976) Model I and Model II respectively. Importantly, these pairs of concepts are not opposites, with ternary, value-rational, and Model II leadership emphasizing integration rather than simple goal achievement.

Such distinctions relate to men in several ways. The 'binary' type exhibits some of the features of rigid masculinities, while the 'ternary' type can be compared with the other-directedness and empathy of dominant feminine psychologies. To put this another way, caring in relation to a third external object, person, or ideal, is a socially sanctioned element in the psychology of many women. This corresponds closely with Chodorow's (1978) approach to the reproduction of mothering in female psychology (ternary), and the excessive individuation of male psychology, as the boy attempts to enforce a separation from the mother, upon whom there was previously dependence. However, such models of the psychological roots of men's, and indeed women's, management rarely give sufficient attention to the social and organizational contexts in which that management occurs.

CRITICISMS OF THE SEX DIFFERENCES AND SEX ROLE APPROACHES

Many of the distinctions so far discussed rest on assumptions of clear differences between women and men – either the so-called 'sex differences' or 'sex role' approach to gender. There are now many studies that point to the shortcomings of these kinds of approaches. Fundamental difficulties concern what exactly is it that is being measured, especially in sex role studies – is it observed behaviour, expected behaviour, self-perception, or perception of others (Eichler, 1980). Maccoby and Jacklin's (1974) assessment of over 1,400 published studies on the subject showed that assumptions of differences between women and men, in terms of achievement, motivation and intelligence were false, and differences in social skills were rare. Differences in aggressiveness between boys and girls, and men and women, were widespread, but even these vary according to society and social context (Jacklin and Maccoby, 1975). More recent research has shown women to be as aggressive as men in some situations, although men may still tend to initiate aggression more than women (Towson and Zanna, 1982).

One example of the relevant empirical data is that from the American Human Engineering Laboratory/Johnson O'Connor Research Foundation which has been administering aptitude assessments since 1922 (Durkin, 1978). This has revealed no discernible differences between women and men on: analytical reasoning, eyedness, foresight, inductive reasoning, memory for design, number memory, objective personality, subjective personality, pitch discrimination, rhythm memory, timbre discrimination, tonal memory, tweezer dexterity. Statistically significant differences were found in eight areas. Women were superior in: finger dexterity, accounting aptitude, flow of ideas in activities using persuasion and verbal fluency, observation, formation of associations between known and unknown words, non-concrete puzzle solution. Men excelled over women in: grip, and rapid assembly of three-dimensional puzzles.

'Sex differences' and 'sex role' approaches have been further undermined in a number of recent comparative studies of women and men managers and leaders. Boulgarides (1984) surveyed 108 business managers of each sex in 10 Los Angeles areas, and concluded there were no significant differences in their decision style or values. Recent reviews (Donnell and Hall, 1980; Powell, 1988) of research literature on possible differences between female and male managers, in terms of managerial behaviours, managerial commitment and motivation, managerial stress, and subordinates' responses, have found few consistent differences. Indeed, there is some evidence that women managers display more achievement motivation than men, presumably as a way of overcoming gender discrimination. Real doubts now exist over the connections, if any, between sex role behaviour and managerial style. Instead, gender differences in management that are observed may be related to social context, very much in line with the general theory of 'situational leadership' (Fielder, 1967). This broadens the evaluation of management to the nature of that context.

ORGANIZATIONAL CULTURES

Attention to culture has come in recent years from the realization of both limitations on individual managers and management and the ineffectiveness of structural changes in organization. Management is not just what men managers or women managers do, the performance or style of managers, but processes between and across people, in this context women and men. Organizational cultures can themselves be understood as examples of male-dominated cultures – 'Fellowship' culture (Olmosk, 1972) is usually between 'fellows'; 'Club' culture is often a men's club. It is not by chance that Handy's typology is itself a development of Michael Maccoby's (1978) corporate leaders – 'the jungle fighter', 'the company man', 'the gamesman', 'the craftsman' (sic).

Culture can also have prescriptive value in moving beyond bureaucratic and matrix organizations to post-industrial Theory Z models of management, that embrace the benefits of what are elsewhere seen as opposed, possibly 'masculine' and 'feminine' tendencies (Ouchi, 1981). Organizations are social spaces where responsibility, collective and collaborative decision-making, longer-term orientation, worker autonomy, indeed integration, can all be pursued (Peters and Waterman, 1982). The implications that such cultural change and self-learning might have for gender relations (Mills, 1989), and specifically for men, are, however, rarely spelt out, even though such change depends partly upon change in men.

FEMINIST AND RELATED CRITIQUES

Feminist and other radical critiques have addressed men's management in a number of different ways. Most obviously, critiques have been developed in relation to the behaviour of particular men leaders and their frequent sexism. Pollert (1981), for example, in her study of a tobacco factory, discusses the way in which the authority of male supervisory staff over women workers is maintained and reinforced by sexist language, jokes, and innuendo. The frequent sexism in managers' behaviour is particularly crucial for women, such as secretaries, who work closely with managers. More generally still, management, and therefore predominantly male management, can be analysed as a distinct class grouping. Management by men can be understood as an important contribution to the maintenance of capitalist patriarchy.

A number of recent feminist studies have taken up the theme of the simultaneous deconstruction of 'men'/ 'masculinities' and management in the context of patriarchy. These include Rogers (1988) on men-only organizations and Cockburn (1989, 1990) on a large retail organization and its management. The latter study includes an analysis of the mechanisms of the reproduction of power used by men, particularly men as managers in the organization, as follows: assertion of the 'main aim'; autonomous labour market policy; the evasiveness of power; leaving domestic ties to women; defining when difference is legitimate; organization sexuality; and shaping women's consciousness. These approaches to management reflect debates in and around feminism on the rethinking of the meaning of work itself, in light of developments in feminist epistemology (e.g. Beechey, 1988). Such studies along with those by men sympathetic to feminist and gender analysis (e.g. Collinson and Hearn, 1944a) provide the basis for a more detailed assessment of the variety of interrelations between 'men', 'masculinities' and management.

MANAGEMENTS AND MASCULINITIES

The remainder of this section considers the interrelationship between management divisions/differences and masculinities which some recent studies have begun to highlight. Certain writers, particularly within the labour process tradition, have recently argued that in attempting to retrieve the agency of management from an exclusively structuralist analysis, assumptions of management omniscience, intentions, unity and cohesion must be rejected in favour of a focus on the contradictions that characterize managerial control. These contradictions are embedded, firstly in the relationship between management/labour, and men/women, secondly within management itself, thirdly within and between different men and masculinities (Collinson and Hearn, 1994b).

Ideologies and strategies of both direct managerial control and labour response are also highly gendered and reflect specific masculinities. Kanter (1977, p. 22), for example, has argued that scientific management with its emphasis on rationality and efficiency, is infused with an irreducibly 'masculine ethic'. A central assumption of this strategy is that only men hold the requisite qualities of the 'new rational manager'. These include: a tough-minded approach to problems, analytical abilities to abstract and plan, a capacity to subordinate personal concerns in order to accomplish the task, and a cognitive superiority in problem-solving. The human relations emphasis on shared interests and mutual responsibility has been associated in other studies with the masculine managerial strategy of paternalism (e.g. Lown, 1983). Instead of a coercive or dictatorial approach, managers insist on a reciprocal working relationship and call for moral co-operation and the development of 'personal', trust relations. Furthermore, contradictions between women and men in relation to management/labour hinge on the way such gender divisions may both reinforce and impede 'economic' imperatives. In this respect, it is interesting to note that the category 'men management', combining as it does gender and economic categorization, is not in general or sociological use, even though 'men management' is an important social grouping within contemporary patriarchies, assisting the reproduction of men's gender class power.

A second contradictory element is the variety of divisions and differences within management itself, in terms of hierarchical, spatial and functional differentiations. Management is not an integrated totality, rather it is a set of arenas for diverse, hierarchically oriented careers and (potential) promotions. Such competitive strategies reflect the way in which (middle-class) men in managerial positions routinely define themselves and are defined as the privatized breadwinner whose primary purpose is to 'provide' for their families. Competition for career progress often comes to be synonymous with conventional masculinity. Thirdly, there are contradictions between different men and masculinities. I have already noted how management is a means of differentiation of men, both between managers and non-managers, and between different types of managers. Thus 'managerial masculinity' might be understood as a form of hegemonic masculinity; and at the same time, particular managerial masculinities may operate by managerial specialism, for example production management. Then there are the various institutional and interpersonal associations of 'masculinities' and managements. Being a manager may confirm facets of 'masculinity'. Managers may be 'macho', authoritarian, entrepreneurial, democratic, even be against oppression. Differences between management men and masculinities may be interrelated and intertwined with other social differences, around age, ethnicity, locality, sexuality, and so on, as already discussed. Managerial masculinities may be simultaneously heterosexual and homosocial.

Whether the entry of women into managerial positions will facilitate the deconstruction of hegemonic masculinities remains an open question.

Nevertheless, the possibility of a challenge to men's taken-for-granted dominant masculinities in turn could facilitate the emergence of less coercive and less divisive managerial strategies, as well as a fundamental rethinking of the social organization of the domestic division of labour. It is to initiatives and interventions of this kind I shall now turn.

CHANGING MANAGEMENTS

Research on and analysis of men, masculinities and managements provide some of the background for developing ways of changing management, and men in management. They also raise a large number of questions and implications for changing management in specific and practical ways. For example:

- How should men respond to the social changes affecting women and men?
- What kind of involvement can men usefully give in equal opportunities programmes?
- What forms of training, counselling and management development do men need to change oppressive management leadership and other patterns?
- How might new forms of masculinity contribute to and change men's management?
- Is it possible for men to be leaders against sexism in organizations? What can men do in anti-sexist policy development?
- What are the implications of leadership in men's groups and other informal contexts outside organizations for men's management in formal organizations?
- Are there forms of management for men that involve giving up leading?

The responses that men have made to feminist initiatives in organizations, management and elsewhere, range from the deliberate and the conscious to the un-self-conscious, from the positive and welcoming to the ambivalent, and on to the antagonistic backlash. Similarly, within formal organizations, men have responded with hostility to women, liberal accommodations, corporate equal opportunities policies, as well as positive action and leadership against sexism. Some men have attempted to answer them by seeing them as promising a defeat of traditional male-dominated management, or indicating the need for a retreat from management. Paternalistic leadership has been shown to be inappropriate, and shared leadership frequently advocated (Kokopeli and Lakey, n.d.). Part of re-evaluating men's management has been directed at men's behaviour towards both women and men in mixed-gender groups. Moyer and Tuttle (1983) suggest the following 'common pitfalls' for men in such situations:

- 'hogging the show';
- being the continual problem-solver;
- speaking in 'capital letters';
- defensiveness;
- task and content focus, to the exclusion of nurturing;
- put-downs and oneupmanship;
- negativism;

- transfer of the focus of discussion;
- holding on to formal powerful positions;
- intransigence and dogmatism;
- listening only to oneself;
- avoiding feelings;
- condescension and paternalism;
- using sexuality to manipulate women;
- seeking attention and support from women while competing with men;
- running the show;
- protectively storing key group information for one's own use;
- speaking for others.

There are parallels here with recent work on 'the continuum of male con-trols over women' (Adams, n.d.). Although their prime context is violence to women and children in the home, their listing of other male controls is equally applicable to group, organizational and management contexts.

(1) Anger:
  - yelling;
  - threatening gestures, body posture, and movements;
  - destroying or throwing things;
  - verbal threats.
(2) Psychological abuse:
  - defining reality categorically and unilaterally;
  - withholding positive attention, praise or approval;
  - interrupting, not listening;
  - ignoring the woman;
  - ridicule and name-calling;
  - criticism, especially that which is demeaning and/or persistent.
(3) Gender role issues:
  - withholding sociability;
  - controlling resources;
  - controlling sexual behaviours;
  - controlling behaviours about housework, childcare;
  - controlling woman's mobility;
  - isolating the woman from friends or family.

The use of these and similar controls by men in doing what is called 'manage-ment' is to be avoided.

In contrast, attempts have been made to specify more closely what respons-ible action looks like:

- limiting our talking time to our fair share;
- not interrupting people who are speaking;
- becoming a good listener;
- getting and giving support;
- not giving answers and solutions;
- relaxing;
- not speaking on every subject;
- not putting others down;
- nurturing democratic group process;
- interrupting others' oppressive behaviour (Moyer and Tuttle, 1983).

While some of these prescriptions are highly contestable, and even on occasions contradictory, they do indicate the direction that non-oppressive action can take. These sentiments have been consolidated in what Kokopeli and Lakey (n.d.) call 'tactics of structure' and shared leadership:

- determining overall goals and direction;
- consensus in direct action;
- decentralization;
- study groups, since knowledge is a form of power;
- meeting facilitation techniques, such as the use of co-facilitators; silence after proposal and before brainstorms; buzz groups; process observers; agenda review; co-operative games; and group evaluation.

In these and other ways, men's management and leadership as both theory and practice have been subject to re-evaluation. Indeed the interrelation of theory and practice is itself a way of re-evaluating management and leadership. The reformulation of men's management takes several forms: questioning management processes, devising new ways of working in mixed-gender groups, seeing the applicability of men's groups in organizational contexts, such as training and organization development. This, therefore, includes attention to the relevance of these questions to formal, mainstream (or malestream) organizations – in schools, the health service, business, commerce, and so on. For example, a recent Women in Social Services (Social Services Inspectorate, n.d.) booklet addresses the question of men's attitudes, and suggests that it is important that men in management training or personnel posts have opportunities to explore myths and stereotypes, and different 'communication' patterns and styles of behaviour. It notes that 'male awareness programmes' can enable men to explore these issues, both personally and organizationally. These could include:

- how they developed their male identity and learned about being a man;
- what prejudices they were encouraged to adopt;
- the good and bad things about being a man;
- how attitudes and prejudice can change;
- how their organization reflects male values;
- ways of achieving change within the organization in both attitudes and behaviour (also see Ruth, 1986; Farrell et al., 1986; Equal Opportunities International, 1989).

Finally, I shall put forward some more specific suggestions for making both men and management less oppressive (Hearn, 1992a). In doing this, I think it is fair to say that it is quite difficult to make positive suggestions, and especially so without being unnecessarily optimistic. So, what is to be done, and especially at a time of limited resources?

(1) If there are to be more women in management, it needs to be accepted that there will be fewer men in management – that is, unless there are major changes in the structuring in organizations, management and hierarchy. Getting the question of fewer men in management on to the policy agenda, or at least on to the table for discussion, is rather difficult. One thing that national professional and managerial associations could do, for example, would be to set targets, national targets, for

changes of this kind for top management in different sectors, industries and professions.

(2) There is a need to ensure there is a minimum mass of women in management, so that this group can develop its dynamic. If there is not that minimum mass, then that too should be on the policy agenda, at different levels in the organization.

(3) Changes that are already happening to organizations – such as budgetary changes, legal changes, geographical and locational issues, or whatever – can be seen as offering new opportunities for challenging men and men managements.

(4) Those men who are in management or remain in management need to be challenged in terms of dominant models of masculinity. To put this another way, much conventional or 'normal' masculinity, including conventional managerial masculinity, could be seen as unreasonable behaviour. Changing men's behaviour in organizations and managements challenges what is seen as 'normal' masculinity. Men managements need to attend to this, to sort these problems out, to begin to look at themselves as men, and not just as managers, and to change relations with both women and other men.

(5) In challenging dominant models of masculinity, all the issues that are looked at in men's groups (such as those listed above by the Commitments Collective) are relevant. In particular there is a drastic need for men in management to give greater priority to domestic and other 'private' and caring responsibilities.

(6) If men wish to address these questions in work time then attention has to be given to the use and distribution of training resources. It is necessary to ensure that all women employees have at least as much time and resources as men do for such training and related needs. More reasonably, the distribution of training budgets to women or men could work in inverse proportion to the number of women/men in management or elsewhere in the organization.

(7) Men can be asked to consider explicitly how we can assist equal opportunities policies, and how we can stop blocking equal opportunities policies (Cockburn 1989, 1990, 1991; Collinson et al., 1990). This may involve attention to two models of equal opportunities policies: one that creates new rules to break the domination of informal masculine culture; the other that breaks down bureaucracy (Ferguson, 1984), perhaps giving more autonomy to different managers and workers. Needless to say, both of these models have their problems. Examining men's participation in equal opportunities policies also necessitates distinguishing different 'types' of men, what they do, and how they may or may not benefit differentially from equal opportunities policies. Introduction of equal opportunities policies may benefit, albeit very slowly, some men, for example black men or men with disabilities. Equal opportunities policies may highlight the contradictions facing different men. There are also more specific issues in appointments to top management, such as the tendency to appoint men through external rather than internal applications. The spelling out of equal opportunities policies has rarely considered the implications for white, heterosexual, able-bodied men or the part they might play in assisting such policies. This is usually an unspoken subject, fundamental as it is.

(8) If men are unlikely to move from management directly, it might be considered how they might move 'temporarily' – to free up such possibilities. This might involve some creative thinking such as exchanges with women, shifts to specialized or lower-level positions on the same pay, external secondments for, say, two years. Such practice can raise difficult trade union and equal opportunities policy issues, but these are some ways of creating the space for women, and women's experience of management.

(9) There is a major need to attend to the problem of sexuality in management. Most organizations and managements have particular dominant sexual cultures that are dominated by heterosexuality (Hearn and Parkin, 1987; Hearn et al., 1989). This might or might not include the occurrence of explicit sexual harassments – but harassment is not just a question of incidents: more usually it is a matter of the whole environment and culture. It may involve the whole process of the organization – the language used, the presence of men, the use of body language. One major problem here is that most versions of heterosexuality are associated with hierarchy and power. So when, for example, it is recommended that men managers support women staff, this has to be placed in the context of the dominant patterns of heterosexuality. This does not of course obviate the need for specific policies on sexual harassment, heterosexism and violence even if drawing them up can be difficult (see Chapter 12).

(10) Men can be asked to clarify where they stand in terms of, for example, anti-racism, anti-sexism, pro-feminism, gay-affirmation, etc. This may well involve acknowledging ambivalence, rather than pretending that there is some 'pure' position. It also necessitates avoiding any sense of being more advanced or further on than 'other men'. In the light of this, men can be asked what is being done and how long term any commitment is. In looking at things this way, I think it is important on the one hand to see nothing as 'too trivial' for attention while, on the other, seeking to change the whole 'set' of the organization: the particular and the global can often go hand in hand.

CONCLUSION

All these recommendations and, indeed, other possibilities discussed in this chapter raise real questions about how it is that men might be managers and leaders in ways that are less oppressive and/or non-oppressive. It is for all these reasons that management of and by men, and the relationship of men, masculinities and management, are on current agendas – in the whole range of organizational and group contexts, in the public sector, the private sector, and various 'partnership' corporations. For if there is concern with the introduction of non-discriminatory and equal opportunities practices in organizations and management, this has consequences not just for women and others suffering discrimination, but also for men. Critically re-evaluating men's management theory and practice necessitates attention to power: challenging men on what we are doing, if anything, against sexism and in support of a changed relationship of gender and management. For women's organizational position to change, so must men's – for the test must be, whatever some men's good intentions, has there been change in power between women and men?

REFERENCES

ADAMS, D. (n.d.) The continuum of male controls over women. Unpublished article, EMERGE, 280 Green Street, Cambridge, MA 02139, cited in Mederos, F. (1987) Patriarchy and male psychology (unpublished paper).

ADORNO, T.W., FRENKEL-BRUNSWIK, E., LEVINSON, D.J. and SANFORD, R.N. (1950) In collaboration with Aron, B., Levinson, M. H. and Morrow, W. *The Authoritarian Personality*, Harper & Row, New York.

ARGYRIS, C. (1976) *Increasing Leadership Effectiveness*, John Wiley & Son, New York.

BALES, R. F. (1950) *Interaction Process Analysis: A Method for the Study of Small Groups*, Addison-Wesley, Reading, Mass.

BASS, B. M. (1981) *Stodgill's Handbook of Leadership*, Free Press, New York.

BEECHEY, V. (1988) Rethinking the definition of work, in J. Jenson, E. Flagen and C. Reddy (eds) *Feminisation of the Labour Force*, Polity Press, Cambridge.

BOULGARIDES, J. D. (1984) A comparison of male and female business managers, *Leadership and Organisation Development Journal*, Vol. 5, no. 5, pp. 27–31.

BOWMAN, G. W., WORTHING, N. B. and GREYSE, S. A. (1965) Are women executives people? *Harvard Business Review*, July–August, pp. 14–28, 164–178.

BRADLEY, H. (1986) *Men's Work, Women's Work. A Sociological History of the Sexual Division of Labour in Employment*, Polity, Cambridge.

BROD, H. (ed.) (1987) *The Making of Masculinities. The New Men's Studies*, Allen & Unwin, Boston.

BURNS, J. M. (1978) *Leadership*, Harper and Row, New York.

CARRIGAN, T., CONNELL, R. W. and LEE, J. (1985) Towards a new sociology of masculinity, *Theory and Society*, Vol. 14, no. 5, pp. 551–604.

CARROLL, S. J. (1984) Feminist scholarship on political leadership, in B. Kellerman (ed.) *Leadership – Multidisciplinary Perspectives*, Prentice-Hall, Englewood Cliffs, NJ.

CHODOROW, N. (1978) *The Reproduction of Mothering. Psychoanalysis and the Sociology of Gender*, University of California Press, Berkeley/London.

COCKBURN, C. (1989) Equal opportunities: the short and the long agendas, *Industrial Relations Journal*, Vol. 20, no. 3, pp. 213–25.

COCKBURN, C. (1990) Men's power in organisations: equal opportunities intervenes, in J. Hearn and D. H. J. Morgan (eds) *Men, Masculinities and Social Theory*, Unwin Hyman, London.

COCKBURN, C. (1991) *In the Way of Women. Men's Resistance to Sex Equality in Organisations*, Macmillan, London.

COLLINSON, D. L. and HEARN, J. (1990) Unities and differences between men and masculinities. (2) The fragmentation of management and the management of fragmentation. Paper at British Sociological Association Annual Conference, 'Social Divisions and Social Change', University of Surrey, April, Mimeo. University of St Andrews.

COLLINSON, D. L. and HEARN, J. (eds) (1994a) *Managements and Men*, Sage, London.

COLLINSON, D. L. and HEARN, J. (1994b) Naming men as men: implications for work, organisations and management, *Gender, Work and Organization*, Vol. 1, no. 1, pp. 2–22.

COLLINSON, D. L., KNIGHTS, D. and COLLINSON, M. (1990) *Managing to Discriminate*, Routledge, London.

COMMITMENTS COLLECTIVE (1980) Anti-sexist commitments for men . . ., *Anti-sexist Men's Newsletter*, No. 9.

CONNELL, R. W. (1987) *Gender and Power*, Polity, Cambridge.

DELMAR, R. (1986) What is feminism? in J. Mitchell and A. Oakley (eds) *What is Feminism?* Basil Blackwell, Oxford.

DONNELL, S. M. and HALL, J. (1980) Men and women as managers: a significant case of no significant difference, *Organizational Dynamics*, Vol. 8, pp. 60–77.

DUBIN, R. (1979) Metaphors of leadership: an overview, in J. G. Hart and L. L. Larson (eds) *Crosscurrents in Leadership*, Southern Illinois University Press, Carbondale.

DURKIN, J. J. (1978) The potential of women, in B. A. Stead (ed.) *Women in Management*, 1st edn, Prentice-Hall, Englewood Cliffs, NJ.

EICHLER, M. (1980) *The Double Standard*, Croom Helm, London.

Equal Opportunities International (1989) Men, masculinities and leadership, J. Hearn (ed.) Special issue, Vol. 8, no. 1.

FARRELL, P., BOYDELL, T. and PEDLER, M. (1986) Training for women and men working together, *Journal of European Industrial Training*, Vol. 10, no. 7, pp. 34–43.

FERGUSON, K. (1984) *The Feminist Case Against Bureaucracy*, Temple University Press, Philadelphia.

FIELDER, F. E. (1967) *A Theory of Leadership Effectiveness*, McGraw-Hill, New York.

HANDY, C. (1978) *Gods of Management. How They Work and Why They Will Fail*, Souvenir, London.

HANMER, J. (1990) Men, power and the exploration of women, in J. Hearn and D. H. J. Morgan (eds) *Men, Masculinities and Social Theory*, Unwin Hyman, London.

HEARN, J. (1987) *The Gender of Oppression. Men, Masculinity and the Critique of Marxism*, Wheatsheaf, Brighton; St Martin's, New York.

HEARN, J. (1989) Leading questions for men: men's leadership, feminist challenge and men's response, *Equal Opportunities International*, Vol. 8, no. 1, pp. 3–11.

HEARN, J. (1992a) Changing men and changing management – a review of issues and actions, *Women in Management Review*, Vol. 7, no. 1, pp. 3–8.

HEARN, J. (1992b) *Men in the Public Eye. The Construction and Deconstruction of Public Men and Public Patriarchies*, Harper Collins, London and New York.

HEARN, J. and COLLINSON, D. (1990) Unities and differences between men and masculinities. (1) The categories of men and the case of sociology. Paper at British Sociological Association Annual Conference, 'Social Divisions and Social Change', University of Surrey, April, Mimeo. University of Bradford.

HEARN, J. and COLLINSON, D. L. (1994) Theorising unities and differences between men and masculinities, in H. Brod and M. Kaufman (eds) *Theorizing Masculinities*, Sage, Newbury Park, CA.

HEARN, J. and PARKIN, W. (1987) *'Sex' at 'Work'. The Power and Paradox of Organisation Sexuality*, Wheatsheaf, Brighton; St Martin's, New York.

HEARN, J., SHEPPARD, D., TANCRED-SHERIFF, P. and BURRELL, G. (eds) (1989) *The Sexuality of Organisation*, Sage, London/Newbury Park, CA.

JACKLIN, C. N. and MACCOBY, E. E. (1975) Sex differences and their implications for management, in F. E. Gordon and M. H. Strober (eds) *Bringing Women into Management*, McGraw-Hill, New York.

JAGO, A. G. and VROOM, V. H. (1980) Sex differences in the incidence and evaluation of participative leader behavior. Working Paper, Department of Management, University of Houston, Texas, 1980, cited in U. Sekaran, J. G. Hunt and C. A. Schriesheim 'Beyond establishment views: an epilog' in J. G. Hunt, U. Sekaran and C. A. Schriesheim (eds) *Leadership Beyond Establishment Views*, Southern Illinois University Press, Carbondale.

JAY, A. (1972) *Corporation Man*, Cape, London.

KANTER, R. M. (1977) *Men and Women of the Corporation*, Basic Books, New York.

KOHN, M. (1971) Bureaucratic man: a portrait and an interpretation, *American Sociological Review*, Vol. 36, pp. 461–74.

KOKOPELI, B. and LAKEY, G. (n.d.) *Leadership for Change. Toward a Feminist Model*, New Society Publishers, Philadelphia.

KORABIK, K. (1980) Sex role orientation and leadership style. Paper at the Institute for Women and Psychology, Canadian Psychological Association, Calgary, June, cited in U. Sekaran, J. G. Hunt and C. A. Schriesheim 'Beyond establishment views: an epilog' in J. G. Hunt, U. Sekaran and C. A. Schriesheim (eds) *Leadership Beyond Establishment Views*, Southern Illinois University Press, Carbondale.

LOWN, J. (1983) Not so much a factory, more a form of patriarchy: gender and class during industrialisation, in E. Gamarnikow *et al.* (eds) *Gender, Class and Work*, Heinemann, London.

MACCOBY, M. (1978) *The Gamesman. The New Corporate Leaders*, Secker & Warburg, London.

MACCOBY, E. E. and JACKLIN, C. N. (1974) *The Psychology of Sex Differences*, Stanford University Press, Stanford, CA.

MANT, A. (1983) *Leaders We Deserve*, Martin Robertson, Oxford.

MCCLELLAND, D. C. (1961) *The Achieving Society*, D. van Nostrand, Princeton, NJ.

MCGREGOR, D. (1968) *Leadership and Motivation*, MIT Press, Cambridge, MA.

MILES, R. (1980) Organizational boundary roles, in C. Cooper (ed.) *Current Issues in Occupational Stress*, John Wiley, Chichester, pp. 61–96.

MILLS, A. J. (1988) Organization gender and culture, *Organization Studies*, Vol. 9, no. 3, pp. 351–69.

MORGAN, D. H. J. (1991) *Discovering Men*, Harper Collins, London and New York.

MOYER, B. and TUTTLE, A. (1983) *Off Their Backs . . . and on Our Own Two Feet*, New Society Publishers, Philadelphia, pp. 24–9.

NATIONAL WOMEN'S STUDIES ASSOCIATION (1988) Annual Conference, 'Leadership and Power. Women's Alliances for Social Change', 22–26 June 1988, University of Minnesota, Minneapolis. Conference Goals.

OLMOSK, K. E. (1972) Seven pure strategies of change, in J. W. Pfeiffer and J. E. Jones (eds) *The 1972 Annual Handbook for Group Facilitators*, University Associates, Iowa City, pp. 163–72.

OUCHI, W. (1981) *Theory Z. How American Business Can Meet the Japanese Challenge*, Addison-Wesley, Reading, Mass.

PETERS, T. J. and WATERMAN, R. H. (1982) *In Search of Excellence*, Harper & Row, New York.

POLLERT, A. (1981) *Girls, Wives, Factory Lives*, Macmillan, London.

POWELL, G. (1988) *Women and Men in Management*, Sage, Newbury Park, CA.

ROGERS, B. (1988) *Men Only. An Investigation into Men's Organizations*, Pandora, London.

ROSEN, B. and JERDEE, T. H. (1974) Influence of sex role stereotypes on personnel decisions, *Journal of Applied Psychology*, Vol. 59, pp. 9–14.

ROWAN, J. (1987) *The Horned God. Feminism and Men and Wounding and Healing*, Routledge & Kegan Paul, London.

RUTH, S. (1986) Men and equality in organisations: training strategies, *Journal of European Industrial Training*, Vol. 10, no. 8, pp. 9–12.

SCHEIN, V. E. (1973) The relationship between sex role stereotypes and requisite management characteristics, *Journal of Applied Psychology*, Vol. 57, pp. 95–100.

SEGAL, L. (1990) *Slow Motion. Changing Men, Changing Masculinities*, Virago, London.

SOCIAL SERVICES INSPECTORATE (c.1990) *Women as Managers*, Department of Health, London.

TAYLOR, F. W. (1947) Taylor's testimony to the Special House Committee, 1912, in *Scientific Management*, Harper, New York.

TOWSON, S. M. J. and ZANNA, M. P. (1982) Toward a situational analysis of gender differences in aggression, *Sex Roles*, Vol. 8, pp. 903–14.

WEBER, M. (1964) *The Theory of Social and Economic Organisation*, Routledge & Kegan Paul, London.

WEICK, K. E. (1979) *The Social Psychology of Organizing*, 2nd edn, Addison-Wesley, Reading, Mass.

WELLS, T. (1973) The covert power of gender in organizations, *Journal of Contemporary Business*, Vol. 2, Summer, pp. 53–68.

WHYTE, W. H. (1956) *The Organization Man*, Simon & Schuster, New York.

PART FOUR

Home–Work Conflicts

CHAPTER 14

Work–Family Conflict, Social Support and Well-Being

JEFFREY H. GREENHAUS AND SAROJ PARASURAMAN

INTRODUCTION

Work and family constitute the dominant life roles for most employed adults in contemporary society. Thus, employed men and women are increasingly concerned about managing the conflicts experienced in fulfilling the dual demands and responsibilities of work and family roles. Work– family conflict (WFC) is experienced when pressures from the work and family roles are mutually incompatible, such that participation in one role makes it more difficult to participate in the other (Greenhaus and Beutell, 1985). No longer viewed as primarily a 'women's issue', researchers have documented the experience of WFC among women and men, and have provided convincing evidence of the adverse effects of such conflict on their well-being in both the work and family domains (Greenhaus and Beutell, 1985; Pleck, 1985; Greenhaus and Parasuraman, 1986; Voydanoff, 1987; Burke, 1989).

The recognition that extensive WFC has negative emotional consequences has directed attention toward the role of social support in ameliorating work–family stress (MacEwen and Barling, 1988; Frone et al., 1991; Parasuraman et al., 1992; Stephens and Sommer, 1993). Paralleling the research on occupational and life stress (Beehr, 1985; Cohen and Syme, 1985; Cohen and Wills, 1985), researchers on work–family dynamics have assumed that social support enables individuals to reduce or manage the stress associated with balancing work and family responsibilities. From Rapoport and Rapoport's (1971) early identification of the facilitating husband in two-career relationships to more recent assertions regarding the importance of family-responsive employers (Friedman, 1990), social support has been viewed as a significant resource that can promote effective coping and enhance employee well-being in the face of work–family stress.

The limited empirical research on social support in relation to WFC provides, at best, mixed evidence of the assumed benefits of support, and a close review of the literature reveals ambiguity and inconsistency in the conceptualization and measurement of support. Theoretical discussions and critical essays on social support suggest that extant research on the support process has failed to examine the complexities and subtleties of social support as an interpersonal phenomenon embedded in the larger social context of individuals' work and personal lives. Thus, an understanding of the causal mechanisms underlying social support requires an appreciation of the social context in which support is provided and received (Shumaker and Brownell, 1984; Eckenrode and Gore, 1990; Pearlin and McCall, 1990).

The aim of this chapter is to examine the role of social support specifically in relation to WFC. First, we will discuss our conceptualization of the WFC process. Next, the role of social support in the stress process will be examined. Then, we will present a preliminary model that delineates the functions and roles played by social support in the complex web of relationships between WFC and well-being. The chapter will conclude with a research agenda to guide future investigations of social support at the work–family nexus.

WORK–FAMILY CONFLICT

Our view of the WFC process is presented in Figure 14.1. As noted earlier, WFC is experienced when simultaneous pressures from the work and family roles are mutually incompatible. We propose that there are two dominant forms of WFC: time-based conflict and strain-based conflict.[1]

Time-based conflict is experienced when the time devoted to one role, for example the work role, makes it difficult to fulfil the requirements of the other role, for example the family. For example, a meeting of a project team at work might conflict with a long-standing conference with a child's teacher. If neither event can be rescheduled, the individual is likely to experience time-based WFC. A decision regarding which role takes precedence and the intensity of the conflict experienced depend on several factors.

First, the salience of each role and one's personal role definition might dictate the role in which compliance is attempted. For example, a highly career-oriented employee may readily attend to a work demand rather than a family demand, whereas a highly family-oriented employee might pursue the reverse option. Second, the salience of the activity within each role can influence behaviour. An emergency team meeting on a long-overdue project may produce stronger pressures to comply with work demands than a routine request to celebrate a colleague's birthday after work. In a similar vein, being present at a daughter's first soccer match may produce stronger pressures to comply with family demands than a backyard barbecue with a neighbourhood friend. All things being equal, psychological conflict is expected to be most severe when both activities are critical to role performance and both roles are highly salient to the individual. Thus, the employee who is highly career oriented *and* highly family oriented is likely to experience the greatest conflict and emotional strain.

Third, pressures for compliance with role expectations will be particularly strong when it is believed that non-compliance will bring negative sanctions. For example, if a spouse insists that the partner attend a parent–teacher conference while a supervisor indicates that one's presence at a meeting is not critical, stronger pressures will be generated to comply with family

---

[1] Although Greenhaus and Beutell (1985) specified a third form of work–family conflict, behaviour-based conflict, the empirical support for this form of conflict is sufficiently rare to exclude a discussion of behaviour-based conflict in this analysis.

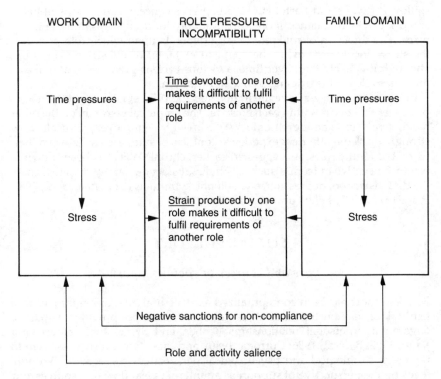

Figure 14.1 Work – family conflict (adapted from Grennhaus and Bentell, 1985)

expectations than with work expectations. Again, we would expect that psychological conflict will be greatest when there are strong negative sanctions for non-compliance in *both* work and family roles.

An important issue in understanding the dynamics of WFC is the direction of role interference. Work interference with family may have different antecedents and consequences than family interference with work (Wiley, 1987; Frone *et al.*, 1992), and consequently may require different approaches for dealing with the conflict. We propose that the direction of role interference is influenced by the individual's reaction to simultaneous role demands, especially in the case of time-based conflict. For example, the employee who chooses to participate in the project team meeting is likely to perceive (in retrospect) that work interfered with family. Had the employee decided to participate in the parent–teacher conference, he or she would have perceived that family interfered with work.

The second form of WFC, strain-based conflict, is experienced when the strain produced in one role spills over or intrudes into the other role. For example, work-related stress, produced by such factors as role ambiguity, role overload, and career frustrations, can produce strain symptoms such as irritability, fatigue, preoccupation, depression, and anxiety (Brief *et al.*, 1981). An employee who 'brings home' these strain symptoms is unlikely to participate fully and happily in the family domain. Interactions with family members can be difficult and trying under conditions of 'negative emotional spillover' (Evans and Bartolomé, 1980), just as concentration and well-being at work can be threatened if one carries family-induced stress into the workplace. The direction of role interference depends upon which role produces the stress and which role is the recipient or target of the strain symptoms, although it is likely that, over time, a vicious cycle is produced that makes it difficult to detect the original source of the strain.

In this discussion we have illustrated specific WFC episodes and the microprocesses that occur within each episode. The empirical research, on the other hand, tends to examine chronic WFC, in which employees indicate how strongly or frequently they experience conflicts or interference between their work and family roles. As suggested earlier, chronic WFC has been shown to produce negative outcomes such as job dissatisfaction, family dissatisfaction, life dissatisfaction, depression, and somatic symptoms (Kopelman *et al.*, 1983; Frone *et al.*, 1991, 1992; Parasuraman *et al.*, 1992).

SOCIAL SUPPORT

Types and sources of social support

Social support has been conceptualized as structural integration into a social network of relationships as well as functional resources provided as part of ongoing interpersonal relationships (Cohen and Syme, 1985; House and Kahn, 1985; Barrera, 1986; Cutrona, 1986), and these two approaches seem to represent sociological and psychological perspectives respectively. We will focus on the perspective of support as an interpersonal flow of resources and tentatively adopt Shumaker and Brownell's (1984, p. 13) definition of social support as 'an exchange of resources between at least two individuals perceived by the provider or the recipient to be intended to enhance the well-being of the recipient'. This perspective emphasizes the dynamic and transactional nature of the support process.

There is growing recognition that social support is a complex, multifaceted phenomenon. Tardy (1985) and Payne and Jones (1987) have distinguished different facets or dimensions of social support: the source of support, the content or type of support, the disposition of support, the evaluation of support, and the direction of support. These subtleties, which may have important implications for the efficacy of support in managing WFC, are not generally incorporated into support research conducted in organizational settings.

Focusing on the content of support, some researchers have distinguished affect, affirmation, and aid as types of support (Abbey *et al.*, 1985). Others have identified esteem, informational, social companionship, and instrumental support (Cohen and Wills, 1985); emotional, social integration, esteem, tangible, and informational support (Cutrona and Russell, 1990); and emotional, instrumental, informational, and appraisal support (House, 1981). Although there is considerable overlap among these approaches, it is clear that some researchers make distinctions that others choose not to make. Moreover, different types of support from the same person tend to be highly intercorrelated (House and Kahn, 1985), and all types of support are perceived to have an emotional component (Barling *et al.*, 1988).

In the interest of parsimony, this chapter will distinguish tangible support from emotional support. Tangible support includes information, advice, and suggestions (informational) as well as aid in time, money, or other forms of tangible help (instrumental). Emotional support includes the provision of esteem, affection, and trust (emotional) as well as feedback and affirmation (appraisal).

The literature also distinguishes support provided by different sources. Much of the research excludes 'formal' sources of support, which include such paid caregivers as therapists, nurses, and attorneys. Research on occupational and family stress often distinguishes support from the work domain (supervisor, co-workers, subordinates, organization) from support in the family or personal domain (spouse, children, other relatives, friends, or neighbours). We will maintain the distinction between work and family sources of support in this chapter.

Functions of social support

How does social support enhance well-being? Figure 14.2 indicates three roles of social support in the stress process. The 'health sustaining' (Shumaker and Brownell, 1984) function of social support, represented by arrow 1 in Figure 14.2, reflects a positive main effect of support on well-being. This main effect has been observed consistently in the literature, and presumably reflects the impact of social support on the recipient's affiliative satisfaction, sense of stability and self-identity, and feelings of self-worth and self-esteem (Shumaker and Brownell, 1984; Cohen and Wills, 1985). The main effect of support on well-being occurs *regardless* of the level of stress experienced by the individual.

The 'stress prevention' (Barrera, 1986) function of social support, represented by arrow 2, is a negative main effect of support on the stressor. In this role, social support reduces the environmental pressures that produce the stress in the first place. For example, cognizant of the pressures generated by

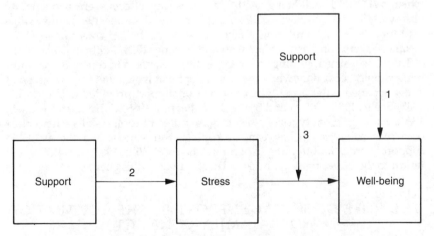

Figure 14.2 Functions of social support in the stress process. Arrow 1 = health − sustaining function; Arrow 2 = stress prevention function; Arrow 3 = buffering function.

a project with a tight deadline, a supportive supervisor might provide additional staff help to an employee that makes the work demands more manageable and prevents the resultant feelings of overload. Although the stress-prevention perspective does not seem to be as widely adopted as the health-sustaining perspective, there is evidence suggesting that social support can reduce the level of stress in the work environment (Beehr, 1985; Ganster et al., 1986; Fusilier et al., 1987) and in the family environment (Frone et al., 1991; Parasuraman et al., 1992).

The 'buffering' function of social support, represented by arrow 3, reflects a moderating effect of support on the relationship between stress and well-being. The buffering hypothesis proposes that support weakens or attenuates the negative relationship between stress and well-being, thereby protecting an individual from the severe consequences of stress. In this role, support directly affects neither stress nor well-being but rather the relationship between stress and well-being. It is believed that support acts as a buffer because it enhances the recipient's cognitive and behavioural coping abilities that enable the recipient to manage the stressful situation more effectively (Cohen and Wills, 1985; Pearlin, 1985; Fondacaro and Moos, 1987). Because of the enhancement of coping skills that are responsive to a particular stressful situation, the buffering perspective – unlike the health-sustaining perspective – asserts that support only promotes well-being in the presence of high levels of stress (McIntosh, 1991).

Empirical research provides inconsistent support for the buffering hypothesis despite its intuitive appeal. For example, although the work stress literature has revealed occasional support for the buffering prediction (Constable and Russell, 1986; Fusilier et al., 1987), many studies have observed either no buffering effect (Aneshensel, 1986; Bamberg et al., 1986; Dooley et al., 1987) or 'reverse buffering', in which the stress–strain relationship is *stronger* under conditions of high support than low support (Ganster et al., 1986; Kaufmann and Beehr, 1986). The results have been equally inconclusive in the few studies that examined support as a moderator of the relationship between WFC and well-being. Although buffering effects were occasionally observed (Suchet and Barling, 1986; Stephens and Sommer, 1993), other studies found either no buffering effect (Frone et al., 1991; Parasuraman et al., 1992) or reverse buffering (MacEwen and Barling, 1988; Reifman et al., 1991).

These inconsistent findings have led some researchers to conclude that buffering should occur only when there is an 'optimal match' between the type of stress experienced and the type or source of support provided (Abbey et al., 1985; Beehr, 1985; Cohen and Syme, 1985; Pearlin, 1985; Cutrona and Russell, 1990). Since different types of stress require different coping skills, 'there must be a reasonable match between the coping requirements and the available support in order for buffering to occur' (Cohen and Wills, 1985, p. 314). We will return to the buffering hypothesis in later sections of this chapter.

THE ROLE OF SOCIAL SUPPORT IN THE CONTEXT OF WORK–FAMILY CONFLICT

In Figure 14.3 is it proposed that all three functions of social support – stress prevention, health sustaining, and buffering – are relevant to a deeper

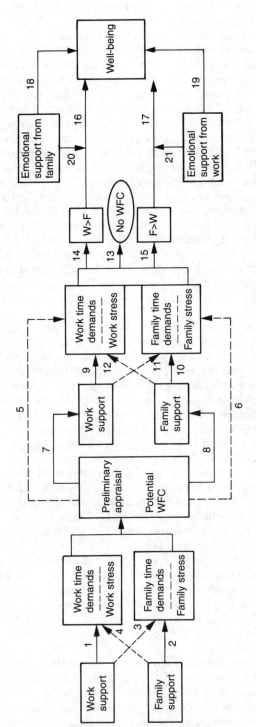

Figure 14.3 The role of social support in the context of work – family conflict. WFC = Workfamily conflict; W > F = Work interference with family; F > W = family interference with work.

understanding of the WFC process. Although both forms of WFC are combined in Figure 14.3 as a space-saving device, we will first discuss time-
based conflict and then examine strain-based conflict.

Social support initially operates to prevent stress. Support from work and
family is expected to reduce the time demands within the respective roles.
For example, a supervisor who extends a project deadline, a co-worker who
takes on additional work, and an organization that has a flexible work
schedule policy can all reduce an employee's time demands within the
work role. In a similar vein, a spouse who participates extensively in household maintenance and a child who prepares dinner can relieve the time
demands associated with the family role. We expect that: (a) tangible support (direct aid, financial resources, information, advice) is more central at
this stage of the process than emotional support (Beehr, 1985), although it is
possible that emotional support can enhance the recipient's self-efficacy
expectations and the enactment of effective coping (Fondacaro and Moos,
1987) which may reduce the time demands associated with a given role; (b)
ongoing or enduring support (Abbey et al., 1985) is critical at this stage; and
(c) support has its primary effect in reducing time demands within the role
in which the support resides (arrows 1 and 2), although it is possible that
informational or emotional support from one role (e.g. advice from spouse)
may enable an employee to reduce the time demands of the other role
(arrows 3 and 4).

Since even the most supportive environments cannot eliminate time demands, it is likely that an individual will, on occasion, experience simultaneous time pressures from the work and family domains. At this point, an
employee makes a preliminary appraisal of the situation's potential for producing WFC. The employee may attend to one role demand, e.g. a work
meeting, over another role demand, e. g. a family gathering, may try to alter
directly the time demands in one or both roles (arrows 5 and 6), or may seek
support from role senders in the work and/or family domains (arrows 7 and
8). If the support is effective in modifying one of the time demands (arrows 9–
12), no WFC is experienced (arrow 13). If the support is not sufficient to
modify time demands, then either work will interfere with family (if the work
demand takes precedence as in arrow 14) or family will interfere with work
(if the family demand takes precedence as in arrow 15). As before, we expect
that tangible support will be most useful at this stage of the role conflict
episode, and that the most powerful impact of social support is within the
role in which the support is provided.

To this point, social support's major function is to prevent or reduce WFC,
initially through the impact of ongoing support on reduced time demands
and then through responsive support resulting from an initial appraisal of
potential WFC. Negative relationships observed between social support and
WFC (Suchet and Barling, 1986; MacEwen and Barling, 1988; Frone et al.,
1991; Parasuraman et al. 1992; Stephens and Sommer, 1993) are consistent
with this perspective.

Note the timing of events inherent in this approach. Ongoing support precedes the initial appraisal of potential WFC, and subsequent support, either
solicited or provided 'voluntarily', follows the preliminary appraisal of WFC
(the 'support mobilization' function described by Barrera (1986)). Moreover,
the time interval between the preliminary appraisal and the resultant presence

or absence of role interference may be extremely brief. This perspective raises some interesting questions, which will be elaborated in the following sections of the chapter: (a) under what conditions does an individual seek support? (b) from which role domains does the individual seek support? (c) what factors encourage a role sender to provide support? (d) what factors encourage an individual to accept the support that is provided? (e) what types of support are most likely to be useful in a given situation?

Continuing the examination of Figure 14.3, role interference is expected to have negative effects on well-being (arrows 16 and 17), relationships that have been amply demonstrated in the literature. Moreover, we predict that emotional support has direct effects on well-being (arrows 18 and 19) as well as buffering effects on the relationship between WFC and well-being (arrows 20 and 21). In particular, we expect that emotional support from the role that is the object of interference will attenuate the negative effects of WFC on well-being. Thus, when work interferes with family, we would expect emotional support from the family role to mitigate the strain produced from the interference, whereas emotional support from the work role would mitigate the strain produced by family interference with work. In other words, the anxiety, guilt, depression, or dissatisfaction aroused from WFC can be more effectively addressed by role senders in the domain most directly affected by the interference.

Although we have illustrated the multiple functions of social support in the case of time-based conflict, the process is similar for strain-based conflict. Social support is expected to reduce the stress associated with the work role (Beehr, 1985; Ganster et al., 1986; Fusilier et al., 1987; Frone et al., 1991; McIntosh, 1991) and the family role (Frone et al., 1991; Parasuraman et al., 1992). Extensive stress in either role is expected to trigger a preliminary appraisal of WFC, which either promotes direct attempts to reduce the stress or encourages the seeking and provision of social support. In either case, the subsequent levels of role stress will determine the presence and direction of WFC, which will have consequences for well-being. Emotional support from each role is expected to have a health-sustaining, main effect on well-being, and emotional support from the affected role is expected to exhibit a buffering effect on the relationship between WFC and well-being.

DEVELOPMENT OF A RESEARCH AGENDA

The preceding discussion undoubtedly raised more questions than it resolved. In this section, we present a research agenda to guide future studies on social support in the context of WFC. The proposed agenda also responds to the call for greater clarity regarding the causal mechanisms underlying the social support process (Shumaker and Brownell, 1984; Cohen and Syme, 1985; Barrera, 1986; Thoits, 1986; Eckenrode and Gore, 1990; Pearlin and McCall, 1990).

Support embedded in social relationships

As Eckenrode and Gore (1990) observed, support is often a subtle part of an ongoing interpersonal relationship. Therefore, an understanding of the conditions under which support is provided, accepted, and utilized requires an appreciation of the characteristics of the social relationship in which support is embedded.

Little is known about the way in which support evolves over the life course or within a specific relationship. Antonucci (1983) described social support as a 'convoy' or protective shield that may explain continuities and changes in social support over the course of an individual's life. This perspective may explain individual differences in the willingness to provide and accept social support.

At a more micro-level, Pearlin and McCall (1990) proposed a four-stage model of marital support that recognizes the rich social environment in which support is provided or withheld. Early stages of a support episode involve a recognition of a problem and an appraisal of the need to provide support to the partner. Subsequent stages focus on the types of support provided and the outcomes of support activities. A developmental view of the support process raises a number of interesting research questions that extend to relationships other than marital partners. For example, how are work–family problems revealed by one individual to another individual? What factors determine whether a specific problem is perceived as sufficiently meritorious to warrant support?

A developmental approach can help reveal the conditions under which social support is provided. Dunkel-Schetter et al. (1987) found that the degree of support provided was a function of a number of personal characteristics of the recipient as well as of an appraisal of the seriousness of the stressful event. Granrose et al. (1992) developed a model of support provided by partners in two-career relationships. They proposed that the amount and type of support provided is a function of three variables: (a) the support environment, which includes the family setting and characteristics of the provider and recipient; (b) the possession of sufficient financial, informational, and time resources to provide support; and (c) the willingness of the partner to provide support, which is affected by social norms, perceived equity, and the expected value of providing support. They offered 10 sets of hypotheses regarding support provision that warrant empirical investigation.

Reciprocity and equity norms may be a particularly significant influence on the decision to provide and accept social support, as well as on the magnitude and types of support given and accepted. Ongoing relationships can be threatened if the provision of support is excessively one-sided (Shumaker and Brownell, 1984; Pearlin, 1985), although intimate relationships do provide greater latitude in reciprocity over time than do more formal relationships (Antonucci, 1983). Thus, providing substantially more support than one receives can dampen a spouse's marital satisfaction (Parasuraman and Greenhaus, 1992). Moreover, perceptions of the equity of support exchanges may be based not only on the relative amounts of support provided and received by the donor and the focal recipient, but on perceptions of the absolute and relative role demands and responsibilities experienced by the two parties. Reciprocity norms may not only limit the amount of support provided in a relationship but can also influence the decision to seek or accept support. Since the acceptance of support implies an obligation to provide future support, an individual may not be willing to accept support if reciprocation is impossible or unwanted (Shumaker and Brownell, 1984).

Reciprocity is not the only social norm that can influence the support process. Undoubtedly, norms develop regarding the appropriateness of seeking or accepting specific types of support from specific sources. Is it appropriate to seek emotional support from a supervisor? How much tangible support is it acceptable for an adult to receive from his or her parents? Does support from a subordinate introduce an unwanted element into the employment relationship?

Future research should examine the extent to which social norms in general and reciprocity norms in particular influence decisions regarding the seeking, provision, and acceptance of social support. For example, norms regarding the separation of family and work roles and beliefs regarding appropriate sex roles may determine whether a supervisor, co-worker or spouse is willing to provide an individual – woman or man – with the necessary support to manage WFC and whether the individual desires to accept the support.

The acceptance and usefulness of support may well depend on the timing, type, and amount of support provided, as well as a variety of personal and interpersonal characteristics. Is the support provided in a timely manner or is it perceived to be too little and too late? Have prior supportive activities by a particular source been successful or unsuccessful? Is a supportive activity seen as a validation of an individual's self-worth or is it seen as a threat to one's self-esteem? We expect that the overall quality of an ongoing relationship would determine whether support is freely sought, provided, and accepted. Yet, the interpersonal nature of the support process is rarely examined in the literature (Pearlin, 1985).

Toward a congruence theory of social support

As noted earlier, the failure to observe consistent buffering effects suggests that for support to be effective, there must be a 'match' between the type of stress experienced and the type of support provided (Shumaker and Brownell, 1984; Abbey et al., 1985; Cohen and Syme, 1985). The central assumption of this approach is that different stress-inducing events pose specific demands and challenges that require specific coping responses. Social support that promotes relevant coping responses will therefore be more effective than support that promotes inappropriate coping responses. Cutrona and Russell (1990) believe that the literature is generally consistent with an optimal match or congruence view of social support. Several linkages must be established to apply a congruence perspective to the resolution of WFC.

First, it is essential to understand the different types of WFC that can be experienced. Although the present analysis focuses on time-based conflict and strain-based conflict, other models have been proposed as well (Small and Riley, 1990). Consensus regarding a typology of WFC will promote consistent conceptual and operational definitions across studies. Moreover, a clear delineation of the different forms of WFC will enhance understanding of the demands, challenges, and threats associated with each type of WFC.

Second, a congruence approach requires an appreciation of the multiple functions of social support. The present analysis incorporates three major functions: (a) stress prevention, in which ongoing or enduring support reduces the environmental conditions (time demands and role stress) that produce WFC; (b) buffering, in which social support attenuates the relationship between stress and well-being; and (c) health sustaining, in which social support has direct effects on strain or well-being. Each of these functions of support can be examined from a congruence perspective. In addition, the support mobilization process, in which initially high levels of anticipated WFC encourage support seeking and support provision, may also depend on a number of situational factors.

Third, it is essential to understand the type of coping that is relevant to each form of WFC. Latack and Havlovic (1992, p. 483) define coping as 'cognitive and behavioral efforts to manage the internal and external demands of transactions that tax or exceed a person's resources'. Although different typologies of coping have emerged, the distinction between problem-focused coping and emotion-focused coping is prominent in the literature (Lazarus and Folkman, 1984). Responding to excessive time pressures may require different coping strategies than responding to excessive stress, just as work-related sources of time pressure and stress may require different types of coping than family-related sources of time pressure and stress.

Fourth, it is necessary to understand whether and how specific types (and sources) of social support promote specific forms of coping. Dunkel-Schetter et al. (1987) provide a conceptual rationale for a causal linkage between support and coping, and Fondacaro and Moos (1987) observed some linkages between support from one's family and the use of problem-solving coping. But considerable research will be required to develop an understanding of these linkages. Does tangible support enhance problem-focused coping? Does emotional support promote active coping by virtue of its effects on an individual's feelings of self-worth and self-efficacy beliefs?

In sum, the development of a congruence approach requires an understanding of the demands posed by different types of WFC, the coping activities relevant to these different demands, and the impact of different types of social support on the utilization of alternative coping activities. To illustrate the benefit of such an approch, one hypothetical conclusion might be that tangible support from either the work domain or the family domain is most useful to prevent the occurrence of time-based WFC, whereas emotional support is most useful to weaken the negative effects of time-based WFC that is currently experienced. Additionally, as implied in the previous section, the development of a congruence approach requires an understanding of specific characteristics of the interpersonal relationship in which support is provided and received.

The role of gender in the social support process

A congruence approach to WFC and social support must examine the role of gender in the support process. It is often speculated that women provide more support to their husbands than they receive from them, women receive more support from a greater variety of sources than men, and women benefit more than men from social support. However, none of these assertions has received consistent support in the empirical literature. Research adopting a congruence perspective should examine not only whether men and women provide and receive different amounts of the various types of support, but also whether different combinations of support sources and types are differentially effective in reducing stress, alleviating strain, and sustaining health.

Although Vanfossen (1986) observed that wives provide more expressive support than their husbands, the difference was small in magnitude. Moreover, Parasuraman and Greenhaus (1992) found no difference in the amount of emotional support provided by husbands and wives. It is likely, however, that women contribute more tangible support to a relationship than men, especially in the area of childcare and daily home maintenance (Hochschild, 1989; Parasuraman and Greenhaus, 1992). Moreover, sex differences in instrumental support may be subtle in the way the support is provided and perceived. For example, Karambayya and Reilly (1992) found that wives are more likely to restructure their work to accommodate their children's needs than are husbands. Significantly, wives' work accommodations tend to be ongoing, whereas husbands' accommodations represent 'special arrangements' to acute family stresses. Given the transactional nature of support exchanges between individuals in ongoing relationships, future empirical research should examine the provision and receipt of support from the perspective of both the receiver and the provider of support.

The literature does not consistently confirm the expectation that women receive more varied social support than men and that women find support more useful than men. Men and women have been found to receive similar levels of support from their supervisors, and sex differences in support from neighbours are mixed. One consistent finding is the more substantial level of co-worker support received by women than men (Shinn et al., 1989; Greenberger and O'Neil, 1993).

Sex differences in the usefulness of support are equally inconclusive and are likely to depend on the type and source of support received. For example, although emotional support from one's partner seems to be equally important for men and women, reciprocity of support (Vanfossen, 1986) and instrumental support (Parasuraman and Greenhaus, 1992) may be especially important for employed women (Vanfossen, 1986). Moreover, although Billings and Moos (1982) found that supervisory support predicted well-being only for men, Greenberger et al. (1989) found that supervisory support predicted job satisfaction only for women, and Parasuraman et al. (1992) observed that work support predicted job satisfaction for both women and men. Greenberger and O'Neil's (1993) finding that women's role strain was mitigated by support from a greater variety of sources (spouse, neighbours, and supervisor) than men's role strain (just spouse support) further complicates the picture.

Additional research on sex differences in support is obviously required, but we propose that such research must be guided by theoretical frameworks that are capable of explaining the differences, and similarities, in the support process as experienced by women and men. Socialization experiences, sex-role stereotypes, organizational culture, and individual attitudes toward combining work and family roles are likely to be useful concepts to guide such research.

Methodological issues

Future research will require designs that are capable of detecting the complexities and subtleties that characterize the social support process in the context of WFC. At a minimum, measures of WFC and social support must be comprehensive and faithful to the underlying theoretical dimensions of the respective concepts. To assess the viability of a congruence perspective, measures of WFC in a particular study should incorporate multiple types of conflict and multiple directions of role interference, and measures of support should assess the type of support, the source of support, and the amount of support. An assessment of the latter variable would be particularly useful in examining the non-linear effects of support on well-being (Cohen and Syme, 1985; McIntosh, 1991).

Since WFC is viewed as a series of episodes that develop over time, in which support both precedes and follows the conflict experience, longitudinal research designs should be used to examine the dynamics of support exchanges among individuals in ongoing relationships. The embeddedness of support in ongoing social relationships indicates the need to examine the dyad (supervisor–subordinate, husband–wife) or the group (immediate work group, family) as the relevant unit of analysis. Thus, the sources and consequences of support need to be examined within the total constellation of support sources available to an individual from the work, family, and personal life domains. Such research would also be strengthened with multiple sources of data gathered from the focal person and members of his or her role set.

While survey-based correlational research using cross-sectional and longitudinal designs is important to the development and refinement of theory regarding the provision and receipt of support, future research should incorporate more qualitatively oriented approaches and intensive interviews to gain deeper insights into the process by which WFC develops as well as the processes by which the need for support is recognized, elicited or sought, provided, accepted, and utilized (Pearlin and McCall, 1990; Weiss, 1990; Coyne and Downey, 1991). Moreover, given the confounding factors inevitably observed in a correlational study (Dooley, 1985), the laboratory experiment, with its manipulation of independent variables, can provide increased confidence in causal inferences, as witnessed in the study by Barling et al. (1988).

CONCLUSION

The literature on social support in relation to WFC reviewed in this chapter reveals that the empirical research has not kept pace with the conceptual developments on the subject of support. The mechanistic application of extant models of stress in examining the relationships of global WFC and social support with outcome variables has contributed to the limited progress in understanding the mechanisms and processes by which social support prevents or alleviates strain, and sustains psychological and physical health. Radically new approaches are necessary to break out of the rut into which research on social support has fallen. Future research should proceed in a number of directions in an attempt to seek answers to many of the questions posed in the earlier sections of this chapter.

Useful research in this area requires an understanding of the conceptual underpinnings of both WFC and the social support process. It is especially important to understand the timing of events in a WFC episode as well as the evolution of supportive activities over the course of a specific problem and an ongoing relationship. Although chronic WFC and cumulative social support are easier to conceptualize and measure than episodic conflict and developmental support, they are not as likely to advance our understanding of the underlying concepts as substantially as the adoption of a longitudinal perspective.

Since WFC exists by virtue of participation in multiple roles and social support is embedded in ongoing relationships, theoretical advancement requires an understanding of role sets, exchange relationships, and interpersonal communications. These topics are often ignored in empirical examinations of WFC and social support, largely because most of the research in these areas adopts an individual level of analysis.

Although considerably more research needs to be conducted on social support in the work and family domains, there is a rich theoretical and empirical history on which to draw. The inconsistent findings in the research literature have demonstrated the complexities and subtleties of the social support process in all circumstances including the work–family interface. We hope this chapter stimulates additional theory-based research that melds a variety of disciplines, methodologies, and time frames.

REFERENCES

ABBEY, A., ABRAMIS, D. J. and CAPLAN, R. D. (1985) Effects of different sources of social support and social conflict on emotional well-being, *Basic and Applied Social Psychology*, Vol. 6, no. 2, pp. 111–29.

ANESHENSEL, C. S. (1986) Marital and employment role-strain, social support, and depression among adult women, in S. E. Hobfoll (ed.) *Stress, Social Support, and Women*. Hemisphere, New York.

ANTONUCCI, T. C. (1983) Social support: theoretical advances, recent findings and pressing issues. Paper presented at the NATO workshop on social support, Château de Bonas, France.

BAMBERG, E., RUCKERT, D. and UDRIS, I. (1986) Interactive effects of social support from wife, non-work activities and blue-collar occupational stress, *International Review of Applied Psychology*, Vol. 35, pp. 397–413.

BARLING, J., MACEWEN, K. E. and PRATT, L. I. (1988) Manipulating the type and source of social support: an experimental investigation, *Canadian Journal of Behavior Sciences*, Vol. 20, no. 2, pp. 140–53.

BARRERA, M. (1986) Distinctions between social support concepts, measures, and models, *American Journal of Community Psychology*, Vol. 14, no. 4, pp. 413–45.

BEEHR, T. A. (1985) The role of social support in coping with organizational stress, in T. A. Beehr and R. S. Bhagat (eds) *Human Stress and Cognition in Organizations*, Wiley, New York.

BILLINGS, A. G. and MOOS, R. H. (1982) Work stress and the stress-buffering roles of work and family resources, *Journal of Occupational Behaviour*, Vol. 3, pp. 215–32.

BRIEF, A. P., SCHULER, R. S. and VAN SELL, M. (1981) *Managing Job Stress*, Little Brown, Boston.

BURKE, R. J. (1989) Some antecedents and consequences of work–family conflict, in E. B. Goldsmith (ed.) Work and Family: Theory, Research, and Applications, Sage, Newbury Park, CA.

COHEN, S. and SYME, S. L. (1985) Issues in the study and application of social support, in S. Cohen and S. L. Syme (eds) *Social Support and Health*, Academic Press, Orlando, FL.

COHEN, S. and WILLS, T. A. (1985) Stress, social support, and the buffering hypothesis, *Psychological Bulletin*, Vol. 98, no. 2, pp. 310–57.

CONSTABLE, J. F. and RUSSELL, D. W. (1986) The effect of social support and the work environment upon burnout among nurses, *Journal of Human Stress*, Vol. 12, pp. 20–6.

COYNE, J. C. and DOWNEY, G. (1991) Social factors and psychopathology: stress, social support, and coping processes, *Annual Review of Psychology*, Vol. 42, pp. 401–25.

CUTRONA, C. E. (1986) Objective determinants of perceived social support, *Journal of Personality and Social Psychology*, Vol. 50, no. 2, pp. 349–55.

CUTRONA, C. E. and RUSSELL, D. W. (1990) Type of social support and specific stress: toward a theory of optimal matching, in B. R. Sarason, I. G. Sarason, and G. R. Pierce (eds) *Social Support: An Interactional View*, Wiley, New York.

DOOLEY, D. (1985) Causal inference in the study of social support, in S. Cohen and S. L. Syme (eds) *Social Support and Health*, Academic Press, Orlando, FL.

DOOLEY, D., ROOK, K. and CATALANO, R. (1987) Job and non-job stressors and their moderators, *Journal of Occupational Psychology*, Vol. 60, pp. 115–32.

DUNKEL-SCHETTER, C., FOLKMAN, S. and LAZARUS, R. S. (1987) Correlates of social support receipt, *Journal of Personality and Social Psychology*, Vol. 53, no. 1, pp. 71–80.

ECKENRODE, J. and GORE, S. (1990) Stress between work and family: summary and conclusions, in J. Eckenrode and S. Gore (eds) *Stress Between Work and Family*, Plenum, New York.

EVANS, P. A. L. and BARTOLOME, F. (1980) *Must Success Cost So Much?* Basic Books, New York.

FONDACARO, M. R. and MOOS, R. H. (1987) Social support and coping: a longitudinal analysis, *American Journal of Community Psychology*, Vol. 15, no. 5, pp. 653–73.

FRIEDMAN, D. E. (1990) Work and family: the new strategic plan, *Human Resource Planning*, Vol. 13, no. 2, pp. 79–89.

FRONE, M. R., RUSSELL, M. and COOPER, M. L. (1991) Relationship of work and family stressors to psychological distress: the independent moderating influence of social support, mastery, active coping, and self-focused-attention, *Journal of Social Behavior and Personality*, Vol. 6, no. 7, pp. 227–50.

FRONE, M. R., RUSSELL, M. and COOPER, M. L. (1992) Antecedents and outcomes of work–family conflict: testing a model of the work-family interface, *Journal of Applied Psychology*, Vol. 77, no. 1, pp. 65–78.

FUSILIER, M. R., GANSTER, D. C. and MAYES, B. T. (1987) Effects of social support, role stress, and locus of control on health, *Journal of Management*, Vol. 13, no. 3, pp. 517–28.

GANSTER, D. C., FUSILIER, M. R. and MAYES, B. T. (1986) Role of social support in the experience of stress at work, *Journal of Applied Psychology*, Vol. 71, no. 1, pp. 102–10.

GRANROSE, C. S., PARASURAMAN, S. and GREENHAUS, J. H. (1992) A proposed model of support provided by two-earner couples, *Human Relations*, Vol. 45, no. 12, pp. 1367–93.

GREENBERGER, E., GOLDBERG, W. A., HAMILL, S., O'NEIL, R. and PAYNE, C. K. (1989) Contributions of a supportive work environment to parents' well-being and orientation to work, *American Journal of Community Psychology*, Vol. 17, no. 6, pp. 755–83.

GREENBERGER, E. and O'NEIL, R. (1993) Spouse, parent, worker: role commitments and role-related experiences in the construction of adults' well-being, *Developmental Psychology*, Vol. 29, no. 2, pp. 181–97.

GREENHAUS, J. H. and BEUTELL, N. J. (1985) Sources of conflict between work and family roles, *Academy of Management Review*, Vol. 10, no. 1, pp. 76–88.

GREENHAUS, J. H. and PARASURAMAN, S. (1986) A work–nonwork interactive perspective of stress and its consequences, *Journal of Organizational Behavior Management*, Vol. 8, no. 2, pp. 37–60.

HOCHSCHILD, A. (1989) *The Second Shift*, Viking, New York.

HOUSE, J. S. (1981) *Work Stress and Social Support*, Addison-Wesley, Reading, MA.

HOUSE, J. S. and KAHN, R. L. (1985) Measures and concepts of social support, in S. Cohen and S. L. Syme (eds) *Social Support and Health*, Academic Press, Orlando, FL.

KARAMBAYYA, R. and REILLY, A. H. (1992) Dual earner couples: attitudes and actions in restructuring work for family, *Journal of Organizational Behavior*, Vol. 13, pp. 585–601.

KAUFMANN, G. M. and BEEHR, T. A. (1986) Interactions between job stressors and social support: some counterintuitive findings, *Journal of Applied Psychology*, Vol. 71, no. 3, pp. 522–6.

KOPELMAN, R. E., GREENHAUS, J. H. and CONNOLLY, T. F. (1983) A model of work, family, and interrole conflict: a construct validation study, *Organizational Behavior and Human Performance*, Vol. 32, pp. 198–215.

LATACK, J. C. and HAVLOVIC, S. J. (1992) Coping with job stress: a conceptual evaluation framework for coping measures, *Journal of Organizational Behavior*, Vol. 13, pp. 479–508.

LAZARUS, R. S. and FOLKMAN, S. (1984) *Stress, Coping, and Adaptation*, Springer, New York.

MACEWEN, K. E. and BARLING, J. (1988) Interrole conflict, family support and marital adjustment of employed mothers: a short term, longitudinal study, *Journal of Organizational Behavior*, Vol. 9, pp. 241–50.

MCINTOSH, N. J. (1991) Identification and investigation of properties of social support, *Journal of Organizational Behavior*, Vol. 12, pp. 201–17.

PARASURAMAN, S. and GREENHAUS, J. H. (1992) An exchange perspective of support provided by partners in two-career relationships: analysis of the determinants and outcomes. Paper presented at the Annual Meeting of the Academy of Management, Las Vegas.

PARASURAMAN, S., GREENHAUS, J. H. and GRANROSE, C. S. (1992) Role stressors, social support, and well-being among two-career couples, *Journal of Organizational Behavior*, Vol. 13, pp. 339–56.

PAYNE, R. L. and JONES, J. G. (1987) Measurement and methodological issues in social support, in S. V. Kasl and C. L. Cooper (eds) *Stress and Health: Issues in Research Methodology*, Wiley, New York.

PEARLIN, L. I. (1985) Social structure and processes of social support, in S. Cohen and S. L. Syme (eds) *Social Support and Health*, Academic Press, Orlando, FL.

PEARLIN, L. I. and MCCALL, M. E. (1990) Occupational stress and marital support: a description of microprocesses, in J. Eckenrode and S. Gore (eds) *Stress Between Work and Family*, Plenum, New York.

PLECK, J. H. (1985) *Working Wives/Working Husbands*, Sage, Newbury Park, CA.

RAPOPORT, R. and RAPOPORT, R. N. (1971) Further considerations on the dual career family, *Human Relations*, Vol. 24, pp. 519–33.

REIFMAN, A., BIERNAT, M. and LANG, E. L. (1991) Stress, social support, and health in married professional women with small children, *Psychology of Women Quarterly*, Vol. 15, pp. 431–45.

SHINN, M., WONG, N. W., SIMKO, P. A. and ORTIZ-TORRES, B. (1989) Promoting the well-being of working parents: coping, social support, and flexible job schedules, *American Journal of Community Psychology*, Vol. 17, no. 1, pp. 31–55.

SHUMAKER, S. A. and BROWNELL, A. (1984) Toward a theory of social support: closing conceptual gaps, *Journal of Social Issues*, Vol. 40, no. 4, pp. 11–36.

SMALL, S. A. and RILEY, D. (1990) Toward a multidimensional assessment of work spillover into family life, *Journal of Marriage and the Family*, Vol. 52, pp. 51–61.

STEPHENS, G. K. and SOMMER, S. M. (1993) Work–family conflict, job attitudes, and workplace social support: investigations of measurement and moderation. Paper presented at the Annual Meeting of the Academy of Management, Atlanta.

SUCHET, M. and BARLING, J. (1986) Employed mothers: interrole conflict, spouse support and marital functioning, *Journal of Occupational Behaviour*, Vol. 7, pp. 167–78.

TARDY, C. H. (1985) Social support measurement, *American Journal of Community Psychology*, Vol. 13, no. 2, pp. 187–202.

THOITS, P. A. (1986) Social support as coping assistance, *Journal of Counseling and Clinical Psychology*, Vol. 54, no. 4, pp. 416–23.

VANFOSSEN, B. E. (1986) Sex differences in depression: the role of social support, in S. E. Hobfoll (ed.) *Stress, Social Support, and Women*, Hemisphere, New York.

VOYDANOFF, P. (1987) *Work and Family Life*, Sage, Newbury Park, CA.

WEISS, R. S. (1990) Bringing work stress home, in J. Eckenrode and S. Gore (eds) *Stress Between Work and Family*, Plenum, New York.

WILEY, D. L. The relationship between work/nonwork role conflict and job-related outcomes: some unanticipated findings, *Journal of Management*, Vol. 13, pp. 467–72.

CHAPTER 15

Role Tensions and Dual-Career Couples

SUZAN LEWIS

INTRODUCTION

Women in management tend more often than male managers to be single, but those who do marry, or live in long-term relationships, are more likely than their male counterparts to have partners with professional or managerial careers (Davidson and Cooper, 1983; Brett et al., 1992). Many more female than male managers thus live in dual-career marriages and must deal with the issues associated with the management of two careers and family life. Both women and men in dual-career families confront these issues, but the impact on their careers is generally much greater for women (White et al., 1992).

Traditional norms governing work and family roles are challenged as dual-career partners negotiate new forms of roles and relationships within the family and the workplace to enable them to combine the two areas of their lives. Inevitably some pockets of conflict and tension persist between work and family in so far as these are constructed as separate spheres, and between new and old forms of roles as they are negotiated and reconstructed. Early research explored these tensions in terms of role theory, particularly sex role theory. Role conflicts, identity dilemmas, attachments to traditional role expectations and ambivalence about emerging degendered roles were explained in terms of early socialization experiences (Rapoport and Rapoport, 1976). More recently two theoretical approaches have proved fruitful in the analysis of dual-career issues: gender theory and a systems approach. Gender theory (Ferree, 1990; Potuchek, 1992; Gilbert, 1993) treats gender as socially constructed and conceptualizes spouses in dual-career families as involved in the process of reconstructing traditionally gendered family and work roles. It emphasizes the significance of ongoing adult experiences, rather than life scripts learned in childhood. These ongoing experiences include not only what goes on in the family but also experiences in systems beyond the household. A systems approach conceptualizes individuals and events as existing in a context of mutual influence and interaction. It acknowledges the interdependence of work and family, the two central systems for dual-career couples (Pleck, 1977; Zedeck, 1992) as well as the influences of wider social systems (Izraeli, 1992).

This chapter draws on gender theory and systems thinking to explore dual-career roles and role tensions. It explores traditionally gendered non-occupational roles challenged in dual-career relationships, which interact with occupational experiences and influence women's career development. As changes in roles and relationships within the family both influence and are influenced by changes in systems external to the family, later sections discuss organizational responses to dual-career couples and others with family commitments.

ROLE TENSIONS AND NEGOTIATIONS WITHIN THE FAMILY

Domestic roles

Despite women's increased involvement in careers and breadwinning, research over time and across cultures continues to document the persistence of inequality in the allocation of household work and in power relations within dual-career families, even among couples with 'modern' ideologies and in countries with an ideological commitment to gender equality at home and at work (Lewis and Cooper, 1987; Hochschild, 1989; Brannen and Moss, 1992; Sandqvist, 1992). When dual-career couples do move towards more egalitarian family roles, men more often share in the performance of domestic tasks than in the management of the household (Berk, 1985; Mederer, 1993). The household management role is a gender boundary which remains contentious and difficult to dismantle.

Women's extra domestic responsibilities can create role conflict and overload and can spill over to affect women's experiences of work, reducing the potential for satisfaction and achievement in their careers (Lewis and Cooper, 1987, 1988a; b). Continuing inequality in the home remains a key factor reproducing inequalities in the workplace. Surprisingly, research indicates that women in dual-career partnerships often report high levels of satisfaction with their partners' relatively modest contributions to family work (Lewis and Cooper, 1987; Brannen and Moss, 1992). It is possible that subtle but real changes are taking place in men's contributions to the family, and hence women are relatively satisfied, but that social scientists have not been able to measure these shifts (Hertz, 1992a; Lewis, 1992). Notwithstanding this point, women's apparent satisfaction with a relatively unequal division of family work has to be contextualized in terms of the meanings attached to their own and to men's family work. Women's expectations of their partners in this respect are often relatively low, and therefore any domestic or childcare work which men do share tends to be overvalued (Brannen and Moss, 1991, 1992; Kagan and Lewis, 1993). Another factor contributing to the maintenance of traditional roles is the social construction of men, in some cultures, as inept at domestic work (Lewis, 1992). This ineptitude can be regarded as a form of dependency, but as has been noted in the field of mental health (Kaplan, 1983), dependency of men on women for domestic services is socially constructed as more acceptable and 'normal' than the types of dependency that women are encouraged to develop.

Gender identity theory explanations have been proposed to explain why the negotiation of the gender boundary around family management creates a greater challenge than changes in the performance of tasks (Mederer, 1993). Psychoanalytical thinkers have argued that caring for others is an important aspect of women's gender identity, stemming from the greater difficulty experienced by female children in separating from their mother and main caregiver (Chodorow, 1978; Eichenbaum and Orbach, 1987). Taking this a step further, the social construction of household work and caring as interlinked may explain why domestic work is constructed as part of the female role (Mederer, 1993) and women may thus interpret withdrawal from the management of family life as a lack of caring. Pushing for men to perform household tasks while retaining overall managerial responsibility for the family may be a way in which women exercise power and retain gender identity. Similarly, performing domestic tasks without taking managerial responsibility may be less threatening to male identity (Mederer, 1993). Certain experiential and cultural factors appear to increase the threat to gender identity in reconstructing domestic roles. For example, a job requiring non-stereotypically feminine behaviour (Silberstein, 1992), or a cultural context that emphasizes familial rather than individualistic roles (Etzion and Bailyn, 1992), may increase women's attachment to socially constructed feminine roles in the home.

The process of making household management and its meanings visible and negotiable is important in changing family roles and may ultimately bring about the reconstruction of household and family management as a valuable function, in which important and transferable managerial skills can be developed by both partners. Such a shift will not occur, however, without similar shifts in orientation to the provider role.

The provider role

There is considerable evidence that women who earn as much as or more than their partners are in a position to negotiate greater husband participation in family work (Hertz, 1986; Potuchek, 1992). However, the significance of women's greater earning power is mediated by the various ways in which their income is defined. For example, wives' income is often devalued subjectively, because it is constructed as expendable in the case of pressing domestic or childcare demands (Brannen and Moss, 1987; Potuchek, 1992). The way in which a wife's income is defined by the partner's, and the meaning attached to this income in terms of family financial support are more central to an understanding of dual-career family processes than the amount women earn. Women who define themselves as co-breadwinners, rather than as generators of a second income, view their income as essential to family support (Potuchek, 1992) and therefore feel entitled to equal consideration in domestic and career decisions. They are, for example, more willing to relocate for a better job than those who define their partners as the major breadwinners (Bielby and Bielby, 1992).

Most women in dual-career partnerships do not define themselves as co-providers (Potuchek, 1992) and therefore do not consider their careers to merit equal consideration. Rather, they reconstruct their own breadwinning role in various ways to enable them to incorporate the importance of their careers, and their earnings, into their self-definition, without totally eliminating the gender boundary which defines men as the major providers. A sex-role theoretical approach suggests that early socialization experiences underpin the apparent persistence of traditional gender expectations. However, Potuchek (1992) found current adult experiences, including career experiences, to be more significant predictors of provider orientation than background factors or socialization. In particular, career success which is associated with greater centrality of career to self-identity, and high earnings on which the family come to rely, increase the likelihood that women will negotiate a co-provider orientation. Organizational policies which enhance equality of opportunities for women and work towards removing barriers to women's career success, may thus play a crucial role in bringing about changes in dual-career family dynamics, which will in turn enhance women's ability to contribute to organizations.

Although women's greater earnings can alter family roles, they can also create tension as new expectations are negotiated. Gender boundaries in the family are most challenged when the wife earns more, or is more successful in career terms, than her partner (Philliber and Hiller, 1983; Lewis and Cooper, 1987). The impact on the quality of the marital relationship, as well as the wife's career, is dependent on gender identity and expectations, particularly of the husband (Vannoy and Philliber, 1992). To the extent that men continue to feel that their masculinity is defined by their performance in the provider role or are protective of the power this role gives them, this situation can be construed as threatening. Some women respond, consciously or unconsciously, by holding back in their career, in what they construct as an attempt to prioritize their marriage (Sekaran, 1986; Cooper and Lewis, 1993).

As with the issue of household management in general, the visibility of the process by which money is managed is an important indicator and determinant of the meanings attributed to each partner's income. Discussions between partners of the mechanisms they use for dealing with money help to reveal gendered assumption while the lack of discussion helps to perpetuate the myth of male superiority (Hertz, 1986, 1992a, 1992b). However, reconstructed roles are fragile, particularly in the context of social and economic threats and insecurities. Hertz (1992b) suggests that the impact of the recession on dual-career families in the USA has been a retreat to more traditional roles. Even among 'modern' couples, she found that the prospect of losing the man's job was more threatening than the woman's job insecurity. She argues that men may be ideologically willing to share the provider role when both jobs are not problematic, but that they may be reluctant to forgo it altogether. The women Hertz interviewed also found this situation uncomfortable and worried about the usurping of their domestic power as main caretaker, if they were forced by economic circumstances to become sole breadwinner (Hertz, 1992b).

The spouse role – giving and receiving support

Orientations to the provider role are reflected in the extent to which relationships diverge from the traditional career man/supportive wife pattern. The construction of a woman's career as equally as, or more important than that of her partner inevitably influences couple dynamics. Divorce and separation rates are relatively high among dual-career marriages. This, of course, may be due to women's economic independence rather than to difficulties inherent in the relationship. Nevertheless, the negotiation of relationships within dual-career marriages occurs in a context where partners must deal, at some level, with societal and internalized notions of male superiority and greater entitlement to career opportunities (Gilbert, 1993). These consciously or unconsciously held beliefs may be particularly challenged by dual-career decisions such as those related to relocation, particularly if a decision is made to move to further the wife's career, or to live apart for career reasons (Cooper and Lewis, 1993).

Occupational factors impact on relationships in a number of ways. Organizational norms of mobility and long hours spent at the workplace to demonstrate commitment can create conflicts and dilemmas for two career-oriented spouses. There is also considerable evidence that stressful work experiences, including overload, conflict, and lack of supervisory support, can affect employee well-being and general mood, which can, in turn, spill over to have negative effects on the perceived quality of the marital relationship (Crouter et al., 1989; Jones and Fletcher, 1992). Exposure to stress at work can create tension within marriage, due to negative moods and preoccupation at home, so it can be argued that the potential for tension is greater when there are two stressful jobs. An alternative possibility is that the dual-career lifestyle offers the potential for a supportive colleague relationship in which occupational problems can be dealt with in a constructive way at home.

A career-oriented spouse may be perceived as a supportive colleague, or potential competitor, depending on both attitudes and economic factors. A genuine desire for each partner to do well is an important buffer against competitiveness, but partners, and particularly men, are more likely to have high aspiration for their partner if they are in a successful position themselves, while conversely, competitiveness is more likely to occur when one partner is insecure or frustrated (Silberstein, 1992).

The ability of both partners to give and receive support is a major factor determining the quality of the dual-career relationship (Vannoy and Philliber, 1992). The potential for dual-career partners to offer mutual career support may be one of the great strengths of the dual-career lifestyle. Social support plays a major role in protecting against occupational stress (House, 1981). However, the processes of giving and receiving support are also gendered, in terms of the nature and quality of support given and in the interpretation of that support. Women tend to talk more than men about work when at home, and particularly to explore interpersonal and emotional dimensions of situations, while men are inclined to problem solve and offer advice in discussing work (Silberstein, 1992). These differences, rooted in gender differences in communication styles (Tannen, 1992) may moderate the impact of support from each partner. Women's emotional support for men is gender congruent and therefore often taken for granted. Men in dual-career families often provide high levels of support to their partners, but this is constructed as optional, and therefore tends to be overvalued. It is not unusual for women to express gratitude for husband support in negative ways, for example in terms of his not interfering with her career (Cooper and Lewis, 1993), or for symbolic support, that would be there if called upon, but is rarely 'needed' (Brannen and Moss, 1991). This is not to deny that any support women receive from their partners, even if overvalued, is real in its consequences, helping women to manage their career and family (Brannen and Moss, 1991).

Nevertheless, the meanings of support between spouses are constructed in ways which reproduce inequalities.

Women's and men's relationships at home, and their struggles with gender stereotypes and expectations are reflected in, and influenced by, relationships in the workplace. Ambivalence about gender expectations underlies the difficulties some male managers experience in relating to women as colleagues and in working with a female superior (Davidson and Cooper, 1983). As more dual-career marriages evolve as real partnerships of equals, and marriages in which the wife is more successful become as normative as the reverse pattern, relationships at work may also change, with potential for more effective communication and co-operation (Cooper and Lewis, 1993). Changing gender scripts at home and at work are therefore crucially interdependent.

Parenthood and other family care

The parental role, especially the maternal role, is arguably the most complex and challenging for dual-career couples. The dual-career lifestyle becomes more difficult to manage and parents experience more role conflict and stress than those without children (Lewis and Cooper, 1987, 1988b). Parenthood also challenges reconstructed family roles. The transition to parenthood is often characterized by a shift to a more traditional division of domestic labour (LaRossa and LaRossa, 1981; Lewis and Cooper, 1988b) and mothers are less likely than childless career women to define themselves as co-providers (Potuchek, 1992). In the UK the return to employment after maternity leave is socially constructed as a choice, even in the context of economic need (Brannen and Moss, 1991, 1992). Consequently, mothers are assigned responsibility for managing career and family, which they have 'chosen' to combine (Brannen and Moss, 1991, 1992). Dual-career couples face the task of renegotiating their roles to incorporate parenthood within a context where the accepted norm is that mothers are primary caregivers, and fathers' contribution, other than as income provider, is optional, a view reinforced by public policy, such as the provision in the UK of statutory maternity leave, but not paternity or parental leave.

There is evidence of a slowing down of career progression for dual-career managerial men and women with young children (Brett et al., 1992). It is not clear to what extent this finding is due to self-selection. However, occupational as well as family roles have to be renegotiated after the transition to parenthood. Fathers have a choice about whether to make their new family status and needs visible, and if they do choose to modify their work schedules, frequently do so in a covert way (Hall, 1990). For women there is no question about the visibility of motherhood. In so far as they have a choice, it is whether to endeavour to make their family needs invisible by conforming to traditional patterns of work or to modify work schedules, often at considerable cost to career advancement. In contexts where organizational commitment is constructed in terms of long hours at the workplace, or where it is assumed that women's attachment to their careers will decline with motherhood, new mothers are often faced with identity dilemmas and difficult career decisions (Lewis, 1991). Careers can be threatened by overtly modifying work for family in these contexts, but the concealment of family needs perpetuates organizational structures which are incompatible with family life.

Work–family tensions are not confined to parents of very young children (Cooper and Lewis, 1993; Kagan and Lewis, 1993). School hours can create scheduling problems for parents who do not have the advantage of flexible hours. The ideology of full-time mothering usually declines after children reach school age but ideologies of mothering vary according to characteristics of the children. For example, mothers of children with disabilities have received scant attention in the dual-career literature, but there is some evidence that they are expected to be available full time for caring on a lifelong basis (Kagan and Lewis, 1993). These ideologies impact on dual-career families feeding the guilt experienced by many mothers (Lewis and Cooper, 1987; Brannen and Moss, 1991) and the construction of mothers' but not fathers' career involvement as a voluntary choice.

Much of the perceived guilt and conflict between the demands of work and the perceived needs of children of all ages stems from the way parental roles are socially defined and children's own perspectives are often overlooked. Solberg (1990) argues that the construction of childhood as a time of passivity and the tendency of researchers to explore children's views indirectly, rather than letting them speak for themselves, have perpetuated myths about children in dual-career families. She argues, for example, that Norwegian school-children, with working parents, far from considering themselves to be 'latchkey children', feel positive about returning from school, often with friends, to a 'vacant' house, with time for themselves before parents return. The extent to which parents dismantle gender boundaries will influence the way children and adolescents experience dual-career family life. For adolescent girls, growing up in a role-sharing family appears to be a more positive experience, as reflected in their own aspirations for career and family, than more traditional dual-career family contexts (Gilbert and Dancer, 1992). An important direction for future research is to explore further children's and adolescents' perspectives on dual-career families.

Another population whose perspectives on and involvement in dual-career families has been neglected is the older generation; the parents of contemporary dual-career couples. Older generation parents can play a significant role in the creation or reduction of role tensions, by their communication of supportive or non-supportive attitudes to their offsprings' lifestyle (Silberstein, 1992), their defensiveness concerning traditional values and openness to change and by practical help in the form of childcare or other instrumental support. In later stages of the family cycle, however, ageing or sick parents, who have traditionally been cared for by daughters or other female relatives not involved in careers, can pose a new challenge which can mirror and often exceed the conflicts associated with childcare (Kagan and Lewis, 1993; Neal et al., 1993).

Organizations may have a crucial role to play, in partnership with government agencies, in facilitating the balance of childcare and careers, through flexible work policies and care schemes (Neal et al., 1993) and through shifts in organizational cultures towards the greater valuing of families. However, in the case of eldercare, relatives themselves may be reluctant to co-operate in arrangements made for them by others, without consultation (Kagan and Lewis, 1993). The perspective of older parents, both in terms of their relationships with and support for the dual-career lifestyle and in terms of their needs and experiences when requiring care at a later stage, is thus needed to contribute to a broader picture of role tensions in dual-career family systems and in the development of appropriate organizational responses.

CHANGES IN ORGANIZATIONAL ROLES AND EXPECTATIONS

Conflict between work and family is not inevitable for those with multiple roles, but is a consequence of social definitions of work and family as separate and unrelated and of the pervasive assumption that employees, especially managers, have the back-up of a full-time homemaker. This is reflected in expectations that committed employees should be available to work long and inflexible hours, to travel and relocate without concessions to family commitments, and in the non-legitimacy of family reasons for absence from the workplace.

Women and men in dual-career families reconstruct their occupational roles in various ways to accommodate family needs. A favoured strategy is to negotiate flexibility at an informal level (Hall, 1990). The ability to be flexible, by, for example, taking time off in the day and working in the evening, can increase the permeability between work and family boundaries (Hall and Richter, 1988), giving dual-career spouses greater autonomy and control over their lives.

Managers are more likely than others to be in a position to modify work schedules for family, but may also be more reluctant to do so. The ability and willingness to modify schedules is mediated by gender, but not in a straightforward way. There is an argument that it may be easier for male than female managers to adapt their working practices for family, in that men who do so may be evaluated positively as 'new men', while women managers are seen as confirming female stereotypes (Silberstein, 1992). Alternatively it may be considered less legitimate for men than women to adapt work for family because it conflicts with gendered expectations (Hall, 1990). The likelihood that informal flexibility will be negotiated also appears to depend on the gender domination of a particular workplace, with the legitimacy of family reasons for modifying schedules being more acceptable in female- than male-dominated contexts (Holt et al., 1992).

The benefits of informally negotiated flexibility are, of course, limited by unequal access across organizations and are often dependent on the attitudes of line managers. Even formal policies depend for their success on the attitudes of line managers, who can sabotage them in a number of different ways (Raabe, 1990). There are clearly limits to what can be achieved by individuals at an informal level, without changes in formal practices and the organizational values which inform them.

The literature on organizational responses to dual-career couples and others with family responsibilities has passed through different phases. The earlier studies focused on the need for change (Sekaran, 1986; Lewis and Cooper, 1987) and described strategies adopted by pioneering companies (Berry-Lound, 1990; Hogg and Harker, 1992). Recent studies have also explored processes for changing organizational culture (Hall, 1990; Milliken et *al.*, 1990; Gonyea and Googins, 1993), and sought to evaluate the impact of family-friendly initiatives (Truman, 1986; Galinsky and Stein, 1990).

The formal policy changes recommended to ease work and family conflict include various initiatives to assist with childcare and eldercare, alternative patterns of work, part-time work with career opportunities and benefits, career breaks, enhanced maternity, parental and family leave, and the re-thinking of relocation policies and anti-nepotism policies (Cooper and Lewis, 1993). Each of these strategies challenges, to some extent, the traditional model of work and can challenge norms surrounding managerial work in particular, but they do not necessarily indicate fundamental changes in or-ganizational cultures. Family-friendly policies may be implemented as a genuine effort to reduce work–family conflict for employees and enhance women's career development, but may also be developed to improve public image or to retain women staff, while the organization continues to value and promote only those who do not accommodate work for family.

Research evaluating the effectiveness of family-friendly initiatives has focused largely on cost-effectiveness and short-term organizational benefits, with less attention to fundamental changes in organizational culture or to the perspectives of employees and impact on families. It has been criticized for methodological weaknesses, including the shortage of longitudinal studies to demonstrate long-term effects or comparative designs examining organiza-tions with and without family-responsive policies, as well as problematic conceptualizations of outcome variables (Raabe, 1990; Gonyea and Googins, 1993). The long-term impact of career breaks on the careers of spouses (usu-ally women) in dual-career partnerships, for example, has yet to be demon-strated. The scarcity of comparative data examining family-responsive and non-responsive organizations may well reflect the reluctance of organizations to participate in research on the basis of what they are *not* doing. Despite these methodological problems, and the inconclusive nature of much of the evidence (Gonyea and Googins, 1993), there are some signs of positive out-comes associated with family-friendly initiatives. These include enhanced recruitment and retention, and associated reductions in costs (Truman, 1986), reduced absenteeism (Ransom *et al.*, 1989), decreased work–family conflict (Neal *et al.*, 1993) and increased worker satisfaction with their schedules, if not with other aspects of the job (Harrick *et al.*, 1986).

More attention is now needed to focus on the way family-friendly initia-tives reflect and influence changes in organizational culture and are experi-enced by employees in dual-career households and their families. We need to be aware that the criteria of effectiveness may differ from various perspec-tives. For example, recent research indicates that the opportunity to work flexibly tends to be used to work longer hours overall (Holt *et al.*, 1992). While this might be viewed positively by the organization and often by the em-ployees themselves, other family members may be happier if their spouse or parent worked rigid, predictable hours, with less permeability of work–family boundaries. The focus on organizational outcomes obscures the poss-ible impact of policies on employees' self-definitions and on gender bound-aries in the family, with their consequences for women's career development. The most well intentioned of family-responsive policies can fail to reduce work–family load if, for example, the recipient retains sole responsibility for family work (Kagan and Lewis, 1993). Although it is beyond the scope of this chapter to discuss the impact of public policies, the impact of policies such as parental leave or care in the community on dual-career couples also needs to be examined in order to inform both theory and practice.

CONCLUSION

Dual-career couples are challenging gender boundaries in family and work, although role tensions and constraints to degendered roles persist and are potentially damaging to women's careers. Organizations are beginning to respond to changes in the family by modifying the traditional model of work and this may, in time, create the conditions for further changes within families. The future research agenda can usefully examine processes of negotiation and decision-making within dual-career families, explore the perspectives of other members of dual-career couples' households and evaluate the outcomes of organizational responses to family needs using broader criteria than those currently employed. It will be particularly useful to chart the processes whereby organizational change impacts on dual-career family roles and relationships and the further impact of these changes in the family on organizational thinking.

REFERENCES

BERK, S. (1985) *The Gender Factory. The Apportionment of Work in American Households,* Plenum, New York.

BERRY-LOUND, D. (1990) *Work and Family. Carer Friendly Employment Practices,* Institute of Personnel Management, London.

BIELBY, W. T. and BIELBY, D. D. (1992) I will follow him: family ties, gender role beliefs and reluctance to relocate for a better job, *American Journal of Sociology,* Vol. 97, pp. 1241–67.

BRANNEN, J. and MOSS, P. (1987) Dual earner households: women's financial contributions after the birth of the first child, in J. Brannen and G. Wilson (eds) *Give and Take in Families: Studies in Resource Distribution,* Unwin Hyman, London.

BRANNEN, J. and MOSS, P. (1991) *Managing Mothers. Dual Earner Households After Maternity Leave,* Unwin Hyman, London.

BRANNEN, J. and MOSS, P. (1992) British households after maternity leave, in S. Lewis, D. Izraeli and H. Hootsmans (eds) *Dual Earner Families. International Perspectives,* Sage, London.

BRETT, J. M., STROH, L. K. and REILLY, A. H. (1992) What is it like being a dual career manager in the 1990s, in S. Zedeck (ed.) *Work, Families and Organizations,* Jossey-Bass, CA.

CHODOROW, N. (1978) *The Reproduction of Mothering,* University of California Press, Berkeley.

COOK, A. (1992) Can work requirements change to accommodate the needs of dual-earner families? in S. Lewis, D. Izraeli and H. Hootsmans (eds) *Dual Earner Families. International Perspectives,* Sage, London.

COOPER, C. L. and LEWIS, S. (1993) *The Workplace Revolution. Managing Today's Dual Career Families,* Kogan Page, London.

CROUTER, A. C., PERRY-JENKINS, M., HUSTON, T. L. and CRAWFORD, D. W. (1989) The influence of work-induced psychological states on behaviour at home, *Basic and Applied Social Psychology,* Vol. 10, pp. 273–92.

DAVIDSON, M. and COOPER, C. L. (1983) *Stress and the Woman Manager,* Martin Robertson, Oxford.

EICHENBAUM, L. and ORBACH, S. (1987) Separation and intimacy, in S. Ernst and M. Maguire (eds) *Living with Sphinx*, Women's Press, London.

ETZION, D. and BAILYN, L. (1992) Patterns of adjustment to the career/family conflict of technically trained women in the US and Israel, Working Paper no. 3507192 BPS, Sloan School of Management, MIT, MA.

FERREE, M. (1990) Beyond separate spheres, *Journal of Marriage and the Family*, Vol. 52, pp. 860–84.

GALINSKY, E. and STEIN, P. J. (1990) The impact of human resource policies on employees: balancing work and family life, *Journal of Family Issues*, Vol. 11, pp. 368–83.

GILBERT, L. A. (1993) *Two Careers/One Family*, Sage, Berkeley, CA.

GILBERT, L. A. and DANCER, L. S. (1992) Dual earner families in the United States and adolescent development, in S. Lewis, D. Izraeli and H. Hootsmans (eds) *Dual Earner Families. International Perspectives*, Sage, London.

GONYEA, J. G. and GOOGINS, B. K. (1993) Linking the worlds of work and family: beyond the productivity trap, *Journal of Human Resource Management*, no. 31, pp. 209–26.

HALL, D. T. (1990) Promoting work/family balance: an organizational change approach, *Organizational Dynamics*, no. 18, pp. 5–18.

HALL, D. T. and RICHTER, J. (1988) Balancing work life and home life: what can organisations do to help? *Academy of Management Review*, Vol. 2, no. 3, pp. 213–23.

HARRICK, E. J., VENECK, G. R. and MICHLITSCH, J. F. (1986) Alternative work schedules, productivity, leave usage, and employee attitudes: a field study, *Public Personal Management*, Vol. 15, pp. 159–69.

HERTZ, R. (1986) *More Equal Than Others. Women and Men in Dual Career Marriages*, University of California Press, Berkeley.

HERTZ, R. (1992a) Financial affairs. Money and authority in dual earner marriage, in S. Lewis, D. Izraeli and H. Hootsmans (eds) *Dual Earner Families. International Perspectives*, Sage, London.

HERTZ, R. (1992b) Financial affairs: money and authority in American dual earner marriages. Paper presented at the international conference on Dual Earner Lifestyles: Culture Policy and Practice, London School of Economics.

HILLER, D. V. and PHILLIBER, W. W. (1982) Predicting marital and career success among dual career couples, *Journal of Marriage and the Family*, Vol. 44, pp. 453–62.

HOCHSCHILD, A. (1989) *Second Shift: Working Parents and the Revolution in the Home*, Viking Penguin, New York.

HOCHSCHILD, A. (1992) Beyond the second shift: denying needs at home or contesting rules at work? Paper presented at the NCFR Annual Conference, Orlando.

HOGG, C. and HARKER, L. (1992) *The Family Friendly Employer: Examples from Europe*, Sage, London.

HOLT, H., THAULOW, I. and MAERKEDAHL, I. (1992) Do working arrangements affect stress and welfare in the family? Paper presented at the National Council on Family Relations Annual Conference, Orlando.

HOUSE, J. S. (1981) *Work Stress and Social Support*, Addison-Wesley, Reading, MA.

IZRAELI, D. N. (1992) Culture, policy and women in Israel, in S. Lewis, D. Izraeli and H. Hootsmans (eds) *Dual Earner Families. International Perspectives*, Sage, London.

JONES, F. and FLETCHER, B. (1992) Transmission of occupational stress: a study of daily fluctuations in work stressors and strains and their impact on marital partners. Paper presented at the 6th European Health Psychology Conference, University of Leipzig, August.

KAGAN, C. and LEWIS, S. (1993) Family, employment and social change in Britain: accounts of women with multiple commitments. Paper presented at the Committee on Family Research seminar on Rapid Social Change and the Family, Palanga, Lithuania, June.

KAPLAN, M. (1983) A woman's view of DSM-111, *American Psychologist*, Vol. 38, pp. 786–92.

LAROSSA, R. and LAROSSA, M. M. (1981) *Transition to parenthood: How Infants Change Families*, Sage, Beverly Hills, CA.

LEWIS, S. (1991) Motherhood and/or employment: the impact of social and organisational values, in A. Phoenix, A. Woollett and E. Lloyd (eds) *Motherhood: Meanings, Practices and Ideologies*, Sage, London.

LEWIS, S. (1992) Dual earner families in context, in S. Lewis, D. Izraeli and H. Hootsmans (eds) *Dual Earner Families. International Perspectives*, Sage, London.

LEWIS, S. and COOPER, C. L. (1987) Stress in dual earner couples and stage in the life cycle, *Journal of Occupational Psychology*, Vol. 60, pp. 289–303.

LEWIS, S. and COOPER, C. L. (1988a) Stress in dual-earner families, in B. A. Gutek, A. H. Stromberg and L. Larwood (eds) *Women and Work. An Annual Review*, Vol. 3, Sage, Newbury Park, CA.

LEWIS, S. and COOPER, C. L. (1988b) The transition to parenthood in two earner couples, *Psychological Medicine*, Vol. 18, pp. 477–86.

MEDERER, H. J. (1993) Division of labor in two-earner homes: task accomplishment versus household management as critical variables in perceptions about family work, *Journal of Marriage and the Family*, Vol. 55, pp. 133–45.

MILLIKEN, F. J., DUTTON, J. E. and BUYER, J. M. (1990) Understanding organisational adaptation to change: the care of work–family issues, *Human Resource Planning*, Vol. 3, pp. 91–107.

NEAL, M. B., CHAPMAN, N. J., INGERSOLL-DAYTON, B. and EMLEN, A. C. (1993) *Balancing Work and Caregiving for Children, Adults and Elders*, Sage, Newbury Park, CA.

PHILLIBER, W. W. and HILLER, D. V. (1983) Changes in marriage and wife's career as a result of the relative occupational attainment on wife's achievement, *Journal of Marriage and the Family*, Vol. 52, pp. 323–9.

PLECK, J. (1977) The work family role system, *Social Problems*, Vol. 24, pp. 417–27.

POTUCHEK, J. L. (1992) Employed wives' orientation to breadwinning: a gender theory analysis, *Journal of Marriage and the Family*, Vol. 55, pp. 133–45.

RAABE, P. H. (1990) The organisational effects of workforce family policies: past weaknesses and recent progress toward improved research, *Journal of Family Issues*, Vol. 11, pp. 477–91.

RANSOM, C., ASCHBACHER, P. and BARUEL, S. (1989) The return in the child-care investment, *Personal Administrator*, pp. 54–8.

RAPOPORT, R. and RAPOPORT, R. N. (1976) *Dual Career Families Re-examined*, Harper & Row, New York.

SANDQVIST, K. (1992) Sweden's sex role scheme and commitment to equality, in S. Lewis, D. Izraeli and H. Hootsmans (eds) *Dual Earner Families. International Perspectives*, Sage, London.

SEKARAN, U. (1986) *Dual-Career Families: Contemporary Organisational and Counselling Issues*, Cambridge University Press.

SILBERSTEIN, L. R. (1992) *Dual Career Marriage: A System in Transition*, Lawrence Erlbaum Associates, Hillsdale, NJ.

SOLBERG, A. (1990) Negotiating childhood: changing constructions of age for Norwegian children, in A. James and A. Prout (eds) *Constructing and Reconstructing Childhood*, Falmer Press, London.

TANNEN, D. (1992) *You Just Don't Understand*, Virago, London.

TRUMAN, C. (1986) *Overcoming the Career Break. A Positive Approach*, Manpower Services Commission, Sheffield.

VANNOY, D. and PHILLIBER, W. W. (1992) Wife's employment and quality of marriage, *Journal of Marriage and the Family*, Vol. 54, pp. 387–98.

WHITE, B., COX, C. and COOPER, C. L. (1992) *Women's Career Development*, Blackwell, Oxford.

ZEDECK, S. (1992) Exploring the domain of work and family concerns, in S. Zedeck (ed.) *Work, Family and Organizations*, Jossey-Bass, San Francisco.

CHAPTER 16

Variations in Career and Family Involvement Over Time: Truth and Consequences

MARY DEAN LEE

INTRODUCTION

The purpose of the study described in this chapter was to increase under-standing of professional women's careers by examining the diversity of women's experiences and involvement in career and family over the lifespan. More specifically, there were three objectives: (1) to assess the accuracy and usefulness of a theoretical framework (Lee, 1993), which suggests six alterna-tive models of involvement in career and family over the lifespan; (2) to gather women's perceptions of the costs and benefits, difficulties and satisfac-tions involved in their own experiences/choices with respect to career and family; and (3) to generate a set of testable hypotheses about the relative merits of the models.

Many writers have called for additional or expanded theory in career de-velopment and adult development to increase understanding of women's career and life patterns (Larwood and Gutek, 1987; Gallos, 1989; Marshall, 1989). The rationale for this need has been based on three consistent findings in the literature. Women continue to take primary responsibility for children, and their careers are therefore more strongly affected by the addition of children (Hochschild, 1989; Gutek et al., 1988; Brett et al., 1992). Secondly, women are having children at very different ages and stages of their lives and careers, from early 20s to early 40s, which results in radically different experi-ences and no single modal career pattern which is consistent with established theories of (male) adult development or career development (Daniels and Weingarten, 1982; Jones et al., 1990). Thirdly, levels of involvement in career and family have different implications for men and women, for which there has been no adequate theoretical explanation (Pleck, 1985; Piotrkowski et al., 1987; Gutek et al., 1988).

Because of this need for further theory development on women's careers and lives, a set of alternative models of combining career and family over the lifespan was conceived in order to: (a) articulate and legitimize the diversity in professional women's involvement in career and family over the lifespan; and (b) provide a typology of different ways of combining career and family which would allow comparisons of costs and benefits to women, families, society, and organizations (Lee, 1993). From a practical point of view, articulation of different ways women actually experience varying degrees of involvement with career and family throughout the lifespan was expected to increase understanding of professional women's career patterns and perhaps provide some insight into how organizations can best offer appropriate support systems to their male and female employees with children. These models were also expected to increase professional women's awareness of the range of options available to them, and to mitigate the pressure to conform to any one particular approach to combining career and family.

The six models were developed based on a review of the literature and were designed to represent the variation in women's career patterns on three dimensions: (1) timing of children; (2) level of involvement in career over time; (3) level of involvement with family over time. The models were meant to capture women's actual experiences, not intentions or values, because it is clear that women's work patterns are determined by many more factors than relative value placed on career and family, for example financial need, marital status, husband's occupation, employment opportunities, etc. Characterization of women's patterns was approached retrospectively and from an external perspective. That is, as an outside observer looking back at any given professional woman's early to late adulthood years (20–60), how would one describe the timing of children and shifting level of involvement with career and family over time?

The focus of this chapter is to describe the results of an interview study which was conducted with a small sample of professional women, in order to flesh out the characteristics of each model, and to generate a set of hypotheses about individual and family outcomes associated with the models. First I will describe the methodology of the study. Then I will briefly describe the revised models and propose a set of hypotheses based on trends found in these women's perceptions of the costs and benefits of their ways of combining career and family – from a personal perspective, as well as from the perspective of the family. Finally, I will conclude with a discussion of theoretical and practical implications of these findings.

METHOD

The sample selection strategy for the study was to provide as much diversity as possible among the women to be interviewed within each category. The plan was to select 6–10 professional women who fit into each of the 6 models, 2 in their 30s, 2 in their 40s and 2 in their 50s or older in order to provide a total lifespan perspective. Within each model, women from a variety of professional occupations were included, from the more traditionally female dominated (like teacher, nurse, social worker) to the more traditionally male dominated (like manager, doctor, lawyer, architect). In addition, an attempt was made to include one or two separated, divorced, or single parents in each category. A snowball sampling procedure was utilized in order to generate a list of approximately 200 potential participants. Then potential participants were selected to satisfy the requirements of diversity within models on age, occupation, and marital status. Forty-five women were interviewed over the course of a year, 1991–92. They were mostly (75%) from two large metropolitan centres in Canada. The others were from cities in the north and southeast USA. The mean age was 42.3 years and one-quarter of the sample were managers, administrators, or executives.

Each woman was interviewed once for 1–3 hours. All interviews were audiotaped, transcribed and then content analysed for common themes within and across models. The interviews were semi-structured and consisted of first asking for a brief life history starting from high school age to the present. All participants were then probed on the following points: (1) career and family aspirations in high school, college, early 20s, 30s, and so on to the present; (2) occupational choices; (3) choice of spouse and the marriage relationship; (4) decision to have children, or circumstances surrounding children's arrival, and the experience of becoming a parent; (5) spouse's occupation; (6) childcare arrangements from birth on; (7) personal involvement with the family; (8) husband's involvement with the family; (9) career pattern. In the last part of the interview, participants were asked to reflect on the difficulties and satisfactions they had experienced in the past and were experiencing in the present, around combining career and family. They were asked to talk about themselves, their own personal disappointments, frustrations, rewards. And then they were asked to talk about their families – their marriages, their children, and the overall quality of life in the family.

DESCRIPTION OF THE MODELS

The six alternative models of combining career and family over the lifespan to be described are proposed to represent the most common ways in which professional women actually behave as they pursue careers as well as families. The models group women according to three behavioural dimensions: (1) timing of children; (2) level of involvement with children and family over time; and (3) level of involvement in career over time. The timing of children was considered early (first child born before age 30) or late (first child born age 30 or later). Level of involvement with children and family and level of involvement in career were categorized as high, moderate, or low at different points in time. In making judgements about the level of involvement with career and family, there was no single indicator, but rather an overall pattern which seemed self-evident from participants' descriptions of their work and family routines, the division of labour in the family, their relationships with their children and husband, their concerns and sources of pleasure in their career and family lives.

Early career orientation sustained

The first model of professional women's involvement in career and family is characterized by a high level of involvement in career sustained across time, and a low level of involvement with family sustained over time. The timing of children is variable, it may be early or late, but does not interfere with the career. Women in this model share the following in common:

(1) Occupation or jobs held require a high level of involvement in career, which includes long hours being routinely spent at work, whether mostly during the day, nights, weekends, and/or as a result of out-of-town travel.
(2) Continuous full-time participation in the workforce throughout the adult lifespan.
(3) Low level of involvement with family, and others (e.g. husband, nanny, housekeeper, etc.) taking primary responsibility for children.
(4) Family involvement is orchestrated around career commitments.
(5) Timing of children may be early or late, but does not interfere with career, since minimal time is taken off from work and others take primary responsibility for children.

The striking personal characteristics shared by the women in this model were: (1) their high level of energy and drive, and (2) their profound and intense passion for their work. They were highly committed to their careers, and their recollections about the most fulfilling or happiest periods in their lives were all related to their work. Their sense of identity was strongly tied to their professional accomplishments. They did not seem highly invested in their role as parent, and they were unambivalent about delegating primary responsibility for childcare to someone else.

Early career orientation modified

This model is very similar to the 'early career orientation sustained' in that there is initially very high involvement in a career. However, women in this model make some adjustments in their careers in order to have somewhat greater involvement with family, at least for a limited period of time. Women in this model share the following in common:

(1) Occupation or jobs held require a high level of involvement in career, which includes long hours being routinely spent at work, whether during the day, nights, weekends, and/or as a result of regular travel out of town.
(2) Continuous participation in the workforce, mostly full time, throughout the adult lifespan.
(3) Children arrive after career is well established, usually after age 30.
(4) A temporary decrease in career involvement at some point after children arrive in order to increase involvement in the family.
(5) Return to high level of involvement in career as children become more independent.

The common thread among these women was their strong commitment to their careers early on, and a continuation of their careers after children were born, but with some changes or adjustments made along the way. In most cases, these women did not anticipate the desire or need to shift their orientation from being heavily focused on career. It became clear to them at some point after a child, or children, arrived, that they wanted, or felt the children needed, their greater involvement in the parental role than was possible if the pre-parenthood work regime continued unaltered. None of these women wanted full responsibility for child raising, and they all relied on other individuals or institutions to play a major role. But they wanted *some* significant involvement in bringing up their children. They were not interested in delegating the responsibility to the same extent as women in the 'early career orientation sustained' model. Their sense of identity was strongly tied to their professional accomplishments, but they were also invested in their parental role to some extent. These women might be best distinguished from those in the 'early career orientation sustained' model by their different posture toward family life. Once children arrived, these women were more attentive and responsive to the ebb and flow of needs within the family, rather than attempting to protect their careers from interferences from the family sphere.

Modification of an early career orientation, in order to accommodate greater participation in the family, was manifested in a number of different kinds of changes in work behaviour, from very minor to more significant. Minor adjustments included such things as rearranging, not cutting back, work hours in order to spend more time with children. For example, a doctor temporarily arranged her schedule to be home at 4.00 p.m. several days a week for about 6 months, in order to get her children into productive after-school routine. Another example was an architect who reduced business travel and also systematically began avoiding special taskforces and committees which usually met in the evenings. One woman negotiated days off without pay for her child's school holidays and sick days. Slightly more significant changes made by some of these women included choosing to change jobs, or remain in jobs, which were less demanding, and didn't require long hours or working nights and weekends, thereby giving more time with children. More radical modifications involved negotiating limited periods of unpaid leave and/or reduced workloads (e.g. 3-day or 4-day weeks), in order to spend more time with children.

Early career and family orientation

This model differs radically from the previous ones in that career and family are both launched early, in the 20s, and a pattern of mutual accommodation of career to family and family to career is established from the start. Women in this model share the following in common:

(1) Moderate level of involvement in career in 20s and 30s, increasing to high as children become more independent.
(2) Continuous participation in the workforce, mostly full time, throughout the adult lifespan.
(3) Early marriage and parenthood.
(4) Moderate level of involvement with family in 20s and 30s, decreasing to low as children become more independent.

All of the women interviewed in this category were strongly committed to their careers. However, they did not conceive of their careers as coming first, either in a temporal dimension or in terms of priorities. And in fact, in several cases, these women's careers took shape gradually as events unfolded. The idea was not to establish the career first, and then once it was stable, to add children. Rather, the idea was to get the career started *and* the family started more or less simultaneously. The assumption was that of course there would have to be compromises made in order to launch a career and family at the same time. None of the women in this model had ever conceived of having only a career, or only a family, and none was able to imagine giving one up for the other. Their sense of identity was strongly tied to both their profession and their role in the family.

Sequencing: career–family–career

This model of combining career and family over the lifespan is quite different from the previous ones described, because instead of involving trying to combine career and family at the same time, it involves combining the two sequentially, where the focus is on career first, followed by a period of focus on the family, followed by a return to a focus on career. Women in this model of combining career and family over the lifespan share the following patterns in common:

(1) High involvement in career in their 20s until some point after children arrive.
(2) In occupations or jobs generally requiring above-average work hours per week.
(3) Interrupted participation in the workforce for at least 1 year, up to 10 or more, in order to focus on family.
(4) High involvement with family during career break.
(5) Moderate level of involvement in career and family when participation in workforce is resumed, until children are independent, after which involvement in family decreases to low and involvement in career increases to high.

The women interviewed in this model were strongly invested in both their professional and parental roles. But when they took a break from their careers, they did not work part time or earn money during this period. Yet all of them intended to or had returned to full-time work after their career break. Their careers were well established before being interrupted, and several had achieved a very high level of success. Those who had not yet returned to their careers had concrete realistic plans to return. Some planned to start part time and build up gradually to full time; others planned to start back full time all at once. All had planned or experienced a change in career direction when they returned to work – in order to be able to continue some significant involvement with children.

Sequencing: family–career

This sequencing model involves high involvement in family first, with a shift later to high involvement in career. Women in this model share the following patterns in common:

(1) Early marriage and parenthood and high involvement in family in their 20s.

(2) No participation, or sporadic and part-time participation in workforce during primary child-rearing years.
(3) Entry or re-entry into workforce to launch career in 30s or early 40s after children are more independent.
(4) Continuous workforce participation and high involvement in career after children are grown.

There were two different ways that women in this model launched their careers. One involved going back to education after children were in school, either to finish degrees and fulfil original career goals, or to pursue a different career through going to graduate school. The other path emerged more out of discontent with the role of being a full-time homemaker. Women who went down this path were either miserable at home as full-time mothers, or content for only 2 or 3 years before wanting to get out and work or do something. Their careers emerged gradually over time as they each found a niche, by pursuing what interested them and by circumstances unfolding in a timely way. For example, one woman, who was a nurse by training, applied for a job in a pain research project, which eventually led to her doing data analysis and other research work and pursuing a master's degree in statistics.

Early family orientation sustained

This pattern involves clear priority being given to family throughout the lifespan, even though there is commitment to a profession. Women in this model share the following in common:

(1) Choice of occupation tends to be in female-dominated fields like nursing and teaching.
(2) Moderate to high involvement in career until children are born, decreasing to low or moderate involvement thereafter.
(3) Pattern of participation in the labour force is sporadic and orchestrated around family life.
(4) Early marriage and parenthood (in 20s) and high involvement with family throughout the lifespan.

The women interviewed in this model had achieved highly variable degrees of success in their careers. Some had not worked at all after their children had been born; others had worked off and on throughout their lives, whenever it could be arranged around the family schedule. Some of the unusual accomplishments of the women in this category included: (1) founding and directing a preschool; (2) performing or exhibiting publicly in the arts; (3) publishing books, articles, poetry; (4) serving as chair of a board of directors of a hospital; (5) receiving a fellowship to do a Ph.D. at a prestigious university.

These women's high level of involvement with family was manifested in different ways. Some felt strongly about always being home for children at lunchtime and after school. Others worked part time and arranged for baby-sitters to cover some of the time they were working. They were all consistent, however, in believing that their putting family first was essential to their children's optimal growth and development, to family harmony, and to their own peace of mind.

FINDINGS

Since this was a small interview study, the findings concerning individual and family outcomes of various ways of combining career and family are presented below in the form of 13 hypotheses. These hypotheses were formulated on the basis of trends observed across the six models.

Individual level outcomes

HYPOTHESIS 1   The higher the level of career involvement sustained over time, the greater will be ultimate career success.

If career success is defined objectively as level of job attainment, it was clear that the women in the two 'early career orientation' models had achieved greater career success than those in other models. However, there were one or two women in three other models, who had achieved very high levels of career success, levels equivalent to those in the 'early career orientation' patterns. This suggests that career success can be achieved through many different patterns of combining career and family.

HYPOTHESIS 2   The greater the match between women's personal preferences and actual experience in level of involvement in career and family over time, the greater will be their career satisfaction.

Career satisfaction, which is usually significantly correlated with career success, is nevertheless quite a different outcome, because it involves a subjective assessment, which means one's achievements are evaluated on the basis of one's own goals and expectations. Career satisfaction was generally high among the women in all patterns except one, 'early career orientation modified', where most were very satisfied, but one-third were very dissatisfied. This dissatisfaction had to do with their being unhappy with the extent of the adaptations they had made in their careers for the sake of the family. Yet they couldn't see any viable alternative, given their husbands' occupations and the career stage they were in when children arrived.

HYPOTHESIS 3   Among those making adjustments in their career involvement in order to increase their level of involvement in the family, those who make structural adaptations will be more satisfied with their careers than those who make contingent adaptations.

Structural adapations include reducing the amount of work one is doing (to three-quarters or half load, for example) or changing jobs to reduce the level of work demands or to increase one's flexibility to respond to family issues. Contingent adaptations involve: (1) rearranging the time schedule or location of work; (2) negotiating a reduced load or flexible hours when needed; (3) extending work time lines and due dates; or (4) arranging for greater assistance from others on projects when needed. Structural adaptations usually involve a single decision point in time which results in substantial change. Contingent adaptations must be continuously negotiated and/or arranged. They therefore require more ongoing monitoring and vigilance to keep things in balance. These contingent modifications also involve repeatedly experiencing the trade-offs between career and family, and making the painful choice of giving less to the career than ideally desired, instead of a one-time structural change in workload. On the other hand, the cost of the more structural adaptation is that it is more visible and often viewed as a choice to be on a 'mommy track', which can restrict opportunities for career advancement in the future.

HYPOTHESIS 4   The greater the match between women's personal preferences and actual experience in level of involvement in career and family over time, the greater their overall psychological well-being.

Women across all six models had experienced or were experiencing significant stress and strain related to juggling career and family. There were also women across all models reporting a high level of happiness and personal fulfillment. Using Barnett and Rivers' (1983) conception of the psychologically healthy woman as one who is able to achieve both a sense of mastery and a high level of intimacy in her life, it was self-evident that all six models are potentially highly compatible with psychological well-being. By definition, all women in the study were in professional careers and were mothers. The key to psychological well-being then becomes finding the desired levels of involvement in career and family at any given point in time, and being able to alter those levels as needed.

HYPOTHESIS 5   Those who are most clear and consistent over time about their desired levels of involvement in career and family will experience the least internal conflict and emotional turmoil about choices.

Those expressing the least internal conflict and turmoil about their choices and priorities were those in the 'early career orientation sustained', 'early career and family orientation', and 'early family orientation sustained' models. They were extremely clear and unambivalent about their lives, even though they acknowledged the trade-offs they had made.

HYPOTHESIS 6   Those whose life patterns go through dramatic shifts in levels of involvement in career and family, for example by adding children to a well-established life oriented around career, or adding a career to a well-established life oriented around family, are more likely to experience greater internal conflict and emotional turmoil around those transition times.

For those in the sequencing patterns the internal conflict about choices and priorities was associated with the periods of time when these women were unhappy with their relative involvement in career and family, but were unable or not ready to make the desired shift toward high involvement in either career or family.

HYPOTHESIS 7   The higher the sum total of women's level of involvement in career and family at any given point in time, the greater the daily emotional stress and strain and the more likely they are to experience psychological or physical health problems.

Women in two models reported the most daily stress and strain in their lives: 'early career orientation modified' and 'early career and family orientation'. These are the women trying to maintain the highest levels of involvement in both career and family simultaneously. They complained the most of fatigue, emotional strain, and health problems they associated with trying to spend the time they wanted with the family while not sacrificing their career. Women in these patterns were also the only ones who consistently complained of having no time for themselves. In addition, consistent with others' findings, the greatest stress across all models was reported during periods when children were under 5, except for women in the 'early career orientation sustained' model. Women in this model did not describe stress and strain experienced when children were young, and in fact they described less psychological strain than those in any other model.

HYPOTHESIS 8   The higher the level of family involvement sustained over time, the higher the parental role satisfaction.

Parental role satisfaction was not as important to some women as to others in the study, but women across all models discussed their feelings about themselves as parents, or in the role of parent. In general, the more involved with family, the more fulfilled they were in their parental role, and the more involved with their career, the less fulfilled they were in their parental role. This meant that those in the two 'early career orientation' patterns expressed the least satisfaction or sense of fulfilment in their parental role, and those in the 'early family orientation sustained', 'early career and family orientation' and 'sequencing: career–family–career' patterns expressed the most satisfaction and fulfilment in their parental roles.

Family outcomes

HYPOTHESIS 9   The higher the sum total of a professional woman's level of career involvement and her partner's level of career involvement, the greater the strain on the marriage relationship.

The marital relationship could only be assessed from the women's perspective in this study. From these women's perspectives, there were very happy and very unhappy marriages in all six models, although there were more unhappy (first) marriages in the 'sequencing: family–career' model than in any other. Women in two other models also described significant marital problems: 'early career orientation modified' and 'early career and family orientation'. There were issues of career competition between these women and their spouses. They described dilemmas of opportunities for promotion which required relocation and uprooting of themselves or their partners and subsequent career sacrifices. They also described conflicts over division of labour in the home, between themselves and their husbands. Finally, they mentioned having no time to spend with their partners after devoting the necessary time to career and children.

HYPOTHESIS 10   In marriages where there are dramatic shifts in role expectations between husband and wife, as a result of (a) children being added to an established relationship where both partners' lives had been previously oriented mostly around career, or (b) career being added to an established traditional relationship between husband and wife, marital conflict is higher and there is a higher risk of marital dissolution.

Women in the 'early career orientation modified' pattern often added children to an established relationship in which both partners' lives had been previously oriented around their careers. The radical change in life-style required a great deal of mutual accommodation and successful conflict resolution around taking on new roles. Likewise, when women in the 'sequencing: family–career' pattern added a career to a traditional marriage, in which the man was the breadwinner and the woman took care of the home and family, the marriage relationship was put through a severe test. All of the women interviewed in this model eventually were divorced from their first husbands.

HYPOTHESIS 11 The happiest marriages are those in which: (a) women's ways of combining career and family are consistent with a traditional gender ideology, where women take greater responsibility for the home and family and the men focus their energies more on their careers; or (b) an egalitarian ideology is shared and implemented early in the marriage.

Those in the 'early family orientation sustained' or the 'sequencing: career–family–career' patterns were enacting the more tradional gender ideology of the husband being the primary breadwinner and career-oriented partner, and the woman being the primary person in charge of the children and home. These women reported the most marital satisfaction. The most egalitarian marriages appeared to be in the 'early career and family orientation' and the 'early career orientation modified' patterns. In the 'early career and family' pattern, the norm was for both partners to make accommodations in their careers in order to maintain the necessary level of parental involvement in the family, or to enable a spouse to main-tain the necessary involvement in career. The husbands in this pattern were more likely than those in any other to have spent or to be currently spend-ing significant time (other than nights, weekends and holidays) with chil-dren as the sole caretaker. Their wives described their partners' involvement with children not as necessarily equal to their own, but as of the same magnitude. A few of the husbands of the women in the 'early career orientation modified' were also described as sharing substantially in the family work. Division of labour in the home was typically not split along traditional gender lines. However, the husbands were not described as having made accommodations in their own career involvement in order to spend more time with the family, and they were unlikely to have ever been in the sole caretaker role for any significant blocks of time. Nevertheless, they did such non-traditional things as care for children at nights and week-ends when their wives were away on business, handle the family food shopping and cooking, go clothes shopping with or for children, make arrangements for babysitters and visits of children to friends' houses, etc.

HYPOTHESIS 12 The higher the level of involvement in family over time, the closer the relationship between parent and child.

A closer attachment or relationship between mother and child was described by women more involved in family and less involved in career. They cared passionately about this relationship, not just during the period when children were young, but also for the future when they would be grown up and gone. These women wanted their children to think of home as a haven, a place they could always return to for support, for renewal. They wanted a relationship of mutual love, respect, and trust. They wanted to know their children well. Those most highly involved in their careers, in the two 'early career orientation' patterns, were most likely to describe a distant or troubled relationship with their children, or at least some concern about that relationship.

HYPOTHESIS 13   The higher the level of involvement in career over time, the greater the concern about children's well-being.

Women in all six models described children who seemed to be thriving and doing very well. At least one woman in all six models also described a child or children having trouble – in school, in relationships, in emotional adjustment, in establishing an independent life as an adult. From the information gained in these interviews, no conclusions or predictions can be drawn directly about children's well-being and these six models of combining career and family.

In general, women more involved in their careers believed that their children benefited from their high career involvement, because they felt they were better mothers at home, due to their having their own independent pursuits and an arena for accomplishment separate from the family. And women who were more involved in family believed that they were better mothers because of their relationships with their children, and because they could invest the necessary time and energy into their children's long-term development as human beings, for example teaching values and how to resolve conflicts with siblings, how to make friends, manners, etc. Only a study which focuses specifically on children's well-being and provides information on both parents' career and family involvement, as well as many other factors, can examine this outcome adequately.

However, looking only at expression of concern about children's well-being, there were three patterns in which women were most likely to be worried about their children. These were the two 'early career orientation' patterns and the 'sequencing: family–career' pattern. Women highly involved in their careers relied heavily on institutional or parental surrogates for care of their children, for example daycare, after-school care, and babysitters, live-in nannies, etc. In cases where there were highly stable and long-term arrangements which were judged to be very high quality, these women were not so concerned. However, with most women, there were periods in their lives in which less than optimal arrangements had been made for childcare under difficult circumstances, and these women were worried about negative effects on the children. In the case of the 'sequencing: family–career' women, they were more concerned about the effects of the marital conflict and break-up on their children, rather than their own level of involvement with children when they were young.

CONCLUSION

Theoretical implications

The question of what determines women developing one pattern instead of another is not the main subject of this chapter. However, a few observations were made which may be valuable to further theory development on women's career patterns.

One individual difference factor which seemed key in women's development of these different patterns was how two basic drives in adult development are dealt with over time. One involves the need to strike out on one's own, assert independence, and strive toward individual achievement or accomplishment. The other involves the need for attachments and a sense of belonging, for interdependence, and for relationships and intimacy. In the past, many viewed developmental maturity for men as meaning increased autonomy and separation from others in the process of finding oneself and launching a career. For women, developmental maturity meant accepting and embracing interdependence and the importance of relationships and achieving intimacy. More recently, it has been proposed that developmental maturity for men *and* women means coming to terms with both of these issues, attachment and separation, but at different points in time. For example, perhaps women start out in early adulthood with the assumption of the importance of relationships, and then later, after their children are grown, explore ways of achieving individuality and productivity. Perhaps men start out exploring and establishing autonomy, seeking accomplishment at work and then later, after mid-life, accept and embrace interdependence and the importance of relationships with others.

However, for professional women, it seems that the ebb and flow of these two forces within, does not follow any predictable pattern. For some women, the drive or inclination toward finding a partner or close relationship comes early and strong and overshadows the drive or inclination to launch an ambitious career. For others the drive to achieve and become independently productive is strong early in adulthood and overshadows the inclination to form a close bond and start a family. For still others, perhaps both drives are quite strong early on. The need for independence and individual striving for recognition and achievement, versus the need to be connected to others and attain intimacy, also probably shifts throughout the life-span in idiosyncratic ways, which shape career and family involvement.

Another underlying dynamic observed in women across all categories was women's need to cope with the inevitable uncertainty in daily life which comes with having children and an expanded circle of interdependent relationships. The greater the expansion, the greater the uncertainty. For example, children get sick and can't attend daycare or school. Children get unexpected invitations to parties occurring the next day, and gifts must be bought on an evening both parents are working late. Babysitters quit without notice, or get sick. Children develop problems in school or in their social circle. Women's emergent patterns of shifting levels of involvement in career and family can be interpreted as simply an overall strategy for dealing with this inevitable uncertainty inherent in being a parent. The different models represent different adaptations given the resources and constraints at work and at home for dealing with these uncertainties. The more resources available in the family, whether husbands, older siblings, in-laws, or hired help, to deal with these uncertainties, the more women are able to maintain the level of career involvement they wish without family needs going unrecognized or unmet. For women who have husbands in certain occupations, or with certain orientations toward the parental role which preclude their being part of the buffering mechanism to cope with this uncertainty, they must find other ways, for example hiring a live-in nanny or full-time housekeeper, even once the children are in school. But such arrangements are never perfect. For part of being a parent means being in this interdependent relationship in which one is inevitably pushed and pulled in ways which may affect the work sphere.

Another factor operating in the emergence of different patterns of combining career and family life was the salience or 'centrality' of the parental role to individual women. It was apparent that among the women interviewed, the importance attached to the role of being a parent varied greatly. Some women said that they had never been very interested in becoming a mother, were not enthralled with being one, and didn't think they were particularly good at it. Others felt it was very important to them to be a mother, to have children, but that it would never be enough. They had to have something else in their lives outside of the family. Still others felt quite content with their primary role in life being mother and wife, even though they pursued professions to a certain extent as well. For some of these women the role of parent was critical to their sense of identity or self-esteem, and for others it was not. For others, being a parent was an important, but not sufficient source of identity, mastery, self-esteem. Men probably also differ in the importance attached to the parental role, which is likely to influence their degree of involvement in career and family. Furthermore, the centrality or salience of the parental role for a professional woman's partner is likely to have an effect on the woman's emergent pattern of combining career and family. For example, a woman married to a man for whom the parental role is highly salient is likely to have a partner more willing to be highly involved in family or willing to make career accommodations for the family, which gives her more options and requires less reliance on hired help or institutions for childcare.

In addition to suggesting the above factors as likely to influence women's emergent patterns of combining career and family over time, the findings also suggest that there are many factors which may make some models work well for some and not others. Certainly, whether there is another parent and that parent's level of involvement in career and family is one factor already alluded to. Another one is the quality and stability of surrogate care found for children in cases where both parents maintain a moderate to high level of career involvement. This supports findings of other researchers in the field (Gottfried and Gottfried, 1988).

Number of children and the overall physical and psychological health of children are also likely to be important factors in the consequences of the different models. The fact that half of the women in the most career-oriented patterns had only one child is probably not coincidental. And in fact, several women had only one child as an explicit aspect of their strategy for coping with career and family commitments. One child who occasionally gets sick, needs you to attend functions at school during the day, needs arrangements to be made for school holidays, etc., is one thing. When it's two children, it becomes complicated and more challenging. When children have serious or chronic health problems, a high level of career involvement is quite difficult unless the husband is highly involved with the family work.

Practical implications

At an individual level there are some interesting and practical implications of this study. As there were some very positive outcomes in terms of career success, career satisfaction, psychological well-being, and parental role satisfaction across multiple models, one can draw the conclusion that women should continue to implement a wide variety of ways of combining career and family over the lifespan, as they respond to shifting circumstances and varying levels of partner involvement in the family. Certainly the findings support the general principle that individuals have to find an approach that suits their peculiar situation, their occupation and spouse's occupation, their investment and their partner's investment in being a good parent, their professionals goals and their spouse's professional goals, their personalities, their children, their community, etc. Consequently, the findings suggest that organizations, communities, and governments should not move in the direction of trying to provide single solutions, or promoting only one or two programmes to support men and women's ability to sustain an involvement in their careers, while also being responsive to family needs. A great diversity of programmes and policies is needed, and the most important component would seem to be flexibility, in keeping with the ebb and flow of family needs and parental resources over time.

A second practical implication of the findings, however, is how do we get more men more involved in the family and taking more proactive responsibility for children. It is evident that professional women are highly creative, flexible, energetic, and tenacious in their various strategies of combining career and family. The women interviewed appeared to take charge of the whole issue of how children should be cared for, almost unilaterally, across models. They are thus the ones making most of the accommodations, pressing for and taking advantage of work and family programmes in the workplace, and living with the consequences of making most of the career trade-offs. The findings from this study suggest a possible direction for increasing level of involvement of fathers in the family.

It has been pointed out earlier that the husbands of the women in the 'early career and family orientation' model were different from those in all other models. They spent significant time caring for their children when their wives were working. Half of them worked an atypical work schedule when their children were young, so they were primary caretakers for a big chunk of every day. These men made career accommodations on account of the family. They were more involved in the daily management of family life. This suggests that a critical variable in women's career and family patterns might be to what extent and how early and profoundly their partners experience the raw and physically powerful reality of having their lives changed by the addition of a baby. Most women, unless they adopt, experience this reality by going through 9 months of pregnancy and often at least 3 months of breast-feeding. Forever after, their lives are not the same, regardless of how they handle their careers. Perhaps the raw physicality of becoming a parent for women creates a powerful kind of link, a sense of interdependence, which results in women being more likely to become proactive about making adjustments in their careers, or whatever it takes to make sure that children are thriving. Perhaps more fathers would develop a similar kind of link and subsequent posture toward the family if they had early substantial experience with being the sole physical caretaker of babies. When two partners, rather than one, are tuned into and responsive to children and what is needed in the family, the burden is lighter on women and they then have more options in their careers. It is not necessary that men and women become equal in their level of involvement in the family. But they should become less unequal, so that it cannot be automatically assumed in the workplace that it is the woman rather than the man who needs a family leave, wants flexitime, or is likely to slip into a 'parent track' for a few years as a means of dealing with the uncertainties involved in being a parent.

A final practical implication of the findings is that there is clearly a need for investigation of children's well-being in relation to parental involvement in career and family. The behaviours and attitudes of both parents, where applicable, must be examined. Women in this study were concerned about this issue from the point of view of their own choices. But the broader question is: What is the critical level of parental involvement with children in order that they develop well, thrive even, and grow up to be responsible, productive citizens and parents to the next generation? This has been a politically unpopular, or sensitive, question because in the past when something has gone wrong with children, mothers have taken the blame. But it is time to defy concerns about political correctness and ask the question: what exactly do children need from parents? The old 'quality time' answer is not good enough. Children in our society are in trouble. We know that parents are spending on average 10 hours less per week with children than they were 15 years ago (Hochschild, 1989). The women in this study who were most confident about their children's ultimate well-being were those in families where either one parent maintained high involvement with the family throughout the children's growing-up years, or both parents maintained at least a moderate level of involvement with the family, regardless of what was happening with the career. Daycare, babysitters, nannies, after-school care, were all considered necessary supports to enable women and men to have careers and families, but they were not viewed as adequate substitutes for parental involvement. But what is the necessary level of parental involvement from the point of view of the well-being of children? Some felt it meant parents spending more than nights, weekends and holidays with children. Others believed spending 'non-work' time was sufficient if it was spent in the right sort of way, or if there was a high-quality, long-term surrogate caregiver in the picture. More research needs to be done on this issue. There is an urgent need to assess just what the critical level of parental involvement is for the general well-being and optimal development of children. Career success for individual women, or men, is a nice aim, but is ultimately a personal or private matter. The health and well-being of children and families is critical to the future of our society.

REFERENCES

BARNETT, R. C. and RIVERS, C. (1983) *Life Prints: New Patterns of Love and Work for Today's Women*, New American Library, New York.

BRETT, J. M., STROH, L. K. and REILLY, A. H. (1992) What is it like being in a dual-career marriage in the 1980's? in S. Zedeck (ed.) *Work, Families, and Organizations*, Jossey-Bass, San Francisco.

DANIELS, P. and WEINGARTEN, K. (1982) *Sooner or Later: The Timing of Parenthood in Adult Development*, Norton, New York.

GALLOS, J. V. (1989) Exploring women's development, in M. B. Arthur, D. T. Hall and B. S. Laurence (eds) *Handbook of Career Theory*, Cambridge University Press, New York.

GOTTFRIED, A. E. and GOTTFRIED, A. W. (1988) *Maternal Employment and Children's Development*, Plenum, New York.

GUTEK, B. A., REPETTI, R. L. and SILVER, D. L. (1988) Nonwork roles and stress at work, in C. L. Cooper and R. Payne (eds) *Causes, Coping and Consequences of Stress at Work*, John Wiley, London.

HOCHSCHILD, A. (1989) *The Second Shift*, Avon, New York.

JONES, C., MARSDEN, L. and TEPPERMAN, L. (1990) *Lives of Their Own: The Individualization of Women's Lives*, Oxford University Press, Toronto.

LARWOOD, L. and GUTEK, B. A. (1987) Working toward a theory of women's career development, in B. A. Gutek and L. Larwood (eds) *Women's Career Development*, Plenum Press, New York.

LEE, M. D. (1993) Women's involvement in professional careers and family life: theme and variations, *Business and the Contemporary World*, Vol. 5, no. 3, pp. 106–27.

MARSHALL, J. (1989) Revisioning career concepts: a feminist invitation, in M. B. Arthur, D. T. Hall and B. S. Laurence (eds) *Handbook of Career Theory*, Cambridge University Press, New York.

PIOTRKOWSKI, C. S., RAPOPORT, R. N. and RAPOPORT, R. (1987) Families and work, in M. B. Sussman and S. K. Steinmetz (eds) *Handbook of Marriage and the Family*, Plenum, New York.

PLECK, J. H. (1985) *Working Wives/Working Husbands*, Sage, Beverly Hills, CA.

PART FIVE

Equal Opportunity and Affirmative Action Programmes

CHAPTER 17

Organizational Initiatives in the USA for Advancing Managerial Women

MARY C. MATTIS

INTRODUCTION

Minorities and women have made meaningful gains in entering the work-force. But there is also significant evidence from research conducted by universities, non-profit organizations, executive recruiters, and the US Department of Labor that documents a dearth of minorities and women at management levels – the so-called 'glass ceiling'.

In 1991, when Catalyst surveyed the *Fortune* 500/*Service* 500 companies, over one-third reported that women constituted from one-half to three-quarters of their non-exempt employees. Another quarter of responding companies reported that over 75% of their non-exempt employees were women.

Women's representation in entry- and middle-management positions has also increased substantially. In the same survey, 42% of companies reported that women constitute fully a quarter to a half of their professional employees; a smaller but notable percentage of companies (25%) reported that from one-quarter to one-half of their managers were women (Catalyst, 1990a).

But while women are beginning to enter the management pipeline in greater numbers, their representation in senior positions has increased little over the 25 years since women began to enter management in US companies. Most studies show that, today, fewer than 5% of senior managers in US companies are women: Korn/Ferry International and UCLA Anderson Graduate School of Management (1990) found that between the years 1979 and 1989 there was only a slight increase in the representation of minorities and women in the top executive positions of the 1,000 largest US corporations. Minorities and women held fewer than 5% of top managerial positions in 1989, up from fewer than 3% in 1979. The US Department of Labor (1991) analysed data from a random sample of 94 reviews of corporate headquarters of *Fortune* 500/*Service* 500 companies between 1989 and 1991. Those data indicated that of 147,179 employees of those 94 companies, women represented 37% of employees and 16.9% of all levels of management, but only 6% of executive-level leadership. Research indicates that women are moving into senior management in some industries more rapidly than they are in others. Currently, the largest percentage of management women (including senior management) is found in the financial services industry (Catalyst, 1990a; US Department of Labor, 1991).

Even within financial services, however, women's representation in senior management varies by subsectors: more women are found in senior management in insurance companies than in banking (Catalyst, 1990a).

Research also shows that women are still concentrated in traditionally 'female' functional areas of companies – staff positions such as human resources, corporate communications, community and governmental relations and on the staff side of marketing and finance (Catalyst, 1990b; US Department of Labor, 1991).

During 1991–93, Catalyst conducted individual assessments of the environment for women and career development opportunities in more than a dozen major US corporations and professional firms. The research, carried out at the request of these organizations, shows that women are becoming discouraged by the barriers found in corporate cultures and environments that continue to block their advancement.

This finding is consistent with that of other studies. For example, a *Business Week* (1992) survey of 400 female managers in US corporations found that almost half of the respondents believe that large companies have done 'somewhat better' over the last 5 years in hiring and promoting female executives, but more than half reported that they believe the rate of progress has slowed down. Seventy per cent of respondents to the same survey also reported that the male-dominated corporate culture was an obstacle to their success, up from 60% of women responding to a similar *Business Week* survey in 1990.

Within corporations, there is also growing awareness and concern about the turnover of valued female talent, especially in service organizations and professional firms where the largest concentrations of female professionals and managers are found.

Employers are beginning to recognize the high cost of turnover of seasoned employees, reported in one recent study (Families and Work Institute, 1993) to average 150% of the annual salary of a manager or professional and 75% of the annual salary of a lower-level employee; another study reported the cost of turnover to be 193% of an annual salary (Galinsky, 1993). Companies are interested in knowing how they can retain valued female employees in order to leverage the investment they have made in their recruitment and training and reduce the high turnover costs they are experiencing. They want to know what they can do about the so-called 'glass ceiling'.

THE ROLE OF AFFIRMATIVE ACTION LEGISLATION

In the USA the focus of affirmative action legislation and enforcement agencies has primarily been on the recruitment of women and minorities. There is no question that Affirmative Action/Equal Employment Opportunity (AA/EEO) has provided, and will continue to provide, greater access to employment opportunities for women and minorities. Beyond Federal legislation, specific industries in the USA are also subject to review by regulatory agencies in the communities in which they operate: for example, the banking industry's employment of women and minorities has, in part, been motivated by the enactment of the Community Reinvestment Act and the representation of women and minorities in public utilities is reviewed by state and municipal commissions that approve rate increases and review bids for contracts.

While such legislative and regulatory efforts have been relatively effective in gaining access to employment for women and minorities, they have not been that successful in advancing women and minorities to positions of significant leadership in business organizations. In reality, a corporation can be in compliance with Federal, State and local guidelines while promoting a very small number of women to senior management positions. The US Bureau of Labor Statistics reporting categories make it all but impossible to monitor the progress of women in management. For example, the reporting category 'Officials and Administrative Management' groups such diverse management tiers as administrative assistant and chief executive officer.

Whether or not it is theoretically possible to mandate and monitor equal advancement of women and minorities to the extent that it has been possible to mandate equal access, the reality is that there has not been the political will to do so in the USA.

To date, policies and programmes to enhance the retention, development and advancement of women largely result from the voluntary initiatives of employing organizations. For corporations and professional firms, the organizations that Catalyst has studied most extensively, this requires a paradigm shift. It requires moving from mandated approaches, motivated by a need to be in compliance with regulatory agencies, to approaches that involve building the business case for diversity, motivated by demographics and by corporate-driven business strategies and bottom-line concerns.

BUSINESS MOTIVATIONS FOR VOLUNTARY EFFORTS BY CORPORATIONS TO ELIMINATE THE GLASS CEILING

The question that follows is, why should business organizations be so motivated? The answer is because, increasingly, US corporations' very survival depends on their ability to attract the most talented human resources. Women currently represent 45% of the workforce. In the future, women will constitute an even larger percentage of the net pool of new entrants to the workforce.

Currently, women represent the most highly educated segment of that labour pool. Unprecedented numbers of women in the USA have prepared themselves for careers in business. Today over half of the bachelor's and master's degrees awarded go to women. In 1990 women were awarded close to half of the undergraduate degrees in business and management, in accounting and in mathematics (US Department of Education, 1993 unpublished statistic).

Furthermore, more women than ever before are committed to careers rather than the intermittent workforce participation of an earlier generation of women. This is evidenced by the following facts: (1) women are working later into pregnancy (O'Connell, 1990); (2) women are returning to work faster after childbirth (O'Connell, 1990); (3) 75% of new mothers have returned to the labour force by the time their children are 2 years old (Rand Corporation, 1991); (4) statistics show that the labour force participation of women with preschool children has more than quadrupled from 1950 to 1990 in the USA (Bureau of Labor Statistics, 1991 unpublished statistic).

Increasingly, employers will be motivated to retain and promote women, not because it is the right thing to do, but because it is the only thing they can do to remain competitive. Already, many corporate executives recognize that to ignore the retention and advancement of women threatens their very survival. In the short run they will experience unacceptable rates of turnover of valued female contributors; in the long run, they will lose their ability to compete in a job market where women constitute the largest percentage of the best and brightest human capital.

Catalyst's research (1990a) shows that companies are highly motivated to increase the representation of women in positions of leadership. And they are motivated by business needs, rather than EEO requirements or social responsibility: 78% of *Fortune* 500/*Service* 500 CEOs cited 'the increased presence of talented women' as a motivation to increase women's representation and 62% cited the 'need to use the most talented human resources'. Findings from this survey also show that corporate leaders are aware of the glass ceiling: 79% of responding CEOs agreed that there are identifiable barriers to women's advancement in US corporations; more importantly, CEOs overwhelmingly agree that 'it is the company's responsibility to change to help meet the needs of management women'.

In order to improve the chances of successfully promoting female professionals and managers, business organizations need to understand the 'glass ceiling' as a series of events in the careers of female managers and professionals rather than a fixed point beyond which advancement is impossible. Even women may fail to recognize the glass ceiling for what it is – a cumulative outcome of attitudinal, cultural and organizational biases that are at work in corporations.

In turn, organizations need to identify, in a deliberate and systematic fashion, the specific barriers and biases in their culture and work environment and develop systematic approaches to eliminating them. These barriers include:

- stereotyping and preconceptions about women's abilities and suitability for leadership positions in business;
- lack of careful planning and planned job assignments;
- exclusion from informal networks of communication;
- managers' aversion to placing women in positions of line responsibility, that is positions that generate revenue;
- absence of effective management training, and failure to hold managers accountable for developing and advancing female employees;
- absence of succession planning, or succession planning processes that fail to look beyond the top 100–200 managers to identify and monitor the progress of high-potential women and minorities;
- inadequate appraisal and compensation systems, leading to inequities in salaries, bonuses, incentives and perquisites;
- failure to collect data and track the progress of women and minorities against that of white male co-workers;
- inflexibility in defining work schedules and work sites;
- absence of programmes to enable employees to balance work/family responsibilities.

Time alone will not eliminate these barriers. Unlike the relentless drive of technology and other inevitabilities historically experienced by business organizations, eliminating barriers to the advancement of women is not something that is destined to happen. In order for real change to occur corporate leaders must: (1) have the *will* to act; (2) *develop and communicate*, throughout the organization the *business case* for retaining and advancing women; (3) *identify* those dimensions of the corporate culture/environment that are *barriers* to retaining and advancing women; (4) *implement initiatives* to eliminate these attitudinal, cultural and organizational biases.

TYPES OF CORPORATE INITIATIVES

For a number of years, Catalyst has been conducting research on corporate initiatives that address the retention, development and advancement of women involving surveys, in-depth interviews and site visits to major corporations and professional firms. In addition, each year Catalyst invites the *Fortune* 500/*Service* 500 corporations, the largest private companies and the largest professional firms to identify initiatives for consideration for The Catalyst Award. The nomination review process and site visits to finalist companies and firms has provided a rich opportunity to learn about what works and, conversely, what doesn't work, in devising and implementing strategies to retain and advance female employees.

Generally speaking, Catalyst's research (1990b) indicates that corporate cultures/environments that represent greater opportunities for women's development and advancement are those in which:

- performance-based contributions are emphasized over face-time, seniority, or information gained through exclusive networks in evaluating success and granting promotions;
- diversity is valued in recruiting and developing employees, because valuing diversity addresses the demographic trends that indicate increasing shortages of white men in the workforce and provides the opportunity for innovation and creativity;
- work and working relationships are organized horizontally as well as vertically and opportunities for lateral mobility are available and supported;
- open communication is the norm; criteria for success are shared with employees; feedback on performance and information needed for career planning is available and accessible; critical information is formally communicated to employees;
- innovation, as well as tradition, is valued;
- flexibility is emphasized in scheduling work and in designating work sites.

In looking at corporate initiatives to address women's recruitment, retention, development and advancement, Catalyst has found it is useful to distinguish between the broad range of policies and programmes that fall under the work/family category (in some companies referred to as work/life programmes) and initiatives that more specifically address women's development and upward mobility in organizations.

CORPORATE WORK/FAMILY INITIATIVES

Among the work/family initiatives that have been implemented in US and Canadian companies are parental leave, family care leave, sick leave for dependent care, adoption assistance, flexible spending accounts, domestic partner benefits, childcare centres, family daycare networks, emergency childcare, preschool programmes, after-school programmes, training and support groups, dependent care resource and referral, relocation assistance, and eldercare programmes.

Implementation of work/family programmes is often the first step in a company's development of programmes to recruit, retain, develop and advance women. Such programmes are fundamental to women's upward mobility, since research shows that 70% of the women in the US labour force are in their prime childbearing years (US Bureau of Labor Statistics, 1994 unpublished statistic).

The impact of work/family programmes on measurable phenomena such as absenteeism and tardiness and retention is clear. A 1990 study showed that 35% of mothers with children under 12 years old had a sick child in the last month; 51% of them missed work to care for their sick child (The Urban Institute, 1990). A *Fortune Magazine* study (1987) reported that 25% of employees with children under 12 years old experienced childcare breakdowns 2 to 5 times in a 3-month period. Breakdowns were linked to higher absenteeism and tardiness, as well as lower concentration on the job and less marital and parental satisfaction. Aetna increased its retention rate for women from 77% to 88% when it instituted a 6-month leave with flexible return-to-work possibilities. Based on a cost of turnover study (Galinsky, 1993) that found employee replacement costs 193% of annual salary, Aetna estimates its savings to be $1 million per year.

A positive impact of work/family programmes on less easily measured behaviours such as productivity, morale and loyalty have also been suggested by responses to opinion surveys: six studies have found lower absenteeism and improved productivity to be the most important benefits reported by employees who were surveyed (The Conference Board, 1991). Eight studies of manager perceptions of the impact of childcare assistance found the major benefits were better morale and lower absenteeism (The Conference Board, 1991). A large study that examined corporate responses to maternity, found pregnant employees who worked for more family-responsive companies were more satisfied with their jobs, felt sick less often, missed less work, spent more uncompensated time working, worked later in their pregnancies and were more likely to return to their jobs (National Council of Jewish Women, 1987, 1993).

Case study – Johnson and Johnson: Balancing Work and Family Programme

In 1989 Johnson and Johnson introduced its Balancing Work and Family Programme. Johnson and Johnson is the world's largest and most comprehensive manufacturer of healthcare products serving the consumer, pharmaceutical and professional market. The company is highly decentralized, with 168 separate companies worldwide.

The Balancing Work and Family Programme includes the following components:

- *Childcare Resource and Referral* – a service that helps employees find, evaluate, and choose appropriate childcare arrangements.
- *On-Site Child Development Centres* – in 1993, there were three on-site centres, with a fourth planned to open in the near future.
- *Dependent Care Assistance Plans* – employees can use payroll deductions to transfer pre-tax earnings to dependent care accounts administered by the company.
- *Family Care Leave* – job-guaranteed, unpaid leave for up to 12 months that may be used by male or female employees to care for a family member; serves as extended parental leave for employees with newborn or adopted children.
- *Family Care Absence* – time off with pay to provide short-term emergency care for family members.
- *Flexible Work Schedules* – the company encourages supervisors to respond to the needs of individual employees who experience changes in family responsibilities by developing flexible work arrangements, including flexitime, part-time work, job sharing, and telecommuting.
- *Adoption Benefits* – in addition to providing family care leave to adoptive parents, the company reimburses up to $3,000 for the cost of adoption and provides adoption referrals, adoption consultation, and support during and after the adoption process.
- *SchoolMatch* – a resource and referral service that assists parents in choosing state or private schools appropriate for their children.
- *Eldercare Resource and Referral* – a service providing information on ageing, expert help in choosing appropriate services, referrals to community services for the elderly, and useful publications.
- *Relocation Planning* – individualized relocation services which may include reimbursement of moving expenses.
- *Employed Spouse Relocation Services* – assistance to relocated employee's spouse in finding a job in the new locale.

According to the company's reports, these initiatives were designed in large part to address the changing composition of their workforce – the increasing numbers of women, two-career families, single parents and the children of elderly parents.

Johnson and Johnson also provided work/family training for managers and supervisors to help them understand the business case for work/family policies and to help them implement effective work/family practices: family-friendly programmes will help the company attract and retain the top-quality employees needed to remain competitive in its industry.

To underscore its commitment to family, the company in 1989 altered the 50-year-old company credo for one of the few times in its history to include this additional responsibility: 'We must be mindful of ways to help our employees fulfil their family responsibilities.'

In 1991, Johnson and Johnson was rated as having the most family-friendly programmes and policies among the *Fortune* 500/*Service* 500 companies by the Families and Work Institute in its publication *The Corporate Reference Guide to Work–Family Programs* (Galinsky et al., 1991). This assessment was made using a quantitative method for assessing the quality of work–family programmes.

Johnson and Johnson has also evaluated the impact of its work/family programmes through use of an employee survey administered shortly after the programmes began in 1990 and again in 1992. Among other findings, the survey showed that between 1990 and 1992, supervisors became significantly more supportive of employees when work/family problems arose and supervisors were also seen as more supportive of the use of flexible time and leave policies. Employee reports indicated that the negative spillover from work to family decreased in the same time period. Contrary to the predictions of proponents of the programmes, there was no impact on absenteeism or tardiness (Families and Work Institute, 1993).

More quantitative studies are needed to demonstrate the benefits of work/family programmes to employers and employees. Early studies seem to suggest that there may be a cost to employers of not providing work–family assistance, whether it be the measurable cost of turnover, the more intangible costs of lower productivity of distracted employees who are worried about their children, or the opportunity costs for a company that cannot compete with so-called 'family-friendly' competitors in recruiting female talent.

Research shows that employees' and managers' assumptions frequently differ with regard to the expected outcomes of providing work–family assistance. A 1990 study of flexible work arrangements showed, for example, that managers were reluctant to offer greater flexibility for fear that employee demand would escalate. In reality, few employees are interested in or can afford to work on a part-time basis. More quantitative research would enable employers to test assumptions against measurable and behavioural results (Mattis, 1990).

While work/family programmes are fundamental first steps for companies that are concerned about the recruitment, retention, development and advancement of women, they are not sufficient to guarantee women's career progression, nor are they universally applicable: women with children do not all have the same level of need for corporate-sponsored work/family benefits, nor do women who never have children.

A review of corporate human resources policies and programmes undertaken by Catalyst shows that concern for helping employees balance their work and family responsibilities does not necessarily lead to an increased attentiveness to other factors that affect women's access to advancement. Therefore, it is important for companies to go beyond initiatives that address work/family balance to those that address other structural barriers in the corporate culture and work environment.

CORPORATE INITIATIVES THAT PROMOTE WOMEN'S UPWARD MOBILITY

Most companies that have 'glass ceiling' initiatives use at least one, and often more than one, of the following approaches:

- removal of cultural and environment barriers to women's advancement;
- early identification of high-potential women;
- leadership development programmes that emphasize lateral moves and line experience;

- flexibility in arranging work schedules and sites.

Specifically, companies have implemented policies, programmes or practices that include one or a combination of the following:

- training (e.g. gender awareness, diversity, sexual harassment);
- mentoring;
- women's advisory and support;
- accountability programmes;
- succession planning;
- rotation/non-traditional employment programmes;
- leadership development and upward mobility programmes;
- flexible work arrangements;
- work/family policies and programmes.

PROGRAMMES VERSUS PROCESS

Corporations are gaining more awareness of the business motivations for retaining and advancing women. In turn, they are looking for ways to enhance their performance in this important area of human resources management. The recent involvement of US companies with total quality management has led to an increased use of benchmarking by companies to measure their performance against that of industry peers. So it is not surprising that some companies are turning to benchmarking in the area of human resources management, seeking solutions from companies that have been more successful in retaining and promoting women.

The fact that companies are beginning to benchmark against the human resources practices other companies use to enhance their recruitment, retention and advancement of women suggests that business is looking seriously at issues related to the underrepresentation and underutilization of women in the ranks of corporate managers and professionals.

The greatest motivation for corporations to eliminate the glass ceiling for women and minorities will come through observing the successful business outcomes experienced by industry leaders, who recognized early on the importance of retaining and promoting valued female talent.

For this reason, it is important to identify and profile exemplary efforts by US companies to dismantle the glass ceiling for women. The remaining pages of this chapter will be devoted to describing several such initiatives.

BENCHMARKING CORPORATE INITIATIVES FOR WOMEN'S ADVANCEMENT

Catalyst's recent research suggests that, today, more companies are concerned about the retention of female professionals and managers than about the recruitment of females into their management ranks, although there are exceptions. Highly technical industries and engineering companies, for example, continue to be concerned about recruitment of women engineers and scientists, but they are also experiencing a new awareness of the need to retain those women currently in their technical workforce.

Financial services organizations, on the other hand, report no difficulty in recruiting talented women on campuses. Their concern, and that of companies in the service sector generally, is with the disproportionate turnover of women they are experiencing, especially high-performing, seasoned female professionals and managers.

When women leave, companies often assume that they are choosing family over a career, opting to stay home with children. Therefore, they erroneously believe that there was nothing that the company could have done to retain these women. Catalyst's research with a group of women who had left their companies through voluntary resignations shows that most of the women left for better career opportunities rather than for work/family balance. Though work/family programmes might have benefited some of these women (as well as some of their male co-workers), such programmes alone would not offer a long-term solution for reducing the disproportionate turnover of women.

This example is given to illustrate common problems inherent in corporate benchmarking practices: (1) failure to identify the real problem; (2) desire for a 'quick fix'; (3) assumption that one solution fits all. The companies described above failed to identify the real reason that women were leaving. Their erroneous assumption that women leave for work/family balance will lead them in search of a 'quick fix', a work/family programme. Whether they select a low-cost programme, such as dependent-care tax savings accounts for employees, or a costly benefit such as an on-site child-care centre, doesn't really matter. The solution doesn't fit the problem – which remains unidentified.

Catalyst has found that the most effective corporate initiatives have more to do with the *process* by which programmes are selected and implemented than with the programmes themselves. In every case, the process began with a recognition and articulation of a business need. This, in turn, provided the rationale for all of the actions that follow. Articulation of the rationale for advancing women in the organization came from senior management and was linked to the specific business needs of the organization.

To be taken seriously, the business case needs to be articulated by senior line managers as well as human resources professionals. Since corporations are in the business of generating revenue, it follows that any initiative, if it is to endure, has to be tied to corporate profitability.

Central to the development of effective corporate initiatives for advancing women is an internal research process designed to: (1) measure human resources performance in the area of the recruitment, retention, promotion and representation of women by level/functional area; (2) identify assumptions; (3) assess employee needs, perceptions, opinions, career goals by gender and other potential discriminating factors. Corporations measure what they value, so it is critical to measure human resources management in corporations in the same fashion other aspects of performance are tracked.

Typically, companies combine internal research with benchmarking to assess both *how* industry peers are doing on selected human resources performance measures, and *what* policies/programmes other organizations are using to advance women. Such benchmarking should not be used as a substitute for internal research and issue identification.

Case study – Bank of Montreal: Task Force on the Advancement of Women

Bank of Montreal, Canada's oldest chartered bank and one of the largest financial institutions in North America, employs 30,000 people in Canada and the USA.

Bank of Montreal's Task Force on the Advancement of Women exemplifies the critical role of research in enabling companies to identify initiatives that are specific to and appropriate for their corporate culture. The taskforce was established to identify barriers to women's advancement and devise action plans to remove them. Women made up 75% of the bank's workforce in 1991, but only 9% of executives and 13% of senior managers. On the other hand, women held 91% of non-management jobs. The question the taskforce explored was, Is there a rational explanation for these discrepancies?

Through an extensive research process – interview and survey responses were received from one-third of the bank's employees, more than 10,000 women and men – the taskforce identified five main assumptions as to why so few women had reached senior positions in the bank. The taskforce then analysed the human resources records of more than 28,000 employees. All five assumptions were proven false; that is, by all important yardsticks (including education, length of service, dedication and job performance) women in the bank equalled or surpassed their male colleagues. The analysis of human resources data provided an unprecedented opportunity to compare perceptions with facts and irrefutably debunk myths about women's lack of advancement.

In its 1991 *Report to Employees*, the taskforce refuted the false assumptions, and set out the real facts. One fact was that time alone was not going to correct the gender imbalance at the bank. At the rate women were advancing in 1991, they would make up just 18% of the executive ranks and only 22% of senior management by the year 2000 (Bank of Montreal, 1991).

In response to the recommendations of the taskforce, the bank's president and CEO committed the organization to dramatic and systematic change to achieve both proportional representation and equality of opportunity at Bank of Montreal.

Bank of Montreal's initiative exemplifies a process that includes the components Catalyst has identified as most likely to result in success:

(1) *Motivation and rationale linked to strategic business goals.* The advancement of women, along with other workplace equality goals, is an essential part of the bank's corporate strategic plan, which was articulated in the following way: 'Our strategy, quite simply, is to make ourselves the Bank of Choice by becoming the Employer of Choice in our industry. When we attract and advance the best people, and give them the support they need to do their best work, they in turn will attract and keep loyal customers.'

(2) *Top-down support.* The taskforce was personally sponsored by the president and this fact was widely publicized within the bank and to the public at large. The president was directly involved in the deliberations and drafting of the report. He also endorsed every action plan. The taskforce leader was a female vice president, who had the full support of the president.

(3) *Accountability*. In the *Report to Employees*, and many other internal communications, the president has made it clear that he is personally accountable for the success of efforts to advance women. The bank made the report widely available to customers and the public, in this way holding itself accountable for this high-profile commitment. The creation of the new position of vice president for workplace equality was the first action plan in the report. By reporting directly to the president instead of reporting to the head of one bank group (as is customary), the vice president for workplace equality is in a position to help bring about the kind of change in the overall bank culture that would be accomplished much more slowly from within the constraints of one bank group. The taskforce established highly visible national and divisional advisory councils to provide ongoing leadership and advocacy throughout the bank. Since the advancement of women is a major business goal, it is fully integrated into the business plan process. All managers (starting at the executive level) establish annual hiring, retention and advancement targets. Then each manager's success in reaching the individual goals, along with her or his contribution to workplace equality generally, is assessed in the annual performance review. Performance evaluation also takes into account a manager's day-to-day behaviour – her or his success as a role model for fair and equal treatment of all employees. The bank's progress in advancing women is measured quarterly and reported to employees in an annual report as well as in occasional interim reports.

(4) *Communication*. In addition to the *Report to Employees*, more than 20,000 copies of which have been requested by outside organizations around the world, and the annual and occasional progress reports, other communication channels were used to publicize the bank's commitment to advancing women, including development and distribution of new or updated policies; new recruitment and interviewing materials; revised corporate sponsorship criteria; revised advertising and promotional materials; a new employee orientation handbook, video and manager's guide; individually labelled copies of the bank's code of conduct; ongoing features and items in internal news magazines and new videos; new or revamped training programmes, such as the awareness training workshop, Women and Men as Colleagues; handbooks and pamphlets about related programmes such as flexible work arrangements; ongoing presentations to employees by the vice president for workplace equality and other staff; speeches and letters to employees from the president; employee meetings with the president; and an updated corporate strategic plan.

(5) *Measurable results*. Results are measured on an ongoing basis and reported to employees. The measurement process includes quarterly business plan updates, regular employee surveys, focus groups, feedback from advisory council members and comments and suggestions from employees.

(6) *Supportive environment*. Every aspect of how the bank does business has been touched by the initiative, including the corporate strategic plan, recruitment, corporate sponsorships, policies and programmes, performance review, code of conduct, orientation and training.

Bank of Montreal's initiative is an example of an integrated approach to the advancement of women. Increasingly, organizations are recognizing that single programmes cannot address the numerous barriers to women's advancement embedded in their corporate culture and work environment. Family and work/life needs of employees call for a whole complex of policies and programmes. Isolated programmes don't work; for example, providing a generous parental leave policy without flexible work arrangements will not help employees who want to balance work and family. The same can be said for women's upward mobility initiatives.

Companies need to be working on a variety of fronts. The most effective initiatives encompass a combination of programmes or systemic approaches to advancing women.

While the research findings regarding the advancement of women for any two organizations might be similar, we would expect their solutions to be different. For example, two US companies that came to conclusions similar to Bank of Montreal – namely, women weren't advancing to senior levels commensurate with their abilities and their representation in management overall – devised different initiatives to address this issue.

Case study – Continental Insurance Company: Accelerated Development Programme

Headquartered in New York City, The Continental Corporation is an insurance provider that employs approximately 16,220 people. Continental's Accelerated Development Programme (ADP) encompasses a number of initiatives including succession planning, mentoring and rotational assignments. The programme is a strategic tool for grooming leaders and ensuring that women – who represent over half of Continental's professional workforce – are equally represented in the process.

Designed by the CEO and his senior officers, the ADP was instituted in 1987 with the goal of cultivating company talent from within. In keeping with Continental's business goal to move more women into visible leadership roles, management ensures that many of the ADP participants are women.

Once a year, employees, who are either self-nominated or nominated by their managers, undergo a challenging selection process that involves written essays, numerous interviews with senior managers and corporate officers and completion of an assessment questionnaire by the candidate's supervisor describing his or her attributes.

During an intensive 3-month training and orientation period at corporate headquarters, ADP participants learn about a variety of company functions and formulate detailed career plans. An average plan consists of three to five assignments, each 12 to 24 months in duration, including at least one geographic relocation. Experiences must include staff, line, home, office, field, project and management positions so participants develop broad-based backgrounds. An adviser, programme manager and supervisor are each assigned to every ADP participant for coaching, providing feedback and developing career plans.

Senior management strongly endorses the programme. The programme is funded by the Office of the Chairman, giving it great significance. This factor also offers supervisors the incentive of having talented individuals work with them in rotations that have no impact on their departmental budget. Aside from providing steady financial support, senior managers help select, train and mentor ADP participants.

For Continental, the programme formalizes the experiences and opportunities necessary to the development of corporate leaders and ensures that women and minorities are not excluded from these key developmental assignments.

Case study – Motorola, Inc.: succession planning with clout

Motorola is an electronics company that manufactures cellular phones, electronic paging equipment, semiconductors and robotics. The company has 100,000 employees worldwide.

In 1986, stimulated by changing workforce demographics, Motorola began developing initiatives to advance women and minorities in the company with the recognition that women were increasingly the buyers for projects (especially in local government) and consumer goods.

Motorola's Organization and Management Development Review (OMDR) is a succession planning and accountability process that is integrated with the company's diversity resources function. The OMDR is used to identify and track women and minorities who have the talent to reach senior levels, and then to plan their development. In an effort to eliminate glass-ceiling barriers to minorities and women within management, Motorola established the corporate-wide 'parity goal'. Goal attainment will require that by 1996 there is a representation of qualified women and minorities at all management levels that mirrors the representation of qualified members of these groups in the general population.

Communication of Motorola's diversity drive is worldwide. Though currently only divisions in the USA are accountable to the OMDR system, divisions in other parts of the world have begun their own diversity initiatives. Memos regarding the parity goal are distributed worldwide.

The director of diversity reports directly to the CEO's office. Quarterly reports on the status of women and minorities are given to the CEO. When a vacancy occurs in a division, the CEO personally contacts the division head in order to discuss the parity goal.

Motorola has continued to evaluate and refine its succession planning process to ensure it will meet targeted goals for the representation of women and minorities in senior leadership positions.

On the work/family front, Motorola has opened two on-site childcare centres at two operating facilities; a third centre, to be located at the corporate headquarters, is in the design stage.

CONCLUSION

Corporate initiatives for advancing women: What works? What doesn't?

Corporate initiatives to advance women are relatively few in number compared to corporate work/family programmes. Most initiatives have not been evaluated in any rigorous sense. In the majority of cases it is too soon to assess the measurable impact on the numbers of women in senior positions or on the more intangible barriers in the corporate culture of these initiatives. The corporations for which initiatives are profiled in this analysis have reported measurable results in advancing women to leadership roles while acknowledging that much remains to be done.

Catalyst's research suggests that corporate initiatives are most likely to succeed where (1) the CEO and other senior line managers recognize and articulate the business case for advancing women and strategies for advancing women are embedded in the organization's strategic business plan; (2) managers are held accountable for the development and advancement of women, results are measured and reviewed by the executive leadership of the organization and incentives/rewards are tied to successful performance in this area; (3) research is undertaken to identify the specific barriers in the culture and working environment that impede women's progress; (4) training is implemented to address stereotypes and preconceptions about women's abilities and suitability for careers in business and to equip managers to coach and develop women who report to them; (5) a system is implemented to identify and monitor the progress of high-potential women and to ensure that they acquire a broad range of experience in core business areas so that they will be able to compete with men for leadership positions in the organization.

Since women are a diverse group, a multi-programme or systemic approach to advancing women has a more positive impact than isolated programmes. Systemic approaches are also needed because biases against women are deeply embedded in corporate culture.

Companies need to be alert to the dangers inherent in benchmarking against the programmes of other corporations without first identifying the barriers to women's advancement that are specific to their culture and work environment. There are no 'quick fixes'; many solutions are needed, only a few of which have been identified at this time.

Finally, corporate leaders must have the will to act that comes from the belief that advancing women is a business imperative.

REFERENCES

BANK OF MONTREAL (1991) *Report to Employees*, Bank of Montreal, Montreal.

Business Week (1992) Corporate women. Progress? Sure. But the playing field is still far from level, *Business Week*, 8 June, pp. 74–83.

CATALYST (1990a) *Women in Corporate Management: Results of a Catalyst Survey*, Catalyst, New York.

CATALYST (1990b) *Women in Corporate Management: Model Programs for Development and Mobility*, Catalyst, New York.

THE CONFERENCE BOARD (1991) *Linking Work-Family Issues to the Bottom Line*, The Conference Board, New York.

FAMILIES AND WORK INSTITUTE (1993) *An Evaluation of Johnson & Johnson's Work–Family Initiative*, Families and Work Institute, New York.

GALINSKY, E. (1993) *Thirteen Consistent (and Sometimes Surprising) Findings From Work–Family Evaluations*, Families and Work Institute, New York, unpublished.

GALINSKY, E. and HUGHES, D. (1987) *The Fortune Magazine Child Care Study*, Families and Work Institute, New York.

GALINSKY, E., FRIEDMAN, D. and HERNANDEZ, C. (eds) (1991) *The Corporate Reference Guide to Work–Family Programs*, Families and Work Institute, New York.

HOFFERTH, S. *et al.* (1991) *National Child Care Survey, 1990: A NAEYC Study*, The Urban Institute, New York.

KORN/FERRY INTERNATIONAL and UCLA'S JOHN E. ANDERSON GRADUATE SCHOOL OF MANAGEMENT (1990) *Korn/Ferry International's Executive Profile 1990: A Survey of Corporate Leaders*, Korn/Ferry International, New York.

MATTIS, M. (1990) Flexible work arrangements for managers and professionals: myths and realities, *Human Resource Planning*, Vol. 13, no. 2, p. 142.

NATIONAL COUNCIL OF JEWISH WOMEN (1987) *Accommodating Pregnancy in the Workplace*, National Council of Jewish Women, New York.

NATIONAL COUNCIL OF JEWISH WOMEN (1993) *Experience of Childbearing Women in the Workplace: The Impact of Family–Friendly Policies and Practices*, National Council of Jewish Women, New York.

RAND CORPORATION (1991) Child Care and Women's Return to Work after Childbirth, Santa Monica, CA.

US DEPARTMENT OF LABOR (1991) *A Report On the Glass Ceiling Initiative*, US Department of Labor, Washington, DC.

US DEPARTMENT OF LABOR (1992) *Pipelines of Progress: A Status Report on the Glass Ceiling*, US Department of Labor, Washington, DC.

CHAPTER 18

Affirmative Action in Australian Organizations[1]

ROBIN KRAMAR

INTRODUCTION

Never have the prospects for the creation of equal employment opportunity (EEO) for women in Australia been so good. However, at the same time, the realization of these prospects is a complex, slow process and continually under threat. Government ratification of International Labour Office (ILO) conventions, State and Federal legislation and the central industrial relations system have provided a supportive framework for the development of initiatives which seek to improve the position and rewards of women in the labour market. Within these structures, many initiatives have become an integral part of the process or change designed to improve organizational and labour market efficiency. These provide an opportunity for the acceptance of employment principles consistent with EEO. Despite these developments, changes in legislation, labour market structures and industrial relations arrangements could alter the structures within which EEO initiatives are developed and, as a result, impede progress to a more equitable labour market for women.

EQUAL EMPLOYMENT OPPORTUNITY:
AN ESTABLISHED PRINCIPLE

The principle of EEO has been accepted by Australian governments as a standard for the operation of the labour market. This follows the ratification of the International Labour Office (ILO) Conventions and Recommendations which specifically address the problems of women workers achieving equal opportunities and equal remuneration under safe working conditions. These Conventions include Discrimination (Employment and Occupation) Convention 1958 (No. 111), Equal Remuneration Convention 1951 (No. 100) and Equal Treatment for Men and Women Workers with Family Responsibilities Convention 1981 (No. 156). The ILO has been particularly concerned with

---

[1] Parts of this chapter appeared in Women in management in Australia, *Women in Management Review* (1993) Vol. 8, no. 3, and are reproduced here with permission.

developing measures which ensure equal access to training and employment with special reference to issues such as the impact of new technology, equality of remuneration, the improvement of conditions in industries and occupations employing large numbers of women, women working as part-time, casual, contractual, home-based or domestic workers and the participation of women in decision-making at all levels. It acknowledges there are problems translating the principle of equality into practice and in integrating the mechanisms into economic, social and political programmes (International Labour Office, 1987, pp. 1–5).

The Australian experience indicates EEO principles can be integrated into wider programmes. This has been achieved through legislation which establishes standards for behaviour in the labour market and the development of economic, social and industrial policies. Anti-discrimination legislation defines the standards for behaviour essential for EEO.

Legislation in five states, the Australian Capital Territory and in the Federal jurisdiction prohibits behaviour which discriminates either directly or indirectly against women. Direct discrimination refers to any action or policy which excludes a person or a group from an opportunity or benefit because of a personal characteristic irrelevant to the situation. Indirect discrimination is more difficult to detect and may not always be the result of conscious intent. It refers to actions or policies which may appear non-discriminatory, but are discriminatory because they incorporate attitudes or assumptions which operate to limit the access of a person or group to benefits or opportunities. The legislation also prohibits sexual harassment and attempts to promote the acceptance of equality of men and women within the community.

This standard of discrimination-free behaviour is the basis of affirmative action legislation and it has been embodied as a principle into industrial relations legislation. Section 93 of the Industrial Relations Act 1988 requires decisions of the Industrial Relations Commission to comply with the Sex Discrimination Act 1984. In addition the application of discrimination-free behaviour has been extended by requiring government contractors to comply with these standards of behaviour, in the Victorian government and in the Commonwealth government.

These principles of anti-discrimination were strengthened in 1992 with amendments to the Sex Discrimination Act 1984. The amendments seek to protect female workers in a more deregulated labour market, provide additional protection from discrimination to workers with family responsibilities and include victimization as a ground for complaint under the Act. The amendments allow for discrimination in new awards or enterprise agreements to be a ground for complaint. An award will be discriminatory if it includes terms which treat employees unfavourably on the basis of sex. This could include instances where discrimination occurs in relation to access to shiftwork or overtime rates, or where allowances or increments are denied to women workers, or where wage rates determined under award classifications are undervalued on the basis of sex.

One of the recent amendments prohibits dismissal on the grounds of family responsibilities. These responsibilities are defined as those associated with the care for or support of a dependent child of the employee or any other immediate family member who is in need of care and support.

The definition of an immediate family member is quite broad and includes a spouse, *de facto* spouse, parents, grandparents, grandchildren, adult children, siblings of the employee or the employee's spouse or *de facto* spouse. It is anticipated this amendment will protect employees with family responsibilities who are dismissed because they are unable to work new work arrangements such as 12-hour shifts or 7 rostered days in a row. These amendments substantially broaden and strengthen the scope of the Sex Discrimination Act and it is anticipated they will promote equity for women in the labour market.

Legislation is, however, only one way Australian governments have sought to create EEO. The Australian government has developed a National Agenda for Women which seeks to create EEO through a variety of policy initiatives. These include strategies designed to improve the stock of human capital by increasing the qualifications and employment experience of women through better access to education and training and the establishment of national goals. These strategies include the National Policy for the Education of Girls in Australian Schools, the National Plans of Action for Women in TAFE and Higher Education, Action for Women: National CES Strategy for Women, and A Fair Go: The Federal Government's Strategy for Rural Education and Training.

The Australian government also recognizes the importance of the provision of childcare for the creation of EEO. It has developed a Commonwealth National Child Care Strategy which includes a variety of arrangements developed to deal with preschool-age children, after-school care, holiday care and occasional childcare resulting from illness. The Australian government has encouraged the development of these initiatives by expanding funding for childcare through the creation of almost 90,000 community childcare places, the extension of the eligibility for fee relief, the provision of incentives to industry to invest in childcare for employees' children and the implementation of taxation arrangements which encourage employers to provide childcare for their employees.

Developments in the industrial relations arena also support the promotion of EEO for women workers covered by awards. In recent years decisions of the industrial tribunals have sought to create a more skilled and flexible workforce while providing wage and salary increases in exchange for productivity improvements. Employment conditions have been rewritten to provide for skill-related career paths. These career paths are meant to provide employees with an incentive to expand their employment skills through training and to remove the barriers preventing employees from performing a variety of skills while, at the same time, expanding the range of tasks employees may be required to perform. In addition, employers and trade unions are also required to address any instances where award provisions discriminate against women.

Anti-discrimination and affirmative action legislation are the cornerstones of the Australian government's attempts to create EEO for women. However, this legislation is only one part of a strategy which seeks to integrate women's concerns into broader employment policy issues. Affirmative action legislation has the potential to be a powerful force for creating EEO by making it compulsory for employers to take a proactive approach – they must ensure employment policies don't discriminate against women.

AFFIRMATIVE ACTION

The enactment of the Affirmative Action (Equal Employment Opportunity for Women) Act 1986 (the Act) by the Australian government is an attempt to systematically remove discrimination from employment policies and practices in private-sector organizations and trade unions employing more than 100 employees. Universities are also covered by the Act. The legislation is framed in such a way as to allow employers to develop affirmative action programmes which are consistent with their organizational and industrial culture. However, although employers objected to limits being placed on their discretion in employment matters, the government acknowledged the need for legislation. This need was obvious following the failure of employers to devote sufficient resources or to take adequate action during the 12-month voluntary pilot programme held in 1983 (Department of Prime Minister and Cabinet, 1985).

The Act provides only general guidelines for the development of an affirmative action programme, but it requires organizations covered by the Act to be accountable to a government agency, the Affirmative Action Agency, for the way they develop their programme. These organizations are required to comply with the following eight steps and to provide annually a short report for public scrutiny and a more detailed confidential report. These reports are evaluated by the Affirmative Action Agency. The eight steps to be followed in the development of an affirmative action programme are:

(1) Issue a policy statement.
(2) Confer responsibility for the programme on a senior person.
(3) Consult with trade unions.
(4) Consult with employees, particularly women.
(5) Establish and analyse the employment profile.
(6) Review employment policies and practices.
(7) Set objectives and forward estimates.
(8) Monitor and evaluate the programme.

These eight steps should ensure that:

(a) appropriate action is taken to eliminate discrimination by the relevant employer against women in relation to employment matters; and
(b) measures are taken by the relevant employer to promote equal employment opportunity for women in relation to employment matters.

Although the requirement to establish objectives and estimates suggests one of the aims of the Act is to promote changes in the distribution of men and women across occupations and hierarchies, the Act does not require the establishment of quotas. Quotas require employers to obtain a percentage of women employees regardless of the number of qualified applicants available and are not consistent with the principle of merit which the affirmative action legislation is seeking to promote. In comparison, the establishment of objectives and forward estimates requires the realistic assessment of the aims of affirmative action programmes and an estimation of the number of women who would occupy various positions at the end of a given time period, given the nature of the affirmative action programme and the state of the labour market. Therefore, under the Australian arrangement, any redistribution of women across industries and occupations would result from discrimination-free employment practices. These practices would be characterized by decisions based on notions of merit, skills and qualifications, not practices based on positive discrimination.

Sex discrimination and affirmative action legislation in Australia does not prevent employers from implementing special strategies which allow women to develop and demonstrate merit. These strategies could seek to redress past discrimination so that women are better placed to compete on the basis of merit. Case law indicates the provision of special measures for members of disadvantaged groups such as women is unlikely to be discriminatory unless it excludes others. For instance, in the Proudfoot case in 1992, it was established that different services were required to give women and men equal access to appropriate health services. The provision of services for women did not exclude men from the benefit of healthcare. In addition, it is possible for industrial agreements to acknowledge that different groups of workers require different working arrangements. For instance, agreements can provide different working arrangements for workers with family responsibilities, and consequently provide greater flexibility for employees.

The Affirmative Action (Equal Employment Opportunity for Women) Act 1986 appears to have promoted change. Almost 100% of the 2,342 organizations covered by the Act (99.3%) comply with the legislation by submitting their annual reports to the Affirmative Action Agency (Pratt and Davis, 1993). In addition it is reported that the legislation has raised the awareness of employees and senior management about the way women are discriminated against in the workplace (Braithwaite, 1993, p. 6). By legitimizing a certain standard of behaviour, it also provides managers responsible for EEO matters 'with considerable clout in convincing their managers to address these issues' (Powell and Russell, 1993, p. 24). This clout has been further enhanced by the recent amendment to the Act which requires compliance by government contractors. There are also some excellent examples of initiatives undertaken as part of affirmative action programmes.

Each year awards are made to organizations which develop policies regarded as models of 'best practice' in promoting EEO. These policies are varied. They include management development programmes designed to encourage the movement of women through management positions, the implementation of effective communication channels involving unions and women employees in the development of affirmative action plans, a range of strategies designed to encourage women to move into non-traditional occupations and workplaces such as oil rigs and mines, and flexible employment conditions which allow women to accommodate childrearing and employment (Affirmative Action Agency, 1990; Gibbs, 1991; Pledger, 1991).

Many organizations acknowledge the benefits of these initiatives. These include improved recruiting criteria, the selection of employees with higher qualifications and employment skills, reduced turnover of employees, the ability to attract well-qualified women for positions and the perception among employees that employment practices were more equitable (Powell and Russell, 1993).

Despite these admirable policy advances, 'women in Australia do not enjoy equal opportunity and do not have equal status with men' (Lavarch, 1992). This is reflected in the persistent concentration of women in traditional women's

Table 18.1   **Occupational segregation – July 1992**

MAJOR OCCUPATIONAL GROUP	NUMBER	FEMALE OCCUPATIONAL GROUP (%)
Managers and administrators	215,100	25.00
Professionals	456,000	43.00
Para-professionals	204,300	45.00
Tradespersons	110,900	9.00
Clerks	994,400	77.70
Salespersons and personal service workers	775,600	64.90
Plant and machine operators and drivers	77,500	14.22
Labourers and related workers	399,900	34.68
TOTAL	3,233,700	42.00

- 54.8% of female employees were concentrated in two major occupational groups: clerks and salespersons, etc.
- While 20% of female employees were in professional and para-professional occupations, 22% of these were teachers and 30% were registered nurses.

SOURCE: Australian Bureau of Statistics (1992) The Labour Force, Australia, July, 1992, Cat. no. 6203.0.

occupations and part-time work. They also continue to have lower earnings and membership of superannuation schemes than men (see Table 18.1).

Most Australian organizations appear not to have developed their organizational cultures to support the principle of EEO or to have effectively communicated their EEO policies to employees. Instead, EEO has been developed within the existing power and social structures. This is demonstrated by the continued low level of consultation with trade unions, with only 55% of employers claiming to have consulted with trade unions in 1992 (Affirmative Action Agency, 1992). An audit of affirmative action reports in the state of Victoria suggests, however, that the actual incidence of consultation is much less, with only about 22% of companies consulting with trade unions (Victorian Trades Hall Council, 1992). Similarly, although 79% of employers reported consulting some women employees (Affirmative Action Agency, 1992), a survey revealed the rate of compliance was much less, probably closer to 10% (Powell, 1993). In addition, there continued to be poor compliance with the requirement to establish forward estimates, with only 37% of employers undertaking this task (Affirmative Action Agency, 1993).

Although some organizations have developed innovative techniques using videos and training programmes to communicate their commitment to EEO (Affirmative Action Agency, 1990), there is still a low level of understanding of affirmative action among employees. Even in organizations where senior management have a strong commitment to EEO, knowledge and information does not necessarily flow down to lower levels in the hierarchy (Castleman et al., 1991; Employment Research Group, 1991). Communication and training about affirmative action was found to be most effective when it was relevant to the employee's own situation, involved good presentation styles and provided the opportunity for meaningful and ongoing interaction between employees and trainers (Castleman et al., 1991).

It has been argued that the sanctions and the form of affirmative action legislation indicate it was never intended to bring about significant social change (Thornton, 1990; Graycar and Morgan, 1990; Scutt, 1991). The nature of the legislation has been seen as a way of encouraging the redistribution of people within the existing employment structures, most particularly the promotion of women to senior management positions. It has not been seen as changing organizational priorities, values or systems. The only sanctions for not complying with affirmative action legislation are being named in parliament and not securing government contract work. It has been claimed the sanctions within the legislation are so weak as to be almost irrelevant (Newman, 1991).

Affirmative action legislation has been crucial for establishing standards for policies and behaviour in organizations. It does not explicitly require organizations to recognize the different needs of groups of employees with varying family and personal responsibilities. This has been explained in terms of the masculine values of organizations being left intact (Burton, 1991) and is demonstrated by women being sent off to assertiveness training sessions, rather than creating work environments in which less assertive employees can be productive and prosper (Poiner and Wills, 1991). Despite this tendency, there are some examples of the different needs of workers being acknowledged and accommodated by some organizations.

WORKERS WITH FAMILY RESPONSIBILITIES

Some Australian organizations have acknowledged that a situation of EEO requires recognizing that different groups of employees have different needs in the workplace. Pressures resulting from the globalization of business operations, rapidly changing technology, manufacturing techniques and materials, and the changing demographics have encouraged some employers to develop a more flexible approach to employment practices and work organization. Initiatives designed to accommodate workers with family responsibilities have been acknowledged by some employers as a way of improving organizational performance and developing commitment among employees.

This recognition has been fuelled by the Australian government's ratification of ILO Convention 156, the establishment of a Work and Family Unit within the Department of Industrial Relations and the provision of the Corporate Work and Family Awards to companies judged to be one of the top 10 family-friendly companies.

The Work and Family Unit has developed a strategy for implementing Convention 156 across Australian government policies and programmes. In addition, it plays an important role in research, promotion and the provision of information and advice to industrial parties and the broader community.

The implementation of initiatives designed to accommodate work and family responsibilities is not widespread in Australia. In those instances where they do exist, the policies take a variety of forms. Some have been general and focused on issues such as changing the corporate culture; so it is consistent with organizational arrangements necessary to accommodate workers with family responsibilities. Other arrangements have been more specific and dealt with policies such as the provision of childcare, flexible working arrangements and employee relocation policies. These policies have frequently been developed in the context of broader human resource strategies and changes in the industrial relations system, particularly award restructuring. Parental leave provisions which provide men with the opportunity to take leave for childcare are generally being incorporated into awards.

A key feature of the strategies developed to deal with employees' family and work responsibilities has been the recognition that the working lives of employees will be affected by their family responsibilities. One way of doing this has been to state explicitly the need for employees to manage both their private and work lives. BP has done this in its Vision and Value Statement which 'includes an explicit reference to the need for BP employees to strike a balance between their responsibilities to BP and to their home life' (Aidie and Carmody, 1992, p. 4). The Vision and Values Statement signals the formal intent of the company, and this intent has been operationalized by providing part-time work, and where possible home-based work, a sensitive relocation policy and a requirement for employees to think about their long-term career aspirations and life goals in their development plan.

Organizations operating in the finance industry have been particularly concerned to retain skilled staff with young children. This concern arose because of the pressures imposed by the deregulation of the banking and insurance industry, and the costs of higher turnover associated with the expansion of career opportunities in other organizations. The Commonwealth Bank developed a range of policies in the context of the renegotiation of its award under the structural efficiency principle, as well as in the context of its equal employment opportunity programme. Initiatives include flexible employment arrangements which allow full-time staff to change to part-time employment and vice versa. Part-time staff receive *pro rata* pay and conditions, and are able to attend in-house training programmes. In addition, the bank has emphasized the need for managers to treat sympathetically employee requests for short periods of paid leave of absence in the event of sudden illness of family members.

Banks have typically relied on internal sources of labour. Therefore, in an attempt to provide staff with greater flexibility in planning their career, a career break scheme has been developed in the Commonwealth Bank for both men and women. Career breaks can take a variety of forms and may comprise full-time leave, part leave/part-time work or job sharing for a predetermined period, or registration as a casual employee. Career breaks can be taken for a variety of purposes, including travel, study, care of children or elderly parents or spouse or immediate family members and alternative employment. The break can last for between 12 months and 3 years.

One of the requirements of the career break scheme is that participants maintain contact with the bank. This is arranged formally through a re-familiarization programme which requires that participants spend 2 weeks of every year in a position of the same or similar grade to their pre-break position. Other ways of keeping up to date are through the provision of information packs, attendance at 1- or 2-day seminars and close contact with 'personal points of reference or nearest branch for clarification of matters arising from information packs' (Aidie and Carmody, 1992, p. 10).

Other financial institutions have also developed career break and more flexible work schemes. The focus of these schemes has been a recognition of the impact of work/family issues on the pool of internal labour. The National Australia Bank, Westpac and the Australia and New Zealand Banking Group Ltd have all developed forms of these schemes. However, the Commonwealth Bank's scheme which was developed as part of a major organization restructure and which involved a complete rewriting of the award setting out employment rewards and conditions is the most flexible scheme. The Department of Industrial Relations acknowledges the Commonwealth Bank's scheme as a model for other organizations: 'changes and innovative and dynamic work practices are making one of Australia's largest financial institutions more productive, efficient and competitive – and a better place to work' (Department of Industrial Relations, 1991).

Another bank, the National Australia Bank (NAB), acknowledges that flexible work practices are a key factor in maximizing productivity and enhancing customer service. To achieve this end, they have secured agreement of the Finance Sector Union for greater flexibility in the use of part-time and temporary employees. In addition, they are also trialling 36 job-sharing arrangements and in November 1992 the NAB introduced a scheme which provided staff with up to 5 days' leave per annum in an emergency to care for immediate dependent family members, or other acknowledged dependents including children and the aged. It also provides parental leave, a career break scheme and general advice on childcare by way of an information brochure and childcare directories (Vaneris, 1993).

Some companies have acknowledged that family responsibilities influence not only career patterns, but also absenteeism rates, turnover, employee health and ultimately productivity. Policies which deal successfully with these matters have been explicitly linked to business issues. One instance of this is in Pacific Brands, a division of Pacific Dunlop, where management sought to reduce the high costs of absenteeism, turnover and workers' compensation by changing organizational culture, the authoritarian management style, by opening up communication and introducing greater flexibility into the organization. This was done by making people the focus of the strategies and implementing a two-way communication process. Employees were surveyed about their reasons for absenteeism. In addition, effective communication structures and processes were developed, line management assumed responsibility for workers' compensation as well as for developing trust among employees, and training programmes were developed which include reference to gender issues. These programmes have been effective in reducing the costs associated with injuries, absenteeism and turnover. In 5 years injuries have fallen by 50% and absenteeism has fallen from 10% to 3.5%.

CHILDCARE

Childcare has been acknowledged as a critical issue in the provision of EEO. In Australia, companies interested in providing childcare usually assess the need for childcare among their employees through surveys. Although there are still only a very small number of work-based childcare centres, indications suggest there are a number of companies seriously considering providing childcare, either by themselves or in conjunction with another organization. Such arrangements, however, face a number of barriers. Work-based childcare is expensive and highly regulated, and this certainly acts as a disincentive to employer-based childcare. Employers interested in assisting with the childcare for their employees have therefore developed other schemes such as disseminating information about childcare providers and providing training on parenting to employees. Flexible work arrangements and home-based work have also been developed as a way for employees to meet their childcare needs. Another impediment to the provision of childcare is the recession which has encouraged employers to restructure their organizations by removing levels of management and reducing the number of employees. In such an environment the issue of childcare is not given high priority (Aidie and Carmody, 1992).

CONCLUSION

Ten years ago there was considerable opposition to the creation of EEO among many Australian employers. The legislative framework providing for discrimination-free employment practices and the development of affirmative action measures has forced employers to acknowledge the value of employing women in a range of positions for organizational efficiency. The Affirmative Action Agency reports that

> the environment for affirmative action has changed during the 1980's . . . More attention is being focused on . . . how organisations accommodate work–life cycle and patterns of workers with family responsibilities. There is closer attention to the contribution of people to productivity as an essential aspect of organisational strategy. Affirmative action is increasingly integral to human resource management.

(*Affirmative Action Agency, 1992, p. 1*)

The integration of anti-discrimination principles into legislation, industrial relations arrangements and policies has established a standard for behaviour, and it appears to have slowly influenced employer attitudes towards female employees. This favourable change in attitude has been encouraged where economic circumstances have provoked employers to consider the impact of the costs of turnover, absenteeism and workers' compensation on the organization. Conversely, imaginative arrangements facilitating the employment of women have fared badly in situations where economic circumstances are poor for all employees in the company.

The creation of EEO has been nurtured by the institutional arrangements in Australia. Despite changes in attitudes among many employers, the dismantling of these institutional arrangements could threaten the further development of equity in the labour market. The shift in the industrial relations arena to enterprise bargaining away from a centralized system could disadvantage female workers. This could occur because women workers have inferior bargaining power resulting from their concentration in part-time employment. In addition, under the existing wage-fixing principles, improvements in rewards and conditions are to be based on increases in productivity and output, and unfortunately for women there is great difficulty in quantifying output and productivity in the occupations and industries in which they work. An enterprise bargaining focus requires face-to-face bargaining sessions, a situation in which women are disadvantaged because of their social conditioning to be less aggressive and assertive than men (Distaff, 1992).

The continued development towards EEO in Australia requires the maintenance of existing institutional and legislative arrangements which establish the principle of anti-discrimination. This principle can continue to influence awards and a range of organizational and government policies by being an important determinant of policy development. It would also highlight the need to provide training and education to women so that they could participate more effectively in the new bargaining arrangements and policy formation. This would require providing training to women who work part time and it could necessitate providing training during work time. A further way of enhancing the palatability of policies designed to create EEO would be to develop measures which demonstrate the value to companies of such measures. The Australian experience provides a model of the advantages of legislation for EEO and at the same time demonstrates the importance of integrating anti-discrimination principles into a range of policy domains.

REFERENCES

AFFIRMATIVE ACTION AGENCY (1990) *The Triple A List*, Australian Government Publishing Service, Canberra.

AFFIRMATIVE ACTION AGENCY (1992) Affirmative action into the '90s. Discussion paper, Australian Government Publishing Service, Canberra.

AFFIRMATIVE ACTION AGENCY (1993) Affirmative action: latest data, in V. Pratt and E. M. Davis (eds) *Making the Link, 4*, Affirmative Action Agency and Labour Management Studies Foundation, Sydney.

AIDIE, J. and CARMODY, H. (1992) *Families at Work: Practical Examples from 140 Businesses*, The Council for Equal Opportunity in Employment, Melbourne.

BRAITHWAITE, V. (1993) EEO and HRM: compatible positions but different interests. Paper delivered at the 5th Women, Management and Industrial Relations Conference, Macquarie University, 30 June and 1 July.

BURTON, C. (1991) *The Promise and the Price*, Allen & Unwin, Sydney.

CASTLEMAN, T., SEITZ, A. and CARGILL, B. (1991) Affirmative action case study. Confidential report of first round findings (draft), May.

DEPARTMENT OF INDUSTRIAL RELATIONS (1991) Changes. Pamphlet prepared with the co-operation of the Commonwealth Banking Corporation, Sydney and Canberra, and the Commonwealth Bank Officers' Association, Sydney.

DEPARTMENT OF PRIME MINISTER AND CABINET (1985) Affirmative action for women. A progress report on the pilot program, AGPS, Canberra.

DISTAFF (1992) Women and enterprise bargaining: who benefits? Occasional paper no. 2, National Women's Consultative Council, Canberra.

EMPLOYMENT RESEARCH GROUP (1991) Knowledge of attitudes towards affirmative action and equal employment opportunity. Summary report, Affirmative Action Research Projects, no. 1: Workplace attitudes survey (Part 1), Affirmative Action Agency, Sydney.

GIBBS, A. (1991) Equal employment opportunity implementation strategies at Argyle Diamonds. Paper delivered at 3rd Women, Management and Industrial Relations Conference, Macquarie University, 3 and 4 July.

GRAYCAR, R. and MORGAN, J. (1990) *The Hidden Gender of Law*, The Federation Press, Sydney.

INTERNATIONAL LABOUR OFFICE (1987) *Women at Work Number 2, Equal Opportunities: Trends and Perspectives*, International Labour Office, Geneva.

288 WOMEN IN MANAGEMENT

LAVARCH, M. (1992) Half way to equal. Report of the Inquiry into Equal Opportunity and Equal Status for Women in Australia, Australian Government Publishing Service, Canberra.

NEWMAN, J. (1991) Affirmative action evaluation: opposition support – but there are problems. Press Release, 25 September.

PLEDGER, R. (1991) Ericsson's approach to affirmative action. Paper delivered to the 3rd Women, Management and Industrial Relations Conference, Macquarie University, 3–4 July.

POINER, G. and WILLS, S. (1991) *The Gifthorse: A Critical Look at Equal Employment Opportunity in Australia*, Allen & Unwin, Sydney.

POWELL, A. (1993) Consultation and affirmative action. Paper delivered to 5th Women, Management and Industrial Relations Conference, Macquarie University, 30 June and 1 July.

POWELL, A. and RUSSELL, G. (1993) Managing affirmative action, in V. Pratt and E. M. Davis (eds) *Making the Link, 4*, The Affirmative Action Agency and Labour Management Studies Foundation, Sydney.

PRATT, V. and DAVIS, E. M. (eds) (1993) *Making the Link, 4*, Affirmative Action Agency and Labour Management Studies Foundation, Macquarie University, Sydney.

SCUTT, J. A. (1991) Feminism and the law, the sexes and society (review article), *Womanspeak*, Vol. 14, no. 1.

THORNTON, M. (1990) *The Liberal Promise: Anti-Discrimination Legislation in Australia*, Oxford University Press, Melbourne.

VANERIS, B. (1993) National Australia Bank working towards constructive change. Paper delivered at the 5th Women, Management and Industrial Relations Conference, Macquarie University, Sydney.

VICTORIAN TRADES HALL COUNCIL (1992) *Making Affirmative Action Work*, Victorian Trades Hall Council, Melbourne.

CHAPTER 19

Implementing Equal Opportunity and Affirmative Action Programmes in Belgium, France and The Netherlands

MONIQUE CHALUDE, ATTIE DE JONG AND
JACQUELINE LAUFER

INTRODUCTION

Figures from a 1992 report on the position of women in the European labour market illustrate that in all the European countries women's increasing importance in the labour market shows no sign of slowing even in this period of economic crisis (Meulders *et al.*, 1992).

In the European context, France remains in the group of countries with a high rate of female employment, Belgium among the middle of the curve, and The Netherlands recently left the countries with the lowest percentage of female employment. This general growth is obvious when we look at the evolution of the figures from 1975 to 1989 (Eurostat, 1975, 1989). In 1975, in France women represented 37.8% of the working population, in Belgium 32.5% and in The Netherlands 24.2%. In contrast, by 1989, women made up 43.8% of the working population in France, 38.8% in Belgium and 38.4% in The Netherlands.

However, by 1989, in The Netherlands, the participation pattern of women differs from the other two countries in two respects. First, the participation drops considerably in the age group between 29 and 39. This reduction is a direct result of the fact that many women still leave their jobs when the first child is born. Secondly, it should be borne in mind that 55% of all working women in The Netherlands work part time, which means less than 35 hours per week. In France and Belgium this percentage is considerably lower. Obviously such a participation pattern has an unfavourable effect on the career prospects for women (Doorne-Huiskes, 1989).

During the same period, female students in all three countries increased their numbers in universities and other institutes of higher education. Between 1960 and 1985 the percentage of female students rose from roughly one-quarter to 50% of all students in higher education (Unesco, 1962–89). One needs to pose the question as to whether this increase helped women attain managerial positions in organizations. Certainly, it is in the professional and middle-management functions that women have progressed the most; particularly in administrative positions.[1] For example, in France, they account for more than 60% of accountants, executive secretaries and middle-level insurance professionals. As managers they represented 19% in 1982 as compared to 25% in 1989. They are also progressing in new careers such as marketing, advertising, public relations, auditing, human resources and computing. Nevertheless, as one moves up through the organization, women become fewer and fewer.

According to a study carried out in France in 1987 among senior management of 5,030 major companies representing 50% of gross national product (GNP), 1,237 out of 30,000 top-level executives were women, as were 55 CEOs out of 2,974.

The Belgian national statistics reveal that in 1991 women were underrepresented as managers, directors or top executives: only 33,000 women were occupying such jobs in Belgium, compared with 112,000 men in the same professional group. The 'glass ceiling' phenomenon at the top level is also illustrated in a recent survey (October–November 1993) made by the Belgian economic magazine *Trends-Tendances* on the 100 top managers in Belgium: one woman (recently arrived from the USA) appeared on the list after a long enquiry.

In The Netherlands, according to 1992 figures, women hold 13% of executive and management functions (Centraal Bureau voor de Statistiek, 1992). Compared with 5% in 1985, this is a real improvement. However, among the top-level executives of private-sector organizations represented on the stock market, there is only one woman.

The explanation for this underrepresentation of women in management is a combination of various factors such as sex roles and attitudes of men and women. These attitudes influence the choice of education and professions, limiting women in a smaller range of sectors than men. The responsibility for children and housework restricts the possibilities for women, especially in those countries where public childcare is scarce and where the statutory right to parental leave is shorter than the years between birth and school age. Also, the following enhance their difficulties on the road to the top:

- lifetime employment as a formal and informal rule to career development;
- need of exposure to a variety of situations to acquire experience and show one's talent and one's loyalty to the organization; this also means mobility around the country (or the world);
- availability for at least 40 hours a week, which makes it impossible for most women to combine a managerial job with motherhood;
- appropriate qualifications: especially economic and technical;
- work culture: a male culture with its specific rules and the lack of role models for women;
- trust from the other managers: it is easier to trust someone with the same characteristics as yourself; as long as decision-makers are men, it will be

[1] In this chapter we use the term 'manager' in a broad sense including middle-management functions and professionals such as accountants, top executive secretaries and insurance professionals: generally speaking, individuals with a university degree who exercise a post with responsibilities. Most of the figures for Belgium and France are based on this definition. In The Netherlands the word 'manager' is used in a more restricted sense and confined to the positions with either executive responsibility or with the authority to hire and promote employees in at least one department. Figures for The Netherlands refer to this more restricted category.

more difficult for a woman to be chosen than it is for a man with the same ability and experience;
• personal factors, such as commitment, social image, right connections and confidence in oneself, are also hampering women.

LEGAL TOOLS AND INSTITUTIONAL SETTINGS OF POSITIVE ACTION

The increasing numbers of women on the job market, and the acknowledgement of many obstacles blocking the way to equal opportunity for women, have resulted at the EU level in several legal and concrete measures to enhance women's professional equality.

The principle of equal pay for work of equal value was the object of the first EU Directive, in application of the principle written in Article 119 of the Rome Treaty, and has been translated in all national legislations (Directive, 1975).

The Directive on equal treatment concerns itself with the larger field of recruitment, training, working conditions, etc., on the job market and within companies. This Directive contains the principle that those positive actions aimed at creating equal opportunity between men and women and being defined as temporary measures necessary to correct an unequal situation, are not contrary to the principle of equal treatment. Positive action can therefore allow better access for women to jobs where they have been underrepresented, better career and training opportunities, better relationships with their family and enhanced career responsibilities (Directive, 1976).

While the Directives on equal pay and equal treatment have been incorporated in all national legislations in EU countries, the legal framework regarding positive action varies in each country. Although a Recommendation on positive action has been formulated by the EU (then EC) in 1984, positive action schemes do not appear to be wholly accepted as a means to promoting equal opportunity within organizations (Council Recommendation, 1984).

Depending on the particular country, positive action can either be compulsory – for example in the public sector of some countries – or alternatively, be left to the voluntary initiatives of companies, or else be integrated into the bargaining systems with unions.

While some degree of legal and administrative constraints implementing positive action does exist, Belgium, France and The Netherlands rely more on negotiation and/or incentive as well as on a set of diversified means including: administrative bodies whose function is to monitor and evaluate national positive action programmes; sensitization to social factors through the diffusion of expertise on positive action; and last, but not least, financial means to support pilot programmes or experts' advice to help organizations develop such programmes (Laufer, 1994).

The Netherlands

In The Netherlands, the law on equal treatment of men and women in the labour market allows 'preferential treatment' for women with regard to recruitment, training and promotion in those cases where they are underrepresented.

Preferential treatment includes everything from quotas for women to a coherent set of measures and personnel practices to remove barriers for women in the organization. However, no legal obligations or administrative rules have been formulated to implement positive actions. The government has stimulated positive action by means of brochures and publications and has made funds available for organizations in the public and private sector for half the costs of an emancipation officer or an expert giving advice on positive action. The grant scheme was started in 1991 and will be continued until 1994.

PRIVATE SECTOR   The realization of positive action in the private sector is regarded as the responsibility of employers and workers' councils. The latter have the obligation by law to guard against any kind of discrimination in the organization. The workers' council has the right to ask the employer for figures on the position, recruitment and promotion of women in the organization and can insist on positive action to be taken in those cases where women are underrepresented. In a few organizations the workers' council has actually exercised this power.

THE ROLE OF THE UNIONS   Positive action is one of the issues promoted by the two main Federations of Unions. In 1990 just over half of all current collective agreements (CAOs) had one or more provisions on the position of women. Most common are provisions on childcare, for example the obligation to buy a certain number of places in public childcare facilities for employees (43% of CAOs) or measures against sexual harassment (38% of CAOs). Only 8% of collective agreements contained the obligation to formulate a positive action programme and the implementation of this provision is still considerably lower (Dienst Collective Arbeidsvoorwaarden en Loontechnische Dienst, 1991).

PUBLIC SECTOR   The government as an employer has set an example by deciding that each department of central government should have a positive action plan by 1990. For the central government organization as a whole, targets are set by the Ministry of Home Affairs. These targets are aimed at achieving 30% women in the organization as a whole and 20% women in graduate-level positions.

Belgium

In Belgium the legal framework for positive action includes the law of 4 August 1978 (Title V) on economic reorientation which imposes equal treatment for men and women in the professional sphere. Article 119, included in this law, allows the implementation of positive action in order to promote equal opportunity between men and women. To enforce this law, two royal decrees have been signed. One (14 July 1987) concerns the voluntary schemes to be initiated in the private sector. The other (27 February 1990) concerns the compulsory positive action schemes to be initiated in the public sector. Furthermore, on the basis of another royal decree (7 December 1992), a company, after being given permission to restructure the employment of its workforce, must add a positive action plan for women in its restructurization plan.

PRIVATE SECTOR   From 1989 to 1993, the actual Ministry of Employment, Labour and Equal Opportunities – at that time Secretariat of State for Social Emancipation – had secured positive action agreements with companies which agreed to follow a specific methodology in the way they carried out their programmes. The Ministry provided experts in management, human resources and positive action (paid by the Ministry) to help, and motivate, the companies. The agreements were for one year and renewed tacitly. About 40 companies have signed this convention. However, over the years, and due to the recession, other priorities, or because they maintained they had achieved their aims, only a few of them continued to pursue annual positive action plans, integrating them in their human resources practices.

Recently, the royal decree of 12 August 1993 included an obligation for all the companies to establish an annual report about the situation of employment to the company council or the union representatives.

THE INFLUENCE OF COLLECTIVE BARGAINING   The influence of collective bargaining has been significant in the development of positive action schemes. During the negotiations for the interprofessional collective agreement for 1989–90, the social partners reached an agreement to consider positive action as a negotiation subject. Consequently, positive action was included in the package of work conditions to be negotiated and integrated in the relationship between employers and employees. It also foresaw the creation of a Positive Action Unit in the Department of Labour Collective Relations of the Ministry of Employment and Labour, which should help the negotiators to conceive and realize positive action plans (Ministère de L'Emploi et du Travail, 1991–92). In the interprofessional agreement 1990–91, 13 sectors signed collective agreements mentioning positive action programmes. The next interprofessional agreement (1991–92) included a financial incentive by proposing to finance positive action projects related to training or employment by the 'National Employment Fund' or by the 'Sector Funds'. Nineteen collective agreements were concluded. But it was a long and difficult process to go further than the commitment phase and to actually lay down positive action programmes. Therefore, the strategy of the Positive Action Unit is now focusing more on the companies themselves as well as the sectors.

PUBLIC SECTOR   As the biggest employer in the country, the public sector can play a major role in promoting positive action. As we mentioned earlier, positive action schemes are compulsory in the public sector. As well as the nomination of an equal opportunity officer in each department, these schemes include the publication of an analytical report concerning the situation of women and men in terms of employment, and the setting up of a positive action scheme including objectives, a description of the actions to be undertaken and a timetable and evaluation procedure. An internal working party (civil servants and union representatives) evaluates and monitors the positive action scheme, whereas a general working party (government representatives) supervises the whole programme and prepares an annual report.

France

In France it is the July 13th 1983 law on professional equality which constitutes the legal basis for positive action in the private sector.

PRIVATE SECTOR   Each year, companies must draw up a report on the comparative status of women and men in relation to recruitment, training, promotion, qualifications, working conditions and pay. This report must be discussed with the elected work council.

Companies are also encouraged to negotiate positive action schemes with trade unions to improve the status of women in areas such as recruitment, training, promotion or working conditions. Financial aid can be granted by the state, if the proposed measures are judged to be 'exemplary'. If the negotiation fails, the management of the firm can implement the scheme by themselves.

In addition, since 1987, firms can sign contracts with the government concerning the training and promotion of individual women. These contracts are directed at small and medium-sized businesses which would not initiate negotiations with unions. They are designed to promote a greater number of women in positions traditionally occupied by men. More than 400 individual affirmative action contracts have been signed up to now. Some of these could facilitate access for a number of women to middle management, but in general they have only marginally affected women managers as such.

THE ROLE OF THE UNIONS   In the French system of 'social concertation', equal opportunity objectives can either be integrated in collective agreements or go through the system of consultation of elected bodies at the firm's level: firm's council, committee on working conditions, committee on health and security, etc.

As far as collective bargaining is concerned, several levels of negotiation can be identified. The branch level is the essential one within the firm's level. Firms' negotiations are increasingly important, as is expressed in the 1983 law on professional equality which specifically deals with equal opportunity schemes at the firm's level. At that stage, the results of the negotiation on equal opportunity at other levels are not very encouraging (Jobert Voir, 1993).

In November 1989, a national agreement on equal opportunity was finalized between two major employer organizations and three of the main workers' unions. This agreement concerned the fact that at the branch level, a diagnosis of the situation of women could be made and precise objectives could be set. It also recommended that equal opportunity issues be included in negotiations on technological changes, working time and organization of work. However, since then, only one branch agreement has been concluded.

As far as the firm's involvement is concerned, with few exceptions, company management, rather than unions, has initiated equal opportunity schemes. The rather limited impact of positive action schemes (30 have been negotiated altogether in French firms) has been determined by the limited influence of women in union activities and the economic and employment crisis. All these factors have contributed to unions not pushing positive action programmes (whose efficiency remains to be proved) and to treating the question of discrimination and inequality through negotiations on the issues of employment, working time, classification, salary and training.

PUBLIC SECTOR   As far as public firms are concerned, they are subject to the 1983 law on professional equality, but only four of them have negotiated positive action schemes (Grandin *et al.*, 1989).

Concerning the public sector, the French principle of equality as it relates to the *statut général des fonctionnaires* tends to result in neutral procedures of recruitment and promotion, and limits the possibility of positive action schemes.

While the May 7th 1982 law concerns the principle of equal access of men and women to all public offices, the July 13th 1983 law concerns the rights and duties of civil servants indicates in its Article 6 that no distinction can be made on the basis of sex among civil servants.

However, since 1983, government recommendations have been made to ministries and departments concerning job advertisements, gender distribution on juries training, and the fact that female candidacy for a job should never be disregarded under the argument that family responsibilities could prevent them from fulfilling the job's requirements.

Since the May 1982 law, a report must be submitted every two years to the Parliament and to the 'Conseil Supérieur de la Fonction Publique' evaluating the evolution of the situation of women in the public service.

THE CONTENT OF POSITIVE ACTION SCHEMES

While a systematic evaluation of positive action schemes cannot be made for the EU countries, or even for each individual country, it can be concluded from the following sections in this chapter, that the issue of women in management has certainly not always been a priority in positive action schemes in either The Netherlands, Belgium or France.

The Netherlands

In The Netherlands positive action programmes have mainly been carried out in the public sector. The local authorities in the large cities were the first to plan and implement positive action for women. The city of Amsterdam formulated a positive action plan in 1985. Other large and medium-sized cities, provincial organizations and central government departments followed between 1987 and 1993.

In all of these programmes, attention was given to the issue of women in management and, in many positive action programmes in the public sector, targets were set for the percentage of women in higher positions. In the municipal organization of the city of Amsterdam, for example, the target was as high as 50%.

Specific action has been taken to meet the targets. Where underrepresentation was evident, functions have been reserved for female candidates. Moreover, several public-sector organizations have organized special training courses for women in more junior positions, to help them bridge the gap to management functions. Courses to help women to better balance and plan life and career events, have also been rather popular in public-sector organizations. The courses, which aim at preventing wastage by making women more career oriented, also brought to light the structural problems in combining work and family life. Certainly, one of the main obstacles for women aiming to get into higher management is the clash between family commitments and the requirement of full-time availability. In The Netherlands the difficulty in combining work and family is enhanced by the fact that public childcare facilities are hardly available. Until 1990, only 2% of children under the age of 3 were provided for in public childcare, against 20% in Belgium and France. Over the past 2 years, the number of childcare places has grown to cover approximately 4% of all children under 3. Parental leave was not a statutory right in The Netherlands until 1991. Since then, both parents have a right to reduce their working time to 20 hours a week for up to 6 months. The leave is unpaid, but return to a full-time appointment is guaranteed. The social partners are supposed to improve on the statutory right in their collective agreements. In the private sector, results so far have been very limited. However, in the public sector, a more flexible arrangement has been agreed and the time taken as parental leave is paid for at 75% of the employee's salary.

One of the most common ways in The Netherlands to reconcile work and family life is by working part time. In the public sector the attitude towards part-time work in higher functions is far more lenient than in most private-sector organizations. Usually, the formal policy allows part-time work in all functions for men and women up to the highest managerial level. In practice, the resistance is still great but there are some well-known examples of women working 32 hours a week in some of the highest managerial positions in the Civil Service. As a result of these measures, the public sector accounts for a relatively high number of women in management positions.

In the private sector positive action programmes are far less developed. A survey in 1990 among a sample of 842 organizations with over 100 employees, showed that only 4% had a positive action plan with a reasonably coherent set of measures. One in five of the organizations in the survey did at least something to improve the position of women in the organization (Dienst Collective Arbeidsvoorwaarden en Loontechnische Dienst, 1991).

Concerning women in management, measures such as quotas and reservation of functions or preferential treatment in selection procedures, are never used in private firms. Some organizations which recruit a considerable number of graduates, such as the large banks, have set themselves targets for the recruitment of female graduates. Others monitor their university entrances in this respect.

Some organizations have made use of a special training course for young female managers organized once or twice a year by the training centre of one of the employers' organizations. Others have organized training and work experience programmes for re-entry of women with graduate degrees.

In the largest organizations in the private sector, the need to be mobile all over the country, or even the world, is one of the problems gaining more recognition. Shell has a long-standing career scheme for those couples in which both partners work in the company. Other organizations try to arrange a job for the partner abroad, but they do all this on a strictly individual basis.

Childcare facilities, unpaid maternal leave and paid or unpaid leave in case of sudden illness of children, are among the measures most often taken by companies. In most organizations in the private sector, working part time in a professional function is something that could be negotiated. Even so, in management functions, it is still ruled out in most organizations. However, the subject has started to be addressed. For example, in the banking sector, one of the clauses in the new collective agreement states that part-time work is not to be ruled out beforehand in any function. Furthermore, research is under way in one of the large banks to see what the possibilities for part-time work in management functions are, and to decide on future policies in this respect.

Belgium

In Belgium, positive action programmes began first in the private sector under the incentive of the EU. Twenty organizations were contacted by the national EU expert and subsequently carried out several positive actions in terms of recruitment, training and information for their personnel. Positive action officers from the private and public sectors, as well as personnel directors and representatives of unions, met a few times a year in the Belgian 'EU positive actions network' to share their experiences in this field. In association with the Secretariat of State for Social Emancipation, pilot projects were developed in a systematic and coherent way in both the private and public sectors.

The phase 'actions' carried out by the EU began in 1980 in the private sector when the largest Belgian bank – Générale de Banque (G) – agreed to participate in an international action-research project on equal opportunity in the banking sector.

With the support of the EU, the bank made a video on equal opportunities, which was shown and discussed during in-company management courses as well as to other audiences.

Another large Belgian bank – Banque Bruxelles-Lambert (BBL) – has also committed itself to support the EU action: from 1979 until 1991, a quota of one-third of women has been set among young graduate trainees hired yearly and who constituted the future managers of the company. The actions realized in these two companies included management training programmes for women (Women Managers and Career Development).

Through the EU sensitization programme aimed at industry, Philips Belgium also implemented a quota system for the recruitment of young graduates: the proportion of males to females had to be equivalent to the number of males and females graduating from the specialized fields of education required by Philips.

In 1989, through positive action agreements signed by companies with the Belgian Secretariat of State for Social Emancipation, several companies in sectors with traditional male cultures (such as construction, chemical industry, etc.) have initiated actions in order to open up access to managerial posts previously not held by women. These initiatives illustrated that these male-dominated companies were open-minded and were willing to adapt to the reality of the labour market. While protective legislation (such as restricting night work for women which, with a few exceptions, still exists in Belgium) restricted certain companies hiring women as workers, companies which had predominately female employees and very few, if any female managers, concentrated their energies on access to management for women.

The main focus of positive action strategies concerning women in management has concerned:

- *The area of recruitment.* Most of the companies have offered access to managerial posts previously occupied almost exclusively by men. This was generally implemented after a widely publicized study showing that there were no reasons other than discrimination keeping women out of these jobs.
- *The area of training.* In the public sector: training for women managers from all the ministries. In the private sector: training for personnel managers about positive action integrated in human resources management and sensitization to equal opportunity and training for women (management, assertiveness, career development).
- *The area of career development.* In several companies, training and advice in career development for women are accompanied by a more systematic introduction of performance evaluations.

In the public sector, each year a report is drawn up for the government on the state of the advancement of the implementation of the royal decree of 1990, a promotion of equal opportunity between men and women.

In the last report, some results of the application of the positive action methodology were given: 1,109 civil servants were appointed as equal opportunity officers; 899 analytical reports were completed; 281 equal opportunity programmes were established and 444 working parties helped in the implementation of positive action programmes in public administrations (Rapport au Gouvernement sur l'Arrêté Royal, 1993).

As women are underrepresented at the highest level, many measures in the positive action plans concern careers and include issues related to promotion, training and measures to improve access to training. Moreover, they also deal with the flexibility of work time in order to favour a better conciliation of work and family. Also, some innovative measures considered as positive actions are aimed at eliminating situations resulting from 'violation of existing regulations' (Jacqmain, 1992).

Career breaks and part-time work were addressed by laws and collective agreements to promote employment through sharing available labour (part-time: Law 23/6/81 and Collective Agreement no. 35, 27/2/81; career break: Law 22/1/85). Several collective agreements at the sector level have established career breaks as a right and a recent collective agreement qualified as 'suppletive' can be applied in sectors where there are no measures taken on this matter. A career break is often linked with family reasons, even though it can be taken for other reasons. It depends on the agreement of the employer who must replace the person with an unemployed person. Nevertheless, as this implies a reduction or lack of salary, it risks reinforcing the prejudiced view that women are only working for pin-money (De Vos, 1991; Maingain, 1993). As executives and managers are not directly affected by the enforcement of these collective agreements, managers who want a career break can refer to the law and request an agreement with their employer. However, in reality, there are very few cases in the private sector because men and women know that a career break adversely affects their future career, and that they have no job security once they leave their employment.

France

In France, companies have, on the whole, been reluctant to be the main initiators in the implementation of equal opportunity programmes. In a climate of rising unemployment, the need to restructure the workforce, introduce flexible working hours, or implement equal opportunity programmes could only be legitimized when women's mobilization or skills appeared to be the answer to the firm's economic objectives.

However, the emphasis now placed on the development of human resources as a factor for improved business performance, the determination of companies to evaluate more accurately the types of skills they require to fulfil their economic objectives and the introduction of new technologies in the industrial and administrative sectors are the key elements which could provide valuable opportunities for women if integrated within proper change strategies.

About 30 French firms have implemented positive action schemes, the majority of them through negotiating with the trade unions a *plan d'égalité* as defined in the 1983 law. This relatively low figure would indicate that most companies do not feel it necessary to include equal opportunity issues among their objectives or, at the very least, do not wish to assert a specific policy concerning this matter. However, while in recent years much attention has been given in many firms to improvements in the field of human resource management, most firms would stress that these have concerned both men and women.

The measures covered by these schemes include all the areas relating to the status of women in employment: recruitment, career development, training, compatibility of domestic and professional roles, and awareness-raising among employees and management about the issues of equal opportunity (Laufer, 1992).

In the area of recruitment, action schemes have been set up to readjust recruitment policies in favour of women executives, engineers and technicians into jobs where they were underrepresented, and to provide more information concerning vacant positions within the company, so as to encourage more women to apply for them.

In the area of career development, action schemes have helped to promote women to male-dominated managerial positions, to define new career paths enabling women working in administrative functions to enter marketing and sales functions, and to promote the lack of use of individual career and performance evaluations. They have led to a more systematic inclusion of women in career development programmes and to the setting up of working groups to identify and to evaluate the changing content of the secretarial function and its consequences for future secretarial skills.

In the area of training (which is crucial to equal opportunity schemes), efforts have been more directed towards factory workers and employees. Faced with technological changes and a growing demand for higher quality in their products or services, the companies have taken it upon themselves to transform or upgrade the skills of groups of female factory workers and clerical staff, ill-prepared to confront technological changes or to take on positions requiring initiative and greater responsibility. In some other firms, all employees below secondary school level were given courses in economics, banking and communication, which could grant them access to further managerial training so as to allow them to take up managerial positions in the administrative and marketing areas.

In the public sector, while women constitute the majority of civil servants (51.6%) they constitute only 9.4% of top-level jobs. However, they have progressed at the level of heads of services and assistants to heads of department: from 11.8% in 1988 to 15.1% in 1991. This progress is linked to the fact that more women get access to category A (top-level) jobs through the competitive tests. Women now constitute 47.3% of civil servants in category A. However, they constitute only 28.5% of these category A civil servants preparing for a *concours* to get higher-level jobs in that category (Ministère de la Fonction Publique et des Réformes Administratives, December 1993).

Positive action schemes have also included the issues of reconciliation between professional and family responsibility, for example the taking into account of maternity leave for seniority bonuses and the introduction of an interview with the employee's immediate supervisor after her return from maternity leave, to evaluate her career development. These procedures have allowed motherhood to be integrated into women's career development in a positive manner. Some firms have included certain measures to facilitate the access of women to training, taking into account the family role of women.

Part-time work has often been presented as a 'meeting point' between the needs of the firm for more flexible working time patterns and the needs of the female workforce. Even so, if part-time jobs concern only women, it could lead to a new type of job segregation which is not compatible with equal opportunity.

Policies which address themselves to both sexes – such as parental leave (July 19th 1977 law) are in principle an answer to such a goal. However, legal tools, as such, are inefficient when it comes to modifying the traditional gender division of roles within the family. Although some firms allow parents of sick children to take a certain number of days off, a few others have chosen to have insurance policies which provide for childminders to look after sick children at their home in case of minor illness. As to flexible working hours, these can be very varied and range from flexible working hours during the day or the week, to part-time work or time off during school holidays.

In the public sector, part-time work and parental leave systems have also been developing. Twelve point four per cent of the female staff in the A category, 11.5% in the B category and intermediate levels, and 18% of the clerical staff, work part time. Nevertheless, while part-time work in the French public sector is formally well protected in terms of rights to seniority advancement, promotion or training, and constitutes together with maternity and parental leave a distinct advantage for women's desire to combine all their roles, some questions remain as to the impact of such a situation on the career prospects of women.

CONCLUSION

When considering the positive action schemes within the public and private organizations in France, Belgium and The Netherlands, three strategies emerge. We will call them: the affirmative action strategy; the human resources strategy; and the reconciliation strategy.

The affirmative action strategy

The affirmative action strategy is based on the idea that women are under-represented in management positions due to disadvantages in the past and ongoing discrimination, mainly based on sex stereotypes. This implies that there must be an untapped potential of qualified women for these positions, either inside the organization or in the labour market. To remedy the under-utilization of women, targets are set for promotion and recruitment of women for these positions based on their availability. Quotas, 'preferential treat-ment', special efforts in recruitment and monitoring of selection outcomes, are all used to realize the targets.

The lesson to be learned is that the affirmative action approach can only be carried out if an independent outsider monitors the results regularly. In the public sector in The Netherlands, this has been done by the Council of Minis-ters for the central government departments and by local and provincial coun-cils for their organizations. Where monitoring has been carried out consistently over a number of years (as has been the case in the municipal organizations in the large cities in The Netherlands), this has resulted in a relatively high pro-portion of women in management positions in these organizations.

The human resources strategy

The human resources strategy is based on the idea that a personnel policy which guarantees equal access to training and promotion is the best way to improve the position of women and make full use of their potential.

The strategy aims at descriptions of functions, recruitment and promotion criteria and access to training which are free of any discriminatory aspects, such as age barriers or unnecessary restrictive qualifications. Imposing strict criteria for recruitment and choosing candidates by means of encouraging employees to apply, are some of the policies adopted under this strategy. Most private companies in each of the three countries and the public sector in France rely on this strategy to improve the proportion of women in manage-ment in their organizations.

The human resources strategy, in its purest form, does not take into ac-count any differences between men and women due to past discrimination, institutional barriers or differences in family responsibility. These differences, if recognized, are not considered the responsibility of the company. However, it is considered in the interest of the company to stimulate women to realize their full potential by giving them some special support. All schemes which fall under this strategy have in common that the solution to the problem of unequal representation is found at the level of the individual employee. The organizational structure remains unchanged and is not seen as part of the problem.

The reconciliation strategy

Organizations which have recruited and trained female graduates are now beginning to realize that they must offer either them or their partners, or both, the opportunity to care for children and continue a career, or risk the loss of the investment in at least one of them. As long as parental leave is in fact used mainly by women, questions remain as to the impact of these schemes on the career prospects of women.

In each of these three countries a few large and progressive organizations have already started to explore more flexible career paths, which include the possibility of temporary part-time work and career breaks in middle management and professional jobs. One of their motivations is that the need for more flexibility in career paths coincides with the need for flexible work arrangements felt in their organizations.

We also need to acknowledge that managers, both male and female, are also vulnerable in relation to unemployment. Indeed, the present uncertainty of employment has destroyed the old pattern of the linear career previously offered by companies and this in itself could introduce more equality between men's and women's career patterns – both sexes having to learn to cope with change and instability. It is also interesting to note that in the past mobility has always been important for careers and this was a handicap for women. Nowadays, more men refuse to be relocated because their wife risks losing her job. In the meantime, companies are more likely to consider women for relocation, therefore the need for mobility is less discriminating to women in their careers.

As the OECD report *Shaping Structural Change* points out, positive action by employers should include the willingness to change the structures of the organization and especially to facilitate innovative ways to challenge traditional working patterns. More companies now consider that family matters are not only private problems, but that companies should take measures to help this reconciliation regarding home/work conflicts. The type of measures will depend on the national background: in The Netherlands, women are working part time; in Belgium and in France attention is paid to crèches, different kinds of parental leave and other measures. Even so, in the final analysis, positive action by employers is not enough to remove all barriers for women wishing to enter into management positions. Much remains to be done by companies, governments and unions before a new structure will be realized in which both men and women can fully realize their human potential.

REFERENCES

CENTRAAL BUREAU VOOR DE STATISTIEK (1992) *Enquête Beroepsbevolking 1992*, The Hague.
COUNCIL RECOMMENDATION (1984) The promotion of positive action for women (84/635/EEC), 13 December.
DE VOS, D. (1991) Entre travail et familles, les femmes, *Revue du Travail*, October–December, Brussels.
DIENST COLLECTIVE ARBEIDSVOORWAARDEN EN LOONTECHNISCHE DIENST (1991) *Emancipatie in Arbeidsorganisaties*, The Hague.
DIRECTIVE (1975) 75/117/CEE, 10 February.
DIRECTIVE (1976) 76/207/CEE, 9 February.
DOORNE-HUISKES, J. VAN (1989) Women and changing patterns of work: analysis of the situation in the Netherlands. Paper for the 15th Seminar on Social Welfare, Netherlands.

EUROSTAT (1975, 1989) *Enquête Naar de Arbeidskracht.*

GRANDIN, C., MARUANI, M. and MEYNAUD, H. L. (1989) L'inégalité professionnelle dans les entreprises publiques à statut réglementaire. GIP Mutations Industrielles, Cahier no. 34, pp. 35–49.

JACQMAIN, J. (1992) Actions positives dans les services publics, *Bulletin de la Fondation André Renard,* no. 196/197.

JOBERT VOIR, A. (1993) Négociation collective et promotion de l'égalité professionelle. Rapport BIT, Geneva.

LAUFER, J. (1992) L'entreprise et l'égalité des chances, enjeux et démarches. La Documentation Française.

LAUFER, J. (1994) Le difficile chemin de l'égalité, forthcoming, *La Revue Travail,* no. 32.

MAINGAIN, B. (1993) *Vie Familiale et Vie Professionnelle. Etat du Droit, Enjeux et Perspectives* Editions Larcier, Brussels.

MEULDERS, D., PLASMAN, R. and VANDER STRICHT, V. (1992) La position des femmes sur le marché du travail dans la Communauté Européenne. Evolution entre 1983 et 1990. CEE, V/938/92–FR, p. 4.

MINISTÈRE DE L'EMPLOI ET DU TRAVAIL (1991–2) Service des Relations Collectives de Travail. Cellule Actions Positives. Rapport d'Activités.

MINISTÈRE DE LA FONCTION PUBLIQUE (1992) Quatrième Rapport au Parlement sur les Mesures Prises dans la Fonction Publique de l'Etat pour l'Application du Principe d'Egalité des Sexes. December.

OECD (1991) *Shaping Structural Change in the Role of Women,* OECD, Paris.

RAPPORT AU GOUVERNEMENT SUR L'ARRÊTÉ ROYAL (1993) du 27.02.90 portant des mesures visant la promotion de l'égalité des chances entre hommes et femmes dans les services publics. Figures cited by the Ministry of Employment and Labour and Equal Opportunity Policy in a press conference, 25 November.

TRENDS-TENDANCES (1993) no. 42 à 44, Zellik, Octobre à Novembre.

UNESCO (1962–1989) Yearbooks, Paris.

WHO'S WHO PORTRAITS DE FAMILLES (1993) *Trends.*

CHAPTER 20

Opportunity 2000: Good Practice in UK Organizations[1]

VALERIE HAMMOND

INTRODUCTION

More than 20 years after the initial UK sex discrimination legislation, employment statistics confirm that the labour force is still segregated by gender. Women are concentrated in specific sectors, notably distribution and services more generally, and in clerical and secretarial occupations. Men have a greater proportion of career and professional roles. Even in sectors where women form the large majority of employees of professional status, for example in health and education, they hold fewer than 20% of the management jobs overall.

The situation persists despite significant structural changes in the workforce. The number of women in employment increased by 16% between spring 1984 and spring 1993, while the number of men in work remained roughly the same. The number of women of working age who are economically active increased from 66% to 71% over this period, whilst the figures for men declined from 88% to 86%. By spring 1993 women accounted for 44% of employed people of working age. Women, therefore, are an increasingly important source of labour in the UK and form the majority of skilled or professional employees in some key growth sectors (Sly, 1993).

Despite women's presence, contribution and skills, a 1993 survey of 29,000 executives in 533 companies showed that only 8% of top executives in Britain are women, and further up the hierarchy the percentage is even less (Gregg and Maichin, 1993). It noted that women are still paid less than their male counterparts, although regular surveys carried out for the Institute of Management suggest that women managers' earnings have been increasing at a faster rate than men's.

RESEARCH BASE FOR OPPORTUNITY 2000

The business-led initiative known as Opportunity 2000 was developed by a group of 17 chairpersons, chief executives and directors (11 men and 6

[1] Sections of this chapter originally appeared in *Women in Management Review*, Vol. 7, no. 7, pp. 3–10 and N. J. Adler and D. N. Izraeli (eds) *Competitive Frontiers: Women Managers in a Global Economy*, Blackwells, Oxford. Material is included with permission from both respective publishers.

women) drawn from major UK companies and with trade union representation. It operates as one of the 'target teams' of Business in the Community
(BitC) – a charitable venture which provides a meeting ground for top-level
people to work on projects to address social and economic issues which affect
the well-being of the community. This target team was working on women's
economic development and had implemented activities including assistance
for women entrepreneurs, training for women, and guidance on childcare.
Frustrated by the lack of real change for women in the workplace, the target
team commissioned research to investigate alternative strategies which might
be more effective.

Recognizing that a substantial shift in organizational culture would be
necessary before there would be any lasting change for women, the research
carried out reviews of processes used to bring about major organizational
change and compared these with the implementation of equal opportunities.
The premise was that there would be substantial differences in how organizations tackled the integration of women into the mainstream, even though in
most organizations this would constitute a major cultural upheaval for all
staff.

A model was developed from the examination of some 150 international
examples of successful organization change. This showed several clusters of
critical success factors classified around commitment, behaviour, ownership
and investment. Specific factors included the long-term and unstinting support
evidenced by top management and the clear link with a business case for
change. Significantly, actions were many and varied, touching all parts of the
business. They were part of a complex system of encouragement and sanctions
to bring about and sustain a climate for wholehearted change (see Figure 20.1).

The resulting model was then used as a template against which actions
taken to implement equal opportunities could be assessed. Examples were
drawn from North America and Australia as well as the UK and the rest of
Europe. These showed that although there were superficial similarities in
intent, overall the approach for equal opportunity was far less comprehensive. Commitment was partial. Even if there was a champion, that individual
was seldom on the board and was rarely perceived as having real power.
Attempts to change behaviour were most frequently targeted on making
women fit the existing culture. Action to raise awareness of the dominant
group usually relied on the introduction of new policies and procedures,
sometimes accompanied by information sessions. There was seldom any significant effort to build ownership. Communications explaining the objectives
and creating involvement tended to be procedural at best and often omitted
many of those most affected. There was little evidence of the aims or benefits
of equal opportunity being explained or of how it linked to the business
situation. Quite simply, there was insufficient investment in the change in
terms of resources, time or money (see Figure 20.2).

Viewed in this light, it was obvious that until women's development was
regarded as a business issue, there was unlikely to be much change in the
way women are regarded in the workplace. Conversely, corporations like the
Littlewoods Organization in the UK and Gannett in the USA, who had
tackled equal opportunity as a business issue, had long-term strategies to
bring about the change with interlocking actions to promote and support new
behaviours. From this, it was deducted that a culture change approach to the

implementation of equal opportunities would be the way forward. Additional research was completed to understand how to develop and frame the business case.

The BitC target team were involved throughout acting as sponsor and sounding board to the researchers. The target team shaped the ideas and developed the concept of a campaign – Opportunity 2000 – to invite the involvement of other employers. The work attracted the interest and support of government but the campaign was launched by and remains an initiative of employers for employers.

THE OPPORTUNITY 2000 CAMPAIGN

Opportunity 2000 recognizes that legislation and procedural change are not sufficient to bring women fully into the mainstream of organizational life.

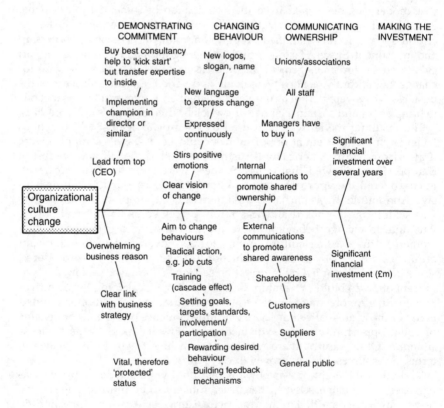

Figure 20.1 Changing organizational culture

A fundamental shift in organizational culture is needed to retain the talent of women which is otherwise lost.

Membership is voluntary but requires payment of a fee related to the number of people employed. Members are required to make three commitments: to set their own goals for increasing opportunities for women in their workforce by the year 2000; to publish these goals; to monitor and report on progress regularly. The campaign addresses and provides materials for different audiences: the chief executive and board, human resource (HR) and equal opportunity (EO) professionals and line managers. Assistance includes individual guidance, publications, workshops, networks, access to ongoing research, developing tools and techniques.

The 17 original members had expanded to 61 by the time of the launch meeting in October 1991. By November 1993 numbers had risen to 216. Membership includes major public- as well as private-sector employers and together they account for around 25% of the UK labour force.

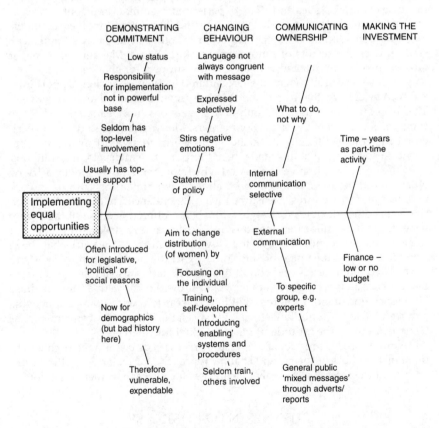

Figure 20.2 Implementing equal opportunities

Each individual member's goals and action plans are in the public domain and the media takes an active interest in progress. In some organizations the goals are quantitative targets. In others, the action plan sets out qualitative goals, usually actions designed to create a more open climate for women. This might involve reviewing the effectiveness of recruitment and selection processes, looking at different options for flexible working within career streams, creating a variety of measures to support carers (of either sex), and introducing specific training where necessary.

REGULAR REVIEWS

Each year every Opportunity 2000 member is required to take part in a detailed review. In 1992 and 1993 this involved the completion of questionnaires, confidential interviews with senior management and with EO specialists and meetings with samples of line managers. Best practice is collected and disseminated. Members are encouraged to take part in joint working groups, to tackle common issues and share experience in seminars and conferences as well as through 'seeing is believing' visits. The latter involves members 'opening their doors' so that colleagues from other firms can visit, talk with staff and see the results of innovatory work practices. Manager-to-manager talk has proved a powerful way of winning support for change.

After 3 years during which the UK suffered a severe recession, Opportunity 2000 can be pleased that its membership has grown by more than 35% per year. The drop-out rate is minimal, only 2 organizations in 2 years, and relates to companies who were the subject of mergers. Many members said they experienced increasing difficulty in financing measures to support their goals, but they also suggested that this made them more creative in developing solutions.

At the end of the first year, a period which many members spent clarifying what should be done, pioneers were already experimenting with new work practices and procedures. Measures including enhanced maternity leave; job share and other flexible work styles were being offered to some staff, as were benefits such as childcare, pensions and healthcare. A striking difference at the end of the second year was the way in which these measures had been extended to a wider range of staff, often with the declared aim of working towards common terms and conditions for all staff. This significant achievement means that women in junior or non-professional occupations, or those who work non-standard hours, will have access to a wider range of benefits as a right. They will not have to ask for special or different arrangements, or be dependent on the attitude of the individual line manager.

An important by-product of the review process is its use as a research tool to monitor the effect of the culture change approach, particularly whether it can withstand the recession and other challenges for top management attention.

BUYING INTO BUSINESS

Putting the case for equal opportunities on the agenda and into the business plan of many major companies has been one of the main achievements of Opportunity 2000.

Members welcomed the visible evidence of support through the appointment of a senior level champion – the Opportunity 2000 manager. In turn, these managers are committed to keeping women's development within the mainstream of organizational policy. The original research had identified six different types of business reason for developing equal opportunities: customer/market orientation; first-choice employer; reducing costs; increasing productivity; increasing creativity and innovation; and belief in the development of all individuals. Opportunity 2000 companies have been quick to build their own cases appropriate to their business need.

Attracting and retaining key people saves money

Boots the Chemist aims to select and retain the best graduates. Women graduate pharmacists generally achieve higher ratings against the company's performance criteria and it has become important to focus on women's development in order to attract this talent to the firm. To increase the number of women in supervisory and management positions, Boots examined its recruitment and promotion procedures and found that by using competence-based assessment techniques, focusing on skills rather than stereotyped roles, the number of women moving into management positions began to increase rapidly.

Reducing costs by funding childcare

Working together and sharing best practice enabled companies to develop ways of measuring the cost of not introducing childcare and other similar policies. The campaign published a booklet – *Corporate Culture and Caring – The Business Case for Family Friendly Provision* – which sets out the information to collect and how to calculate the true costs of continually recruiting and replacing staff. This can be used to review proposals to introduce measures such as childcare, flexible hours or other measures which help to retain skilled women in the workforce. This type of approach encouraged 35% of the Opportunity 2000 members to offer workplace nurseries for some or all staff. For example, East Midlands Electricity and the Wellcome Foundation have negotiated special deals for staff at local nurseries. The Inland Revenue, with 70,000 staff, is already involved in 11 workplace nurseries and 43 holiday play schemes and is currently planning for more.

Others take a longer-term view. Boots the Chemist is developing and sponsoring training for childminders. Still more have found less expensive ways to demonstrate a sympathetic awareness of mothers' (and sometimes fathers') needs. Northern Dairies, for example, keeps a register of local childminders.

Increasing management effectiveness through difference

The Inland Revenue, acting on evidence that women employees have been underpromoted in the past, aims to make use of all its talent and to get women into higher levels of management. It is believed that this will contribute to a change of management style, and that more emphasis on the so-called feminine qualities will help to improve effectiveness. They say they have found mixed teams to be more productive, creative and to deliver more effective results. Flexible work practices are now encouraged and today 15% of staff work part time.

FLEXIBILITY AT WORK

Flexible working patterns are generally becoming more widespread. The traditional career path from trainee to golden handshake is no longer there and men also find that career breaks, retraining and changes of direction are commonplace. It is not such a disadvantage for a woman to return to work after having children.

A survey by Hall (1994), among 320 senior personnel executives, shows that 64% of companies believe that flexible working increased productivity by reducing overtime and idle time and that more than 45% intend to increase flexitime and part-time work over the next 4 years.

Barclays Bank is one of the major organizations to realize that the traditional 35-hour work unit no longer matches its needs. The bank wants to take advantage of technological advantages which do not cut workloads into these convenient slices. They researched caring responsibilities and found that 65% of staff had this responsibility, 38% for the elderly. The social need for flexible working therefore matches the business need.

An aspect of flexibility being studied at Roffey Park is how to manage part-time workers for the optimum result. Management training programmes and textbooks still assume an organizational model based on mainly full-time male employees rather than female part-timers. However, specific skills and approaches are needed to get the best results from this increasingly important workforce.

TRAINING AND DEVELOPMENT

Training is central to the theme of Opportunity 2000 and assists in many different ways – raising managerial awareness of EO policies, sensitizing organizations to inequalities, training internal counsellors to deal with problems of stress or sexual harassment and helping women to break into traditional male territory.

A rising concern among Opportunity 2000 members is to ensure that training and development is gender free. Shell UK monitors the development of its staff for gender bias while Yorkshire Bank pays special attention to the *access* people have to its training programmes. Training methods are changing with long residential programmes giving way to combinations of short, modular courses and open learning systems. The Inland Revenue provides family rooms and access to a crèche for staff attending training at their residential centre. Other firms are prepared to provide temporary help whilst parents are undergoing training.

Many Opportunity 2000 companies have programmes for women. More than one-third offer schemes for non-traditional work or to bridge the leap from junior to senior work. Nuclear Electric, among several others, has positive action to ensure that women do take up the opportunities that are offered. They search out all those women with talent, wherever they are in the organization. The result is that the numbers of women now on the fast track has increased from 9% to 14%.

Employers are increasingly aware of the need for development among men and over half of Opportunity 2000 members offer equal opportunity awareness training to some or to all staff. Around one-third offer programmes which aim to assist women and men to have a better understanding of the other's perspective and experience.

MESSAGES AND REWARDS

Although women's pay continues to lag behind that of men, many Opportunity 2000 employers are acting to change this. Around half of the members have reviewed their reward policies to ensure they offer equal pay for work of equal value. Most already offer, or are working towards, common terms and conditions for all staff. These employers are concerned to ensure that all women in different employment groups have access to best employment practice. A side benefit is that junior women feel less 'separate' from those who are more senior, increasing the likelihood that achievers are perceived as role models. This is important as employers move towards fair assessment and open promotion schemes where it is often left to the individuals to put themselves forward.

SPREADING THE WORD

One of the recommendations arising from the Opportunity 2000 annual report 1993 is that it should develop its role as an ambassador to universities and schools to encourage women to study in non-traditional areas. Lucas Industries is already investing in encouraging girls in school to consider a career in engineering. They encourage them at each point of choice – GCSE subjects, A-level and further education.

At graduate level, some industries have changed recruitment policy to attract women. At Northern Foods women graduates were not being recruited for positions in production or distribution, the 'white hat and wellies' area from which senior managers have traditionally been promoted. A change in the cover of its graduate brochure from an outward-bound activity to an impressionist-type painting resulted in an increase of interest from both men and women.

Several members ensured their aims for women are known and reinforced from beyond the company itself. Yorkshire Bank have made sure, through their marketers, that advertising agencies are aware of their views on equal opportunity. Other members, ranging from Midland Bank, through the Metropolitan Police, the BBC and BP Oil, have set up working parents networks.

OPPORTUNITY 2000 AS A STRATEGIC POLICY

Most progress has been made in those organizations where the development of women is a strategic priority. It is clearly linked to the business plan and, as such, includes a variety of interlocking actions which support the achievement of the stated objectives at all levels of the organization. Opportunity 2000 includes a number of examples. Three are selected here as case studies representing quite different types of organization in the public and private sectors, the macro and the micro.

Case 1: The National Health Service

The National Health Service (NHS) is Europe's largest employer with over 1,000,000 employees, more than 790,000 of whom are women. Despite the existence of a huge resource of well-trained and qualified workforce, women are underrepresented in senior decision-making roles in virtually all areas of the NHS. In 1991 only around 18% of all management roles in the NHS were held by women.

The loss which arises when women cannot achieve their career potential has huge financial implications. For example, it has been estimated that it costs up to £250,000 to train a medical consultant, yet difficulties of creating a career within the NHS means that fewer women doctors continue into specialist or consultancy roles. Some simply leave, finding it easier to combine a career and family life elsewhere. This is a doubly serious situation since, as women comprise 52% of the population, a similar proportion of the patients – the client group – are also women. It is vital for women's voice to be heard as both consumers and providers of healthcare.

To remedy the situation, the NHS knew that radical action would be necessary especially as another major change – to trust status – was already under way. This meant the creation of new structures and roles on a massive scale. If women were to play a significant part in the decision-making of the new NHS, then it would be vital to create the environment for this at the outset.

The NHS was the first public-sector employer to join Opportunity 2000 in 1991. At around the same time, the NHS created a Women's Unit within the management executive (the most senior tier of management for the whole service). With a staff of 10 and a high-profile careerist to manage the unit, other organizations might envy the resource allocation but it is worth remembering that this equates to one staff member per 100,000 employees.

An early task of the Women's Unit was to build an advisory group and to develop goals for ministerial approval. Dealing with a broad remit which covered women in all NHS occupations, eight goals were set for achievement by the end of 1994. Four of these goals set numerical targets relating to women general managers, accountants, medical consultants and members of trust boards or authorities. The other four goals relate to personal development, promoting flexible working, career breaks and maternity leave and ensuring that women and men have equal access to nurse management positions. In comprehensive guidance, actions to be taken from the centre and locally were identified. Decisions are made at the local level and trusts and authorities were asked to produce their own action plans.

The approach is active and experimental. Bold initiatives include the creation of nursing bursaries for management study – overnight creating the largest pool of women (150) studying for MBAs that the UK has seen. These are NHS professionals who have the capacity to be future leaders. Other training elements deliver specific skills in areas ranging from clinical work through to finance and management.

A career development register, a service available to women at senior levels which gives access to individual coaching and counselling, also works with recruiters and promotors to hunt and find the best talent. Women are not guaranteed jobs through this process. They are supported and encouraged to focus their ability to compete more strongly. The process of applying for a high-level post – chief executive or director – thus becomes a learning experience with value even if the individual is not successful at first. The register, itself run by two job-sharing women, has been successful in challenging many assumptions and stereotypes about women. There are now nearly 500 high-calibre people on its books. As important as its role for women, the register is also a key tool for managing development in a time of turbulence and flatter structures when there is very little clarity about career routes. It therefore carries implications for the way men's as well as women's development needs could be handled in the future.

Another key component is the provision of development centres. These provide an assessment for the individual (not her manager) of her strengths and developments needs. These elements, together with a range of training programmes, enable women in the NHS to take charge of their own careers.

The task is a large and ambitious one and the NHS is a leader nationally and internationally in a field in which there is a growing interest – a strategic approach to managing a largely female workforce to maximize return on investment and provide flexible career opportunities for women and for men.

Case 2: Rank Xerox (UK) Ltd

There are similarities and differences in the situation for Rank Xerox. Although international and well respected in the USA for its approach to women's development, the UK numbers are more modest, with women being in the minority. As in the NHS the decision-making roles were generally the province of men but there were fewer women in the career stream. The company enjoyed a reputation for aggressive marketing and a strongly masculine culture. Few women were able to conform to the pressures of this environment, many simply left.

To change the situation and to benefit from a larger pool of talent, Rank Xerox used its membership of Opportunity 2000 to develop its own strategic approach. Women's development was given 'vital few' status among a group of strategic initiatives selected each year by the board as a key business priority. This high profile guaranteed that the impact on women's development was considered alongside every major business issue. The board itself went through an equality workshop and this has been followed over a 2-year period by workshops attended by all employees.

The workshops raised awareness but also identified the barriers to opportunity and recognized that tough action would be needed to break down stereotypical views of men's work and women's work. Drawing on its experience of introducing a culture for quality, and perhaps also on its marketing orientation, Rank Xerox set a clear target for women to hold 25% of the management posts by 1995 (from 15.5% in 1993). To achieve this change, the company embarked on a comprehensive set of actions ranging from targeted recruitment under the banner 'We only discriminate on ability' with positive action advertisements, through enhanced maternity leave, to a succession planning process that challenges assumptions. The result has been the emergence of a climate which is perceptibly more open to women and they now hold 15% of the management roles.

Case 3: The Macro Group

A much smaller member of Opportunity 2000, The Macro Group, with 361 employees, is Britain's most successful distributor of semiconductors. The company is distinguished by its financial success and by the presence of women throughout its structure in a male-dominated industry. In the difficult trading period of the early 1990s the company has increased in size by 50% and profits have at least doubled. It too has adopted equal opportunities as a strategic planning tool.

The Macro Group sought flexibility and women offered this in abundance. Team and cross-functional working are corporate characteristics. There are few boundaries between jobs and employees are encouraged to be involved in areas that interest them. Macro backs its belief in high-quality staff by responding quickly and imaginatively to their needs. The result has been the development of many strong female role models; 11 of the management team of 18 are women. They have not been held back because they had children or worked part time – in fact 3 of the 5 sales managers work part time. Difficulties are a challenge not a problem. The company approach is to look for a solution that meets the individual need and keeps the talent with the firm.

A major success factor for the company is thought to be the ability of the employees to 'multiplex', that is to work and care about several things at the same time. In their experience, it is a skill very many women have. As the managing director remarked, 'If a woman can get her entire family up, fed, clothes ironed, packed lunches made, husband off to work, children to school and still arrive at work at a normal time, it's no wonder she can run her department well.' This company acknowledges the reality of so many women's lives *and* finds a way to maximize their involvement at work.

Macro joined Opportunity 2000 to make a public commitment and to share their experience of creating an environment in which women *and* the company can thrive. However, they also have an eye to the future knowing that the attention will bring them to the eye of potential recruits of high calibre.

CONCLUSION

Achievements and future outlook

After 3 years Opportunity 2000 is three years into its allotted timespan. It has moved from being a campaign with all the connotations of temporariness into a mainstream policy issue. It has been adopted by some of the UK's largest and soundest employers and it has been sustained through one of the most difficult periods of recession. It has been able to demonstrate that progress can be made in difficult times, as well as in good.

Perhaps most significantly Opportunity 2000 has stimulated discussion and action beyond its own activities. One spin-off group, Employers for Child Care, lobbied the government for more realistic provisions and regulations surrounding the care of young children. Myriad networks and local groups for HR practitioners exist to exchange information about new work practices. Companies now seem genuinely concerned to understand and to take action with regard to the roadblocks which many women still experience.

Against this, surveys continue to show that women's earnings are consistently lower than those for men. And women, themselves, frequently feel that Opportunity 2000 has little to do with them. In one sense, they are right for the initiative does not address women directly but instead tries to change the climate in which we all work. However, it is vital for Opportunity 2000 itself to hear the view of the group whose interests it represents. A worrying aspect is demonstrated by a Mori Great Britain Omnibus Survey (1993) which showed that fewer than 1 in 10 people knew of Opportunity 2000. It will be important to include women among the target groups for future involvement.

Future research issues

Predictably Opportunity 2000 has generated a great deal of comment and criticism but women's development, in all its forms, has secured a place on the corporate agenda. The issue is not now why do it, but rather how to do it. The original 17 champions might feel that this was their question but the research issues are now much clearer.

Among the critical aspects still to be addressed are: salary drift – why it happens, how to prevent it; women's motivation – what causes stops/starts/ pauses; what women bring – more research on difference in styles, skills, abilities; women and men at work – understanding where there is potential synergy and what causes unproductive conflict; career management issues – how to incorporate flexibility and deal with the issue of flatter structures.

Many of the Opportunity 2000 members are already involved in studying these and other issues. All have become used to receiving requests for information or for access and most have shown a spirit of openness to participate in the new research agenda. The jury is still out on whether Opportunity 2000 will create a sustainable change for women, but it is clear that the campaign has already succeeded in raising widespread debate and, more important, action.

REFERENCES

GREGG, P. and MAICHIN, S. (1994) Is the glass ceiling cracking? Gender compensation differentials and access to promotion among UK executives. National Institute of Economic and Social Research, Discussion Paper No. 50 (October).
HALL, L. (1994) Juggling act, Personnel Today, 8 February, pp. 21–4.

HAMMOND, V. and HOLTON, V. (1991) *A Balanced Work Force, Achieving Cultural Change for Women: A Comparative Study*, Opportunity 2000/Ashridge Management Research Group, Berkhamsted.

MORI GREAT BRITAIN OMNIBUS SURVEY (1993) *Attitudes to Women in the Workplace*, September.

OPPORTUNITY 2000 (1992/1993) Annual Reports, December 1992 and December 1993, Business in the Community, London.

SLY, F. (1993) Women in the labour market, *Employment Gazette*, November, pp. 483–502.

INDEX

Index